I'M EVE

I'M EVE

Chris Costner Sizemore
AND
Elen Sain Pittillo

DOUBLEDAY & COMPANY, INC.
GARDEN CITY, NEW YORK

To

ACIE and ZUELINE COSTNER
Parents, Friends, Gentlepeople

in appreciation for their acceptance and
endurance, and because they touched my
life with love and understanding.

Chris Costner Sizemore

Foreword

Chris Sizemore, about whom you will read, is a treasured friend. So is her double cousin, Dr. Elen Pittillo, who has co-authored this book.

Opportunities to know and enjoy true friendships are rare enough; in the cases of Chris and Elen, they are really "once in a lifetime" experiences. Meeting them and others of their family members has enriched my professional understanding, and even more so, my personal life. You will read in the book how we happened to discover each other.

The fact that Elen and Chris were willing to share their identity is in itself no small miracle for a professor of clinical psychology who spends most of his time in the classroom teaching academic psychology. To have had Chris as a patient would have been challenging; to have her as a friend is delightful.

I remember well the publication of *The Three Faces of Eve* (1957) and my vicarious meeting with Eve White and Eve Black. What a fascinating account of her neurosis—dissociative reaction, multiple personality type. Then came the professional film *A Case of Multiple Personality*, which allowed one to be present at a few moments of therapy with the real Eve. The film, more than the book, brought Eve to reality, and one could see the dissociative state in action.

Chris experienced a hysterical neurosis, dissociative reaction, multiple personality type. Such neuroses are treatable, and the response is generally favorable. In dissociative reactions one typically sees an altered state of consciousness, a change in the sense of identity, or sometimes both. Other types of dissociative reactions are: somnambulism (sleepwalking); amnesia (loss of memory, past experiences, etc.); and fugue state (escape from one's

vii

past to take up an entirely new life). Multiple personalities have apparently been active since early childhood for Chris. The book clearly brings to life the existence of early childhood multiple personalities. Hysterical seizures are usually accompanied by a clouding or loss of consciousness. Hysterical seizures may take the form of isolated spasms or of convulsions involving the whole body. The seizures are thought to represent distorted pantomimic expressions of underlying sexual or aggressive urges and often are accompanied by crying or by hysterical laughter. All of these classical symptoms are exemplified in the book, although they are not identified as symptoms going together to make up the syndrome called hysterical dissociative reaction, multiple personality type. Multiple personalities are rare, but the case history of I'M EVE may possibly be repeated in the life of other children.

Dissociative hysterical amnesia, the blotting out of important, sometimes traumatic experiences, is a precondition to both fugue states and multiple personalities. This is beautifully illustrated in Chris's early life, when she denied doing things (repressed them) and as a result received punishment for acts she could no longer remember doing. The recovery of the forgotten memories in dissociative amnesia may occur spontaneously, be achieved through hypnosis or by the administration of drugs. In Chris's case, all three types of recovery of the forgotten memories are illustrated.

One experiencing a fugue state, based on unconscious phantasy, may appear "normal" to the casual observer, but actually be assuming an identity quite different from the real one. The many personalities that Chris experienced may be viewed as representing periods of prolonged and more stable fugue states. Some personalities were longer lived, while others existed for only short periods of time.

The treatment for any form of hysteria is some form of uncovering therapy that will provide or allow the patient to develop insight into the unconscious phantasies and blocked-out memories, thereby translating the somatic and personality symptoms into their underlying psychological equivalents. Included in the various types of therapy providing these insights are psychoanalysis, psychoanalytically oriented psychotherapy, or hypnosis. Chris has been subjected to all of these forms of treatment as she moved from one physician/psychiatrist to another. Her treatment programs are well described in I'M EVE and the earlier writings of Drs. Thigpen and Cleckley. The present state of Chris's adjustment attests to the effectiveness of the present treatment program under the direction of Dr. Tsitos. You might possibly see Chris on television shows, and you might see her in person now that she has revealed her identity. You can then see for yourself the extent to which she has worked through her neurosis and arrived at her present state of adjustment.

In evidence of her present state of adjustment, I was extremely pleased to present Chris and Elen to a professional audience. Chris and Elen individually presented information on early childhood experiences and then answered questions from the audience. This experience was truly one of the highlights of my teaching career. I must add that another highlight from this same experience was that of observing with great pride the manner in which my graduate students received Chris and Elen, and the way the students formulated professional questions that were most appropriate to the occasion and topic under discussion. Another highlight in my teaching career that happened earlier than those mentioned so far was that of having the pleasure of teaching Elen in a graduate course in personality dynamics.

I predict that I'M EVE will be received with equal but different enthusiasm by the lay public and mental health professionals.

W. Scott Gehman, Jr., Ph.D.

Durham, North Carolina
May 27, 1976

Author's Note

This book was born because of my conviction that the true facts of my life were not known, and that I had a story to tell; because the world had the impression that I had recovered from my dissociative problem, multiple personality. I have known twenty-two personalities and have lived to tell of their demise. I have attempted to present my story openly, freely, and with dignity and feeling.

It is my life as I have lived it. These are my memories and impressions; and my emotions. Much of the information is taken from my large collection of letters, newspapers, and magazine clippings, and from many personal tape recordings.

This book has been written for two purposes: as personal therapy and documentation; and hopefully to open a door through which the reader may journey: there to ponder their own conclusions, better understand and accept the mentally disturbed, and more importantly, if there be the need, someone may see a light in the darkness and take hope.

Chris Costner Sizemore

Fairfax, Virginia
July 4, 1976

Preface

Like Topsy, this book just grew. Its original two purposes—to provide a vehicle for Chris to explore critically her own life, and to correct the world's general impression that she had recovered from her dissociative reaction of multiple personality—soon grew into a third. It became increasingly evident as the flood of information from relatives, and Chris's own long-repressed memories, poured out, that there also lay the considerable task of documenting and describing the incidents in her life in such a manner that students of psychology could clearly follow the sequence of events. Great effort was made to leave out no pertinent facts, yet to paint a composite picture of the true color of her environment and heritage.

All events, except those taken from before her birth and her very earliest childhood, are her own memories and her own impressions. Where her impression differed from that of a relative who also remembered the event, her version was recorded, on the premise that it was her reaction and her experienced reality that affected and molded her. Even those recorded episodes beyond her memory, as the events surrounding her birth, were crossreferenced by several relatives. Much information was drawn from her vast horde of letters, clippings, and documents, with direct quotations used where it was legally possible, and paraphrasing employed where it was not.

Most of the technical information, diagnoses, and prognoses included in Part II were drawn from "A Case of Multiple Personality" by Corbett H. Thigpen and Hervey Cleckley, published in *The Journal of Abnormal and Social Psychology*, Vol. 49, No. 1, January 1954, pp. 135–51. Dialogue between doctor and patient used in Part II was taken from that which had already been published in *The Three Faces of Eve, The Final Face of Eve, American Weekly Magazine, McLeans* magazine, and *Life* magazine; that which was taken from the transcript of the professional film *A Case of Multiple Personality*; and that which Chris herself recalled.

None of her doctors—Dr. Corbett H. Thigpen, Dr. Tibor Ham, or Dr. Tony Tsitos—were approached for any technical information. They were visited to gain a general impression of their attitudes toward the patient, to determine what kind of role each played with her, and to learn how each viewed her future.

Special care was taken to avoid assessing any blame, or any cause and effect, between person or event and their subsequent effect on the patient, except where Chris herself felt there might have existed some relationship. In such a case, the relationship was reduced to probability only, by the use of terms like "perhaps" and "who knows."

Since neither of the authors was a certified mental health professional, no attempt was made to reach any sort of conclusions concerning the cause, either environmental or hereditary, of Chris's strange case of mental illness. The diagnosis by Dr. Thigpen of her condition as multiple personality was merely recorded, as was any other event in her life. Whether or not her life before and her life after bear out this now famous diagnosis is neither confirmed nor denied; her life is merely described, leaving conclusions to interested readers.

Much gratitude is owing to members of the Hastings family. The family generously lent their support by divulging information about themselves and their family from the past, exhibiting not only their pride in their family, but also often a rare ability to reveal and to laugh at their own childhood antics. Chris's own immediate family spent endless hours describing her life and their involvement in her illness.

Special thanks are given to Dr. W. Scott Gehman, who provided his extensive library for research, and his own psychological training and knowledge, to smooth the way when seemingly imponderable questions arose or the right word refused to arise; and to Janet Robinson, our typist, who only slowed down once, a bare two weeks, when her twin girls were born, a considerable feat,

xii

which she managed to accomplish on December 19—my birthday and Chris's wedding anniversary.

If this book can be one tiny light shining in the dark maze of mental illness, its purpose will have been accomplished.

Elen Sain Pittillo

Durham, North Carolina
May 30, 1976

Acknowledgments

It is my pleasure to express my appreciation to the following members of my family for their generous assistance in gathering endless hours of information, and for their patience and encouragement: Mr. Don Sizemore, Dr. Robert Pittillo, Jr., Dr. Elen Pittillo, Mrs. Taffy Fecteau, Mr. Bobby Sizemore, Mr. James Fecteau, Mrs. Elyse Walton, Mrs. Louise Edwards, Mrs. Elise Weaghington, Mrs. Mamie Lee Sain, Mrs. Anne Harvley, and Mr. Crafton Hastings.

I wish to thank Dr. Tibor Ham, Dr. Tony Tsitos, Dr. Raymond Dunovant, Dr. Corbett Thigpen, Dr. Hervey Cleckley, and Dr. W. Scott Gehman for their kind co-operation. Last but not least, I express a warm, heartfelt gratitude to Lisa Drew, senior editor of Doubleday, for her understanding and wise counseling during the writing of I'M EVE.

All names in the book are authentic, legal names except Fanny, John Lake, Rena Outz, Missy Mims, Miss Prince, Polly Strom, Hattie Sue Williams, Ralph White, Amos, Dodge, Mattie, Lennie, May, Sally, Willie Moon, Moody, Luke, Ruth, Willie, Al Thorne, Joe Clark, Tom and Sarah Byrd, and Mrs. Anderson. These names are fictitious to protect the identity of living persons who wish to remain anonymous or who were impossible to locate.

Introduction

Our culture discourages the experiencing and expression of feelings; the individual is expected to conceal his emotions, often even from himself.

Society, with its contradictions and conflicting values, perplexes the psyche of the individual and gives him very little choice.

Chris had little choice. She escaped reality by utilizing a very complicated and distorted lifestyle, classified by society as an emotional disturbance.

It was expected that knowledge of human behavior was going to alter her confused life and accomplish the monumental task of delivering a healthy adult. This is hypocrisy, because it just doesn't happen that way: Patient and physician have to work together to deliver to our society a "functional individual."

I wonder who is the accomplisher—the physician or the patient. Chris is a person—a complexed, perplexed, complicated person who tried, and she herself finally revealed herself.

Maybe I played a part in her life, but she herself tried to understand and analyze her own self. This took courage, pain, and determination. Her book is her therapy and will influence her future happiness and health.

This book is greatly concerned with the biographical aspects of Chris. Form, analysis, and medical terminology, though unavoidable at times, are kept to a minimum. It is easy to make a mystique out of form and analysis.

The layman will analyze; this is human nature. For many people it might lead to personal growth and strength. In more than one respect, this book is "her" life.

Tony A. Tsitos, M.D.

Annandale, Virginia
June 17, 1976

"... Ye shall know the truth, and
the truth shall make you free."

Jesus Christ

I

THE SEPARATION
(1927–46)

Prologue

I am frightened, just a little frightened. There is no place for me to go now. I have always needed someplace to go; from the very beginning I have needed someplace to go, and now I have no place. How do I know the place is gone? I just know—I can feel that it is gone. Just as I have always known that it was there, even before I understood what it was, I now know that it is gone. If knowing the truth makes one free, it also makes one naked, exposed, unguarded, afraid.

Where are they? Where did they go? Before, they have always come when I needed them. I was we; now I am I. "I" is so cold, so alone. Who am I? Where are we? O, my God, is this sanity, is this what they have been trying to bring me to? Why didn't they leave me alone? They're all so sure, so confident, so smug. Why did they have to tell me? I didn't believe them at first, I was angry, I felt betrayed. I knew what I knew, and they knew, too. Everybody knew; it is even written in books.

How can something that has always been true, become false just because they say it is? But it did become false; even as they were saying it, it became false. And I knew that it did. With all of my being struggling to hold it, it vanished. My place, my world, my selves—vanished.

My head aches, my stomach is churning, I sweat, and, God, how my head aches! They will come, I know they will come. They have always come. In a moment I will feel something slipping away from me, going to sleep, but not quite. Then somebody else will be there and I can watch—or, blessed oblivion.

3

It's true. Nobody came. The headache stopped and I am here, alone, all alone. The capsules don't help anymore either. Can capsules that have always worked become false if they say they are false? What else that I believe in is false? Is everything an illusion that can be destroyed when they cry "false"?

They tell me that I am real, that I have always been here and been real—the only real one. But how can it be? I knew them, saw them, touched the work they produced, kept the possessions they left, felt their parting agonies. I have notes they wrote in the diaries, paintings. And all those turtles, and bells, and cards.

Am I to believe that I did all that? Have I lived forty years in fantasy, and now am unable to recognize reality? I must think. If I can just think it through, calmly, perhaps I can see where I am. When did it begin, when was the very first time someone came? Oh, I'm so confused, I can't think. I've got to think. My mind, my being depend on my remembering. Maybe they always were there, even before I can recall. But when did I first know? Think.

It was not Eve, not Eve White or Eve Black—anyway, that's just what the doctors called them. But I was Eve, I know I was Eve—and now I am not Eve. They say I was Eve and that I am still Eve, but she is gone—she left, she died, they died. If I were Eve then, did I die, too? My mind closes, it shuts it out. Can you die and still live? No! I won't think about that yet. I've got to think about the beginning. If Eve did not come first, who did? When was the first someone else? . . . Think. . . . Think. . . .

1

The Red-haired Stranger

Before they pulled him from the water, they thought he was dead. Head and shoulders caught in the bushes, and body floating face down with its arms and legs spread-eagled, he looked as if someone had carefully placed him. He must have fallen into the irrigation ditch at some point along the road and had not been discovered until the men left the house for work in the morning.

Christine, unnoticed in the excitement and hurried activity, watched every move. She had heard Uncle Amos's excited shout and his urgent call, "Acie, come quick!" She had run to the door with her father but had been told to stay in the house. The command only slowed down her two-year-old rush, and she reached the ditch only shortly after her father.

The ditch was bordered by a low hedge of bushes on the near side, and had to be crossed by a wooden foot bridge to reach the road. The water at this point due to the recent heavy rains was nearly waist deep on a grown man. Amos had already lowered himself into the water from the bridge and was trying to grasp the floating body.

"It's ole man Williams," he said. "He musta got drunk and fell in. He hasn't moved; I think he's dead."

At the word "dead," Christine's breath stopped. She had heard that word before, and it was mysterious and frightening. Whenever it was used, people changed and became serious, and sometimes they cried. She looked at her father now to see if he would cry, but he was only squatting on the bridge looking down at the scene in the water.

"He's been missin' two, three days," he said quietly. As Christine watched motionless from the bushes, Amos tried to grasp the man by the clothes, but his body bobbed and turned like a cork in the water and was always just beyond reach. Acie slipped down into the water and caught him by the arm.

"He's slick as a greased pig; been in the water a long time. Prob'ly all night."

As Acie tried to lift the arm over his shoulder, the man's body turned. The sun just topping the trees across the rose field struck full on the face. The rather long red hair streaked sideways in thin strands across the forehead, the eyes were closed, the mouth was partly open. The flesh on the face was stark white and glistened like crystal, the lips were purple and rigid, and the teeth shone a yellowish brown beneath the red mustache. There was a purple bruise on the chin, which matched the garish lips. For what seemed an eternity the awful face grinned mirthlessly from its elevated position in the water, then it slipped with a sucking splash face down into the water again. It sank out of sight in the murky water, then bobbed to the surface, making little waves and sucking noises at Christine's feet.

She wanted to move back, to run, to cry; but she was frozen. Her head swam and her sight blurred, her chest hurt, she could not breathe. She could feel the warm sun on her face, she could feel the sharp prick and jab of the bushes, she could even smell the sweet scent of the tube roses. But her mind and being were filled only with the face and consciousness of death.

Almost against her will, she opened her eyes. The scene had changed little. The two men were slowly dragging the awkward body through the water to the bank beside the road. But there was someone else in the picture now, someone who had not been there when Christine closed her eyes. On the bridge looking directly down upon the scene in the water stood a little girl. Her dark red hair shone brightly in the morning sun, and the first thing Christine noticed was that her bright blue eyes were calm and unafraid.

As Christine fascinatedly watched this stranger quietly and intently gaze down from the bridge, her father and uncle struggled to drag their burden from the water. His head hung down with his hair and clothes floating jerkily about him as the disturbed

6

water splashed and waved. When they reached the bank on the far side at the road, they tried to heave the body out of the water. The wet, glistening skin slipped away under pressure, and the soaked body was heavy and awkward. Amos climbed onto the bank and pulled the body by the clothes, while Acie pushed the legs out of the water. Both men were slight of build, and they sat panting on the bank, unable to talk for a moment.

"He must be twice his usual weight," Christine heard Uncle Amos say. "You'd hardly know him except for his hair and clothes. I'd know that red hair and flowered jacket anywhere. But he's alive, I think."

Christine suddenly heard her mother call her name from close behind her, and tearing her eyes away from the scene in the water, she looked across at her father. Seeing that he had found her, she thought, "I'm going to get whipped, but they will have to whip that other little girl, too."

Hearing steps behind her, Christine turned to find her mother frowning and angry. "*Teeny*, where have you been? I've been looking all over for you. You know you're not to go near the ditch! The monster's goin' to get you yet!"

Acie stood up and shouted, "Sister, get her out of here and back to the house, and don't you come any closer either!"

"Honey, what's wrong? Oh, my God, what's happened? Don't tell me something's wrong."

"Now, don't get upset, Sister. It's just ole man Williams, he fell in the ditch. Go on back up to the house, and I'll come up and tell you."

"Oh, Acie, honey, I just *knew* something was going to happen, I just knew it. Don't anybody tell Mama! Amos, don't you tell Mama. You know how she is, and . . ."

"Now, Sister, I told you, go *back* to the house, and take Top with you. Do I have to *take* you back myself?" Acie took several steps toward the bridge.

Zueline, holding firmly to Christine's hand, gave her a little jerk ahead of her and sharply swatted her twice on the backsides.

Christine began to wail loudly, jumping up and down and dancing around her mother. "No, no! She, not Teeny, girl, girl!" And she pointed toward the bridge, looking for the child who had

7

watched the forbidden scene. But the red-haired stranger was not there, she was gone, and Christine could find her nowhere.

Zueline, already upset and angry, became more provoked at Christine's attempt to blame someone else. "You are a bad girl, you must not tell fibs! Mother does not like bad girls who tell fibs. I told you not to go near the ditch, the monster would get you! Now, see, the monster got ole man Williams." And she continued to sharply smack Christine's buttocks and thighs as she half dragged, half marched the yelling child down the lane.

Was that the first one? I know she was there, I saw her. Even if no one else saw her, I saw her, I saw her. She was standing on the bridge, and she watched. I didn't watch. But I knew what she saw. How could I know what she saw? Think. Think! If she was real, what did she look like? I know, I can see her! She was little and skinny. She had the skinniest legs and the knobbiest knees. Her hair was cropped short just below the ears and was straight bangs across the forehead. It was dark red, and she had freckles, lots of freckles. I've never seen so many freckles. Her eyes were big and blue, the blue of the sky just before rain. She was real! I can even remember her clothes. She had on a straight sleeveless dress and wore an old, shapeless sweater. Her feet seemed too big for such a little girl, and her socks were all stretched and pushed down around her ankles. But she was real, I know it. No matter what they say. But was that the very first time? I can remember others. Were they the same one each time, or were there others then, too? When was the first Eve, or have they all been Eves? Little Eves, big Eves. How will I ever put it all together? There was another time, it could have been the first. . . .

"Teeny, will you, please, move back! You've been under my feet all day. Every time I turn, you're in the way." Zueline was churning milk at the fireplace, and two-year-old Christine, curious and energetic, was in the middle of everything her mother did. They were in the bedroom off the kitchen, since that room had a fireplace, and Zueline had earlier in the day put the milk in front of the fire to sour. She had finished churning the milk, and had taken up the butter and put it in a bowl of cold water. She had spanked Christine's hands to keep them out of the butter, out of the churn, out of anything available. She kept up a running chatter to the child, "You are a bad girl." "You will drive me crazy." "Why don't you run play with your toys?" The little girl seemed not to hear the exhortations. She cried when spanked on the hands or backsides, but it was more yelling than crying and only briefly deterred her from the forbidden action.

Zueline had set four glass jars on the stone hearth to warm, so that they would not break when she poured up the warm milk from the churn. She reached down for a jar and began to dip milk into it with a long-handled dipper. As she held it, it unaccountably broke in her two hands. Realizing that the child was directly below the broken jar, she hugged the jagged fragments to her body. A large shard of glass sliced into her left wrist.

Christine watched the bright red blood pour over her mother's arm and stain the front of her dress and apron. It mixed with the white milk from the broken jar and puddled in red and white patterns on the stones in the hearth. The child was paralyzed with fear—her mother's arm was cut off, and she was going to die! She heard her mother's voice from a long way off urgently repeating, "Baby, go get Daddy. Go get Daddy. Hurry, Baby, hurry, get Daddy!"

Christine felt her head buzz and grow light, her stomach knotted, her mother grew dim and wavered. She backed away and ran to the bed in the corner. The soft feather bed seemed to enfold her, and she pushed her head under the feather pillow. She felt safe and warm; the feathers smelled musty and tickled her nose. She began to itch, not just her nose, but all over—her whole body. When she could stand the discomfort no longer, she withdrew her head and sneezed. Her eyes watered, her nose ran, and she had red splotches on her face, neck, and arms.

Through the watery haze, Christine saw a small red-haired girl standing near the fireplace watching the terrible red blood spill over her mother's arm and onto the stones. She was dressed in a yellow checked apron dress with white knee stockings, and her dry blue eyes were calm and unafraid, and at the urging to "go for Daddy," she turned and quietly hurried from the room.

Christine watched as the other child stood near and observed her father tightly bind her mother's arm with torn strips of white

9

cloth. The bright blood stained the white cloth, but it no longer dripped onto the floor. She heard her mother say,

"Acie, I thought you would never get here. The baby didn't seem to understand me. She has been in my way all day. She could have been killed if I had dropped that broken jar on her head! Christine, where are you?"

As the child lifted her head from against the bed, the first thing she noticed was that the small red-haired girl was gone. Her mother was sitting on a chair holding her injured arm close to her body. Christine wondered if the arm would fall off if she turned it loose.

Acie called to her, "Come to Daddy, Baby. You were a good girl to come get Daddy. Sister, I believe she's catching a cold. And look at all these red spots on her! She's eaten something that's given her hives."

"Oh, honey," Zueline fretted, "I'll be glad when we get back home. Mama would know what to do. Everything just seems to be going wrong! You promised me we would go back when that awful thing happened to old Jim!"

"We're goin', honey, we're goin'," Acie soothed softly.

Christine, held tightly in her father's arms, had noticed some red stains on one of her white knee stockings. She wondered if her leg would fall off when he put her down.

That could have been the first time, and it was the same child as the one at the ditch. And that's the same place. I've heard Mother say that we only lived there three months. We moved away from all the rest of the family. I think Daddy liked it, but Mother missed her family. Wallace! That's it, the name of the place was Wallace. And that's where something awful happened, it happened to a black man named ole Jim. I wonder if anyone came then. If I could just remember how it happened. Oh, God, how much do I actually remember, and how much have I just heard others talk about? Think. I know I heard the whistle. . . .

When the whistle began to blow, Zueline looked up sharply from the peas she was shelling into a pan in her lap. She was sitting on a chair in the doorway of the bedroom so that she could watch Christine playing on the porch. If not closely watched, the child would wander away, and her mother was in constant fear that she would fall into the irrigation ditch and drown. Zueline was abjectly afraid of water herself, and she tried to prevent the child from going near the ditch by daily warning her about "the monster in the ditch."

Christine heard the whistle, also. She jumped up and looked down the path toward the sawmill. The whistle blew twice a day, at noon and at 6:00 P.M., and it meant that her father was coming home. At her mother's loud wail, "Oh, my God!" Christine turned toward the house. Zueline was looking at the clock on the mantel. It was only ten twenty-five. She put the pan of shelled peas on the chair and took off her apron. As she hurried down the porch steps, she smoothed her black hair behind her ears and felt the neat knot at her nape. No matter what the circumstances, Mama had taught them to be neat and never to leave the house with an apron on.

She knew that there was only one reason why the sawmill whistle would blow at this time of day, and keep on blowing in that awful, screaming way. There had been an accident at the mill. She snatched the startled child up in her arms as she went by, half praying, half babbling to the child as she ran.

"Oh, my God, what has happened? Acie, Acie, honey, please, be all right! Oh, God, don't let anything happen to him! Mama said something terrible would happen if we came to this awful place! Oh, Acie, honey!"

The sawmill was about a quarter of a mile from the house down the road. But Zueline did not take the road; she cut across the tube rose field, unmindful of the plants catching at her dress. Some of the roses were beginning to bloom, and the fragrance was strong and sweet in the morning air.

On the far side of the field, the big pine forest began. Christine, bouncing to her mother's lumbering gait, looked up dizzily at the crazy swaying of the tall, incredibly slim trees. The whistle, which had grown to earsplitting loudness as they drew nearer, suddenly stopped as they broke out of the trees and into the clearing. The silence was a deafening hum in the ears. The scene laid out before them seemed to have been stopped in midaction. No one was moving. The mill, long and narrow, with its belts and wheels, was still. The mighty saw, its huge round blade gleaming in the sun,

11

was quiet, but its teeth were bared and ready to scream angrily at the push of a lever.

The men were all grouped around the blade. They stood unmoving, staring down into the sawdust pit beneath the sawblade. They were unaware that the woman and child had crossed the clearing until they heard Zueline's scream. Acie jerked his stunned gaze from the scene at his feet, and his face registered his horror for the first time, mirrored from that on the face of his wife, and from the fact that his two-year-old daughter was calmly looking down into the pit.

The man in the pit lay face down on the sawdust pile. He lay in three unconnected segments. His body was neatly sliced in half just above the waist. The two halves falling into the pit on either side of the saw had grotesquely lined themselves up a horribly small distance apart. Bright red blood poured from both ends of the severed body and was hungrily soaked up by the dry sawdust. The glistening puddles never widened. The fact that the wild pouring never seemed to accumulate made the spilled amount appear to be greater. One arm was flung out over the partially buried face, as if he had been diving into water. The other arm lay quietly by his side, severed midway in the upper arm and lying, turned at an odd angle, beside the body.

Zueline clutched the rigid child to her, and babbled the only human sounds except labored breathing, "Oh, dear Jesus, I knew something had happened! I felt it was going to happen. All that blood! Oh, Lord, Acie, his arm is cut off!"

It was a measure of her ability, and her constant practice, to dwell on minor details to avoid facing the major issues, when she commented on the severed arm and ignored the divided body.

Acie, fighting a nightmarish feeling of immobility, moved around the pit and, roughly taking both the woman and child into his arms, moved them away from the horror in the pit. "He's dead, Sister, that's all, he's just dead," he told her soothingly, as if that fact lessened the horror and made a man, divided into three parts, something that the living could accept.

Several things registered indelibly on Christine's mind. So *this* was death. She had heard the word before, and she knew that it changed people. It never made them happy, and often it made them very sad. But she had never *seen* death before. It did not make her sad; it struck a new fear and a tense dread deep in her being. Her head hurt, and her stomach felt sick. And all that blood, red and so freely pouring! Her mother had said that his arm was cut off. All that blood meant that his arm was cut off, and it *all* meant death.

One incongruous scene would remain impressed into Christine's mind for the rest of her life. As the halves of the man lay that incredible distance apart, his belt, which he had placed around his waist several hours before, remained undisturbed and as neatly in place as when the severed hand had fastened it. This commonplace and largely unnecessary component was unobtrusively continuing to perform its mundane function long after the vital components had ceased to sustain life.

Nobody came. All that horror, and I just looked on. I looked at it—no one came. Where was the red-haired child who came the other times? I can see it all so vividly, even now. Or really, how much do I actually remember seeing, and how much did I hear Mother and the family talk about? They talked about it so much, and described it all so many times. And Mother would always say that I was the only one not affected by it—I was too little. But it could have been the beginning of it all. So much blood, and the arm cut off. The blood running into the sawdust. Blood running off Mother's arm, and Mother's arm cut. Wondering if the cut arm would fall off. The cut-off arm and the blood meant the man was dead. Mother's cut arm and all the blood meant death, was like the man in the pit. Turn him over and he was the man in the ditch. Death was bad, not to be looked at, horrible! Was that why I did not look those other times, and the other one came and looked? Was it too horrible to be repeated? Could I not stand the blood and the cut and the death, and the others had to come? Did they come because they had to come?

Be calm. If I ever make sense of all this, I can't panic, I've got to calmly reason and think. Think! What does all this mean? All that blood and horrible dying. I couldn't understand it all, but I knew it was terrible—it frightened my mother and father, and everybody. I should not have seen those things. I could not bear to see those awful things. That man cut in three

13

parts. Three parts. OH, my God, there were always three of them who came! The man had three separate parts, and they were always three separate beings. Was it then, looking down on the three separate pieces, that the three of them came into being? But they were not the same *three each time. Or does that matter? Maybe I didn't need the same help each time. Maybe whatever I needed came to help me, just like the red-haired child—I needed someone to watch what I could not look at. So she came and watched for me. But I knew what she saw— without looking myself, I knew what she saw. I think I'm losing my mind just thinking about it. But wait, wait, maybe there's a pattern, a clue. Don't think about how strange it is; just think about what happened—just exactly what happened.*

All right. Everything seemed to have to do with death. Was there anything else *having to do with death that I can remember? I have only one scene in my mind—one impression. There was a little white box sitting on the back seat of a car. . . .*

It was February. A nasty, cold, rainy February, typical of Carolina in midwinter. It had been raining for several days, with a low, muddy, gray sky and sharp, gusty winds. They had held an umbrella over the little white casket when they took it out to the car. At the last minute, Mamie Lee, tearfully watching her brother carry the little box, had exclaimed, "Wait, wait, let me put a blanket over him!"

Her husband soothingly told her, "It's all right, Mother, it's all right," and motioned for Amos to take his little burden out into the rain.

The cars were lined up waiting to take everybody to the church. Mamie Lee left the house for the car. As she crossed the porch, the rain-filled wind tore at her black veil. Her thin body swayed in the wind, and she leaned heavily on the arms of her father and her brother Dodge. Following her from the house was her mother, leaning on the arm of her brother Ernest. She was also veiled and dressed in black. It was Mama's custom to have a "light stroke" at funerals of members of the family, and now each time she gave a slight moan, everybody looked anxiously at her. Junior had been only five months old, however, and was the first baby to die since

Mattie Willow, Mama's own baby; and that was so long ago that nobody could remember what happened. Some of the brothers and sisters present had not even been born when Mattie Willow died, and the others had been small children themselves.

The family left the house to join in the funeral procession. The last to leave the porch were the father, Ellis, and his brother Acie. As Ellis put on his hat, he voiced a concern to his brother,

"I'm afraid there's going to be water in the grave. I don't see how it could keep from it with all this rain."

Acie, holding ten-month-old Christine in his arms, answered, "We waited till this morning to dig the grave, and we covered it with tarp. The cemetery is on a hill and ought to drain pretty fast."

"Maybe you're right. I hope so. Mamie Lee has been worried all night about leaving Junior out there in the rain. If the grave has water in it, I don't know what she'll do."

Acie answered, "I'm worried about Sister, too. She could be a problem herself. And their mother is no help either. If she faints out there in that red mud!"

Ellis looked at his brother with the first amused look to cross his face in weeks, "Don't worry, she is not going to faint in the mud. Come on, let's go."

As they came up to the car, Christine, looking down from her father's shoulder, saw the small white casket on the back seat of the car. She heard her Aunt Meme sobbing, "Oh, my baby. My baby, you are too little to be dead." And she heard Granny moaning, "Why did he have to die?" All the family were crying, some aloud, others quietly. Most of the men had their handkerchiefs out.

Christine knew there was a baby in the box—a dead baby. Why was the baby in the box? People held babies, and looked at babies, and played with babies. Did being a dead baby mean being shut up in a box and taken away, and did it make everybody cry? Christine knew that she was a baby, everybody called her Baby. It was nice being a baby—but it was not nice being a dead baby.

Was that when the fear began? Way back then? Was I so impressed with the grief, so unable to understand and cope with the emotions that they all turned to fear and dread? Did the

15

natural, innocent death of a baby become translated into that mutilated horror in the sawdust pit? Did death, even in the abstract, become so terror-filled and unbearable that retreat was the only means of holding onto sanity? Did the others come because I could not live with my reality? But other people face these same realities. Why was I different? Others have stood and faced fear, while I ran! Why? Why? There must be some answers. Do all people have this potential? Or was I born lacking something or having too much of something?

It must go back farther than I can remember. There must have been happenings to groom my being for these kinds of reactions. But if I can't remember, how can I ever know? Maybe others, those living when I was born and even before I was born, can tell me something, anything that will show how I got to be this way.

2

Christine

Zueline was sick almost from the moment she conceived her child. Not only did she suffer headaches, nausea, and fainting spells, she also had intermittent bleeding and threatened constantly to lose the baby. She was also very frightened, a fact that she tried desperately to hide. Mama had borne eleven children, ten of whom were still living, and she had never had any trouble. Of course, she had felt faint and weak and had rested a lot, all the women from the good families became delicate during that time, only field hands had *no* trouble at all; but Zueline knew that she was having a lot more trouble than Mama ever had.

Zueline was the oldest girl in the family and the third child after her two older brothers, Robert and Dodge, and she had been aware of her mother's condition during her confinements with the younger children. Even though Mama had complained a lot and had required much waiting on, Zueline knew that she had not been really sick, at least not the way Zueline was now sick. It frightened Zueline to feel that she was not measuring up to her mother's standard. She was the oldest girl, and she was expected to be an example for the other girls. Mama was always pointing out to her how she fell short of her own examples, and Zueline had a deep dread, that she could share with no one, especially Acie, of having to face her mother's criticism if she did a less than acceptable job in this all-important business of producing a child.

Mama had even had two boys before she had produced a girl. All men, of course, wanted a boy, a son, to carry on the family name, and it was so much better to have a boy first. The heir would be assured, and the son would be older and a help and comfort to his mother if anything happened to her husband. Also, men had a first and most important place in the family—not that girls were unimportant, but the men had a first place—and having an older boy taught the younger girls to look up to and respect menfolk. In some families—good families, too—older daughters had been known to take a liking to men's work and to develop into very rough, unladylike women, who even allowed themselves to become browned by the sun. Mama said these women were no better than field hands.

Zueline desperately wanted her baby to be a boy. If it were, it would appease Mama for the fact that Acie was someone whom nobody knew. Not only that, he was not even from South Carolina—he was from *North* Carolina! He didn't even own any land! Worst of all, he talked differently. Even though Zueline loved him dearly, she did wish he would not say "you'uns." Why couldn't he just say "y'all," like everybody else?

Zueline also lived in constant fear that she would mark her baby. She was careful not to look at ugly things or think ugly thoughts, especially thoughts about the booga man or the devil. She had warned Acie and her young brothers not to frighten her. Acie was such a big tease, and she suspected that he did not believe in her fears; but he was always gentle with her. Above all, she would not cook or eat liver. A lot of women had marked their babies with liver spots.

Zueline had been much happier since her sister Mamie Lee had married Ellis, Acie's older brother. He had come down to Greenwood County looking for timber to cut. The cotton farmers had never recovered from the ravages of the boll weevil, and they were happy to sell off the virgin pine timber from their land. When Ellis came back to set up his sawmill and lumber camp, he brought with him two of his younger brothers, Lester and Acie.

There was much competition between the boys from the North and the local boys for the attention of the local girls, but it wasn't long before Zueline and her younger sister Mamie Lee were dating the two Costner boys. Dating was mostly the gathering of young people at somebody's house, going to church together, or meeting at an occasional box supper, but it soon became generally understood that Zueline and Acie were a steady couple. Ellis was twice

18

sixteen-year-old Mamie Lee's age, which displeased Mama, but he was too "well fixed" to be seriously objected to.

It was almost two years before Acie and Zueline were married. Part of that time he was away in Alabama working in lumber camps. When they were married they moved into a tiny house at Ellis's lumber camp. Ellis, Lester, and Amos, Zueline's younger brother, lived with them, and she did all the cooking and laundry for the four men. She also cooked the noon meal for all the men who came daily to work at the sawmill.

She was lonesome and missed the large, noisy household she had left. It was fun having her own house to run, but she also missed Mama and felt guilty about all the things that she was no longer doing for her. She well knew that Mamie Lee, still at home, would never take on her abandoned chores. Mamie Lee really stood up to Mama, and in a crisis she ran to Papa. He would always take up for her. Everybody knew she was his favorite. He even let her cut her hair off like a flapper and wouldn't let the other girls. He had named her after his favorite sister, who had burned to death when she was a young woman.

Ellis soon rented a bigger house having three large rooms, and Acie, Zueline, and Amos moved in with him. Soon he married Mamie Lee and brought her to live there with them. In spite of her sickness, this was a very happy time for Zueline. Having her sister with her was almost like being at home again. Mamie Lee loved to sew, and while Zueline continued to do most of the housework, her sister worked all day making clothes for the baby. Soon Mamie Lee herself became pregnant, and the two sisters spent the days and the long winter evenings planning for their babies.

One night, in the seventh month of her pregnancy, Zueline waked with severe pains in her stomach. She roused her husband,

"Acie, honey, wake up! I'm hurting, oh-h-h, Lordy, I hurt. Do you think it's something I ate? I just knew I would do something wrong!" And she sat up in bed and began to cry, holding both arms around her swollen stomach.

Acie, slim as a rail in his long-handled underwear, got out of bed and sat beside her, holding her close against his side. "There, there, honey, it'll be all right. Don't cry. Where does it hurt?"

"It hurts all over," she wailed. "I think the baby is coming, and nobody is here to help me. What will I do? What will I do?" she moaned softly, rocking back and forth. She was covered by a voluminous white nightgown, and with her long black hair falling around her tear-stained face, she looked like a frightened child.

"Now, don't get scared, honey, it's probably just gas and will ease off in a minute. Stand up and try to walk." Acie tried to help her up from the bed.

"Oh-h-h, I can't! My legs are numb, it feels like the whole bottom is falling out. Oh, Acie, what will I do? Is the baby coming?" Her face was contorted with pain.

"Maybe he is coming early, honey." Acie looked at her, showing his concern on his face. "I'll get Amos up and send him for Doc Crafton. Now you just lie back and rest."

As he crossed the room, his large bare feet feeling the chill of the smooth board floor, he thought how unfortunate it was that Ellis and Mamie Lee were away and there was no car. But who would have thought that Sister would get sick now? It was more than six weeks before the baby was due. Maybe it was just as well; she had been sick the whole time; it would be a relief to get it over with.

He opened the door into the big room in the center of the house. It served as kitchen, dining room, and sitting room. Across the room on the opposite wall was the door leading into the other bedroom. Seventeen-year-old Amos usually slept on a cot in the middle room, but tonight, in the absence of Ellis and Mamie Lee, he was sleeping in the other bedroom. He sat up instantly when Acie opened the door and called him.

"What's the matter, Bud, anything wrong?"

"Sister's took bad sick. Baby's prob'ly coming early. You'll have to go for Doc Crafton. Take the mule. And hurry, boy, she's really bad this time." Acie turned back into the big room and began to punch up the smoldering coals in the fireplace.

Amos, hastily pulling on his clothes, sat down on a chair to tie his shoes. Acie instructed him,

"It's five miles. Should take about an hour. Leave the mule and ride back with Doc; I might need you. Tell him there's no bleeding yet, but the pain is all the time, and bad. And tell him to hurry."

As they crossed the room to the door, Zueline's soft moaning

20

turned into a high, thin cry of pain. Both men, neither scarcely more than a boy, stopped and looked toward the room. Then Acie jerked the door open and pushed his brother-in-law into the chill spring night.

Amos touched him on the shoulder. "I'll hurry, don't you worry none, I'll be back with ole Doc Crafton in no time." And he disappeared toward the barn on the run.

As Acie turned back into the room, he had two thoughts uppermost in his mind: Why did Mamie Lee have to be away at this time? At least she could have comforted Sister; and that he had better get a fire going in the stove for hot water and coffee. Zueline's cries broke into his thoughts and turned his steps toward her room. He heard the gallop of the mule pass the house and fade down the road.

It was almost two hours before he heard the sound of the T-Model pulling into the yard. He had the door open before Amos and the doctor were out of the car. Dr. John Neal Crafton was in his early sixties. He was a small man with dark skin and a thin rim of gray hair around his bald head. He handed his hat and coat to Acie and formally addressed him,

"How do you do, Mr. Costner. How is your wife?"

"She's pretty sick, Doc. The pains are bad. And it's not near time for the baby."

"Well, let's have a look at her. Bring as many lamps as you have." Acie led the doctor into the bedroom, saying over his shoulder to Amos,

"Git all the lamps lit and bring them in."

Zueline lay on the rumpled bed. Her eyes were red and swollen, and her face glistened with sweat. Her long, straight black hair, usually so neat, was damp and thready on the balled pillow. As the doctor approached the bed, she smoothed back a strand stuck to her wet cheek. This was her first female examination by a doctor, and at the moment she was not sure which emotion was stronger, desire for help from the little man, or fear of him.

When the doctor came from the room a few minutes later, Acie took a hesitant step toward him. He did not know the old doctor very well, and he could read nothing in his grave, dark face.

"Doc . . . ," he began. The doctor interrupted him,

"There's nothing I can do for her, son. She's trying a breech birth. We've got to get her to the hospital. They have equipment to help with those things."

Acie looked down at the boards at his feet. His brilliant blue eyes were worried and unsure when he looked again at the doctor. "What's a breech birth, Doc? Is that bad?"

Dr. Crafton looked at the young man kindly. "It can be, son. It means that the baby is coming the wrong way, backward. Zueline is a little woman. And even though her baby is small, she will have a lot of trouble birthing it the wrong way. She needs to get to the hospital as quick as possible. If the baby can be turned before it gets too far down, she'll be all right. She'll have to go to Augusta. Do you have a car we can use?"

Acie was beginning to look really worried. "No, Doc, I don't have no car, and my brother's got his'un and won't be back until tomorrow afternoon. Is that too late?"

The doctor began putting on his coat and hat. "No matter," he said calmly. "We'll take her in mine. She'll have to lie down in the back seat. Wrap her in blankets and put a quilt and some pillows on the seat. Boy," he said to Amos, "go out and snap in the side curtains. You'll find them under the right-hand front seat. I think I'll have another sip of that coffee while you get her ready. Don't let her stand, or even sit any more than you can help."

Amos spread the back seat with a quilt and pillows, and Acie carried his wife out and laid her as comfortably as possible in the narrow nest. He turned to Amos as he climbed up into the car beside the doctor.

"Tell Ellis to come to the hospital as soon as he gets here."

The young man stood shivering in the chill early-morning air, watching the single red light wink and diminish as the little car bounced over the rutted, single-lane road. He was very excited by the events of the night and very much impressed by the quiet, efficient little doctor. He was later to name his only son, Crafton, after this man who delivered him.

The story of what treatment Zueline received in the hospital was never quite clear. The best explanation that filtered down through the years was that "they turned the baby with hot water bottles." At any rate, the turning did not take—Christine was born by breech birth. Ellis brought Zueline home late that same day with instructions to keep her in bed, use hot water bottles for pain, and feed her only warm—not hot—soup to keep the nausea down.

The pain never really let up, and Christine was born almost two months early, about 3:00 A.M. two weeks later, April 4, 1927. Dr. Crafton, along with a neighbor woman and a black woman, had been with Zueline since early morning. The difficulties of the birth were lessened because the baby was so incredibly small. She only weighed approximately two pounds. Her tiny head was covered by an enormous shock of fluffy, dark red hair. Her eyes were not the cloudy, indeterminate blue of most newborn infants, but a bright, clear, cat's-eye marble blue.

Zueline, exhausted by her ordeal and the many sleepless nights and days of pain, was almost asleep when the doctor brought the wrinkled red mite and placed it at her breast.

"It's a girl, Miz Costner," he said gently.

Zueline looked at the crumpled red face with its unusual fluff of hair, which, even damp, was scarcely a darker shade than the face itself, and thought, "A girl, a red-haired girl! What in the world will Mama say?" She began trying to think of any red-haired relatives in her family who could have caused this startling fact. There were the Horn cousins, of course, but they got their red hair from their father's side, which had no blood connection with the family. Mama and Papa were distant cousins, and all the relatives except Mama's brother Jim, who had jet-black hair, lived right around Greenwood County. Sister well knew that there was no red hair in the Hastings family. Acie had never mentioned whether he had any red hair in his family. That had to be the answer! The baby could take after his side of the family just as easily as her side, and there must be red hair in the Costner blood.

It was, however, a question that she never asked her husband, or any member of his family. Perhaps not knowing the answer was safer than receiving a negative answer. As it was, she always replied that the child "took after Acie's side of the family" when she was questioned about the hair. And fortunately the hair gradually darkened until it was brown by the time the child was six, and eventaully it became almost black, always retaining its fluffy, cloudy effect.

Zueline went to sleep cuddling her baby to her breast, strangely comforted and satisfied by the feel of the grasping little mouth on her nipple. Her last thoughts were ambivalent: She fiercely loved this tiny red girl, yet she wished with all her being that it had been a dark-haired boy.

When she awoke it was to a quite different household. Ellis had brought Mamie Lee home, and he had also brought Mama. Since Mamie Lee was four months pregnant, it had been decided that she should not stay and witness the sounds and sights of the birth—it might excite her and cause her to lose her own baby, or at least to mark it. She had been taken to Mama's. When Ellis brought her home, Mama came, too. It was to become a tradition in the Hastings family: The Family! Whenever one of her daughters—and she had six living—delivered a baby, the husband would come for Mama for a couple of weeks. Her greatest contribution was her knowledge of such things as navel bands, poultices, douches, breast pumps, and the like. It also was a comfort to the new mothers—it allowed them to become children again, and in this time of great need, just before assuming the demanding adult responsibility of a new baby, it was good to be taken over and cared for by "my own mother."

And finally, it was a sort of tribute to Mama. This man may have taken her daughter away, always over Mama's tearful, frantic protest that she could not lose her girl, but now he had to come to ask for her help to care for this very same daughter whom he had vowed so fiercely that he could take care of. It was a part of the humbling process that Mama so adeptly used, that allowed her to rule her large family for all of her eighty-six years.

When Zueline awoke she found that the two women had taken complete charge of the household and her baby. Mamie Lee was exclaiming over the fact that all of the clothes she had made for the baby were too big, and Mama was busy reorganizing the household. Amos's cot was moved into Zueline's room for Mama, who felt that she should be close to watch over the mother and baby during the night, and a pallet was put down each night in the middle room for Acie and Amos.

Zueline secretly wished that Acie could be with her at night— they had had no time alone together since this whole thing started—but Mama knew how things ought to be done, and she did not dare oppose her. The baby was to sleep with her at night, but during the day, except at feeding times, the baby was to sleep on the cot. Zueline loved to feel the tiny body nestled against her and to feel the incredibly small mouth sucking at her breast. She had decided to name her baby Christine. This broke with family tradition in two ways. First, it was not a family name, and second, it was not a double name. All girls had two names, usually drawn from members of the Family, past and present, or from close friends. Zueline could have added a second part of a relative's name to Christine, but she didn't, and only her secret heart knew why she broke with this important family habit.

She had always liked the name Christine—there had been an Uncle Christopher way back on Mama's side—but she had not ever thought of giving it to a child. She and Mamie Lee both had talked only of boy babies and had called them Junior, after their fathers; she had not even planned a girl's name. Feeling that her baby was different because of its red hair, and knowing that people, as they always did with red-haired children, would raise half-formed questions concerning its parentage, she perhaps hesitated to form what might prove to be an unwelcome alliance between her innocent child and a reluctant relative. It surely had not relieved her fears to have Mamie Lee exclaim,

"Oh, Sister, it's a girl, and what an awful head of hair!" Her use of the term "awful" literally meant "full of awe." It was commonly used to describe something unusually large or abundant and was in no way derogatory, and Zueline well knew this, but she *had* mentioned the hair. And why not? Not only was it red hair, it was also a lot of red hair. Everybody was going to notice all that red hair. She had also been deeply hurt when Mama, after having bathed the baby and brought her to the bed for a feeding, had commented in her aggressive manner,

"Sister, where *did* you get such an ugly child? It's so skinny and knobby, every bone shows."

Mamie Lee quickly replied, "Oh, Mama, I think she's cute. She'll fill out and be fat as a butter ball in no time."

Mama grunted, "No doubt about that, she nurses as greedily as a boy. But with that coloring, she'll probably have freckles." It was her only reference to the red hair, which to Zueline appeared to be the deliberate avoidance of a distasteful subject. Mama sometimes did that—just ignored something that displeased her, as if her refusal to recognize it robbed it of its substance.

For whatever the reason, Zueline chose to give her baby a completely individual name and to identify her with no one.

The household settled down, and the confusion of baby crying, diapering, feeding, and the numerous other jobs related to caring for a new baby became routine. Women reign supreme at such times; and the three men, feeling awkward around such delicate goings-on, stayed out of the house and out of the way as much as possible. They let themselves be bossed about how to hold the baby, marveled over such things as tiny toes and fingers, and showed proper concern over the soft spot on the little head.

Zueline's breasts had been sore and sensitive from the first nursing. She had a lot of milk, and Christine drank very little. During the second week her breasts and nipples grew hot and swollen and she began to run a fever. The milk was no longer clear and thin, but cloudy and curdled, and Mama said the breasts had risen and the baby could not drink the milk. Dr. Crafton was sent for. He pumped the milk from the painfully swollen breasts and put the baby on cow's milk; but it was evident from the first feeding that this new milk was not agreeing. When the doctor returned, he ordered a feeding of canned condensed milk weakened with water. Christine thrived on the new milk and nursed it from a bottle until she was ten months old, when she suddenly refused her bottle and never again drank milk.

When she left her mother's breast for the bottle, Christine was held by a different person for each of her feedings. Each body felt different, each voice sounded different. Her mother cuddled her snuggly and warmly; her aunt was busy inspecting her and touching her body with cool, impersonal hands; her grandmother very firmly and positively settled her and intermittently fed and burped her; her father and uncles awkwardly and loosely held her and made loud, rough noises. If this were not confusing enough, they also called her by different names. This was a tradition in the Family inherited from their English ancestors. Everybody had two or three pet names, which they were called by as often as by their given names. The women had such names as Fan, Babe, Sal, Duck, and Sister, and the men were called Son and Buster. Younger children who could not pronounce "brother" and "sister" called their older siblings "bubber" and "tuta," and these names lasted a lifetime. Almost every name had its diminutive—Robert was Bob or Bobby, Mary Ann was M.A. or Aunt May—and some names had corruptions, such as converting Mamie Lee to Maje and Meme.

Some names had no obvious explanations and had meaning only to the Family. One woman, the family youngest, was called Little Sugar and Big Toe her entire life, while another father called his daughter Piggy until she was an adult from the game of "This little piggy goes to market," which he played on her toes when she was a baby. Some names, especially male names, did not lend themselves to nicknames, and men could not, of course, be called by pet names. Nevertheless, most men acquired unexplained names, which the other men knowingly called them. Ellis was called Dick by his admiring younger relatives.

Parents most often referred to their youngest child, no matter what age, as "the baby," and husbands and wives addressed each other as Sugar, or Mother and Daddy after the children began to arrive. A person could have several nicknames, perhaps acquiring one that stuck and was used by most people, or having several, each one used by a different person.

Her Uncle Amos began immediately to call Christine Carrot Top, which was shortened to Top or Toppy. Her aunt called her Teeny because "she is not just tiny, she is tee-niny!," her father called her Daughter. Her mother called her Christine or Daughter, and Mama just mostly called her Young'un.

Mama, leaving many admonitions behind her, soon went home, and the household settled into its new normal routine. Zueline, feeling well for the first time in months, cooked, cleaned, and did the laundry. Mamie Lee, four months pregnant, played with the baby and made baby clothes. Christine was so small that no matter how tightly they pinned the tiny garments around her, they usually later found her entirely inside her clothes—head, arms, legs, everything.

It was a good time, a happy time, and as the child grew and filled out she became extremely active and receptive to attention. She recognized all the adults in her little world, and never minded being handled by strange adults and children alike when they all made their weekly pilgrimage to Mama and Papa's for Sunday dinner. She was the only baby in the family. The next youngest children were her cousin and her aunt, Mama's baby, Anne, who were both three years old.

In her own house, Christine was the only darling of five adults, who showered her with constant attention, which she had to share with no one. When she was five months old, however, the picture changed. Her little cousin, Junior, was born—a chubby, dimpled, black-haired baby boy. He naturally claimed a lot of attention—he was a boy, the first boy grandchild in the Family.

Christine, from the first, was jealous of him and showed her first signs of stubborn, mischievous behavior. She especially loved her Uncle Ellis and showed signs of jealousy whenever he held his baby. She cried and fussed and reached for her uncle. Ellis tried holding both her and the baby, one on each arm, but Christine would not allow that, and pushed and kicked at Junior.

She was told that she was a bad girl and that she must love her little cousin. Being a bad girl was a new experience for Christine. She knew that it was rejection, not love, and she felt the rejection. This little cousin was the cause of her unhappiness and the loss of her first place in the Family. The baby's cradle seemed to her to symbolize all of his new importance. Ellis had made a wooden cradle for his baby. It sat on the floor on rockers, and was moved from room to room so that someone could always watch over its precious contents. Christine wanted desperately to be put in the cradle, and she cried and reached for it, until one day someone understood and laid her in the little bed.

Her own bed was a small low green wooden box, which her father had made for her. It was pretty and loved by the little girl, but she always thought it took second place to that cradle.

Junior's short little life only lasted from September to February, and Christine's earliest memory is of his little white casket lying on the back seat of the car on that rainy day when he was buried. They all suffered the loss of the tiny, placid-tempered boy, all except Christine. She became doubly precious to those in her household, for they now knew that a child, no matter how loved and cared for, could one day just be gone, leaving an aching, empty hole. The aggressive, demanding, often comic little girl did much to relieve this terrible ache. She so freely loved her grieving aunt and uncle that they could not help showering her with their thwarted and unused devotion. They became Meme and Unc,

28

and during this period they formed a bond of love with Christine that was to last a lifetime. During her later darkest hours, they renewed this love and gave her the shelter and protection of their home. No matter how confusing and misunderstood her life was to become, her Aunt Meme always defended her and loved her dearly, often more warmly and openly than she did her own daughter.

During the following two years, the two couples became unusually close. Perhaps only in this kind of relationship, brothers married to sisters, could this kind of unrestrained closeness exist. Each one lent a quality vital to the needs of the others, each one felt warm, needed, comfortable, and secure in his place, and each one gave and received love, affection, and acceptance.

The two sisters were only a year apart in age. Both were hardly more than girls, pretty, and fun-loving. Here, however, their similarities ended. Zueline, though calm and even-tempered, had a lively sense of humor and was always joking and laughing. She openly revealed her fears and worries, and unhesitatingly praised and deferred to others. She was a homebody and in no way vain. She loved to cook and to keep her house, but she was not a meticulous housekeeper and made no pretense of always cleaning and putting away. People were comfortable in her presence. Though she kept herself neat and clean, she often went around her house, a part of the day, with her small, chubby feet bare.

Her sister could not have been more different. Mamie Lee both fussed and was fussy. In many ways she was a paradox. She could love fiercely, though never warmly, and she could reject just as fiercely and coldly. She never really unquestioningly accepted any other than her blood kin. Blood kin were accepted irrevocably, and reasons could always be found for their questionable behavior; usually blame was placed on others: "They caused him to do it!" Others, including friends and in-laws, enjoyed her eternally tentative acceptance, which degenerated at the first hint of a question, into a knowing smile and a nod of the head, followed by comments such as, "I'm not surprised." She made a great fuss of cleaning, and indulged in it all day long, with many intermittent periods to rest and talk, or go places and do other things.

The two brothers, one a traveled, experienced man of the world in his late thirties, the other a boy just turned twenty, had a friendly, if reserved relationship. Acie had been only a baby when his oldest brother had left home at seventeen. No word was heard from Ellis for ten years, when he suddenly returned. He had changed his name from Ellis Costner to Ernest Sain to avoid being traced by his family. Unaccountably, he had chosen two names that would have drawn immediate attention to himself if his presence had been sought: Ernest was his brother's given name, and Sain was his mother's maiden name. He later legally changed his name to Ernest Sain to satisfy his military records and to simplify his own clouded identification; but by his wife and her family, he was always called Ellis.

Acie was a gentle man, patient and even-tempered. He was very slender, of medium height, and had curly black hair and startlingly blue eyes. He had a ready smile, loved to joke and tease, and even though he lived in a section famous for its bootleg liquor, he never drank. In after years, when life dealt him a cruel blow, he never lost his calm, balanced composure, his sense of humor, or the mischievous twinkle in his eye. He loved his vivacious little daughter, and throughout her troubled, confused life, he quietly gave her acceptance and love, neither questioning nor directing her. Never creating a disturbance nor being upset by those who did, he placidly moved through his life—perhaps too placidly for the aggressively energetic child.

Acie felt the importance in his work was second to his brother's and wanted to strike out on his own. When he heard of a sawmill needing an experienced foreman, he applied and was hired. When he talked it over with his wife, Zueline immediately began to worry.

"Where is it, honey?" she asked. "I just thought we would live here for a long time. Is it far away?"

"It's near Wallace, North Carolina," he answered. He was aware of her fears, but having grown up in a family with no sisters and a no-nonsense mother, he was never able to fully understand his wife's superstitions and hesitancies.

"Is it near where your folks live?" Zueline asked timidly. She was not so sure that living near her in-laws would be better than living among total strangers. Her family was of direct English descent on both sides; and Acie, replying to her questions about his ancestors in a disinterested, vague way, had indicated that his background was German, French, and Scotch-Irish. What a mixture! She knew they talked strangely, but maybe they even ate strange food and went to a different kind of church. She was almost relieved to hear her husband say,

"No, it's all the way to the other end of the state. And, honey, we prob'ly won't be there long. I don't know how big the stand of timber is."

"Well, if we won't be there long. I just wonder what Mama is going to say," she answered, revealing her greatest concern.

The following Sunday when the Family gathered at Mama and Papa's for dinner, the move was discussed by the entire family. It was their custom to feed the men at the first table; children, up to about age thirteen or fourteen, were fed at a table in the kitchen, or in the summer on the porch; the women ate after the men at the second table, and the two oldest girls remaining unmarried at home, finished up what was left and cleared away the table. The wives often hovered around the table while the men ate, and they helped serve the plates of their husbands, who always got the choicest cuts of meat and the best pieces of chicken. This custom, of course, was merely another indication of the high esteem in which men were held in this tradition-bound family; but if asked, they would have answered that menfolk had their talk and womenfolk had theirs. It was a great day in the life of a boy when one of the adults would tell him to "come on and eat with the men." He would be very embarrassed and protest, several adults would question whether he was old enough, and there would be much joking and teasing; but he would that day have been admitted into the rarefied air of the world of the men of the Family, and entitled to all the rights and privileges thereof.

There was one noticeable difference between the men's table and the women's table: the formality of eating habits. The men were precise and formal in their table manners and got down to the business of eating. Talk mostly had to do with the weather, crops, and politics. Religion was considered female business and left, along with morality, to be discussed by the women. There was a definite order observed and respected: The older and more important men did most of the talking, while the others listened attentively and nodded in agreement. The women, busy around the table serving, did not enter the men's conversations, and if they addressed one of the men, it was in hushed tones.

When the men finished eating, they, in one body, left the table. If it were hot weather, they went out on the porch to smoke; if it were cold, they gathered in one of the rooms around a fireplace; and sometimes they walked down to the barn to see the livestock, or out to the edge of the fields to view the crops.

As soon as the men left the table, the women dished up more food from the warming pots on the big wood-burning stove, and seated themselves to eat. The wives always sat in their husbands' places, often using the same plates with fresh silver. In contrast to the men, who never ate with their fingers, the women relaxed, kicked off their shoes under the table, and ate chicken and sopped gravy with their fingers. They seldom used knives, considering them men's tools. The talk was gossip, but it was not vicious. Since the women did not get out much—mostly Saturday shopping trips to town—the information exchanged was what their husbands had brought home to them during the week.

After the women finished their meal, the two oldest girls left at home ate their dinner and cleared the dishes. Since this chore was assumed by girls at about the same time boys were joining the men's table, it served as a sharp indicator of the favored position of the men. The women joined the men, and the talk became general. It was during this time that the Family discussed the move to Wallace, North Carolina. Mamie Lee, having already whispered it to her younger sisters, Elise and Tobitha, could contain herself no longer.

"Mama, did you know that Sister and Acie are planning to move?" she casually announced.

Mama, seated in a big rocking chair and fanning herself with a round cane fan, leaned forward abruptly and frowned, "Move? Move where? What do you mean, 'move'?"

Zueline, wishing that she could have told Mama herself, but secretly glad that it was out, answered quickly, "It's Acie's work, Mama. He's got a job as a foreman, and it's not all that far away."

"What kind of a job have you got, Acie?" asked Papa in his quiet voice. Nick Hastings was a big man with sandy hair, a full, thick blond mustache, and twinkling hazel eyes. He was Mama's opposite in temperament—calm, generous, and seldom serious. He loved to tease, and he played practical jokes at every opportunity, on anyone available, even his own children. He was, however, a man generous to a fault and much respected by his family and his community.

Acie turned gratefully toward his father-in-law, knowing that he would listen and approve. "It's a timber job, Mista Hastin', down in the eastern part of the state. The work's got too big for the owner to handle, and he wants a foreman with experience. I hear there's lots of timber down there, never been cut. Near Wallace, North Carolina."

"North Carolina!" loudly interjected Mama, stopping her rocking and fanning and looking with shock at the faces in the gathered circle. "You're not going to take Sister way off there? Why, they'd be all strangers, and no telling what kind of people, either. Why, I just won't hear of it!" And she resumed rocking and fanning herself furiously.

"Now, Mama," began Sister nervously, breaking off when so many eyes turned in her direction.

Dodge, Zueline's brother, spoke up, addressing himself to Ellis, "I thought there's lots of timber around here to cut. Things slacking off around here, Dick?"

" 'Nough timber in these parts to last years," Ellis admitted.

Mamie Lee spoke confidently, "I don't see why Sister and Acie have to leave; Acie's doin' fine workin' for Ellis."

Acie, unruffled by all the talk, spoke generally, to no one in particular, "I have a chance to run my own job, start out on my own. Foreman ought to pay pretty good, and I could run it on my own."

Zueline, twisting a handkerchief, looked at him and spoke supportingly, "I know, honey. And, Mama, maybe it won't be for long." She beseeched her mother.

Mama, never looking at her, gave a loud, "Harumph!" and continued to rock and fan.

It was family business, and the whole family discussed it. Even the younger brothers and sisters made comments: The boys thought it would be adventuresome, the girls declared that they would be afraid to go so far from home. Finally, Papa turned to his other son-in-law and asked,

"Ellis, what do you think? Would it be a smart thing to do?"

33

Ellis, who seldom gave advice even when asked, hesitated a long time before he spoke. "A man's got to go where the work is. He's got to be willing to follow the job," he said quietly, looking around at the faces turned to him, all of which, except Mama's and Papa's, were below thirty years of age.

"Oh, Sugar!" Mamie Lee reproached her husband, but Papa turned to Acie and said,

"Well, Acie, wish you weren't taking Sister so far away, but a man has to make a living. Come home whenever you can."

"Thanks, Mista' Hastin'," Acie answered, looking briefly at his father-in-law, then quickly down to a stick he was turning in his hand.

"Well!" Mama pronounced. "Nothing good will come of this. You just mark my words! Going so far away from your family, nothing good will come of it. Something bad will happen. You just mark my words," she prophesied, nodding her head knowingly as she rocked and fanned.

So Acie, Zueline, and two-year-old Christine moved to Wallace, North Carolina, Amos deciding at the last minute to go along with them. They only lived there three months, but in that time Zueline was more than once to mark Mama's words. Terrible things did happen, things that made a deep impression on the adults—but things that so engulfed and shocked the child that they altered the whole pattern of her life. Christine from birth was unusually sensitive and aware, and she responded to her world, both animate and inanimate, much more deeply and completely than most people, and surely extremely more so than those immediately surrounding her. She was, her entire life, a finely tuned instrument on which the sights, sounds, emotions, and indifferences of life played. They produced in her exquisite, harmonious melody as well as terrifying, heartrending dissonance. Her mobile, sensitive face always reflected her every emotion, and the clear, crystal blue eyes twinkled merrily or teared sadly at emotions, which left other faces calm, unaffected, and insensitive by contrast.

Zueline had led a very sheltered life, but it was so by virtue of lack of exposure, not from protection. She simply had never encountered the horrible, the unpleasant, the revolting; therefore she had no skills available to help her protect her child from the hurt-

34

ful experiences of life, until the child could build some inner defenses to shield herself.

Zueline's one concern was to protect Christine from physical harm, never even remotely suspecting that emotional injuries were crippling her precious child, to the degree that her entire life would be a desperate struggle to eliminate her emotional crutches. Junior's death had instilled in Zueline how easily and quickly a child could be lost, and that no matter how desperate the measures taken, a little physical being is fragile. And Junior had been such a normal, healthy, robust baby, while her own had had such a puny, precarious start. Also, she had completely internalized the fears, superstitions, and old wives' tales that had accumulated in her family, and these made her task of guarding Christine a formidable one. She lived, all of her life, in constant fear of violating one of her dreaded superstitions. She was always able to relate any upsetting turn of events, from a cut finger to unexpectedly unpleasant weather, to a long-ago broken mirror, or to a recently overturned salt shaker. The very fact of her constant dread of committing these forbidden acts made her, of course, more prone to do so.

Zueline made the job of protecting Christine a full-time endeavor. Christine was energetic, full of curiosity, and constantly getting into trouble. She started to walk at ten months, and this broadening of her operational environment caused her mother constant concern and redoubled efforts in keeping up with the busy little feet. Living in Wallace, so far away from her family and their constant help and advice, made Zueline acutely aware of her burden of responsibility.

Their house was just outside the small rural town and sat on the edge of a large field of commercially grown tube roses. The land was flat and sandy, and the tube rose field was irrigated by water from a large ditch, which ran parallel to the road. The house sat a small distance from the road and was reached by crossing the irrigation ditch on a narrow footbridge. Zueline was deathly afraid of water, as were all the women in her family, and she dreaded every crossing of the bridge, which had no guardrails and was constructed close to the water. When she walked across, the movement of the water and the reflected motions that could be seen through the cracks in the boards, as well as on both sides, made her head swim, causing her to feel that she was about to be engulfed. She always held tightly to Christine, and cautioned her to walk in the middle of the bridge and to hurry across. This fear was so instilled in the child that all her life she would not voluntarily cross a dock, pier, or any narrow bridge over water, and she always suffered paralyzing fear near bodies of water.

Zueline was always afraid that the child would wander away from the house and fall into the ditch, so she daily cautioned her about it. Since Christine was such an active, curious child, and for the most part heedless of her mother's constant admonitions, Zueline backed up her warnings with a threat designed to make the little girl afraid to venture near the ditch. Zueline told her that the monster in the ditch would get her. Zueline's description of the monster was most picturesque and was a combination of those animate beings of which she was most afraid. It had a long, snakelike body covered with dark slimy scales, and a fishlike head sporting large bulging green eyes.

Christine was never able to visualize the monster until after she had seen ole man Williams pulled from the water, and then it became in her childish fears a cross between him and her mother's description. It had red hair, bulging green eyes, and the elongated body of a man. Strangely, it was always wearing a belt!

A belt. The man cut in half by the saw was wearing a belt, also. Why did I put a belt on the monster? The monster only came after I saw ole man Williams pulled from the water, and he didn't have on a belt—he wore a flowered jacket with his overalls. But the man cut in half had a belt on his severed body. Did the childish mind connect one horror with another? Did it all become one—one terrifying nightmare to be repeated over and over? Was that why the little girl with red hair came and watched the second horror? Was it too unbearable to watch a second time? But I saw what she saw! Does that mean that it was really me and not one of the others? I've got to believe it was someone else; how could I have deceived myself all those years? And I saw her, I can describe her! But wait; the monster, the monster must have a deeper meaning. . . .

The child even believed that the monster could leave his ditch

36

and prowl around. Mr. Williams had, before his accident, visited the house several times, and Christine thought the monster was partly Mr. Williams, since in her mother's words "the monster got Mr. Williams"; therefore it could go where Mr. Williams had gone. Especially at night was she afraid. Her mother was afraid of the dark and wanted to be inside in a lighted area after nightfall. She did not want to enter a dark room without taking a light with her, and she always took her child into the house when night began to fall. She told the child that something would get her if she stayed out after dark. Christine had never been afraid herself until the monster came, but from that moment she was sure that it lurked behind every door, around every corner, and was everywhere outside waiting to gulp her up at the first opportunity. She felt that she was especially vulnerable if she had been a bad girl.

And Christine was always a bad girl. It appeared that her mother's plea for her to stop an action was a mandate for her to continue. Even as a small child, scarcely more than an infant, those things most irresistible to her were those that had been forbidden. Zueline, never having known a child with this sort of aggressive, irrepressible temperament, was daily driven to exasperation and despair.

"Christine, what *am* I going to do with you? You are a bad girl! If I have told you once, I have told you a hundred times not to do that," she would alternately storm and plead with the child when she caught her in the midst of something forbidden.

The child would always loudly and positively protest that she had not done that which she was being accused of, even when she had been caught in the very act. That which upset her parents the most—for her father was often called upon to witness the misdeed and to mete out the punishment—was the fact that the child would never capitulate and confess to having committed her actions, even when faced with unqestionable evidence. She would stanchly declare that she had not eaten unwashed berries from the vines that she had been in the act of pulling and eating when her mother found her; and she would tearfully maintain this stand even when showed the berry stains on her hands and face. She would wail, "She did it," and protest her innocence even while being spanked.

37

I remember, and it was so frustrating. It was always happening. All of a sudden, without knowing how I got there, I would be someplace watching that other little girl doing something that I had been told not to do. I would want to do it too, and I wondered why she could do it and I couldn't, but I was satisfied just to watch. But when Mother came, she grabbed me and accused me. She never accused the other little girl. And she never spanked the other child. I always told her I hadn't done it, but she never believed me—she never said a word to the other little girl. And the strangest thing always occurred: When Mother found me, the other child always went away; she just disappeared. Did Mother frighten her away? I remember the berries; I was not supposed to eat the berries from the bush. And I never ate them—she always ate them. I watched her. She got berry stain on her hands and face and dress. But when Mother found me watching her, she accused me of eating the berries! When I tried to show her it was the little girl, she was gone. And the stains were on my hands and face and dress. I could taste the berries in my mouth. But I hadn't eaten them. I know I hadn't. But why couldn't Mother see her? I saw her, and I showed her to Mother. Could Mother not see her because she wasn't there? All those times she came and did all those things, was she never really there? I can't believe that. There are other times I can remember her. Especially about the shoes . . .

"Christine, what *are* you doing with your shoes off? You bad girl! If I've told you once, I've told you a hundred times not to take your shoes off! This is the third time this morning. What am I going to do with you?" Zueline bore down on the child, who sat in the middle of the porch with her shoes and socks off. She had one shoe in her hands trying to fasten the button strap.

As her mother ungently grabbed her from the floor and gathered up the shoes and socks, Christine began to loudly wail and protest, "No, no, I didn't, she take shoes off! Not Teeny! She take shoes off!"

Her mother, angry and frustrated by this behavior, spanked the child's outer thighs with her hand, "Now, Teeny, don't you lie to me! You *did* take your shoes off! There's nobody here but you. There's *nobody* else here. Tell Mother the truth; tell Mother you took your shoes off." She set the child on the floor, holding her firmly by the shoulders.

Christine rubbed her red, injured thigh and loudly protested through her tears, "Teeny *not* take off shoes, Teeny *not* take off shoes. Girl take off shoes!"

Zueline, at her wit's end, pled with the child, "Now, Teeny, you listen to Mother. You did take off your shoes. Tell Mother that you took them off, and Mother will love you. Mother will hold you and sing to you." She gave the child a slight shake.

Christine looked at her mother. Her red eyes, runny nose, and tear-streaked face made a pathetic, heartrending sight, but she stubbornly persisted, "Teeny not take off shoes."

"All right, Christine, you just can't play anymore. You will just have to go to bed because you are a bad girl. Mother is going to tell Daddy you have been a bad girl, and Daddy doesn't like bad girls." She carried the wriggling, wailing child into the house and put her to bed.

I did not take the shoes off. I remember, and I know I didn't take them off. I can clearly see the little girl doing it. She was sitting on the floor. The shoes were black, and they had one strap that buttoned across the top. I could unfasten the button, but I could not fasten it back. It was easier to try to rebutton the strap if the shoe was off. I wanted them off to work with the button, but I didn't take them off. She took them off. And I wanted the socks off too, to play with my toes. It felt good to play with my toes. Daddy used to play with my toes when he tucked me in bed at night. He pulled my socks back and forth between my toes and said he was cleaning out the toe jam. And he wiggled each toe and played "Piggy Went to Market." It was fun, and I wanted to play the game on my toes. But I didn't take them off. I wanted them off, but I didn't take them off! She took them off. Or did she? Did I just make her up to do what I was forbidden to do? Did she come to do what I couldn't do, as she came to watch what I couldn't watch? Was she really me? But that couldn't be. If she was me, who was watching? I couldn't watch myself do something. That's insane! This whole thing is insane. Am I insane? No, no, I won't be-

lieve that. I can't believe that. There's got to be another answer. . . .

Lying to one's parents was considered by the Family to be the greatest wrong that a child could commit. A parent would say to his child while questioning him about a suspected misdeed, "If you have done this thing, it is bad enough; but if you lie to me about it, that is worse, and I can never trust you again." If a child were accused of an unacceptable act, the parent would bring the child before the accuser and question him, saying, "I will ask him if he did it. He will not lie to me; I have brought him up not to lie to me." And he would believe what his child said. If it was later proved that the child had lied, the parent would make a public, personal apology to the offended party, punish the child, and make any possible restitution for the injury. The child would be in disgrace, and always remembered in the Family for the lie. One could commit all kinds of offenses and be forgiven, and even excused; but lying, and especially to one's parents, was unforgivable.

And Christine so obviously lied. Not only did she so shamelessly lie, but she accused another of having committed her own undeniable acts. It seemed much worse to her mother that this "other person" did not even exist. She could have understood Christine's accusing another child, but her habit of falsely blaming a nonexistent person baffled and deeply hurt Zueline. She wondered if there had been someone with such a faulty character in Acie's family that the child took after. And she had known from the very start that that red hair had boded no good. However, the hair was beginning to darken; perhaps these other qualities would fade also.

Zueline's whole life's philosophy was to wait and see and to hope that "things turned out." She was completely uncompetitive and felt no great ambition either for herself or for her husband and children. She simply wanted them to be happy and comfortable, and she felt that this could best be obtained in close proximity with the Family.

Acie was different. Though young, he had the desire to be independent—a trait that remained with him throughout his long life in spite of two misfortunes that thwarted his drive for worldly success. He knew that his brother, though generous, was a strong and dominant man, and he did not want to tie his destiny to Ellis's. It would be a comfortable, secure life, but he would always be only No. 2, never No. 1, and therefore never completely independent. His move to Wallace was an attempt to strike out on his own. But he was not a selfish man, and the knowledge of Zueline's unhappiness in being separated from her family was a constant source of worry and concern to him. He loved her very much, and his pride in being his own boss and managing an entire operation, however small, paled when compared with his desire to please her. She was not the least interested in discussing his work with him, having been brought up to consider that men's business and not really appropriate for women to try to understand, and she longed to have a woman with whom to talk over her women's concerns. She fretted and worried and, though never by nagging, she communicated her fears and frustrations to her husband by constantly talking about bad luck and the awful things that had happened in this terrible place.

They made only one visit home during their short stay in Wallace, and by that time Acie had about decided to return. Zueline was overjoyed at being with her family again. She related to them the strangeness, the loneliness, and all of her troubles in trying to cope with a foreign, far-off environment. The Family was gratified to know that its suspicions concerning other places were real and true and just as bad as imagined, and Zueline was strangely comforted by the knowledge that her problems had not been due to her inability to adjust, but to unexplained factors beyond her control that were attached to strange places. She even welcomed Mama's stern reminder, "I told you so!" If Mama had known in advance, surely there was nothing she, Zueline, could have done to change things.

When told of the two accidents, that of ole man Williams and ole Jim, occurring so close together and in such close proximity to Zueline, the Family expressed horror, wondered how she had stood the shock, and exclaimed at the "great deal" that she had been put through.

It was a tearful farewell. Mama firmly commanded, "Now, Acie, you bring Sister and come on home, you hear."

Papa kissed Zueline and shook Acie's hand, saying, "Son, come on home. There will always be a place for you here. There's plenty to go around for all of us."

As the T-Model drove away down the lane rutted by wagon wheels, Zueline cried quietly into her handkerchief, Christine waved and shouted "Bye," and Acie bit his lip and frowned as he thought of the decision he shortly would have to make.

They stopped by and spent the night with Ellis and Mamie Lee on the way back. Christine was overjoyed at seeing Unc and Aunt Meme again. She was for all the world like a puppy in her attempt to "show out" for her Unc. She rolled on the floor, tried to stand on her head, and aggressively demanded his constant attention. She prattled "Look, Unc," and strove diligently to find things to show him.

She had always loved fried Irish potatoes, a dish that Ellis himself could eat three times a day. She remembered this, and one of the first things she said to her uncle was, "I want 'taters! I want 'taters." He was delighted, and he instructed the women to fry potatoes for the child for every meal while she was there.

It was a happy visit. Mamie Lee was seven months pregnant and happily looking forward to the birth of her child. She told her sister all about her progress, described her weaknesses and her increasing delicate condition, and bemoaned the fact that Sister would be away when the baby was born. She stanchly proclaimed that she and Ellis had no preference as to the sex of their baby, and wished that it only be whole and healthy, but in her secret heart she wanted a boy to replace her precious lost Junior. There were plans, of course, for Mama to come to see to things until Mamie Lee could manage alone.

Zueline related the details of her sojourn in a foreign land, and was rewarded by her sister's exclamations of horror and protests of "Sister, I don't see how you have stood it!" She felt, perhaps, the least bit guilty when Mamie Lee remonstrated with Acie, "Acie, you have *got* to bring Sister home. Mama's girls are just not built to stand awful things like that!"

"Bullshit!" Ellis pronounced, quietly but succinctly. Perhaps it was the worried look on his brother's face that prompted his comment. At any rate, Acie's gloom lifted at the knowledge of his brother's support.

Both women looked properly shocked, and Mamie Lee chided

her husband, "Sugar, you ought to be ashamed. And in front of Christine, too."

The brothers sat before the fire and talked into the night, long after their wives had gone to bed. Acie confided his concerns to his brother: Zueline's unhappiness, her desire to return home, his own indecision. Ellis listened quietly. He felt deep concern for this brother who was almost fourteen years younger, and who had been only a baby when Ellis had left home so many years ago. Ellis also felt a responsibility for Acie's welfare. Ellis had brought his young brother South with him over his mother's protest. She could remember only that Ellis himself had been Acie's age, seventeen, when he had left one day, to return for the first time ten years later. And he had been home only occasionally and briefly in the ten years since. She had told him that many times she had thought him lost or dead, and had cried her pillow wet many nights. He had assured his mother that he would take care of his younger brother, and he took this assurance very seriously. However, he hesitated to influence him in his decision. He felt that the plotting of one's own life was the making of a man, and he wanted Acie to be independent and on his own. Yet he knew how the young man was torn by the emotional forces pulling on him. He merely counseled his brother,

"A man's got to do what he thinks he oughta. Decisions ought to be made for the future and fit into a plan. A life can't be chopped up piecemeal and amount to anything. But a man's still got to do what he feels is best."

When they left to return to Wallace the next morning, the sisters tearfully clasped each other while the brothers seriously shook hands. Christine climbed into the car beside her mother and crowded over to make room on the seat. She looked up at her uncle standing beside the car, patted the seat beside her, and said, "Git in, Unc."

The tension broke, and they all laughed at the irrepressible child, but all five had heavy hearts as the car drove away. Christine alone was crying.

As they watched the car disappear, Mamie Lee almost tearfully spoke to her husband. "I wish they didn't have to go back. Sugar, why didn't you tell Acie to stay?"

Her husband put his arm around her as he looked thoughtfully down the road and across the autumn fields. The morning air was crisp in the bright, clear sunlight, and the tall pines whispered gently in the light breeze.

"I don't think they'll be gone long, Mother," he told her quietly.

He was right. In less than a month they returned, this time to stay. Acie had quit his job, but he might have been laid off anyway. None of them could imagine on that gentle October day in 1929 that it was the peaceful quiet before the storm that was to throw the entire country into turmoil and to change the course of all their lives.

It was the eve of the Great Depression.

3

An Ugly Duckling

"Sister, where *did* you get such an ugly child!" Zueline had heard this word used by her relatives to describe her child since the very day Christine had been born. Though critical, and certainly not complimentary, it was not designed to be harsh or cruel. And Zueline did not take it as such. She was not offended and did not, at least openly, resent the description; she only quietly and confidently answered with an old saying that was familiar and often used in the Family: "An ugly child, a pretty woman." Her confidence was not merely assumed; she truly believed the saying, just as she did all the other old sayings and superstitions that abounded in her family. Everyone else believed in the truth of these words also.

Christine was loved and accepted, and she had a definite place in her large family, but she was different. She was the despair of everyone! In a day when children should be seen and not heard, she was loud, boisterous, and completely obvious. The usual adult devices such as cold stern looks, raised eyebrows, loud "harumphs," pointed fingers, and the like, which usually completely and instantly squashed obstreperous children, had absolutely no effect on the irrepressible child. Even verbal admonitions and scoldings, carrying dire threats of physical punishment, made little and very brief impression on her behavior. And then, to the final insult of everyone and to the despair and utter embarrassment of her mother, when the inevitable spanking came Christine would loudly scream and deny having done what was precipitating her punishment. This was bad enough, and caused the older adults to sternly shake their heads; but when she accused a nonexistent "she" of committing her acts, they registered shock and commented, "Sister, you must do something about that child; no good will come of this."

Not only was Christine fiery, aggressive, impetuous, and lavish with her every emotion, but she was also as remarkably different physically as she was in temperament. The premature thinness of her body did not lessen as she grew; it became merely accentuated by her stretching frame. She was a gangly, loose-jointed child with the knobbiest knees and hands and feet, which by contrast to the thin arms and legs, seemed much too large for such a small body. Her square-boned face framed by the fluff of disordered reddish-brown hair appeared too heavy for the slender reed of a neck. The enormous brilliant blue eyes were made even more startling by her milky white skin, which, just as Mama had predicted, was soon sprinkled with large tan freckles. They almost completely covered the small, round, button nose inherited from her paternal Scotch-Irish ancestors.

Zueline tried diligently to keep her daughter clean and neat. She started out every morning dressing her in little clothes bedecked with lace and frills, most of which had been made by Aunt Meme, and instructed her about keeping clean. But Christine could not. She just seemed to attract dirt, and in an amazingly short time she would be ruined: The red hair, once so carefully brushed and curled, would be in wild disarray, the white knee socks would be stretched and hanging in unsightly bunches around the bony ankles, and her clothes would be streaked with dirt and hanging at shapeless angles on the thin little body.

Christine did not seem to mind being called "skinny" or hearing herself described as ugly, and she accepted her disheveled condition as innate and not anything over which she had any control. Since her mother never became upset by or in any way protested these damaging allegations, the child therefore believed them to be true and regarded her condition as simply natural and indefensible. "Ugly" was a word that had many meanings in the Family. An unmade bed was ugly, an unweeded flower plot was ugly, weather and behavior could be ugly. Things that looked, or tasted, or smelled, or felt different from what was regular or used to were also ugly.

Vanity in women was not considered an admirable trait; therefore little girls were never told that they were pretty—it might "turn their heads." The qualities stressed as desirable were: being virtuous; having good manners; being neat and clean; and above all, acting like a lady. Poor Christine! She seemed destined to measure unacceptable on every point. Although she never felt rejected by the Family, the atmosphere was obviously one of resigned, exasperated acceptance, and she well knew that she was not admired and that she did not inspire others to be proud of her. She grew up, as did many other of her little girl cousins, feeling plain and unattractive, and lacking even the comfort that the other girls took in "being little ladies."

Acie, though returning home, was determined to remain independent of family. He had, however, reckoned without the Depression. During their absence, Ellis had bought the Miller place, a farm having one large house and two smaller tenant houses; and Acie moved his family into the large house with Mamie Lee and Ellis, until he could find work. There was no work, and much to the delight of Zueline and Mamie Lee, the arrangement became permanent. Acie worked on the farm and helped out at the sawmill. They lived at the farm together for two years, and it was here that Elen was born.

"Look, Teeny, what Santa Claus brought Aunt Meme," her mother seriously announced to her one day when Christine was almost three years old.

Mamie Lee, extremely thin and weak from the birth of her child, held down a tiny bundle for Christine to see. "Sit down and you can hold her," she offered.

As Christine sat down in her little yellow rocking chair, her most prized possession, the five-day-old baby was carefully placed in her arms. Elen, asleep, was dressed in a little white knitted sweater and cap, and as her soft round body and pudgy little face nestled close to Christine, the older child felt a strong surge of love and possession. She closed her arms around the helpless baby, held her close to her own thin body, and firmly announced,

"My baby!"

Her aunt, greatly amused, but pleased, remembering her earlier rejection of Junior, assured her, "Of course, she's your baby."

It was Christmas, the day for gifts, and perhaps that explains it. Perhaps the generous and loving atmosphere of Christmas nurtured, that day, the beginning of an unusual, enduring, and lifetime relationship. Christine from that moment considered that this little cousin belonged to her, and that it was her sole responsibility to care for her, to make her knowledgeable on all subjects, both real and fancied, and to generally oversee her upbringing. Elen, completely and unquestioningly, accepted the proprietary attitude of her older cousin, always following her lead and trusting her totally. For the first time Christine was absolutely accepted for what she was, and openly and fiercely admired above all others. In return for this cherished and needed acceptance, she lavished on this little cousin all of the attention and care that boundless energy could muster. She shaped and molded the younger child in ways that influenced Elen's thoughts and actions for the rest of her life. Elen, years later in recalling some choice bits of information that Christine had fed her as a child, declared that her entire adult life was simply one long experience of exploding the myths that Christine's active and colorful imagination had created.

The new baby was named Mary Elen for her cousin May and for her Grandmother Rebecca Elen. The child was called by her full name through all of her growing-up years; and later, as an adult, she shortened her name to Elen. In those first few years, Christine felt at times sharp pangs of jealousy because of the attention given to Elen, but Christine's love far outweighed her other emotions, and she never disliked the younger child even when being unfavorably compared to her.

Christine did, however, once unceremoniously dump her from the cradle. It was the same cradle that Christine had so coveted for herself when Junior had slept in it, and now here it was again, with another baby in it. It didn't matter that it was occupied this time by her own baby. Outraged, she promptly turned it over and rolled the wailing Elen out onto the floor. Her motives were completely misunderstood. She had no desire to hurt the baby; she simply had an overpowering wish to claim that elusive cradle for herself.

During this period, one event occurred that was to remain imprinted in Christine's mind as a gross unfairness that she, as a child, could not understand, and even as an adult, after understanding came, seemed unaccountably to still resent. When Ellis installed a new water pump in the well, he fixed it to the ground with a wide apron of concrete. While it was still wet, he pushed Elen's bare foot into the concrete and made her footprint on the apron. When Christine saw the footprint, she wanted to make one of her own. Her uncle simply told her that he could not make her footprint in the concrete. Unaware that the child did not realize that Elen's print was made when the concrete was wet, and that it was impossible now to make any kind of print in the hardened mixture, he did not explain why he could not do as she asked. Undeterred by what seemed to be his unwillingness to help, and spurred by her resolve to imprint the concrete, she worked many hours determinedly pushing her foot against the hard apron. When her efforts were so totally frustrated, she alternated them with the equally impossible task of trying to erase Elen's print. The adults, observing her labors, thought her actions were amusing and cute, and never even vaguely suspected the deep rejection that the child so poignantly felt.

Christine thrived and grew like a weed, and her energy knew no bounds. Since there were always several adults around and no obvious nearby physical hazards, her mother felt that she was safe playing outside. She had the run of the place, and she slaved mightily from early rising until the much-resisted bedtime, "helping" everybody work. She was constantly underfoot and in everybody's way, but she was a pleasant, comical little being to have around, whose curiosity and enthusiasm were infectious even to the exasperated adults. Their reprimands for the disasters she caused were most often given with laughter and without the needed convincing sting.

The farm raised chickens, bred stock cattle, and operated a dairy. Later, as an adult, Christine was to become afraid of animals, but as a child she loved them all, both large and small, and she spent much time in the dairy barn watching the processes of extracting the milk and preparing it for market. The barn was inhabited by several cats, whose job it was to contain the ever-flourishing rat population. Operating on the philosophy that a lean cat with a hungry belly made a more diligent ratter, since he ate what he caught, than a sleek, lazy, well-fed one who only hunted for sport and pleasure, farmers forced barn cats to fend for themselves. The barn cats were constantly hanging around and mewing for a handout during milking time. The milkers would often divert a stream from the milk pail and empty a teat on a yowling cat's face. Some of the cats became very adept at catching a great deal of the warm milk in their mouths. At any rate, cats so favored ceased their clamor and sat quietly and contentedly licking and washing the sweet milk from their faces.

Christine was always delighted by this act, which was performed as often for her benefit as for the cats', and wanting as always to be helpful, she decided one day to feed a cat herself. Unnoticed, she seized one of the less wary cats and, with instructions to "drink, kitty, drink milk," she stuffed him headfirst into the cream separator. It had large paddles designed to keep the milk agitated and in constant motion for a period of time. The paddles caught the hapless cat, dragged him under, and drowned him. His milklogged body was found floating on the surface of the hair-flecked milk by Ellis, who declared, when delightedly relating the story, that the cat had a contented smile on his milk-soaked face.

This was not the first cat that Christine had so generously "helped" in this manner. A few months earlier she had assisted their house cat in his efforts to get at the milk by cramming him into her mother's churn. When Zueline came for the milk, she was horrified to find the drowned cat's tail limply trailing down the side of her churn. Equally concerned over the loss of the milk and the cat, and the child's denial of having done such an unlovely deed, she soundly spanked the protesting Christine. The child was saved from a spanking the second time, however, by her beloved Unc, who could not bear to see her punished.

He called to her as she ran from her irate mother who bore down on her, "Come to Unc! Get in Unc's pen and she can't get you."

The child ran to her uncle, and standing between his knees, enclosed in his arms, she looked out tearfully but confidently at her frustrated mother.

Ignoring the larger issue of the ruined milk, Zueline, halfway between laughter and tears, exclaimed, "But Ellis, she drowned the cat!"

Hugging the little girl to him, Ellis philosophically comforted both mother and daughter, "It's all right, Sister, we had too many cats in the barn anyway."

Mamie Lee, critically watching this oft-played scene, and feeling that she must add a final corrective touch to every situation, admonished her husband, "Sugar, you are spoiling that child rotten! Sister can't do a thing with her now." It was true. Ellis, having grown up in a family with all boys, was a pushover for little girls.

The laundry, a hated chore, always seemed to fall to Zueline. Before she married it had been her job, and after she later moved back near home, she weekly left her own work undone for a day to go help do Mama's wash. She was uncomplaining, but Acie resented this; and just as soon as he was able, he hired a woman to come in and do the wash, or he took the dirty clothes out to a "washer woman." When they lived together at the Miller place, she and Mamie Lee always did their laundry together on the first pretty day of the week.

The clothes were washed out in the backyard near the well for easy access to water. A fire was built under the large black iron pot, which was a necessary fixture of every household. The dirty clothes were put into the boiling water in the pot and periodically stirred with a long, smooth stick selected and kept for just that purpose. The white clothes were washed first, and the colored clothes made up a second load. Two large tin tubs filled with water sat on a board erected between two trees. The clothes were removed from the boiling pot and carried on the end of the stirring stick to the first tub, where they were washed additionally by hand, stubborn spots being scrubbed on a tin washboard. The second tub contained the rinse water. Finally, the rinsed clothes were hung on the line, or often on low bushes or nearby fences, to dry.

Washday was a scene enacted weekly in every household, and it took an entire day. Christine loved washday, and imitated her busy mother's every motion. One day as Zueline was busy scrubbing clothes at the tin tub, she heard the child scream. In attempting to emulate her mother by punching up the fire under the boiling pot, she had gotten too close and caught her clothes afire.

"Oh, dear Jesus, Christine, what have you done?" Zueline cried, throwing her hands over her horrified face. She ran to the screaming child and began to beat at the flames with her bare hands. Mamie Lee, hearing the cries, rushed from the house, snatched up Christine, and doused her in the tub of rinse water.

The flames were instantly extinguished, and miraculously the child was not badly burned. The only severe injuries were under the arms, where Mamie Lee had held her, but they were extremely painful and caused lifetime scars. Dr. Crafton prescribed that a covering of beaten eggwhites be placed over the burns. However healing this treatment might have been, it in no way lessened the pain, and the four adults spent several miserable days and nights walking the floor with the tormented child.

Lightning rods were a new invention, and they were being hailed as man's savior from the damages of lightning. A rod was placed on each gable and on the highest points of the roof of a building. From each rod ran a thick twisted metal wire down the side of the building and into the ground. The theoretical principle on which the lightning rod operated stated that since lightning struck the highest point, it would be attracted by and would strike the metal rod, which would then conduct it down the metal wire, where it would be dissipated into the ground. Practically, the rod followed the theoretical principle up to the part where the electrical charge would be dissipated into the ground. True to prediction, the rods did attract lightning, and a building so equipped was almost certain, sooner or later, to be struck by lightning; but at this point, theory and practice parted company. Instead of conducting the charge into the ground, the rods, unless wired properly, diffused the electricity to all parts of the building, and each beam, stud, and joist became a conductor. A house was literally ripped apart, and often it burned as well.

Word got around, and lightning rods fell into disrepute, but not before many people were duped into using them. Ellis was one of those. Though not foolhardy, and not one to experiment lavishly, he was not afraid of the new and did not shun the unknown. After all, he had studied electricity and electrical wiring, and it did sound as if it ought to work. In less than a year after Ellis had installed on his tin-roofed home the bright new lightning rods with their shiny glass bulbs, they unerringly drew the dreaded electrical charge into the house. It ran across the main gable of the building, cutting each rafter loose from the beam; fol-

52

lowing each nail, it ran down each stud, cutting them loose from the flooring and jumping onto every metal object in every room; it ran around the entire frame of each metal bed, burning a hole in the floor at each bedpost; and it played and shimmered over the iron cookstove like a sentient, mischievous being, knocking down the tin chimney stack in a cloud of soot and flinging all four stove lids high into the air. And then it dissipated into the ground, leaving the theoretical principle of lightning rods intact, if somewhat sketchy concerning details.

The cloud had come up almost instantly, as summer thunderstorms often do. The bright sun suddenly disappeared, and the sky turned dark and threatening. A low distant rumble was followed quickly by a muted flash and a sharp crack. It was nearly an hour before dinnertime, and Zueline and Acie were down at the dairy working with the milk. At the sharp crack they came to the door and looked out. Cousin M.A. and her husband, Moody, had been visiting for several days, and Ellis had taken him over on the hill to show him the new plantings in the orchard. At the first rumble they started for the house.

"Come on, Moody, we better get in. That cloud's comin' up fast," Ellis remarked.

Inside the house, Mamie Lee and M.A. were preparing to feed Christine and Elen their supper. The two little girls were sitting on the side of the table in the kitchen. Mamie Lee had just taken up some fried potatoes from an iron skillet and set it back on the stove, an act that surely saved her life.

To those outside, it later seemed that the deafening clap of thunder came simultaneously with the blinding flash of light. The bolt cut a swath in the muddy air, struck the right-hand lightning rod, followed it down to the house, and with incredible speed outlined the entire building along all of its corners and angles. What must have been seconds seemed forever to those watching. From their stunned, rooted positions, they all began to run for the house, which was smoking in numerous spots, but miraculously did not catch fire.

Zueline's scream, "Christine! My baby! What's happened to my baby?" brought Acie's dulled senses alive. Seeing Ellis and Moody nearing the house at a breakneck speed from the orchard, Acie grabbed his wife and held her; she was struggling and crying hysterically. Whatever was in there, it was better for the men to find it first.

As Ellis grabbed the metal pull on the screen door leading onto the enclosed porch off the kitchen, he swore briefly under his breath. The handle was too hot to hold.

Moody, right on his heels, gasped, "God, Dick, you don't suppose . . ." His voice trailed off.

Ellis just grimly shook his head, and using his handkerchief, he pulled open the door and ran in.

It was only to those on the outside that the house appeared quiet. To those in the kitchen, the whole of the world had become a din of noise and terrifying confusion. The loud clap compressed them with its pressure, and their ears ached and popped. The air, black with falling soot and glaringly brilliant with dancing light, became filled with flying objects. The acrid smell of burning stung the nostrils and labored the lungs.

And then the quiet fell. The drifting, settling soot soundlessly caressed each surface. The eardrums conditioned for the onslaught of sound buzzed against the heavy silence. A moment only, one of those endless, weightless, insensible moments of unfeeling nothingness used to prepare the human organism to withstand the unbearable.

When Mamie Lee turned to the table, she looked first at Christine, who was making quiet, whining noises.

"Christine! Are you all right?" she managed to gasp.

The child, her face soot-streaked, tears beginning to form in her wide, scared eyes, whimpered, "I didn't do it, Aunt Meme."

Mamie Lee then turned to her own daughter. Elen, not yet two years old, sat calmly on the table. Other than her sooty face, she seemed untouched by the harrowing episode. Her mother spoke to her, and the child did not answer—she showed no reaction at all. Mamie Lee, already strained to the breaking point and ready to believe that anything could have happened, panicked. She grabbed up Elen and shook her, crying hysterically.

"Oh, my baby, my baby, she can't hear! She's been struck deaf! Oh, May'rellen, speak to Mother! Oh, my Jesus, she can't hear!"

M.A., jolted out of her stunned condition, took the child from her mother, saying,

"Oh, Mamie Lee, your baby's all right. She's just scared.

54

There's nothing wrong with her." And seeing Ellis burst through the kitchen door, she asked the child,

"Who is that, Baby, who is that man there?"

Elen reached her arms for her father and smugly replied, "My daddy."

The promised land—that's what Acie always called it. It was the land where one put down roots. It was the land that produced yield in proportion to one's labors. And it was the land that held the promise of the good life. The country was in the midst of one of its darkest hours. There were no jobs, there was no money, people were hungry. Ellis was never afterward able to pinpoint exactly why he pulled out of the lumber business and sold his thriving interests. Perhaps he half consciously noted subtle little signs in business, which added up to a growing uneasiness; perhaps he only knew that he now had accumulated enough capital to invest in much-cherished land; but, at any rate, he withdrew his money from lumber and bought one of the best farms in the entire area— the Butler place.

Land to a southerner has an interesting meaning, and one that is inbred and historical. Even at its peak, the South never had a great deal of money, and a man's wealth was reckoned not in dollars, but in acres. A lot of ready cash was not required. Life's necessities were produced by the land, and those staples not available from the farm could always be purchased when the crops were sold, or bought on credit against the next harvest yield. If a man were really strapped for cash, he could always sell off some timber, or as a last desperate measure, sell a small portion of land.

To most, this was extremely painful, but some who had inherited their property but not a feeling of responsibility and pride for their heritage, made a business of this gradual disposing of land. Personally he lived well during his own lifetime, but paternally he passed nothing on to those destined to follow him. This had been the fate of the Hastingses, leaving the present family simply poor, with a splendid heritage that only enriched their conversation, not their pockets.

This was the point at which most had arrived when the economic disaster struck. Ellis, whether through wisdom of the changing times or through chance prompted by his desire for land ownership, avoided economic failure by having fortuitously invested his money in a fruitful, well-equipped farm. He lost less than nine hundred dollars when on that black Friday the banks took their extended holiday. He had built and paid for a new house; stocked his farm with cattle, fowl, and mules; cleared new ground and planted an orchard; and stored seed for the planting in his new granary.

The place had two tenant houses: a large one, just down the hill from the new house; and a smaller one, across the pasture on the hill. Acie and Zueline moved into the small house on the hill, and Nick Hastings, the last of a long line of proud land owners, lost his place and moved the ten members of his family into the large house. It must have been cruelly devastating for Papa and Mama to be living in a tenant house, even one belonging to their daughter and son-in-law, but their offspring—both married and unmarried—were delighted to be all together again.

Mamie Lee's cup of pride surely ran over, but she constantly stressed at the time, and also in later recountings, that they just all lived there together, and that Acie and Papa could not possibly be tenant farmers, since Ellis owned the land. Relatives could not possibly be sharecroppers! Mama and Papa had six unmarried children still living at home: two boys, Amos and Ernest, and four girls, Elise, Tobitha, Myrtle, and Anne. Dodge and his wife also lived with them.

Though times were severe, the large, gregarious family found time to play. They were together constantly, but Saturday night was planned and special. They gathered, usually at the new house, to make fudge and to dance to the Victrola. They rolled up the rugs, pushed back the furniture, and danced into the night. The older girls were dating, and their visiting boyfriends joined the fun. Going to church was itself a social event, and Sunday afternoons were spent taking automobile rides with visiting young men —suitors and cousins. Unmarried girls were not permitted to be alone with a suitor, so the young marrieds felt no hesitation in joining a courting couple; in fact, they were often prevailed on to do so by the couple, who wanted to escape the house and Mama's watchful, disapproving eye.

It was at about this time that Elen became old enough to be, not just Christine's baby to play with and to mother, but her playmate, cohort, confidante, and friend. The two girls were totally different. Where Christine was boisterously aggressive, Elen was quiet, shy, obedient, and totally uncompetitive. And they were as startlingly different in appearance as they were in temperament. The younger girl had a small, heart-shaped face; blond hair; dark brown eyes; and the dark skin of her father. She was a full-term healthy baby, and grew to be small-boned, with slender, rounded limbs. She emulated the straight, almost military bearing that her father proudly sported, and she was as neat and clean as her fussy mother could desire. Even though she followed her older cousin's every step, she remained spotlessly immaculate, a fact that by contrast made Christine appear even grubbier.

Christine never seemed to mind being unfavorably compared with Elen, and showed no noticeable resentment to such admonitions as "Watch Elen and do like she does. See how clean she is?" Christine's only defense was, "But she's just cleaner than me!" She simply accepted Elen's neatness and her own mussed condition as natural and unchangeable states over which outside control was ineffective. And the fact that she knew that admiring Elen wanted desperately to be just like her no matter what her condition, and not the other way around, lessened the impact that this harsh criticism might have carried.

Elen conscientiously emulated her older cousin's every action, trying to be like her in every way, and especially did she want a nose like hers. When she was four years old, Christine rounded her small button nose even more by breaking it. Her father, fearing that the busy, heedless child would burn herself on the wood-burning cook stove, had put up a gate between the bedroom and the kitchen. Finding that she could not open the gate, yet determined to "help" her mother, she tried to jump over. She fell, striking her nose on the gate. Zueline, as she always did in a crisis, threw her hands over her eyes at the sight of the child's bloody face and ran out of the house calling for help. Acie ran into the house, determined that Christine's nose was broken, and took her to see Dr. Crafton. She had black eyes for weeks and a permanently soft nose. In later years when she described to Elen the trip to have her nose repaired, she said that Dr. Crafton had placed wet cigarette papers to her nose, and that was what made it so soft and wiggly. Elen, who wanted everything to be just like Christine's, detested her own thin, firm English nose. The two

57

children endlessly applied wet cigarette papers, filched by Christine from their own fathers' pockets, to Elen's nose, but to no avail. No matter how many papers they used, or how hard they wiggled it, Elen's nose never reached the desired delicious softness of Christine's.

4

"Let's Pretend"

Life was a game to be played, and Christine was all the actors. She was never just Christine, unless, as often happened, some unfortunate infringement upon the surrounding adult world jerked her abruptly back to reality. And seldom has a child been immediately subject to the control and direction of as many adults as she. Her extended family, with which she daily interacted, contained a round dozen of assorted adults ranging through teen-age aunts and uncles, married aunts and uncles and their spouses, and parents and grandparents. In a close family relationship of this sort, the authority of all adults over all children was recognized; therefore each child, to survive, had to quickly become familiar with the idiosyncracies of each adult, knowing full well that there was no appeal or recourse, unless some blatant injustice had been committed.

The Family made no pretense of being a democracy, and wasted no time in the adjudication of equal rights. It was indefensibly and proudly an autocracy, unquestioningly and strictly adhering to its precise pyramidal hierarchy. Papa, of course, as the paternal head of the Family, stood at the apex of the pyramid. He and Mama most often agreed on the larger, more important issues, which it was their prerogative to decide, as it was traditional that husband and wife present a united front to the world. If there were disagreement, they worked it out in private, the husband having the final, decisive say. Publically and outwardly before the world, even before the family, husband and wife were in accord. Privately, the women, in hushed tones, confided to their

59

favorite contemporary the exasperation they felt toward a stubborn, immovable husband. Seldom, however, would a daughter confide such feelings to Mama, who would right smartly and caustically inform her daughter that a wife always deferred to and followed the lead of her husband. Mama, of course, used herself as the perfect example of this golden rule, avowing, "I always follow your papa, just like my mama followed my papa." The very idea of being a weak link in this chain of women who somehow had proved strength and courage by being obedient followers caused these girl-wives, no matter how strong-willed in the privacy of their homes, to diligently strive to appear docile and subservient to their husbands in the presence of others.

Each generation rested on a higher level in the family hierarchal structure than the generation younger, and on a lower level than the generation older. Due to the practice of having large families, there were always four generations living. It was not unusual for a mother and her older daughters and daughters-in-law to be producing babies at the same time, causing age overlapping at the extreme ends of generations. A large family was a justifiable reason for exhibiting pride. The father of a numerous family had personal as well as economic cause to view his accomplishment with pleasure: He had without doubt proved his manhood, but he had also produced free labor for the ever-present, time-consuming work necessary to running a successfully productive farm. This was, of course, but another reason for the desire for, and the cherished position of boys—they were needed for the physical, outdoor labor innate to farming. The demonstrated ability to produce offspring was also a source of pride for women. However, since the begetting process was such an unmentionable subject, it is an inexplicable wonder that the begotten product could have been so openly exhibited and lovingly claimed. It was as if the little human, like Athena, sprang fully formed from the intellect of its parents, and morally bypassed the shamefully base physical act of its human parents by imitating the immaculate conception of the divine.

The Family indulgently frowned upon loose morals among men, but it definitely branded loose women with a large scarlet A. Authority was also meted out according to a strict code. Most was bestowed automatically as a result of uncontrolled factors, such as sex and age, while some could be gained through one's efforts, such as the accumulation of property and the attainment of acclaim in the larger community. The oldest living generation, regardless of how senile and ineffective they became, was always tenderly treated with respect and veneration. Here sex distinction even seemed to fade, and the oldest women were accorded equal place with the old men. Within the other generations, however, males obviously enjoyed a favored position. Even across generation lines, the men dominated the women. A mother could take her sons and sons-in-law to task as she might not her husband and brothers, but they were not bound to seriously consider her advice, even though they respectfully received it, as they were so bound by instructions given by their older male relatives.

The youngest generation was the lowest level in the family structure, and the children in this generation were the property of everybody. Though cherished and protected, they had no innate rights whatsoever, being considered simply the raw material whose only *raison d'être* was the faithful continuation of the family line. The old saw "Children should be seen and not heard" was strictly adhered to, but was interpreted as "seldom seen" and "never heard unless asked." Children were sent out to play if small, or given tasks to perform if older, and they were not allowed to hang around and listen to the talk of adults. Single women were not privy to the talk of the married women; and a single girl simply could not be close friends with her married peers, on the theory that their knowledgeable talk would corrupt her thinking, causing her to bring less innocence to her husband when she married. A husband was cheated unless he could teach his wife "everything."

Children earned privileges by growing up and becoming adults. Little people were constantly being told, "You are too young to do that," "You are not old enough to do that," "You can do that when you grow up," etc. Right and wrong, good and bad were not absolutes; they were relative to and equated with age; and to the child the world of the adult was secretive and mysterious and desirable beyond all belief.

So stringent and implacable was this containment and restriction of the young from the privileges of the adult world that those who finally passed through the privations of childhood and were admitted, simply by having lived long enough, into the rarefied atmosphere of the grown-up, jealously guarded this status; and they in their turn, just as their elders before them, protected their rights from the encroachment of the young.

The black sheep of the Family was simply one who broke with tradition, a family member who did not faithfully mirror the accepted image. One, of course, fell into disgrace by committing some shameful act that ran afoul of the law, but there were other routes by which one could attain disrepute within the Family that were completely ignored by jurisprudence. The Family might even stand by a member who had committed murder, if the act resulted from an attempt to defend insulted honor, but only implacably unyielding rejection could be expected by the hapless member who violated the family codes. This most often happened by marrying someone unacceptable. An in-law, at best, always ran a poor second to the sorriest blood member that the Family had to offer; but the prospective mate had always to be approved, however reluctantly, by the parents. Many sons and daughters of the good families, through the years, had been disinherited for stubbornly persisting in taking a mate who, through reputation or questionable family background, failed to meet family standards.

Daughters, of course, had one sure way to ruin: unwed motherhood. Even "fast" girls were risking banishment, and mothers often warned their courting daughters, "I would rather see you in your coffin than disgraced." And they meant it. Parents could decently mourn a daughter who had died of a respectable disease or accident, and they could take comfort in the sympathy of friends and in the knowledge that the loved one was "asleep in Jesus"; but the disgraced girl, even if her partner married her—and no one, not even the girl's parents, expected a man to ruin his own life with such a foolish act—was forever a black sheep, disowned by her family and friends, and never again able to hold up her head around decent people.

Sometimes one became a black sheep merely by moving away from home ground to the nether regions. This wayward one might possibly be slavishly portraying the proper image in some far-off place, but since his behavior could not be observed, and since it was not wise to trust the unknown, and since it was strange enough anyway to move out among foreigners, it was best to assume a suspicious attitude before one's worst fears were realized rather than to foolishly trust and experience later shock. The knowledge of this resultant treatment, as well as the inbred distrust of the unfamiliar, turned many potential rovers into homebound daydreamers. This tradition not only bred inhibiting suspicion of outsiders and distant places, but it also tied young men to the Family apron strings long after the farm, as a result of crop reverses and dwindling acres, required their physical services. Its self-defeating philosophy, instead of encouraging them to think universally and to try their own wings abroad, contained them as barely literate gentlemen farmers, boozing and birdhunting, leaning heavily and confidently on a decayed, crumbling structure.

How long can basically intelligent people exist in this state of self-delusion without undermining their own inner strength? Only as long as the dominating, strength-lending older generation is operative. When this borrowed support is withdrawn, as it always is in time, only the dream remains. Pockets of strength, miraculously gleaming in the worn, rotten weave, are too scattered, too separated by yards of dusty, disintegrating warp and woof to preserve the fabric intact. The tapestry is strong, its colorful scenes bright and bold only in the embellished, oft-spun web of tales lovingly tended by the few proud, remaining adherents.

The fabric was already weakening and the bright pictures fading when Christine was woven into the material of the Family. The obvious deterioration of its moral fiber, as well as the astonishingly rapid decline of its physical resources, alarmed the Family into more guardedly closing its ranks and more suspiciously warding off undermining dangers from without. Any sign of deviant behavior within the fold was attacked critically, and every effort was made to mold the moist, pliant clay of its young into the acceptable form. Christine's clay, though utterly shapeless and desperately desirous of the security of a definite pattern, stubbornly and with the desperation of a drowning soul, resisted the overpowering current of her family's inflence to mold her in its own image. She had a changeling's innate urgency to follow after a strange tune, alien to the ears of her kin, whose faint, haunting melody taunted her senses and called to her to step out of the drab reality of mere existence and float into the aesthetic beauty of soft silk, melting color, lilting rhyme, sensuous movement, and entrancing thought.

When the sensitive beauty hunger of her mind faced only frustration and lack of fulfillment in her tiny world, Christine created to survive. Could she have been protected from this suffocation of the soul until she had matured sufficiently, she might have saved herself by creating her own world of beauty through her considerable talents. But tragically and unintentionally, through the fault only of her own peculiar environment, she was raked too early by raw, hurtful experiences. Her family, motivated by a consuming desire to protect its own tarnished uniformity, never realized that into its midst had been born the potential to refurbish its tattered fabric, to restore its faded glory. The creative intelligence of the child could not be contained, and its overflow was interpreted, at its best, as unrestrained curiosity, and at its worst, as uncontrolled naughtiness. Her self-image was daily buffeted by damaging traumas, but her intelligence would not let her sensitivities perish. Paradoxically, to survive intact, she splintered; she created other selves to endure what she could not absorb, to view what she could not comprehend, to do what she had been forbidden, to have what she had been denied.

Christine craved beautiful things, but because of her father's straitened financial circumstances, she received, as a child, few ready-made toys and playthings. The most beautiful object that she had ever seen was Elen's little red wristwatch. Its band was made of flat, bright-red china squares held together by two elastic threads strung through either side of the sections. The face was round with black numerals and black hands, which actually moved when the little winding stem was turned. The elastic stretched to allow the watch to be slipped over the hand, and then it fit snugly around the wrist. Elen, usually generous with her toys, would not allow Christine to wear the new treasure. Each afternoon the little girls were put down on the floor on a quilt pallet for a short nap. On this particular day, Elen removed her watch, as she had seen her father do each night before he retired, placed it on the pallet, and lay down, announcing,

"I'm napping."

Christine also lay down, but she did not follow her little cousin to sleep. Her entire being was focused on the overpoweringly desirable watch, shining so brightly and redly in the golden sun. Did she sleep? Did she dream that the small girl, clad only in white knitted underpants, her reddish brown hair cut short and pulled back from a side part, had urgently reached out and grasped the precious watch? Could it have been a dream, in which the exquisite pleasure of caressing the smooth, gleaming prize turned to the nightmare horror of watching the little girl with eyes squeezed tightly shut and bared teeth clenched, furiously jerk the watch apart, sending its bright red links violently flying like a startled covey of tiny wild things? It was no dream! Christine heard a gasp behind her,

"Christine, what *have* you done? How could you be such a bad girl? You will get a whippin' for this!" Her mother bore down on her and grabbed her away from the pallet. She continued to scold her in a loud whisper to avoid waking Elen, dragging her roughly from the room.

Christine, astonished and frightened by the sudden attack, began to cry tearlessly, looking wildly around the room for the guilty little girl. She was not there; and Christine herself was holding the ruined treasure in her own hand, the torn elastic spiraling raggedly down from the dismembered band, whose red links lay scattered in telltale splashes like drops of vital blood, over the quilt and the floor.

"Mother, I didn't do it, I didn't do it!" She yelled as the first blows of Zueline's angry hand began to sting her bare thighs. "The girl did it, she did it! I saw her do it! Stop! Stop, Mother, I didn't do it!"

Zueline, angry and hurt by her child's utterly wanton deed, and thoroughly exasperated by this shocking denial, renewed her attack on the already scarlet legs. "Don't you lie to me, Christine! You did break the watch, you've still got it in your hand. You're a bad girl to lie! Mother doesn't love bad girls who lie. And what will your Aunt Meme say? Unc and Aunt Meme won't love you either!" Zueline, close to tears herself, was voicing one of her own nagging, half-formed fears.

Tears were streaming down Christine's freckled face, her hair, loosed from its pin, was streaked over her drowned eyes and pasted slickly to the wet cheeks, and her nose ran profusely. She was no longer coherent but blubbered wetly, drawing in her breath in long, shuddering gasps.

65

Mamie Lee came into the room frowning, "What in the world?" she asked.

"Oh, Mamie Lee, I'm so sorry." Zueline apologized, looking worriedly at her disapproving younger sister. "Christine broke Elen's new watch. We'll try to get her another one. I just don't know what got into her." She well knew that even the small cost of the inexpensive toy would be difficult for Acie to pay, but she had to offer.

Mamie Lee surveyed the scene before her: the scattered red evidence of the crime, Elen still miraculously sleeping, Zueline close to tears, and the shattered, snubbing child tenaciously clutching the torn toy in her hand. She distastefully wrinkled her thin, sharp nose, rather absently ordering,

"Sister, wipe that child's nose. Quick, get it before it runs any further." She was constantly wiping children's noses and cleaning the sleep matter from their eyes; other crimes had to fall into proper place and wait for attention while these urgent corrections were made.

Zueline, taking a plain white handkerchief from her apron pocket, knelt before her sobbing daughter and began to clean the ruined face. She was relieved to be faced with a smaller task that she could perform to everyone's satisfaction, gratefully leaving to others the larger, more complicated business of straightening out the dilemma of Christine's misdeed. Zueline tenderly held the child's thin, shaking shoulders as she mopped the red, swollen face. The wet, clinging hair, when pushed back, revealed enormous blue eyes drowned in a sea of misery, and the entire little face contorted into a heartrendingly pitiful grimace. The mother wanted desperately to enfold the hurting child against her own aching breast, but she calmly continued to clear the still-pouring face. After all, one did not comfort a child for his naughty deeds; the suffering would teach a lesson and serve as a deterrent to future, perhaps larger, crimes.

Zueline's handkerchief was soon a balled sopping mess, and she absently wished that she had another. Mama had taught them to carry several at all times, and she had always tried to do as she had been told, but, just as now, she forever seemed to be just short of what was needed. That small wisp of cloth was the badge of

66

women, and no woman in the Family, if possible, was ever without at least one.

Mamie Lee produced another handkerchief from her pocket, and soon the child stood before the adults, blotched face quiet now except for an occasional hiccup, small, naked body shivering in spite of the warm summer sun, one hand still rubbing the fiery, smarting thigh. Her aunt tried to reason with her.

"Now, Christine, tell Aunt Meme. Why did you break the watch? Was it an accident? It's all right, you can tell Aunt Meme." She coaxed, leaning down to the child.

Christine, looking pleadingly at her aunt, trusting her to believe, pointed at the pallet in the next room, "She did it, Aunt Meme! That little girl did it! She just tore it up." And the child showed her aunt exactly how the watch had been broken.

Mamie Lee straightened up, frowning severely, "I don't know, Sister, what in the world you are going to do!" She began to pick up the scattered red links, putting them on the pallet beside the sleeping Elen.

"I told Ellis not to get things like that for May'rellen, she's just not old enough. Don't tell her what happened, there's no use in her blaming Christine. She'll think it just broke. Come on, we'll never get this dress cut out." And she left the room, having already dismissed the incident from her mind.

Zueline surveyed the scene before her: her own child standing vulnerable and alone still clutching the ragged watch, the other child sleeping peacefully and unaware. She felt that there was something wrong, something that begged to be done, to be corrected, but her limited world gave her no clue to the enormity of the problem budding in her precious daughter. She could only behave as she had been taught: A child had been naughty, and she had been punished. Zueline had performed the distasteful but time-honored task of the parent, as she had been taught to do; she knew no other way. She had not spared the rod, and now she could not spoil the child by petting her.

The child has grown. As I grew the little girl grew, too. But this time it is all so hazy, so vague; if only I could remember more clearly. But I know definitely that she was larger. She seemed to be about five years old, and I would have been five, too. Her hair was reddish-brown, but she had the same blue eyes. But something was different this time. Before, the little girl did only what I wanted to do, but did not dare. This time she did an act all on her own, something I would never want to do. I would never want to hurt Elen, or tear up anything Elen had. But she did. She maliciously tore up the watch, and simply because Elen had it and she did not. That was deliberately mean. And I would never be mean to Elen, I could not be mean to her, I loved her too much. But if it was really me, what does it mean? Did I really want to hurt Elen, punish her for being selfish? But I could not because . . . oh, I don't know why, just because; and the other one came—came to do . . . do what? To do my mean acts and leave me innocent. No, I won't believe that. That's monstrous! That's, that's like Jekyll and Hyde! And that was just made up—just a story—not true.

It was not like that. All right, all right, then what was it like? The child had grown, just as I had grown. Did she look like me? O God, who knows what one looked like as a child? I can vaguely remember myself, but I remember more about doing things than what I looked like doing things. I do remember being shocked by what she did. What else can I remember? . . .

Christine, left alone, sat down on the pallet and waited for Elen to wake. Slowly and cautiously, as if holding a live being that might escape, Christine opened her tightly clasped hand and studied the ravaged watch. Her thoughts were ambivalent. She first, fleetingly, felt glad that beauty that was not hers, was never hers, was destroyed; and she felt a surge of power that she had ruined another's creation. She did not want Elen to love and to be proud of something that another had done. She, Christine, made beautiful things for Elen all the time. Almost as quickly came hurting sadness that any beauty was marred. Christine truly loved beauty, craved it; and her soul was repelled by the ugly, the squalid, in whatever form it attacked her sensitivity. Her narrow world, in such difficult times, admitted pitiful little of material beauty. She knew only a constant, frightening struggle for the bare necessities that make life possible, with nothing left over for even the smallest extra bit that makes living more than mere existence. But

Christine knew, no matter how formless and intangible her thinking, that there was a different world, a world filled with brilliance, with color, with lilting sound, with lulling silence, with soft silk to caress the body and sweet scent to perfume the hair. She could not have voiced this knowledge; it existed in her only as a restlessness, a drive, a resistance that prevented her being engulfed by her drab, deadening world. Her voiceless knowledge allowed her to find pleasure and happiness only in her world of pretend, her escape. Any ugliness, even in her own being, had to be splintered off and denied.

She was now facing seriously, for the first time, a problem that would haunt her for years: how to explain to an unbelieving world her inability to deal with the unlovely. Whenever it reared its unsightly head, whether within her or from her surroundings, her sensitive psyche cringed and failed to meet the critical test, crucial to developing into an integrated, whole person capable of dealing with life and all of its blaring brilliance as well as its subtle nuances. Having been penetrated too deeply, too early by the harshest that life had to offer, her ability to cope with raw reality was seared and warped, causing the burgeoning creativity within her to soar to its zenith and produce her greatest work of art—her own defense mechanism. This rare creation, however, had one great fault: It was so fine and exquisitely wrought that Christine herself was unable to recognize it and claim it as her own. She was left in utter bewilderment and despair, faced with the impossible task of explaining denied and dissociated behavior to a judgmental and disapproving world.

On this first occasion, she simply created, out of the material available to her, a small, isolated fantasy that she thought her trusting little playmate would believe. Whether partially through her perception or totally by accident, it was a story so universally encompassing in scope that it boggled Elen's mind completely, leaving no space for hurt, blame, or anger. Christine merely told her that the sun had broken her watch. And the child, just waking and blinking into the bright sun, seeing the watch parts neatly lined up and gleaming redly in the hot glare, had not the slightest doubt that it had happened exactly that way. For years she was careful to keep her cherished belongings out of the sunlight, remembering sharply the lesson she had been taught about the watch; and interestingly, a surprising number of obvious facts along the way supported Christine's fantasy. Didn't the sun fade fabrics, melt butter and similar substances, wilt and kill fragile plants, and drive fainting ladies into the protecting shade?

The adults, even after hearing Elen's explanation for the disaster, did not betray Christine, and only admitted the facts when the almost-adult Elen seriously demanded to know if it could really have happened. Surprisingly, on learning the truth, she felt no resentment; she only ruefully began to analyze her other accumulated beliefs about the sun's powers to determine if they checked out with science or fit neatly into her cousin's fantasy.

On moving to the Butler place, Christine had acquired another playmate—Anne, Mama's baby. Anne was nine years old when the Family all got together in the Promised Land, and she was a young lady wise far beyond her years. Being the last of eleven children and a pretty little girl, she was spoiled beyond all reclaim and allowed to get by with all the mischief and meanness that had been denied the older children. This was also according to family tradition: The baby was always spoiled and always remained "the baby" throughout the entire life of the generation. The term applied even after the parents were deceased, older siblings referring to the youngest as "the baby of the family." And Anne took to spoiling like a duck to water, using coy, cute ways to attain her ends if possible, but never hesitating to employ lying and cheating where necessary.

The next oldest child was a boy, Ernest, and in a day when everybody, especially boys, had to put in a day's work, chubby Anne with her blue eyes, peaches-and-cream skin, and dark honey hair was petted and allowed to run free long after she should have been performing serious tasks. Never called Anne, she acquired the pet name "Little Sugar," by which she was called for the remainder of her life. Barely five feet tall and never thin, she grew chubbier with age, but her merry eyes never lost their twinkle nor her personality its impish mischievousness.

The family grapevine is a wonderful wireless instrument, quite like the game of gossip in that the farther away from the source the information is repeated, the more distorted it becomes. Sometimes the vine protrudes an unplanned runner from the main stem, and information, unnoticed, is illegitimately siphoned down, becoming incredibly garbled along the way. Anne was one of these unsuspected branches, and her ability to fall privy to choice bits of forbidden information was simply uncanny. Her already distorted version was, in a highly embellished form, passed on to Christine, whose partial understanding, more than simply supplemented by her active imagination, came finally to saturate Elen, that dry little sponge whose almost total store of early information came by way of this prolific though questionable source. Even as a middle-aged woman, Elen was still suffering that all too familiar but always shocking experience of having voiced a truism of old and seeing on the faces of her listeners a look of incredulity and derisive humor. When younger, she would hotly defend her derided bit of information, and suffer later the untold embarrassment of learning the truth; but as she matured, she learned to spare herself and even to enjoy the revelations by blithely admitting that her source was not infallible.

The three girls played together daily; sometimes all three, often only two, Christine being the lone switch member. She played as a twosome with Elen or with Anne, but Anne and Elen never played together without Christine. One of their favorite games was riding the turnstyle gate, which was located in the pasture fence between Anne's and Christine's houses. Luckily the gate was three-sided, offering a position for each rider. As circus riders, daredevil pilots, or just great soaring birds, they took their places, gave themselves a push, and rode for long, airborne hours on the magic gate.

"Run away and join the circus" was a game that held their fascinated attention for hours. Since they had not the faintest notion of what a circus was, Mr. Barnum would have been much surprised at the acts attributed to his enterprise. Their one bit of legitimate information about circuses came from Amos, who had two acts that he was perfecting so as to be ready when he ran away and joined the circus. It is a comment on the close-knit clannishness of the Family that a twenty-two-year-old man, unfettered by responsibilities, would consider it necessary to "run away from home" when he decided to leave the nest and seek his independent fortune. At any rate, he spent most of his spare time practicing his skills for his new career: bareback riding and snake handling.

71

Amos, to the delight of the three little girls, would stand on the bare back of a horse and ride with the wind down across the large pasture. He could even perform facing backward. Christine, a particular favorite of his, perhaps because he had been present at her birth or maybe because he just felt a kindred restlessness in her, was his special confidante.

"Top, bareback riding is the greatest," he confidently assured her, "and circuses are always looking for good riders. I'll teach you, and we'll perform together."

Alas, this dream, as is the way with dreams, never came to fruition. Zueline, on hearing of the glamorous plans, put a stop to even the talk of Christine's riding a horse. Why, everybody knew that horseback riding was no decent pastime for a girl, making their hips spread and their legs bow, and bareback riding was downright scandalous. It was also dangerous. Zueline was frightened of horses, they not being animals with which women came into contact, since men harnessed, drove, and plowed, and she did not want her daughter to develop any kind of friendly relationship with those high-spirited, unpredictable animals.

"One of these days Amos is going to get killed," she predicted, "and I am not going to have you getting killed with him."

Even though Christine pled to no avail with her mother, she believed her words, and for years she thought that riding a horse would eventually kill one. Ironically, when she rode a horse twenty years later, for the only time in her life, it threw her and did almost kill her, eerily bringing to mind her mother's superstitious belief. Christine also began to notice women with large rears and bowed legs, knowing that their horses were tethered nearby, and she passed on this important bit of lore to Elen.

"Mrs. Turner is fat like that and has crooked legs because she rides a horse. That makes her fit around the horse," she instructed. It made sense to Elen, as she stored it away with all her other important trivia for future reference.

Amos's other circus act, snakehandling, also horrified Zueline. Some of the abundant supply of snakes on the farm were poisonous, some were harmless, but to most women, a snake was simply a snake and was to be scrupulously avoided. Amos, fully realizing the tenor of his audience, performed with flamboyance, grabbing the snakes just behind the heads and holding them high in the air while their shining bodies coiled sensuously about his arm. He sometimes really warmed up to his art and would grab one by the tail, viciously snapping it in the air in an up-and-down motion, killing it by severing the spinal cord. Zueline, wisely afraid that Christine would try her hand at snakehandling, told her that Amos cast a spell on the snake so that he could handle it, and that if you didn't know to cast the spell, the snake would get you —"get you" being left undefined but ominous. Christine, pondering that perhaps only mothers were afraid, asked her father if snakes would get you. When Acie admitted that he was also afraid of snakes, she became properly frightened herself, a state that coincided with and was fortunately reinforced by Amos's being bitten. Even the best in the trade sometimes encounter a particularly difficult specimen, and the fearless handler sported an ugly swollen arm for several days. The child's learning that poison from the dying snake caused the painful injury reinforced Zueline's story that the spell had to be cast just right or the snake would get you. The child, terrified, had nightmares about parts of her body turning to snakes; and her mother, cuddling her in her arms, assured her that snakes could not get into the house. Ironically, Zueline was now trying to allay the very fears that she had striven so diligently to arouse. Alas, the mother had once again protected the physical being at the dire expense of the mind.

The three houses in the Promised Land were lined up down a small lane that ran between two large cotton fields. Ellis had built his house at the end of the lane in a grove of pine trees. It was a six-room white frame house, tin-roofed and trimmed in dark green. The inside walls were painted soft colors; the floors had rugs; and wonder of wonders, there were two sitting rooms, a mark of real elegance. A farm family had really arrived when it possessed a house having a parlor that did not have to double as a bedroom, and Mamie Lee's parlor even contained a three-piece set of overstuffed furniture: a three-cushion settee and two armchairs. They were covered in dark mushroom velvet with picture-decorated cushions, depicting gladed scenes of overfed ladies languishing in dim wooded bowers. This was the "company room," of course, and was used only on special occasions, at all other times being kept dark and closed up, giving it that eternally faint, musty parlor smell. It was this room that helped to give Elen her

73

long-held impression that the forbidden is the most beautiful and tantalizingly desirous. She was constantly told not to put her feet on the parlor chairs, not to touch its pretty objects, and not to play there with her toys. Her favorite secret sin was to slip into the dim remote room and do all the delicious forbidden things, once even jumping from seat to seat on the wondrously springy cushions. It was also here that she hid to perform the scandalously naughty "bad girl" deeds, such as play with her new-found navel and try mightly to view her hidden genitals. She and Christine had, of course, shown their private parts to each other, and Christine had said that all girls were made alike, but how could one be sure if one could not compare. It was a real revelation the day Elen discovered the hand mirror.

Farther along the lane, down the hill from the new house, sat the house where Mama and Papa lived. It was a six-room weathered house, the kind that, never having been painted, ages gray and beaten. Having a wide front porch, a small side porch, and two bedrooms upstairs, it sat in a clean-swept, sun-baked red clay yard under two enormous old oaks. With the turkey pen to the right and the garden on the left, the house itself backed right onto the barbed-wire fence enclosing the lush, green, clover-filled pasture. Mama and Papa had once owned fine, elegantly appointed furniture, but fire, that tragic destroyer of life and possessions, swept away all in one bitterly remembered night. Their home was burned after their fortune took its headlong plunge downward, making it impossible to rebuild or to replace their lovely old belongings. They had since lived with their numerous family in amply large, though rented, houses, and their furnishings were mismatched, made-do pieces supplied by begrudging and even remindful relatives. Mama, who was herself from a large family and the youngest girl, was discreetly criticized by her older sisters for continuing to produce children after her material circumstances became so acute. There was a sage nodding of heads that accompanied statements about Nick's inability to pull himself out of his difficulties and that it was no wonder with "all those mouths to feed!"

The lane stopped at Mama's house, but a path, leading through the turnstyle gate, led down the pasture to the spring at the bottom of the hill and continued up another hill on the far side to

Acie and Zueline's house just outside the pasture fence. It was quite far on foot, but it was in sight and well within hollering distance. In the absence of telephones, and often automobiles as well, this significant means of communication was reserved for special occasions, usually pressing emergencies. One never ignored a halloo, taking it as a distress signal, and always sent an answering one before dropping immediate tasks and hurrying to the aid of the caller.

Acie's house could not be reached by car from Ellis's and Papa's houses; there was only the path through the pasture, but it had its own lane winding through the fields and pine forests from the main road. It was a three-room house having a large kitchen and two bedrooms, one of which had a fireplace and doubled as the sitting room. It was not a fine house and its furnishings were not elegant, but then it was really not lived in much, either. Acie was away working all day, and Zueline spent most of her time down the hill at Mama's so that she could "help out" with the work. When the men came home for the midday meal, Acie came to Mama's kitchen, knowing that his wife would be there and that she had done part of the work of preparing the food.

Christine almost never played during the day at her own house, since she left with her mother early each morning and went down to Granny's. She played with Anne or went up the hill to play with Elen, who also loved to go to Granny's to play. Most of the time the three little girls played contentedly together, and if there was discord, Anne was the inevitable instigator. It was almost impossible for this mischievous little demon to "play by the rules"— she always had a secret, devious angle—and often Elen, still scarcely more than a baby, fell victim to her cunning tricks. One favorite trick was to play Follow the Leader, coaxing the small child through several simple monkey see, monkey do acts. After Elen finally caught on and was enjoying the game, Anne would run in her ringer. Once Anne, as the permanent leader, pretended to sit in a fresh pile of manure that an obliging chicken had just deposited on the porch, generously showing her unspoiled panties and bragging in the accepted Follow the Leader chant, "*I can sit in chicken shit and not get any on my pa-ants!*"

Christine, old enough to be aware of all the little subtleties of the game, took her turn and faithfully followed the leader, showing in turn her own clean panties while repeating the victor's chant. But poor Elen, unaware of the trickery at work in the game and believing that she could do anything the older girls could do, if only she followed the leader, sat carefully and heavily on the offending little mound. She then confidently turned her rear to the eagerly awaiting audience and began to chant. Her first suspicion that the magic had not worked came with Christine and Anne's loud laughter, and it was fully and horribly confirmed when her own investigating hand discovered the thick, gooey mess clinging to her ruined pants. Heartbroken, she ran crying into the house to her grandmother; and even though she did not accuse her playmates, Mama, at a glance, took in the facts of the situation and soundly spanked the older girls. Elen, not understanding why they were punished, believed for years that if she only knew how to play the game, she would be able to perform this wondrous feat.

Christine was in a unique position between her two playmates, one three years younger and the other three years older, and she always got punished when there was mischief involved. It seemed that excuses could always be found for the other girls—Elen was too little to know better, and Anne was too old to do that kind of thing and needed a good talking to; but Christine, like Goldilock's pudding, was always just right for being eaten up by some avenging adult for every infraction of the rules. She never seemed to mind the leniency shown toward Elen, knowing that the child simply meekly followed along; but she highly resented and loudly protested Anne's escape from the switch, when it had usually been her fertile brain that had conceived the idea causing the trouble.

A woman's place, especially the rural woman, was in the home. Consequently, little girls, from babyhood, were encouraged to ready themselves for their predestined task in life. Every little girl had a playhouse, ranging in elegance from an elaborate little construction scaled down in size and stocked with miniature furnishings to the make-believe structure built only in the mind of an imaginative child and stocked with broken items from the adult world and "let's pretend" treasures from fairy castles. Christine and Anne had a playhouse of the latter variety under a big oak tree near the spring just below Mama's house. The spring was a lovely place, all cool and green, and completely overhung by the intermeshing limbs and leaves of shading, protecting trees, while underfoot was a thick carpet of soft, lushly green grass and clover. The spring, backed up against a mossy bank, formed a large pool of clear crystal water that lightly gurgled and rippled as it overflowed its lip and began its long journey of currents and eddies to the Savannah, that sluggish, wide red ribbon to the sea.

Playhouse confines consisted of rows of small stones and sticks, and necessary pieces of furniture such as tables and chairs were indicated by placing boards across bricks. One important task of little homemakers was setting the dinner table and eating pretend food from the dishes—pretty pieces of broken glass that the little girls were constantly searching for. Elen often played in the spring playhouse, but she also had her own playhouse in a pine thicket across the lane from her house. It was nestled under a little hill and had the prettiest dishes, much prettier than those at the spring. Christine had helped her find the lovely bits of colored glass, but she never claimed them for her own; they belonged to Elen.

Anne almost never played up the hill in the pine playhouse, but she kept a secret watch on all of its goings-on, and from time to time she stole a particularly nice dish. When it was recognized on her own table, she airily announced that she had one like theirs. Christine knew that she had taken the treasures—she had even seen her snooping around the pine grove—but Elen never knew. One day, Anne persuaded Christine to help her burglarize the playhouse and steal all of Elen's dishes. They waited until the little girl's nap time, and their well-laid plan might have worked if Ellis had not spotted them in the act of committing their dastardly deed.

Never having much confidence in physical punishment, since a great amount of it had had a negligible deterrent effect on him as a child, Ellis dealt very successfully with youngsters by treating them as adults, just scaling the verbal exchange to their level of comprehension. Amused, he observed their crime, allowing it to be carried to fruition; and the next day, making no reference to the stolen dishes, he casually announced to Christine,

"Well, guess the sheriff will come today. He didn't make it yesterday, but he said it was against the law to steal."

Everybody knew about the sheriff. Children were taught from the cradle to respect and obey the law and to fear lawmen; and mothers even used the sheriff to calm the hysterical behavior of temper tantrums, saying, "You had better stop that. The sheriff will get you!"

Christine, well aware that the sheriff was second only to the booga man in his ability to "get" bad children, flew to the task of replacing the dishes and removing the evidence of the crime. In far less time than it had taken both girls to remove the bright, colorful bits of glass, she alone had them all back in place, and she had learned an important lesson about theft: Stealing was a wrongdoing that was handled by the law, not parents. And having learned from past experience that she was the one who always got punished no matter who was involved, she did not even expect Anne to help right the wrong, knowing full well that the sheriff, when he came, would talk sternly to the older girl, but that he would surely get her and drag her off to jail, whatever that was.

The sojourn in the Promised Land was short, but each day was brim full with adventures, most of which were of the forbidden variety. Anne had learned the art of rabbit tobacco from her older brothers, and she and Christine had their own secret cache, some of which they had picked and dried according to the age-old, word-of-mouth method, and some that they had stolen from other secret caches. Their supply was under Mama's house up next to the chimney, a warm place both summer and winter, and the brown stalks with their grayish foliage dried crisply and pungently. Female clothes were not adorned with the large, useful pockets that were a natural part of the male garb, and little girls were often reduced to transporting secret objects in their pants. These homemade bloomers, gathered and roomy but held securely at the waist and legs by elastic, were capable of holding an amazing amount of hidden treasure. A little girl carrying a bloomerload walked with an extremely odd gait and often made strange rattling noises, depending on the cargo she was carrying.

Christine and Anne transported their rabbit tobacco from its hiding place under the house to the smoking place behind the tool shed in this unusual manner. If the busy adults had only noticed, they would have seen them staggering along with spraddle-legged shuffles and pained expressions on their faces—dried rabbit tobacco sticks and scratches awfully when carried in one's panties. It's amazing how the act of secretly smoking matures the conversation. The little girls, having rolled their leaves in paper and licked it down the side to make it stick in the accepted roll-your-own fashion, lit up, leaned back against the shed, and launched into the current adult topics—usually sex.

Sex was a subject that was never discussed across generation lines and was seldom mentioned across widespread age lines even within the same generation, and it was a topic never broached by anyone to a child; consequently, children grew up with extremely erroneous and strange misconceptions of that all too natural phenomenon, their information gleaned out of context from secretive adults and teasing, misleading older youths. Anne, with her uncanny talent for "overhearing," was a veritable storehouse of misinformation and mismatched truths. Living among so many unmarried and newly married siblings, she fell privy to constant whisperings about this ever fascinating subject; and when the information became skimpy, she generously filled in the gaps with her own fertile imaginings.

It is a paradox and patently unfair that adults, who so scrupulously strive to prevent their young from gaining any knowledge concerning sex, are so quick to blame them when they exhibit false behavior based on their incomplete knowledge. Anne and Christine, through their faulty grapevine, had unearthed the interesting bit of information that a man could easily insult a woman in the area of sex doings, and that this kind of insult was hotly disapproved of by everyone, especially by fathers and brothers of the insulted lady. Anne found a place to use this newfound knowledge with near-disastrous results. Mr. Will Moon, an elderly, gray-haired man whose farm adjoined the Butler place, was a good friend to Ellis, and Mr. Moon was in the habit of cutting across the two farms and walking over to visit with his friend instead of driving his car the long way around by the road. His shortcut brought him out into the lane between Ellis's and Papa's houses. As darkness was falling one evening, Mr. Moon, on his way home, spotted Anne and Christine sitting behind a barn playing. Realizing that the little girls should not be out alone so late, he tried to send them home. When Anne protested and im-

79

pudently told him to mind his own business, he took each child by the hand and led them down the lane to the house. Papa thanked him for his good-neighborly deed and promised to severely "speak to the girls."

Anne, furious with Mr. Moon for "meddling in where he didn't belong," and trying desperately to avoid one of Papa's dreaded "talkings-to," struck out in defense,

"He insulted me, Papa," she tearfully told. "He put his hands on me." This was the way she had heard being insulted described.

Nick Hastings reacted just as all the whispered stories predicted that a father should; in fact, he reacted much stronger than his spoiled little daughter ever dreamed or desired. Papa roared,

"What do you mean? Look at me, girl, what do you mean, 'He put his hands on you?'" He gripped her by the shoulders, glaring down from his six-foot height.

Anne, frightened, but equal to the moment, glanced at her angry father, ducked her head shyly, and primly answered, "Oh, you know, Papa, I can't say it, but you know."

Papa, an honest, straightforward man, put on his hat and headed across the field to confront his neighbor with the accusation. They both returned and questioned Anne, who stubbornly and heroically held her ground. They then went, with Anne tearfully in tow, to question Christine, who had been taken up the hill to her own home. Guileless and frightened, the younger child repeated everything exactly as it had happened. Papa apologized to Mr. Moon as one gentleman to another and promptly thrashed wailing Anne on the spot. Mr. Moon went home saddened though vindicated, but he never again cut across the fields; he always drove his car around by the roads when he came to visit with his friends.

Anne sulked and was mad with Christine for days. "You are a tattletale," she accused her. "If you hadn't told, I could have had that uppity ole man put in jail!"

Christine did not know what "uppity" was, but she thought for quite a long time that gray-haired old men were bad and ought to be put in jail. It did not occur to her to doubt Anne then, or all the other numerous times when she was being educated by her little playmate in how things got done. Anne was the one to burst Christine's bubble of illusion concerning the Easter Bunny, in-

forming her that those colored eggs were not bunny eggs at all—
they were only regular chicken eggs, dyed to look like bunny eggs.
Anne's plan was to steal Mama's eggs from the hen nests before
they were gathered each day, hide them until Easter, and then
have lots of eggs to eat when the great day arrived. Everything
went according to plan up to the part about eating them on
Easter. When the buried eggs were carefully dug up on Easter
Eve, the offensive, nauseating smell emanating from them convinced Christine that bunny eggs were very different from hen
eggs, and Anne's credibility concerning the whole Easter Bunny
affair was in serious doubt for several years.

The sweet shrub is one of nature's little extra gifts, a bonus, and
available only to those who actively seek it out. It grows wild on a
rather scraggly, nondescript bush, and is itself a slightly repulsive
little growth. Its treasure is its scent—somewhat reminiscent of
deliciously ripe bananas; a full, sweet, heavenly waft overpowers
the senses, tingles the nostrils, and converts the doubter into a lifetime sweet shrub sniffer. Women tied several of the aromatic balls
in the corners of their handkerchiefs, and placed them in dresser
drawers with their personal garments, and lovers have always
brought them to their ladies as "sweets to the sweet."

Searching for sweet shrubs was forever an intriguing pastime for
women of all ages, Christine and Anne being no exceptions. They
mostly had a free run of the area immediately surrounding the
three farmhouses, but some places were clearly off limits, as was
the Negro house on the far side of the pasture. There were several
good reasons for this being a forbidden spot: It was too far away,
the small girls would be a bother to the busy tenants, and then
there was the always vaguely stated belief that black men would
"get" little girls. Both girls were well aware that under no conditions were they to travel to this interesting place, it had been
stressed many times; but one day while searching for sweet shrubs
down in the pasture, Anne casually suggested,

"Let's go to the nigger house, I dare you!"

"We can't go, you know we can't go there. We'd get a whippin'," Christine protested vehemently.

"You're a scaredy cat," Anne taunted. "Anyway, they'll never
know."

Christine wanted very much to go. She had been several times with her mother, and it had always smelled like such good things to eat. She was hungry now, and the house was just over the hill, almost in sight.

"I dare you!" Anne taunted. "Come on, let's run!" she coaxed.

Temptation intermingled with her own desire was suddenly beyond Christine's endurance, and even as she stood there shaking her head, she saw an ugly little girl with huge freckles and square-cut bangs cross the creek and start up the hill toward the Negro house. Christine watched everything they did: play with the little black children, eat cornbread and black strap molasses, and start home at dusk just as their fathers came up the hill looking for them. She ran, horrified, up to her father, exclaiming,

"I told them not to do it, Daddy. I didn't go I just watched!" And Christine pointed to Anne and the ugly little girl.

"Top, don't you lie to me!" Acie sternly scolded his child, embarrassed that his father-in-law was witnessing her degrading lie.

Christine turned to find the other girl who had accompanied Anne on the forbidden trip. The other girl was not there. Anne stood alone before her father, her head down, her face contrite, the perfect picture of a remorseful, chastened child who had learned a lesson.

"I did it, Papa, and I'm sorry," she confessed sorrowfully.

Christine, totally unable to comprehend the meaning of the scene and desperate to convince her father of her own innocence, pointed to the empty air and loudly protested,

"She did it, Daddy, she did it! Daddy, I promise you, I didn't!" In her strength of emotion, she seized her father's hand and pulled him toward the spot where she had last seen the ugly little culprit.

Acie, exasperated beyond understanding, jerked his hand from his child's grasp, and holding her under his arm, with her thinly clad rear protruding, soundly spanked, with his bare hand, his screaming, kicking daughter. When he set her down on the ground again, he shook his trembling finger at her, roughly admonishing,

"Now you just hush that fuss. Hush it, I say! I will break you from your lying. I *will* break you! Now you go home, and I don't ever want to catch you over here again."

They all started for home, Anne walking meekly beside her father, the smaller issue of running off having been lost in the greater sin of lying. As they neared the parting fork in the path, Papa spoke gently,

"Don't be too hard on her, Acie. Chaps will be chaps."

Acie answered, his voice hard, "You know she can't go through life not facing up to things, Mista' Hastin'; it wouldn't be right to let her grow up that way. She's got to take life as it really is. Life's hard enough without trying to run away from it."

They went their separate ways, the father holding the child's hand as they climbed the hill in the gathering dusk. The brightest stars were already winking in the dark gray sky, made strangely translucent by the last glow of day, and the dew on the soft grass soothed Christine's hot little feet. She felt suspended between earth and sky, a good place to be, surrounded by the comforting, concealing darkness and untouched by the harsh reality of earth.

When the tale was told to Zueline, she tried to soothe the upset child, and mildly remonstrated with her husband when it was revealed that Papa had not also spanked Anne. Acie answered patiently,

"I am not responsible for raising Anne. And Top deliberately lied to me. She can't be allowed to get away with that. She has got to learn to face up to things. She shouldn't get *you* all worried up in your condition, either."

"Honey, she don't know anything about that. How could she?" Zueline gently smiled, rocking her daughter against her thickened body.

Nobody saw her. Daddy wouldn't lie about it. Anne might lie about it to keep from being punished, and Grandpa might tease me, but Daddy wouldn't lie, and he wouldn't tease me and then whip me about it. Why was I always the only one to see her? And why was I always whipped for her naughtiness? Why didn't Anne or even Elen get blamed for what she did? She was so ugly this time: skinny and sloppy and all those horrible freckles. What did I look like at that age? Everybody said I was ugly, too, and I was always being told to hold up my shoulders and straighten my clothes. And I did have awful freckles. God! Do you suppose that was me? No! It couldn't have been! Anne could have told them it wasn't me, she saw her, she played with her all afternoon. But Anne was always playing tricks on me, she wouldn't help me. But that does prove that it wasn't me— Anne must have seen her. If I just think there will be other times when someone else saw her . . .

Christine was shortly to be faced with one of the hardest realities of her life: the loss of first place, if not in the hearts of her parents, then surely in their time and attention. The six-year-old child could not see into their hearts; she only knew that she no longer had first choice of their energies and their efforts. Poor Christine, just at the age when she was least able to deal with the trauma of a new baby in the family, she was faced with this always disrupting, unsettling event in her own house. And it was not just one baby, it was two babies; Zueline gave birth to two beautiful, blue-eyed, black-haired, identical twin girls. Christine had not only irrevocably lost her cherished position as the baby in her home, she had also lost it to *two* little interlopers: the babies!

5

The Babies

Matched sets have always held a peculiar kind of fascination for people. Those things, animate or inanimate, that are unique, rare, one of a kind, are revered and desired as collectors' items; but a matched pair, with a similarity close enough to be termed identical, does not often occur in nature, being, in fact, so rare that those things that man deliberately fashions as mirror images are objects of curiosity and admiration. One vase from an old Chinese dynasty is an *objet d'art* worth a fortune, but two matched Ming vases are priceless museum pieces, guarded and locked behind glass as if even the raw, unfiltered gaze might damage the precious treasure.

The great miracle of nature is to be found in the total lack of perfect reproduction in all her uncountable hosts of creations. Man is fascinated by the rare occurrences in nature of near identicalness. He stares, he closely examines, he marvels, and he shakes his head in wonder at the close resemblance.

The introduction of a new sibling into the family circle is always, to varying degrees, traumatic, but no single child can possibly hold his own when pitted against the fierce competition of the natural phenomenon of identical twins born into the family. And Christine's competition was perhaps fiercer than most. She turned six in April 1933, and her identical twin sisters were born the following August 13—the only twins in the entire county, and they remained so for more than thirteen years.

Full-term, perfectly formed babies, they were yet incredibly small, weighing only 2½ and 3 pounds. Though nature had fashioned them from the selfsame genes, their nine-month sojourn in the uterine environment had by birthtime altered them to a measurable degree, and even the imperfect human eye could catalogue minor differences. Still, they were fascinatingly similar, and stories concerning the confusion surrounding their alikeness sprang up and were eagerly retold, gathering color as they went. One such story had to do with Zueline's inability to distinguish between the infants. She would be asked to say which was which and then be slyly watched as she studied the babies and made her choice, which was always met by indulgent protests of disbelief. Zueline, torn between pride over the attention given her children and fear that she was not competently controlling this unusual and demanding situation, would, half vexed, affirm, "You *know*, a mother knows her own children!"

A few months after the birth, one baby fell from the bed and gashed a small wound on the bridge of her nose, leaving a tiny white scar. This accident forever settled the question of identity, adding to the retold tales that now Zueline had to surreptitiously scan the little visage before confidently making her pronouncement. Mostly, however, they were referred to with group anonymity as "the babies," a name they carried into adulthood. They were born in the little house atop the hill across the pasture in the Promised Land. Mamie Lee and Mama attended the birth and performed the customary tasks of heating water, providing rags, and holding lamps for Dr. Raymond Buist Dunovant. It was a fairly easy process as births go and occurred, as so many seem to, in the dark of the night. When it had become evident that the birth was near, it was arranged for Ellis and Elen, along with Christine, to spend the night down the hill at Mama's house. This plan placed Ellis and his car near enough to hear Acie's halloo if he needed help. The doctor had also left his car at Mama's and walked the path through the pasture to the house on the hill.

Dr. Dunovant, a tall, slender man just over thirty, had twinkling dark blue eyes and a wry sense of humor. The air of unhurried calm surrounding him allayed the rising hysteria of fear and promoted confidence in medical skill, possibly the doctor's greatest asset, other than his own training, in dealing with, not only the patient, but also the anxious kith and kin. In delivering the twins,

86

his worth was established, and he became the doctor for the Family for more than forty years, spanking their newborn bottoms to encourage life, caring for their health, and closing their eyes in death. He stopped by Mama's on his way home that night and told the anxious, expectant relatives about the surprise in the little house on the hill. One could speculate about his thoughts as he slowly drove the miles of rough dusty roads that warm summer night. Thoughts about the courage and determination of people who, though drowned in the black depths of the Depression, rejoiced in the birth of babies; thoughts about the kind of world those babies would live to see, a world of which the mind could not yet even conceive; and thoughts about the interweaving of his own life's thread into the fabric of a family, a community, a nation of little people, daily and desperately struggling against devastating and only partially understood economic forces. For his long night's labor, he charged Acie fifteen dollars.

And on the eve of this wondrous event, the involved men fared no better than had their brothers before them in similar circumstances. Ellis, the brother of the new father, noisily fell out of his bed at the very moment of birth; and Acie, the father, showed up at the birth with his pants on backward. Father Freud and his disciples would have had a field day with these symbolism-fraught incidences; and the amused relatives, though only partially understanding the psychological implications of their tales, related them with leering relish in the presence of the weakly protesting, secretly pleased men.

Life on the farm begins early in the day, but on the morning after the babies were born, life was astir even earlier than usual. Everyone wanted to see the twins, and the talk was of nothing else. Christine, Anne, and Elen were too excited to eat and had to be restrained from crossing the pasture before the little house on the hill was ready for visitors; but just as soon as the sun was up, the three little girls set off down the hill in the heavy dew. Christine's pride was almost more than she could contain. She ran, she jumped, she babbled. Never a calm, introspective child, she now loosed her emotions in a torrential outburst that was indulgently accepted and encouraged by the pleased adults, who were feeling their own juvenile stirrings of family pride. The absence of the usual reprimand for her comic antics whipped her noisy acrobatics to a fever pitch and precipitated a spontaneous, warm glow inside her. It was wonderful to have babies, it changed things, it made people happy and tolerant and accepting, and it set Christine apart fom Elen and Anne. *They* didn't have any babies, and she, Christine, had two. It was wonderful. Alas, she was too young to realize that her glow was only reflected from the true source, and that her glory would always be of a lesser, paler variety. The course of her entire life might have been changed if the importance of this first blush of pleasurable pride had been recognized and nurtured to permeate her natural generosity.

Elen had no such feelings of pride; she felt cheated, and deeply suffered from the gross injustice of the whole affair. She, in contrast to exuberant Christine, was calm and unemotional, and her unruffled exterior gave no indication that she considered an act of blatant partiality to have been committed by someone. Eventually the brunt of the blame came to rest on Dr. Dunovant. She was completely ignorant of the entire process of begetting babies on that morning when the wondrous announcement was made, but one phrase penetrated her childish darkness: "Dr. Dunovant brought the babies." He must have brought them in his car from town; he even drove right past her house and took both of them up the hill and gave them to Christine. Why didn't he stop and leave one of them at her house? She was to wonder for years if he would have done just that if she had been home that night, and as a result she never wanted to spend Christmas away from her house—Santa Claus might well pass her up just as the doctor had done if she were not in her accustomed place.

None of these abstractions concerned Anne. Wise beyond her years, as ever, she was busily pursuing the mechanics of this new venture. She had unobtrusively tuned in on all the vital channels of news crisscrossing the family scene that morning, and by the time they were allowed to leave for the official first viewing, she was overflowing with choice half truths and brilliantly mismatched facts, which she passed on to her awed, gullible little nieces. As they passed the spring where the washing was done, she marched them over to the washtubs and pointed out the bloody sheets and rags that had been used during the delivery. This sight had a profound effect on Christine. All that blood! Blood meant death. Was her mother going to die? Had she already bled to death? Christine's pleasure and pride evaporated in an instant, never again to return to that first pristine purity, and she experienced her second reaction to her new sisters: If her mother had died, they had killed her! She hurried up the wet grass of the hill with unformed fear drumming in her ears and choking off her breath.

Elen was also deeply struck by the bloody rags, but she did not associate them with death, only birth. Having been carefully shielded from all knowledge of the female monthly cycle, and having a shy nature that allowed few questions, she always afterward experienced exultation whenever she accidentally discovered evidence of her mother's menstrual flow among the soiled laundry, to be followed closely, however, by disillusioned dejection when no baby resultantly appeared.

When they arrived at the house, dew-damp and out of breath from running, Acie and Mamie Lee took them into Zueline's room to see the babies. Unsuspecting Christine was due for another shock. The babies were in *her* little green bed! There was a baby at each end of the bed. It was not a matter of sharing the bed with them, they had completely taken it over—there was no room for her. They were sleeping, and as she looked down at them, she thought how little they looked and how round and pretty, and what a lot of black hair, just like Mother's and Daddy's. She especially noticed that they didn't have any freckles. Acie pulled back the light blanket to better show them off, each clothed in identical little white gowns piped around the neck in blue. Acie was so proud.

Showing his large white teeth in a wide grin, he fairly crowed, "There's the babies!"

Christine, looking into her father's radiant face and fully comprehending the meaning of his words, registered her third shock of the morning: These little beings had not only taken over her bed, they had also usurped her place in her family. She was no longer the baby, *they* were the baby—the babies! Elen was still Unc and Aunt Meme's baby and Anne was still Grandpa and Granny's baby, but now she was nobody's baby.

"I'm not first with anybody," she thought, and tears began to cloud the enormous blue eyes.

No one noticed then or later the distressed child who went

unheeded for the next few days, as relatives and friends gathered to view the natural wonders, who were named Rebecca Elise and Lennie Louise. Rebecca was for Acie's mother, and Lennie was for Mama's mother, insuring that they were properly named for members of the Family; and since tradition also demanded that twins carry rhyming twin names, they were also called Elise for Zueline's younger sister, and Louise simply because it rhymed with Elise. Before the first day was out, however, they had acquired pet names: Rebecca Elise became Becky, often shortened to Beck, and Lennie Louise became Tiny, because she was the smaller of the two.

Becky and Tiny were, from the hour of their birth, favored children. Attention was naturally accorded to them by friends and neighbors because of their similarity, and attention was demanded by them of their family, simply because they were two. It takes twice as much time to feed, diaper, bathe, and otherwise care for two babies as it does to care for one baby. Even with the help given her by her nearby relatives, Zueline industriously labored from morning till night tending to the demands of her helpless infants. Acie, in the evening, cared for them as much as he could to release his harried wife to do her other necessary chores. There was no time for Christine. The bewildered, hurt child watched this busy scene in which she played no role. In a well-intentioned effort to protect the abormally small and seemingly fragile infants, her parents did not allow her to hold them, scarcely to touch them, and she was constantly cautioned to be careful when she even ventured near. Yet she observed that others were permitted to hold them, they were constantly being passed from lap to lap; but she, the sister, was kept from this important, cherished privilege. Were they not her sisters, her babies? She had been allowed to hold Elen, and she had cuddled and rocked other babies from time to time. How was this different? These questions burned through her confused thoughts, and these privations seared her raw sensitivities. The unheeding adults had no conception of the basis for her unhappiness; they only knew that she had become difficult to deal with, and the frustrated child was as completely oblivious to the frailty of the babies as she was to the reputation for unpredictable actions that her erratic behavior had earned her.

Her churning frustrations soon crystalized into a deep resentment of her little siblings, which was not really resolved until the death of Acie and Zueline, more than forty years later, removed from the then middle-aged sisters this primeval barrier to their attainment of an unblemished relationship. Christine was able to say, only after her father's death, when the issue had become forever academic, that she now knew that she had *really* been first with him all of her life. Strangely significant is the fact that his death, the most feared and dreaded of all deaths to her, even though his constantly deteriorating state of health left no hope for recovery, was the one influencing death of her entire life that precipitated no traumatic personality modification. It was, in fact, the beginning of the end of her ability to escape her realities in that so familiar manner. And the resolution of the female oedipal again, and still, remains shrouded in swirling mists, permitting only occasional glimpses "seen through a glass darkly."

At the first opportunity alone with them, Christine hastened to wreak her pent-up vengeance on the infants. Discovering them one day unattended in her little green bed, she stood for a moment immobile, staring down at the twin causes of her growing unhappiness and the sudden demise of her favored position in her home. Her stomach lurched sharply, her breath caught in her throat, and her vision swam and blurred. When her sight cleared, she saw, standing by the bed, a pathetically thin little girl with bowl-cropped, uncurled, stringy hair, whose bony little face, perched on an incredibly slim neck, sported a mass of large brown freckles and enormous bright blue eyes. She watched passively, abstractly, as the ungainly little figure, barefooted and dressed in a short, straight shift, roughly threw off the bed covers and began systematically to torture her little sisters. The strangely familiar child sharply poked her grubby little fingers in their sleeping eyes, and when they began to wail and kick, she grabbed their tiny feet, and squeezing mightily, fiercely bit the red, flailing toes.

Zueline, struck with electrifying fear at the terrified screams of both her helpless babies, rushed, praying volubly, from her work in the garden. Unable to endure the suspense of the longer route around and into the house, she flew to the outside window of the bedroom. Her horrified gaze confirmed, regardless of the unknown casual factors, her heretofore only half-formed, but well-grounded, fears, and she loudly banged on the closed window in a frantic attempt to interrupt the scene laid out before her unbelieving eyes.

Christine, hearing the urgent sound at the window, dragged her fascinated gaze from the strangely satisfying drama being enacted on the bed, and saw her mother's horrified face staring at her. As Zueline hurried around the house, Christine, though breathless with excitement and anxiety, felt confident that this time her mother had seen this other child for whose bad behavior she was always being blamed. She was now gone, of course, but her mother had caught her this time, she had slipped up and looked in the window and saw her doing those naughty things. That's the reason she had looked so mad.

Zueline burst into the room, brushed past Christine, and examined the screaming babies. On determining that they were not seriously harmed, her outrage, no longer contained by primary concern, flooded full-force on her unprepared daughter. The maternal instinct to protect helpless young completely dominating her, Zueline roughly pushed Christine away from the bed.

"How dare you do that to my babies!" she fairly screamed her wrath.

The little girl, her sense reeling both from the physical and the mental shock, fell heavily upon the floor.

Her eyes, wide, vague, and uncomprehending, gazed stupidly at her furious mother. She slowly put her dirty little hand over her trembling mouth, a move which seemed to break the iron grasp of the shock, and tears began to well up in staring blue eyes.

"But, Mother . . . ," she whimpered brokenly.

Zueline, out of control, perhaps for the first time in her even-tempered life, grasped her child by the arm and shoved her to the bedside.

"Look, just look what you've done!" she raged, pointing to the puffy red skin around the babies' eyes. A fingernail scratch oozed tiny balls of crimson on one squeezed, wrinkled eyelid.

"But, Mother, you saw her, you saw her do it! I . . ." Christine's defense was abruptly choked off as Zueline, unable to bear under these circumstances both her child's wickedness and her lying, shook her roughly and slapped her sharply on her bare thighs.

"Christine, you just shut up now, I'm not going to have any of your lying. I am sick and tired of your lying. You just look here what you've done!" And Zueline, beside herself with anger, shame, and despair, pushed her gasping child down close to a tiny leg.

Around the incredibly small calf and ankle were deeply imprinted glowing fingerprints, and sharply cut into the little rounded toes were perfect, purple teeth marks. Her mother methodically forced her to view the ravages on each of the four damaged feet.

Christine, totally unable to comprehend her mother's behavior, wailed,

"No, no, I didn't do it, she did it! That ugly little girl did it. You saw her, Mother. She bit your babies, Mother. I didn't bite your babies!"

Zueline, her anger as suddenly withered as it had burgeoned, sat down on the bed and took up her crying babes, one cradled in each arm. As best she could, she rocked and comforted them, soothing,

"There, there, baby. It's all right. It's all right. Mother's got you now. Mother will take care of you." And she alternately hugged each little body and planted kisses on each little head. How could she comfort her other child, also? Even had she understood her oldest daughter's consuming distress, she simply was physically unable to even stroke her. Had there been only one baby, she could have drawn her daughter into the closed circle of mother and baby, she had enough love; she merely lacked physical capacity.

Christine, huddled on the floor, drowned in the silence of exclusion, knew only that her replacement had been complete. Was Zueline overprotective of her infants from that moment? No one surely could blame her if she were. Being one of the oldest in a large family where there were always little ones and regularly a new baby, her experience, which was all she knew, had taught her that one always loved and cared for the helpless young. She was entirely unable to comprehend her child's wicked, wanton behavior toward her little sisters, and she must have pondered in her secret heart what evil possessed her child, and where she, herself, had gone wrong to visit such sins on the head of her strange child.

Mother saw her. I saw Mother looking in the window; I saw the awful look on Mother's face when she saw that ugly, dirty child hurting the babies. Mother came running into the house to

make her stop. Why did she hit me? At first, I thought she hit me because I hadn't made the ugly girl stop. But she accused me of hurting the babies, and she knew I hadn't hurt them. She knew it—she saw what happened. But wait! Let me think. Now, I know that Mother would not be so mean as to accuse me of doing something that she knew I did not do. I used to think she did that, but now I know better. I still don't understand it, but I know that she would not do that—she was never mean to me, and she never falsely accused me unless that awful child—she— did something mean and then disappeared. Then Mother, and Daddy, too, always blamed me. The only explanation that makes sense is just exactly what they said—that there was no one else there—just me. But I can't believe that, I won't. I would not hurt helpless babies. That would make me a monster. There's another reason, I know there is. And anyway, I couldn't have been as ugly as that awful child—Mother wouldn't have let me get that dirty and unkempt. Think, think of the other times. . . .

At about this time Christine began to sleepwalk. The experience was of short duration, lasting only about two months, and it did not recur again for forty years. The dream accompanying these short dissociative fugues—these nighttime flights to escape intolerable reality—was a pleasurable fantasy. Christine rose lightly, smoothly from her strange, solitary bed, floated out of the dark house, and glided gently over the housetops against a background of bright, twinkling stars strewn thickly across a black velvet sky. She was wearing Elen's nightgown, the one sprinkled all over with green sprigs topped by pink flowers, and bordered at the neck, hem, and sleeves with tiny lace ruffles. And it fit her, too, long enough to cover all except her little pink toes, just like it did Elen. Zueline heard her and put her lovingly, laughingly back to bed, totally unaware, as would most mothers have been, that her daughter's behavior resulted from deep conflicting feelings over aggression and that it was markedly schizoid in character.

Christine spent almost her entire time now playing with Elen, and Christine loved to visit her Aunt Meme's house. It was filled with intriguing and beautiful wonders, and though she regularly wreaked small havoc and was eternally into mischief, her aunt welcomed her and loved her dearly. Mamie Lee was determined to mold her little niece into an acceptable image, the model of which was, of course, Mamie Lee herself. For all their lives, the aunt was constantly instructing the niece, cautioning her against impetuous behavior, admonishing her to "hold up your shoulders," and generally teaching her the catechism of the lady. Christine was not offended by this seemingly high-handed behavior, taking it in the loving spirit in which it was given and considering it a compliment when someone would comment, "That looks exactly like something your Aunt Meme would wear."

In the afternoons, Mamie Lee would bathe the two little girls in a large tin tub on the big table on the screened-in back porch. In contrast to Elen's stiff, straight little frame, Christine was like a soft, rubber, water-filled balloon, so pliable and sensitive to the touch that she melted away at one point only to bulge out at another. As the washcloth stroked down her back, the spine swayed with incredible concavity, while the round little stomach ballooned convexly in the front. The resultant squiggle of a figure tormented the aunt, who direly warned that slouchy posture indicated a slouchy nature, and that ladies held up their shoulders and pulled in their tummies and their rears. She pointed to Elen as a shining example of good posture, while she firmly pushed in Christine's protruding front. Alas, it was all doomed to failure! Mamie Lee did not have enough hands to push in all the bulges at one time; Christine, desperately trying, was still unable to understand the process and became more misshapen the harder she worked; and Elen, aping her idol, was busily ruining the model by jutting out her own abdomen. Christine knew, however, that in those daily sessions she was receiving loving care and attention, and the bond between aunt and niece grew so strong and lasting that Elen, completely accustomed to it and in no way resenting it, believed all her life that her mother loved the niece more than she loved the daughter.

Christine was attracted to trouble like iron to a magnet, and its seriousness ran the gamut from turning the pearl white handles of the gas jets on Mamie Lee's newly converted cookstove to spoiling the drinking water by blowing bubbles through her soapy fist dipped into her aunt's big oaken water bucket. These were, however, happy days, good days, and they gave her a measure of needed acceptance during the harrowing first few weeks when her mother's entire attention was, of necessity, commanded by the insistent demands of two infants.

Nothing in all her experience, unfortunately, had prepared her for her next encounter, for she was shortly to be thrust, totally unready, into her first participation with the outside world, the general other—that extended environment containing overwhelming numbers of unpredictable strangers.

In September 1933, she entered the institution especially designed by civilized man to socialize his young: school.

6

The World Without

The world is big and frightening. It capriciously buffets even the seasoned veteran in the art of living, whimsically cradling his dreams one moment, only to dash all his hopes the next. Regardless of how intensive has been the preparation, or how gentle has been the entry, that first step into the world beyond the protecting palisades of the family circle is sobering and tarnishing. This process, by design lonely, maturing, and cleaving, is, however, absolutely necessary for the purpose of rending those nuturing bonds that are essential for coaxing life and growth into the human infant, but that are also deadeningly detrimental to the child's continued maturation into a self-sustaining adult.

Nature determined that approximately nine months of uterine nurturing was sufficient to prepare the human offspring for the traumatic thrust into the world within the family; and society, just as omnisciently, decreed that approximately six years of familial nurturing was adequate to ready the child for its second forcible thrust—the one into the fierce competition of the world without. School, the institutionalization of this second thrust, is specifically tailored to ensure that the young, on this first unaccompanied sortie into open society, will experience and internalize those facts, beliefs, and values that will allow society to perpetuate itself. The fittest survive. But the fittest in what? Strength? Intelligence? Endurance? Adaptability? Wealth? Beauty? Unfortunately the need varies with the individual circumstances and the particular moment in time, making it impossible to know in advance exactly with what to equip the emerging fledgling.

97

Christine approached her initial encounter with the world with-out as she did every new experience, full of eagerness and enthusi-asm. She felt no apprehension, no fear, these came later; now she was all thrilling anticipation. Two burning reasons whetted her desire for wanting to start to school: writing and painting. She had always intensely hated her name, *Christine*—it hissed and whined nasally in her ear. *Anne* and *Elen* were soft, breathy sounds that lulled one's thoughts; but her own name grated un-pleasantly, always sounding like a criticism, never a caress. She had never seen her name written, but she had an idea that it would strike the eye more favorably than it struck the ear. The very first thing she wanted to do on the very first day at school was learn to write her name.

All things beautiful intrigued her, and she had discovered that one learned to make beautiful things in school. Anne had learned how to make pretty pictures in school, and she even had a box of precious crayons that she sternly forbade Christine to touch, with which she colored them. She fashioned paper dolls out of card-board for Elen, and dressed them in lovely paper clothes deco-rated with those carefully shepherded crayons. Christine also longed desperately for paper dolls, and she knew that school was her only hope of getting them.

The third reason why she needed school was unknown to her; she felt it only as a deep urge, a painful gnawing, an unassuageable hunger. She needed her own experience, to be shared with no one; something that was particularly and uniquely hers, that she could reveal and share if she so chose, but that she could hoard and conceal if the need demanded. School often provides this essen-tial service, it being, in fact, one of its major premises; but for Christine, already hypersensitive and rubbed raw from too much hurt and too little protection from harmful criticism, its failure was miserable, swift, and complete.

School offered only one fare, served in an identical manner to all, with little attempt at individualization to make it more palata-ble for finicky appetites. Christine had known from her earliest memory that she fell short of reaching some pretty important standards maintained by her family, but she had grown to believe that she could set all that straight by going to school, where one learned how to do things right. She had never been in a school before, and no one had explained what it was like, but she had an idea that it was something like Sunday school. Her family didn't go to church regularly, but Christine always loved to go, and she had even been in a church play once. It was one of her fondest memories. Her mother had made her a new dress and had been so proud of her; everybody had been proud of her, and she often remembered with a nice warm glow how she had stood on the stage and looked out at all the smiling, admiring faces. She had felt important, like a good person, and she desperately yearned for more such experiences.

When the magic day dawned, Christine, never one to sleep late, was awake and impatient to be gone long before the necessary time. Acie dressed her while Zueline cared for the babies and made breakfast. Zueline also prepared the child's school lunch: a boiled egg, a biscuit, and a precious piece of fried ham. On most days the lunch would consist of biscuits and fatback; but today, this all-important first day, the mother wanted her child to have a grand lunch. Wrapping the warm, savory food in newspaper and tying it with a white grocery string, she handed it to the eager little girl with these stern instructions:

"Now, Christine, you be good! Don't drop your lunch, and don't get your clothes dirty. And now, you listen to Mother, you mind the teacher and do everything she says. Ya' hear? Do you hear me, Christine?" She gently shook the child, who was so obviously eager to be off.

"Yes, Mother. Bye, Mother," hastily replied the totally uncomprehending Christine. She hugged her lunch tightly, too tightly, and ran for the door.

Acie, watching the scene with amused eyes, smiled at his frustrated wife, hugging her briefly as he followed his impatient daughter out into the faint, misty light. "Don't worry, Mother, she'll be all right. This will be the making of her. The teacher will straighten her out."

Zueline worriedly shook her head, feeling that she should have been able to give the child better instructions, and she had even let her go without hugging and kissing her good-bye. Looking out at her husband and child crossing the packed red clay yard in the moist, warm dawn, her heart was torn between protective love, which longed to recall the dancing child for a tender kiss, and ma-

ternal pride, which yearned for her daughter to show up well at
school. Pride won out, and she called sternly,

"Christine, you keep your socks pulled up, and don't give the
teacher any trouble. The teacher is always right!"

Christine, her socks already beginning their inevitable descent
down the thin white legs, marred here and there by the old signs
of winter boils and the scrapes and scratches of boisterous play,
chattered happily to her father as they moved down the dew-wet
path.

"I'm gonna learn to write my name today!" she announced as
she ran a small circle around him.

Acie, trying to keep the child out of the tall, dripping grass at
the sides of the path, scolded, "Top, stay on the path. Your shoes
and socks are soaking." It did not occur to him to warn his daughter that all her expectations might not be met on the very first
day, but it is also questionable whether the exuberant child would
even have heard him. She had early earned the name of "head-
strong," which merely meant that she accepted no one's advice or
warning on any subject—she had to travel every path herself, as if
it had never been traveled before. It was a trait that was to cause
her much trouble all of her life.

However, on this beautiful morning, all was right with her
world. The red-gold sun, just topping the wet, shadowy trees,
caught and brilliantly shattered each crystal drop on each luscious
green blade. The pasture was a velvet mound strewn with a king's
ransom of glittering jewels, and the child, herself an imp of nature, was prevented from gathering them only by the fast hold of
her practical, earthbound father. The spreading light, striking the
towering trees at the spring, revealed for the close observer the
first bronze hint of autumn. A thready puff of mist still blanketed
the overhung spring bower, outlining all of the intricate spider
lace in tiny glowing seed pearls.

Christine, vacillating between her strong admiration for all
beauty and her equally strong rejection of any beauty that she
could not possess, alternately destroyed some of the shining creations with one swipe of her commandeered stick, and meticulously
avoided damaging others. Clumsily jumping the stones fording
the creek and wetting miraculously only the toe of one shoe, she

ran ahead of her father up the hill to Mama's. As she pushed through the stile gate, she began to loudly call,

"Anne, Anne, are you ready? Are you ready to go?" Pushing upon the never-locked door to the kitchen, she burst into the room, announcing, "I'm going to school. Today, I'm going to school. I'm going to learn to write my name!"

Mama, busy with pots at the big black iron cookstove, turned and looked briefly at her breathless grandchild, "Goodness, Christine, you'll wake the dead! What are you doing up so early?"

Acie, coming in the door, took off his old sweat-stained summer straw hat and hung it on one of several nails tacked for that very purpose along the wall. "Miz Hastin', she's been up since before daylight. Sister wanted me to bring her as I come to work so's she wouldn't have to cross the pasture alone while the cows are near the lot."

"Wouldn't hurt her, Acie. Sister has always been afraid of cows. She didn't take after me. My papa used to say that all animals loved me. You've just got to let them know who's boss, that's all." And Mama, barely five feet tall, drew herself up to her full rotund height. In spite of her diminutive size, she was an impressive figure, carrying her weight as a badge of pride in her womanhood —as the mother of eleven live-born children, ten of whom were still living. A successful woman was one who bore children, ran a decent, moral home, kept a firm hand on daughters and a watchful though indulgent eye on sons, and grew comfortably old in the full knowledge of her lasting place of honor, authority, and affection in the hearts of her ever-expanding family of in-laws and grandchildren. And Mama—Anne Surilla Hastings, née Smith— was successful. She also had very definite ideas concerning those traits in girls that must be developed early to insure their success in finding suitable husbands and fulfilling their roles as women. Of prime importance was a quiet, mannerly, ladylike demeanor in the presence of adults and especially in the presence of men.

Mama was considerably worried about Christine. This strange, stubborn grandchild frustrated her, never seeming to respond to any of her heretofore never-failing methods of whipping into shape those undesirable qualities in young females, or at least of driving them underground until the girls were successfully launched. Mama's way was never gentle and cajoling, and her concern made her manner particularly stern with Christine. The child, never realizing that her grandmother was diligently striving as best as she could to prepare her for a harsh, unyielding world, saw this commanding, authoritative figure as a mean, bossy old woman who loved Anne and Elen better than she loved her. The child had no way of knowing that her granny had given her much loving, tender care when she was an infant; and as she now watched her heap love on the new twin babies, she felt that she had never been enveloped in that soft, suffocating embrace and had never been moistened by those profuse, damp kisses.

On this day, separated by one whole generation, they faced each other in the warm, good-smelling kitchen, and there was no common ground on which they could meet. The child, silently begging for acceptance, looked longingly up at the frowning woman; the frustrated matriarch, feeling a personal defeat in having to send this raw, unacceptable family representative out into the world, stared mutely down at the child. Feeling her thwarted concern turn to helpless anger at the injustice of it all, Mama brusquely directed,

"Sit over there behind the stove on that stool and dry out. You don't want the teacher to see you wet." She turned to Acie, "Now, you just go on and don't worry any, the girls will take care of the young'un."

As Christine silently turned to her seat of banishment behind the stove, she threw her grandmother a secret look of unalloyed hate. Quickly masking her burning blue gaze, Christine thought spitefully, "She's mean and old and ugly and wrinkled and I hate her, I hate her, I hate her!"

Soon the kitchen was filled with bustling activity. Mama had four children who went to school, but only three were starting today. The fourth, twelve-year-old Ernest, was already out in the fields with the men. Most of the farm boys were several weeks late starting school each year, since their free labor was needed to help harvest the late crops. The three girls clattered down the bare stairs and ran head on into Mama's instructive scolding,

"Girls, girls, you'll wake the dead with all that noise. I'm glad the men are all out of the house and can't hear you. They'd be shocked! Elise, the button is unfastened at the back of your dress; Myrtle, straighten up your belt, and you're about to lose a hairpin.

Sugar, have you put anything on your cheeks to make them red?" She never missed a beat in her work as she ran her practical eye over them.

The three girls dutifully did as they were told, murmuring the appropriate answers. Anne solemnly declared, crossing her heart as proof, that her cheeks were unsullied, then she soulfully rolled her big blue eyes and winked her untruthfulness at Christine behind the stove. She was ten years old and endowed with a sweet, angelic face that belied the teasing, impish nature inherited from her father. Her face, most often lighted by a bright, innocent smile, could, however, quickly turn to stubborn pouting when she was crossed; and she had early learned when to use each ploy to her best advantage. Her loyalty and generosity knew no limits, and though she often led Christine into trouble and caused her much resultant misery, she loved her little niece and gave her much needed companionship and acceptance.

The other two girls, Myrtle and Elise, fourteen and seventeen, respectively, though constant companions, were a study in contrasts. Myrtle was a Smith, taking after Mama's side of the family. She was a gentle, sweet-natured girl with brown eyes and long brown hair worn in a braided wreath around her graceful head. She had an incredibly tiny waist and beautiful rounded arms with lovely dimpled elbows. She strove never to hurt a single creature, and though destined not to raise her own children beyond infancy, her loving manner caused her nieces and nephews to each feel that she loved them best of all. Elise, a true Hastings, had flashing dark eyes and glossy black curly hair worn close to her head. Born a rounded, chubby child, she, more than the others, resembled her mother in size and temperament. She was brusque, straightforward, and hearty in manner and emotion, often throwing back her head and bursting forth into deep-throated, ringing laughter, faintly reminiscent of her father's loud guffaws. Serious and industrious, without an envious or malicious bone in her body, she marched through life giving abundantly of her endless love and her fierce loyalty to those who were strong enough to bear her blunt honesty.

The three Hastings girls on the first day of school in the fall of 1933 were dressed in printed cotton shirtwaist dresses that Elise had made on Mamie Lee's sewing machine, brown tie-up oxford shoes, and white turn-down anklets. Their dresses were identical in style, all having been cut from a single pattern with much skillful tucking up and letting out to accommodate the wide variance in figures. Neat, freshly scrubbed, and very proud, they held their heads high in the full knowledge that even though the family fortunes had suffered, its principles had not, and that their blood was as good and as ancient as any the country had to offer.

Christine, feeling terribly alone and isolated, watched the warm flurry of action, desperately wishing that her dress matched theirs. She had never had a dress like that with a belt—hers were always loose shifts—and she longed for turn-down anklets instead of her awful knee socks, which forever sagged and bunched around her ankles. She began to feel ugly, and her fears were confirmed when her Aunt Myrtle led her from behind the stove and, taking her own comb from the pocket of her dress, tried to smooth the flighty hair. As a last-ditch effort to improve the ornery strands, she firmly tucked them behind the child's ears, noting in her calm, low voice,

"I wish Sister hadn't let Acie cut Top's hair so short. There's just nothing you can do with it now."

Mama, still feeling the fringes of her puzzled anger over this little urchin born into her family, frowned,

"Wet it, Myrt, see if that will help. You take her to her teacher today, and go back for her this afternoon. Keep her as clean as you can on the way to school. Tell the teacher who she is; she might not know since her name is not Hastings. And let the teacher know that you are responsible for her." Mama, in her own way, was trying to give the child every advantage, knowing that gentle, well-liked Myrtle would provide the best care for her. Frivolous Anne would have deserted her immediately, and no-nonsense Elise would have given firm instructions once and then washed her hands of the whole affair if she had not been obeyed.

As they were leaving the house, Christine noted another serious deficiency in her preparation for school. Each of her three aunts carried a small bag in which she stored her lunch, pencils, extra handkerchief, and other items necessary to a young lady at school all day. The bags were made of heavy denim and had been cut and sewn by Elise. The child wished that she had one and wondered if she would get one at school. Ironically, it was on this

Zueline

Mamie Lee

Acie, Zueline,
Chris, and the babies

Ellis and Elen

Mama (Chris's grandmother)

*Papa (Chris's grandfather)
and the babies (Becky and Tiny)*

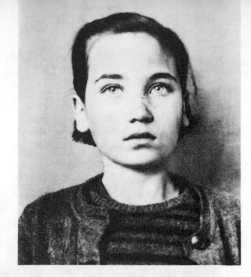

Chris at ten years

"The Attic Child"
by Chris Sizemore, 1975

JIM TINGSTRUM

small, seemingly insignificant lunch bag, completely overlooked by the anxious adults, that the success or failure of Christine's school career, and perhaps her entire life, depended. While larger and apparently more important preparations were being attended for her, this tiny, critical detail was overlooked.

When the four girls, spanning the entire range of Edgefield County's educational offering, started out on their long walk to meet the school bus, the sun was just clearing the tallest trees on what promised to be a cloudless, sultry Carolina day. This early, however, the air still held the faint, misty chill of the night, causing the girls to hurry through the shadows under the trees and out into the warm sun. They were thinly clad and prevented from suffering cold only by the exertions of their walk, which took them up the rutted, washed lane, past the turkey pens, the barns and cattle lots, and the granary to Ellis and Mamie Lee's house on the hill. As they walked by the quiet house, Christine thought of all the things she would have to tell Elen when she returned in the afternoon. She would show her how to write *Christine*, and she would make her some paper dolls. Just thinking about it excited the child and, forgetting her shortcomings, she began to dance and skip down the dusty lane, bringing from Elise a stern reprimand,

"Teeny, stop that playing! You are old enough to go to school now, and that's old enough to walk like a lady. Look how dusty your shoes are!"

Myrtle gently answered her sister. "Honey, she can't learn it all in one day. I'll clean her up in the basement when we get to school."

Elise tossed her black curls and, straightening her own thoroughly neat dress, tartly observed, "Well, I wouldn't want your job."

The lane, level and straight with a narrow grassy strip separating the worn, hard-packed wheel ruts, ran between two gleaming white cotton fields. The long, curved rows, shaped to fit the rolling slope of the land, bore stiff, dry stalks heavy with puffy white fiber ready for picking. Each exploded boll had to be picked by hand, and it took the men and boys several weeks of backbreaking labor to harvest the fields. Some women picked cotton, but Mama, no matter how straitened the family affairs, would not allow her daughters to become field hands. The lane opened into a single-lane road that ran down into the Red Hill section; here the girls turned left and walked the half mile through the tall pine thicket to the big road, a wide, scraped thoroughfare that ran from Edgefield to Modoc. The air under the gently swaying trees was still misty and cool and softened all sounds with its cathedral quiet. It was a lovely parklike forest with the incredibly tall slim trees standing uncrowded and apart, and the uncounted seasons of falling needles carpeting the wide avenues with a soft rust mat. The early sun, beginning to filter through the evergreen fronds, shafted in straight bolts through hidden openings to crisscross the glade with slanted, gleaming beams. All was fresh and hushed with muted buzzing from small winged things, and only an occasional raucous blast from a crow to profane the peace.

The Red Hill road dead-ended into the Modoc road, one of the most important and traveled roads in the county, and it was here that the girls met the bus, which could be heard, grinding and gearing its stops, long before it topped the hill and rumbled to a halt in a cloud of yellow dust. It was typical of that American institution—the school bus—big and squat with *Edgefield County Schools* painted in bold black on its bulging muddy orange sides. As the brakes screamed in protest, the rubber-edged double doors grated open, and Myrtle half lifted, half pushed the suddenly immobile Christine up the two steep steps and into the unique transit environment of the school bus.

The three older girls, who had carefully smoothed their hair and critically checked their clothes before sedately mounting the steps, were immediately loudly and laughingly hailed by last year's acquaintances, who squeezed over to make room for the new arrivals. It resembled a reunion of old friends who had been separated for years instead of just the short summer vacation. The bus, already more than half full, bore mostly girls, and this would be the case for several weeks, when the male riders would begin to pick up as the crop harvesting leveled off.

The driver grated his gears, and the bus lurched drunkenly and shuddered loosely before lumbering down the hill. The new riders, still unseated, squealed in mock fright and fell awkwardly over laughing companions into waiting places saved especially for them. The comments ran thus:

106

"I *love* that dress! Where *did* you get that material?"

"Oh, this ole thing! Now, aren't you so sweet to say that. I just *love* yours!"

"This old rag! I just didn't have *anything* to wear."

"What *have* you been doing all summer?"

"Nothing, just *nothing!* I haven't been anywhere but to town."

"I haven't seen a soul, either."

"If wonder if we have any new teachers?"

"I hope we have some good-looking *men* teachers."

"Just any ole kind of men teachers would help!"

"You've cut your hair. I just *love* it!"

"Aren't you sweet, but it's too curly to fall right. I *hate* it!"

"Mine is just a mess. I can't do a thing with it!"

And on and on . . .

The school bus had its own definite hierarchy, with some seats being more important than others, such as those at the very front and those at the very back, but the seating was mostly according to age. An adult-sized wooden bench ran down each side of the wide vehicle, and the larger, older riders sat with their backs to the strange slide-down windows, which were forever stuck, either up or down. Through the middle of the bus ran two low backless benches for the little kids. These benches, slanted up under the knees, threw the children back to back and prevented them from sliding off onto the floor. Since there was nothing for anybody to hold onto, the riders swayed and bumped laughingly into each other's shoulders, as the old bus jerked and bounced over the rutted, washboard roads.

It all seemed like great fun to Christine as she sat crammed between two other children, leaning heavily against the back of an unseen child behind her. She swayed from side to side, clutching her lunch on her elevated knees and wondering how far her feet were from the floor. Her one fear was that she would not be able to get out of the bus and would be left alone all day. Looking around for her aunts, she saw Myrtle and Elise talking animatedly to strange people, and Anne was way at the back of the center bench, busily whispering secrets into the delighted ear of another stranger. Christine felt lost and alone.

The bus soon smoothed out as it struck the paved streets of Edgefield, only to bump jerkily again as it wheeled onto the washed and rutted gravel of the school yard. Everybody scrambled to his feet at the same time, and there was a suffocating crunch toward the door. Christine, unable to see anything outside and buffeted on all sides by strange bodies, felt cold fright tighten her chest and stinging tears well in her eyes. Moved slowly but relentlessly forward, she soon reached the door and was firmly grasped from behind and swung out onto the ground by big strong hands that she never saw. Standing there surrounded by hurrying, unheeding people, her courage was entirely gone. Then she heard her name,

"Christine, this way." And Myrtle took her hand and led her through the crowd.

"Aunt Myrt," the child pleaded, not knowing for what she was asking; and her aunt, pushed for time and busily recognizing old friends, was unaware of the desperate note in the trembling voice.

As the crowd thinned, Christine looked up and saw the biggest building she had ever seen, bigger even than the Court House. Edgefield High School was a three-story, red-brick building that housed all eleven grades. A concrete sidewalk ran the entire length of the building, and where it joined the wide sweep of walk leading up to the broad entrance steps stood a long, narrow concrete fountain holding four water spigots turned up for drinking. Inside the front entrance was a wide foyer sporting a bulletin board and two tables and leading into the main hall, which ran the length of the building. At each end of the hall was a stair leading up to the top story and down to the bottom level—the basement. The floors, built of long narrow boards, smooth and dark from years of use and oiling, were maintained by sprinkling them with an oily compound to keep down the dust. The compound, resembling dark-brown damp sawdust, was periodically removed and renewed; and its pungent smell, along with the acrid dust of chalk, daily assaulted the breathing apparatus of students and created the "schoolhouse smell," an odor peculiar to school buildings.

Myrtle and Christine entered the building through an end door and descended the half stair to the basement, where the first-grade rooms were located. The furnace room and the rest rooms were also to be found on this level. In fact, the practice of placing rest rooms in school basements was so prevalent that a student, on seeking permission to go to the rest room, asked his teacher, "May I go to the basement?"

The hall and the rooms were crowded with people, little people and adults, going in and out, or just standing. Several children were crying and clinging to embarrassed mothers, who, no matter what their words of reproof, proved, to the close observer, to be clinging just as tightly to their frightened offspring. Myrtle took Christine into the girls' rest room, sponged her face with her dampened handkerchief, recombed her fly-away hair, and pulled up her socks, admonishing all the while in her sweet, calm voice,

"Now, sit still, Top, and don't squirm in your seat. Do exactly what the teacher says. And I will come and pick you up after school."

She pulled the reluctant child along the dim, cool hall and into a classroom. It was filled with rows of tiny school desks constructed of polished boards, fastened to black iron frames, which were nailed to the floor. The writing board of each desk, equipped with an inkwell, a pencil tray, and a shelf for supplies, was fastened to the backrest of the desk directly in front. Many of the desks already contained small, serious-faced first-graders; and in a ragged row along the wall stood several self-conscious mothers.

Myrtle pushed the frightened, wide-eyed child up to the teacher's desk and spoke respectfully to the plump, serious woman seated on a straight wooden chair,

"Miss Waldrop, I am Myrtle Hastings from out at the Butler place, and this is my niece, Christine Costner. She is my sister's girl. She is starting to school today."

Eiron Waldrop, a veteran teacher of thirty years, put her hand up to the bunned hair at the nape of her neck and unsmilingly observed the trembling child. She knew her work well, and she knew what was expected of her, being well aware that each child had been warned about "the teacher" and what the teacher would do with naughty children. She was not married. Teaching was considered a full-time job, and women teachers who married were not allowed to continue teaching, on the premise that their interests would be divided and that they could not devote their full time to their work. Perhaps there was also the thought that carnal knowledge was not proper for women who taught innocent children. Parents expected teachers to mold their sons and daughters into upright, responsible citizens and to smooth off the rough edges. Teachers were highly respected in the community and were accorded an automatic place of honor; in return, they lived a fishbowl existence of exemplary morals and ideals, and they sternly initiated the community young into the serious business of preparing for life.

"Oh, yes, Myrtle," she replied cordially, "I remember you, and I know your family. Leave Christine with me. Pick her up here after school until she learns her bus." Rising from her chair, she put her firm hand on the child's shoulder and strongly urged her away from Myrtle.

"Come, Christine. I will show you your place," she instructed with calm, unsmiling authority.

Christine felt her aunt loosen her grasp, and she felt her own tight hold on the familiar hand break apart under the unrelenting pressure of the strange, cool fingers on her shoulder.

"Aunt Myrt . . . ," she gasped as big tears began to form in her frightened eyes.

"Now, Christine, you go with the teacher, and do everything she tells you. Be a good girl," Myrtle gently directed the child. Only fourteen herself, the older girl could not know the terror of being abandoned in the bowels of this huge, dark building, surrounded only by strangers and strange things. Since she herself had started school in a rural one-room building where the teacher was a family friend and where several of her older brothers and sisters were also students, Myrtle had no conception of the child's terror. And anyway, she had to get to her own class. Everybody had to go to school.

"Just run along, Myrtle, Christine will be fine," Miss Waldrop declared, ending what her long experience had taught her could become a difficult situation if allowed to prolong.

"I'll come for you when school's out, Top. Stay here and don't get lost." And, completely putting the child out of her mind, Myrtle hurried off to begin her own new school year, confident that her little charge was in good hands and that she was successfully launched on her school career.

Miss Waldrop, her generous figure clad in a dark blue crepe shirtwaist with long sleeves, led the no longer resisting Christine to a little desk near the back of the room, informing her,

"This is your seat. This is where you will sit."

And that's exactly what she did. For many hours, even days, she just sat. There were no magic crayons, no pictures to paint, no name to be written—just sitting.

Soon a bell rang. A harsh, grating clang, it assaulted the ear with shock even when it was expected, but to the unprepared it was truly an electrifying experience. The small children, all huddled in their strange new seats, started violently at this unpleasant attack, and were saved from reaction only by the teacher's behavior. As soon as the bell ceased, Miss Waldrop rose from her chair, and keeping the large light-oak desk between her and her pupils, she smiled faintly, folded her white, well-manicured hands at her ample waist, and addressed her new charges,

"Children, I am Miss Waldrop, your teacher. We are going to learn many things this year. First, I want you to learn where you are to sit. You must always sit in your own seat. If you want to say something, please, raise your hand and I will call your name. You may not speak out without permission, and you may not leave your seat unless you are told to do so. Now, children, listen carefully, I am going to tell you to do something. Listen carefully. Everybody, get up and put your lunch boxes and bags on the table at the back of the room. Everybody now. Get up and put your lunches on the back table."

The children, hesitantly at first, then following the lead of the bolder, more mature ones, quickly began to carry their lunch containers and put them on the long, low table. Christine, too busy looking and feeling, did not even hear the command. She rose only because everybody else did, and she carried her lunch simply because she had never yet turned it loose. She stood by the table, hesitant and alone, until the teacher instructed,

"Put your lunch on the table, Christine, and come back to your seat."

The confused, lost child did as she was bidden, seeming only to hear commands when they were directed solely to her, when she heard her name called.

Miss Waldrop continued, "We are glad to have so many mothers come to school today. They are going to leave now, but they will be back to pick you up when school is out."

As the mothers, looking fondly at their little ones and waving shyly at them, began to slowly file from the room, Christine thought, "I didn't know mothers came to school. Why didn't Mother come with me? I'll tell her, and she can come with me. Everybody's mother is here but mine." And the tears stung her eyes again.

The morning was interminably long. The teacher asked questions and called children up to her desk. She often looked out at her restless students and warned,

"Do not talk. In school, one does not talk."

Christine daydreamed, thought of Elen, and once even fell asleep with her head resting on the hard desk. She wondered when she would learn to write her name, and she wanted to ask the teacher, but Miss Waldrop was always so busy. Once her empty stomach, having had no attention since early morning, loudly protested this long-neglected state, and several children looked wonderingly at her; one tousled-haired little boy even laughed. Miss Waldrop looked sternly in their direction and placed her finger across her pale lips. Christine was horribly embarrassed. She had been warned often about making body noises, and even though this was not one over which she had any control, she was not sure everybody knew that. She tried holding her breath when she felt another explosion building up, but the watery gurgle seemed even louder than before. This time several children giggled, and she felt that everybody was looking at her. Miss Waldrop frowned severely and shook her head at them. Finally, when Christine thought she could stand her condition no longer, the teacher stood up and announced,

"It's recess time, children. I am going to give out your lunches. Then we will go outside for recess. Stay in your seats while I give out the lunches. We will march outside." And she went to the table at the back of the room and began to pass out the lunch boxes.

Christine had never seen such an array of beautiful boxes. They were all colors, some even had pictures painted on them, and they were all shapes—square, flat, shaped like mailboxes, and one was even round. Most were fitted with little carrying handles, but some had no handles and were carried clutched in the arms. There were several cloth bags like Anne's, sewn from colorful material and closed with a drawstring. Christine liked the boxes best, but right now she would have given anything she owned for even a drawstring bag, for it was becoming increasingly obvious that everybody had a special lunch container except her. And there was hers, left to the last, lying alone and glaring on the table. The teacher picked up each lunch, called out the name of the child to whom it belonged, and set it on the child's desk. When she picked up the bedraggled package wrapped in newspaper and tied with a string, she turned it over and looked at it carefully. Christine grew hot with embarrassment, her face burned, and sweat beaded her forehead and top lip.

"Is this a lunch? It doesn't have a name on it. Does this belong to someone?" Miss Waldrop held up the package, slightly grease-stained on one end and with one of its corners torn and ragged, and turned it around for all to see.

Christine timidly raised her hand.

"Oh, so it's yours, Christine. If your name had been on it I would have known."

As she put the package down on the desk, and it seemed to Christine that she slammed it very hard, the boiled egg cracked loudly in the breathless quiet. Several children laughed, and Christine was overcome with shame; she wanted to put her head down and cry, but Miss Waldrop was at the door directing,

"Line up, children. Form a straight line, straight now. Come on, follow me, and no talking, no talking. We'll eat our lunches outside."

The children kept their straight line down the dim hall, up the steps, and out into the bright sunlight. They stopped to eat at a low rock wall under an enormous oak tree. Christine's lunch made a loud crackling noise as she opened the paper, and when the children looked at it, she could not eat. Little children, enormously and indiscriminately attracted to anything different, stare only for this reason; it was Christine herself who caused them to think her belongings funny and wrong. So totally lacking in self-confidence and so incapable of accepting either herself or her possessions, she by her own self-rejection led them to reject her. Her self-degradation and her abject shame for her lunch container caused her to deny the savory lunch itself; and, though famished, she was unable to eat. The others, following her unconscious lead, laughed at the lunch, which was much more excellent than most represented, and they formed a negative first impression of her, offering her ridicule when what she needed most was praise. And the next day was no better.

That night, Christine was quiet, she did not talk about school. But she asked her mother two questions.

"Mother, will you go to school with me?" Phrased unemotionally as if she already knew the answer, she gave no explanation and in no way indicated the importance of this request to her.

"My Lord, Christine," Zueline exclaimed, "you know Mother can't go to school with you! Mothers don't go to school. And anyway, I've got to tend to the babies."

Christine well knew that mothers *did* go to school. There had been many there today. And she knew in her heart that if her mother did not have those awful babies, she would go with her. At that moment, Christine's resentment of her tiny siblings reached a new peak; and it was not lessened by the fact that she had to go to bed in a room alone in a big bed, while the babies occupied her little green bed in the room with Mother and Daddy. Even though the door was left open and light from the lamp dimly illuminated the room, she was desperately afraid and just knew that the monster lurked under the bed. She was careful not to allow any part of her body to stick over the bedside for fear he would bite it off, and she wrapped up, head and ears, even though the weather was hot and sultry.

Her second question was one of pure defense.

"Mother, please, write my name on my lunch tomorrow."

"Did you lose your lunch today, Christine?" Zueline, completely misunderstanding, and fearing only that the child had been physically hungry, lectured her on how to nourish the body, never realizing that it was the little soul that was starving.

At recess time the following day, Christine waited breathlessly for the lunches to be given out, confident that all would be well this time, since her name had been boldly written on the wrapping. She had carefully looked at the name, and it did look pretty written down—much prettier than it sounded. When the teacher picked up her lunch, she said to the expectant child,

"I see you have your name written on your lunch today, Christine. But that wasn't necessary; I would have known that it was yours."

Remembering yesterday's lunch, several children laughed. Christine was mortified. She grew uncomfortably hot and wished that she could leave the hated lunch inside. Even her name looked ugly now. It was an ugly lunch and it was an ugly name! She remained in her seat until the very last, and then straggled along at the end of the line, dreading the shameful ordeal of opening and eating her lunch with the other children. Seeing a door partly opened by the stair, she ducked in and found herself in the furnace room, dim and dusty and filled with a big black machine. Her heart thudded with fear; it looked like a perfect place for the monster to lurk. But her fear of peer ridicule overcame her physical fear, and her burning shame and abject misery, prompted by her gnawing hunger, made the fearsome room preferable to the open-air companionship of her classmates. She quickly tore the wrapping from her lunch and chokingly gulped the boiled egg and the ham biscuit. Stuffing the telltale paper behind the coal bin, she ran from the room and out of the building to mingle with the other playing children.

Thus did she eat her lunch on those days when she could escape from the line and dodge into the frightening furnace room. Always afraid, she never turned her back on the monstrous black thing squatting in the middle of the dirty room, and she never ventured inside more than a few steps; but this lonely, frightful lunch was more appealing than having her already blighted self-image daily buffeted by derisive laughter and scorn.

And thus did school, that great socializing institution, fail Christine. Doing the very best it could, acting on the best knowledge gleaned from the best sources available, it failed her miserably, even to the degree of compounding her problems. Her school career unfolded, as did her life among her family, as a near miss—the loftiest of intentions, the lowliest of results. In the final cataloguing of man's mistakes, surely a prominent place must be devoted to the diligent efforts of educators to force the pliable stuff of the young into the preconceived mold of the past, instead of nurturing each new form to grow according to its own bent into a new, inconceivable future.

7

The Strother Place

Happiness is a gazebo in a rose garden. The gazebo is faded, unkempt, leaf-strewn, its day of luxurious leisure discernible, to the close observer only, in its graceful lines and the very frivolity of its existence. The rose garden is untidy, with loose, rampant weeds, its unpruned bushes sending out ungainly liberated growth destined to produce dwarfed, inferior blossoms, infected by unchecked blight and vermin. But to Christine, totally ignorant of the *raison d'être* of the gazebo—never even having heard the name—it was another world, a place apart, her place!

Happiness is also a second chance, an opportunity to recoup, to start over. In November of 1933, in the very darkest days of the Great Depression, Papa heard about the Strother place. Constructed just before the turn of the century on the Meetingstreet Road, it was a lovely old Victorian mansion commanding many farm acres, virgin forests, and numerous dairy stock. It had changed hands several times and was now owned by an absentee landlord who, maintaining only the dairy, was searching for a family to inhabit the house and to run the thriving milk business on a profit-sharing basis. Papa, investigating, found it too good to be true, and though Mama protested "working for strangers," he moved his large family from the Promised Land, so-called, to apparently greener pastures. Papa, a proud man from a long line of independent land owners, could bear, no longer than was absolutely necessary, the generous though galling position of dependency upon his son-in-law. Ellis would have no difficulty locating a

116

tenant farmer, and he, Nick Hastings, had to hold up his head again.

When the move was announced at Sunday dinner, there were various reactions recorded. Mama, never one to endorse anything new, authoritatively predicted that the move would come to no good end. Mamie Lee, expressing exaggerated shock, exclaimed,

"Why, Papa, what do you mean, move? Who are these people anyway, whoever heard of the Strothers? You're doing just fine here with Ellis. And things are going to get better. Everybody says so."

"I know, Maje," he looked at her fondly, "but this is better for me and Mama. We need to be on our own place, even if it is just rented." He looked at his son-in-law.

"We'll be sorry to see you go, Mista' Hastin'," Ellis responded, looking Papa straight in the eye. "But I can understand your feelings. I would do the same thing in your place."

"Sugar!" Mamie Lee scolded her husband.

"Is it far away, Papa?" asked Zueline worriedly. She sat nursing one of the three-month-old twins, while Elise rocked the other gently to and fro by balancing the straight wooden chair in which she sat, on its back legs.

Mama paused in her rocking, leaned abruptly forward, and pointing her blunt, wide finger at her eldest daughter, answered for Papa, "It's too far away for you to stay out here alone with these babies. Who'd help you if they got sick?"

"Why, Mama, I'd help her!" Mamie Lee exclaimed, her tone hurt and reproving.

"Harumph!" Mama snorted, beginning to rock furiously again. "You're too far away yourself, and you've got your own hands full with your own young'un. Sister will just have to come with us."

"Oh, Mama, I don't know," Zueline hesitated. "Acie, honey, what do you think? We will be way out here by ourselves!" She looked imploringly at her frowning husband.

"Oh, no, Zueline," he calmly answered her. "This is not for us, we will find something on our own." He looked speculatively at his brother.

"Stay on as long as you like, Acie. The place is yours as long as you want it." Ellis nodded his answer to his brother's unspoken question.

"Oh, Sugar, tell them to stay. If Sister leaves, I'll be out here alone!" Mamie Lee beseeched her husband.

Ellis, raising his eyebrow in a characteristic gesture of annoyance, spoke sternly to his wife, "Now, Mother, you let Sister and Acie make up their own minds."

Mamie Lee angrily tossed her head and pouted, knowing that the motion caused her cropped, glossy black hair to swirl becomingly and to fashionably frame her pretty face. But she held her peace. The raising of Ellis's eyesbrow was a warning that few who knew him ignored.

Papa, hearing and weighing all the undertones of the comments, spoke earnestly to Acie, "Son, come along if you like. I would hate to leave Sister and the babies out here alone. And the house is big enough. And Lord knows, there's work enough for an extra pair of hands."

"Honey," began Zueline, pathetically clutching her tiny child to her breast. The squeezed infant, perhaps sensing its mother's anxiety, began to softly wail.

Acie, looking at the forlorn picture made by his pleading, frightened wife and her crying babe, felt his command of the situation slip, but he stubbornly persisted,

"We'll talk it over, Sister. We can't make a decision now. We'll talk about it."

"Well, you just mark my words, Sister will just have to go. She can't stay here. It was different before she had the babies, then she could be dragged around from pillar to post all over the country. But now, she has the babies, and she's got to have help!" Mama emphatically made her pronouncement.

And Mama's self-fulfilling prophecy soon was realized. When Papa moved his happy horde, nine strong—leaving behind only Amos, who had married and moved in with his new in-laws—into the Strother place, Acie, against his better judgment, went along, deserting his Promised Land to please his wife. Suddenly the long-vacant old mansion was peopled by fourteen new inhabitants: Mama, Papa, and their five single children; Dodge and his wife; and Acie, Zueline, and their three children.

It was the most beautiful house Christine had ever seen. Standing about one-half mile from the road behind a thick grove of oaks, hickories, and poplars, it was approached by a narrow, winding, rolling lane that crossed about halfway along its length a small, rocky creek. At the bridge over the creek began the roses. Even in early November, when Christine first traveled the lane, and even though they had not been carefully tended in years, the roses were blooming. They were all colors—pinks, yellows, reds, whites—the whites looking like fat globs of wet snow against the dark green. The roses and their sweet perfume served to distract the traveler, and suddenly around the last bend the green-and-white board house rose in dignified correctness behind its terraced approach. Christine's breath caught in her throat; she did not know anything could be so beautiful. The first brightly delineated sheen of its splendor was faded—gone, but replacing it shone the patina with which neglect and antiquity drape fine things.

Christine did not see the shabbiness, the blurred outlines, the droop and sag of age and abandonment; she saw only the dignity, the spaciousness, the way the house seemed to naturally belong in its setting, almost as if it sprang unaided from the sod and nestled comfortably into its groves, its terraces, its outbuildings, its pastures. Her instant, spellbound love for the house was not unrequited, it was a mutual *affaire*. She did not have to molest and rape; her chosen love willingly, lovingly opened her hidden nooks and crannies, revealed her secrets, her beauties that went unnoticed to less sensitive, less observing eyes. The dark, smooth wood of the wainscoting and the stair newel kissed and caressed Christine's yearning hand; the beveled fan glass over the door and the onion-skinned stained glass in the attic window revealed naked beauty to her starved gaze; the cool, deep-ceilinged space of the rooms complemented her loneliness and provided an appropriate mounting for her soul; the numerous unexpected windows, doors, steps, and levels provided the essential variety and mystery without which such an *affaire* rapidly reduces to humdrum habit, to ritual, to routine.

But it was the gazebo, the little frivolous froth of a building with its green conical roof supported by miniature grooved columns, its tiny circumference encircled by wide, gently ascending steps, and its low green wooden seats that beckoned to Christine's love-starved psyche and carried her to the lofty, rarefied heights of romantic adventuring. The gazebo was made for love. It performed no essential task; its absence left no vital duty undone. It existed simply to shade the too bright sun from a too delicate brow, to afford temporary shelter from a sudden gentle summer shower, to provide open exposed privacy to a man and a maid under the protective gaze of the familial eye.

The gazebo and the child had both languished long under their neglect, and they recognized each other on sight. The lonely little temple enfolded the starved little soul, and to some measure, by the beauty of its offering, compensated for the dearth of inspiration heretofore afforded Christine from both persons and places. Here she escaped to wonder, to conjure, to ponder. Lying on her back on the low green seats, watching the ever-changing kaleidoscope of shapes in the puffy white clouds scudding across an impossibly blue sky, she created the world to her own specifications, and her fertile imagination knew no bounds.

It was a happy time. The magnificent old house, constructed in a time of plenty for beauty and comfort, restored to the family its sense of things right and proper. Across the entire front of the house ran a deep porch bound in by wooden railings interlaced by the thick ropes of an ancient wisteria vine. In fact, the house was covered on three sides by wide porches, onto which every room on the first floor offered numerous windows and doors. Huge double doors, bordered on either side by glass panels, opened into a wide hall cleaving the entire length of the house and opening through another pair of identical double doors onto a wide porch that ran across the entire back of the house. This hallway separated Mama's side of the house from Zueline's side of the house.

Zueline had two rooms, the larger of which must have once been the library, for its walls were paneled in gleaming dark satin wood to which had once been attached shelves. This room, containing a large fireplace, served as the bedroom for the entire family; while the other, smaller room, offering a narrow fireplace into which the flue of the cookstove was inserted, became the kitchen. Mama also gave her eldest daughter one of the four bedrooms upstairs as a company room. This room was used by Zueline only on those rare occasions when some of Acie's folks came down from North Carolina, since all other company was mutually shared by both families.

Two small rooms opened from the opposite side of the hall; one was Mama's parlor and the other a bedroom, and between them was a small hall leading to Mama's rooms, and also the enclosed stairwell leading to the second floor. Mama's bedroom and sitting room was enormous, once having been the drawing room, with wainscoted walls; carved, decorated ceiling; and a huge fireplace. One door from the room opened onto the bedroom of Dodge and his wife, and the other opened into the formal dining room, which in turn gave onto the kitchen. This unique room had a fireplace as well as a chimney for the cookstove, and it opened onto two porches, the back porch and a side porch, spanning the whole right side of the house and onto which also opened the dining room and Mama's bedroom.

Interestingly, Dodge's room also had a door leading to the yard outside. It is ponderable why Mama, who was solely responsible for assigning her numerous family to their rooms, would give her son a room that would allow for his comings and goings to be private and unobservable by the rest of the family.

The second floor, split by a wide hall, contained four bedrooms, each equipped with its own fireplace. Double windows were inset into each end of the hall, and those at the front contained stained glass. The attic, reached by narrow, twisting steps, was unceiled and dark, but it contained one treasure for Christine—another stained-glass window, set immediately above the one on the floor below, and just at her eye level. It caught the afternoon sun, and she loved to sit in its rosy glow and let the lovely warm colors play over her and transform her into glorious beings. A box, made by Acie for her to cache her treasures in, and an old cot stored out of the way, furnished this, her secret place, when the weather prevented her use of the gazebo.

One of Christine's favorite pastimes, often shared with Anne, was to climb out of the second-floor bedroom windows onto the flat roofs of the first-floor porches. From here she could survey the world, and she was ruler of all she saw. The back-porch vantage displayed the dairy barns, the outhouse, and the washhouse; the side porch overlooked the pasture and the springhouse; and the front-porch roof, screened and sheltered by a huge evergreen magnolia tree, offered a vista all the way to the bridge, complete with flowers, terraces, and the magic little gazebo. Anne and Christine would lie for hours on the sun-warmed green tin of the roof to plan their dreamy futures and to ponder their present fates. Once Anne, furious with her mother over some lost point, ceremoniously positioned herself on the roof and declared that she was going to hold her breath until she died. This scheme, like most of their grandiose plans, came to nothing.

The nights were as magic as the days. Zueline cooked their supper, an almost unvarying fare of hot biscuits, white gravy, and homemade tomato catsup. The babies, by now old and thriving enough not to require constant attention, were already put to bed, and Christine again had her parents' entire attention. After dinner, Acie read to his little daughter from an old dog-eared book of tales. Her favorite story, to be spun nightly if Acie could be persuaded, told of little children lost in the cold, dark woods, and of the little birds that came and covered them with leaves to keep them warm as they slept. Christine always pictured herself as one of the lost children, and sometimes at play covered herself with leaves and pretended to sleep while being watched over by the only birds she had available—some unco-operative, loudmouthed bluejays.

Her parents, to the delight of the child, sometimes softly sang together. Each had favorite songs, and much is revealed about their natures in the themes of the tunes they chose. Acie's happy, calm outlook on life showed in his joy in singing gay, teasing songs such as "Daisies Won't Tell," "Molly and Me," "Home on the Range," and "I'm Forever Blowing Bubbles"; while Zueline's pensive, superstitious disposition surfaced in mournful, bad-luck songs such as "Letter Edged in Black," "If Brother Jack Were Here," "Put My Little Shoes Away," and "Lonesome Turtle-dove."

Mama had an uncanny way of being right, and she just might have been right this time, too. So many people were constantly present, and the twins were so popular with everyone, that both Zueline and Acie had time for themselves and time for Christine that would have been denied them had they not followed Papa when he moved. Zueline, who always smiled and laughed a lot, was particularly happy during this time, and she began to know her oldest child as a person. They walked often in the woods and the pastures, and the mother, only a woman-child herself, talked and confided in the small daughter as she would have in another adult. She sometimes even rocked the child to sleep at night, and she always tucked her in bed, a practice she pursued even after Christine became an adult.

Even into such a sunny haven as this, however, some rain must fall, some days must be dark and dreary. In this case it was the death of Acie's mother, Rebecca Elen Costner, née Sain. But this event, tragic enough in itself, was not the beginning of the story, which had its roots almost a year earlier, in the Promised Land. On one of their rare trips away from home, Ellis and Acie's parents came down to South Carolina to visit their sons. James Cicero Costner was a short, quiet man with striking blue eyes and a full blond mustache. His wife, Becky, his opposite in size as well as temperament, was tall, dark in eyes and complexion, with a sharp, brusque, restless manner. When they all gathered at Ellis's for a daylong visit, Elen was sporting a new toy, a china doll. It was the first thing Christine saw, and it was the most beautiful thing she had ever seen. The tiny porcelain face was incredibly delicate and fragile, and the crystal blue eyes, like her very own, actually opened and closed. When she slept, the black-fringed lashes lay tight against the luminous white skin, and she had real hair, golden bright and curly. She was brand new and Elen held onto her tightly, refusing to allow her cousin even a moment to cuddle the soft stuffed body dressed in a long blue satin dress.

Christine's mercurial temper broke, and she threw a tantrum right in front of the visiting grandparents. Her mother and her aunt, the two southern daughters-in-law, were mortified, but Grandma Becky, in her overpowering manner, attempted to set all straight. She reached into her voluminous dress pocket and took out a small blue enamel cup from which she had drunk water dipped out of the streams along her slow journey.

"Here, young'un," she ordered her granddaughter, "you can play with this."

Christine looked at the lovely little cup. At any other time, under other circumstances, she would have loved it, blue was her favorite color; but compared with the exquisite little china doll, it could only be rejected. And she called her "young'un," that hated name that Granny always called her. She hated this old grandmother, too, and she hated her old cup.

She had started to reach for the cup when all these emotions broke over her, and, drawing back her hand, she yelled,

"I don't want your old cup, and I don't like you!"

Grandma Becky, startled, dropped the cup, chipping a bright blue sliver from the bottom rim. She sniffed,

"Zueline, you're going to have to work on that young'un."

Zueline was embarrassed and heartsick. "I'll see to her right now. I'm so sorry about the cup. I'm afraid it will leak now." And she dragged her protesting child from the room, giving Christine in private a good scolding and shaking. This, however, did not cool the hot anger, and Christine patiently waited until Elen momentarily abandoned her new treasure. She carefully picked up the delicate creation, turned it tenderly in her trembling hands, lovingly gazed into its gleaming blue eyes, and fiercely smashed it to bits on the stone hearth. Even the sound spanking she received did not entirely erase the pleasure that glowed in her avenged heart.

A year later, Grandma Becky lay dead. Ellis, Mamie Lee, and Elen picked up Acie, Zueline, and Christine, and they all went together to the funeral. On that sad day, Christine and Elen were playing under the high back porch with some gourds when the older girl saw something blue shining in the dirt. It was Grandma Becky's drinking cup, the chipped rim showing a rusty, ragged hole. As she held the cup, the whole scene washed over her: the mean old woman, her mother's anger, the injustice of the china doll, everything. At that moment, Mamie Lee and her sister-in-law, Ruth, came to get the children. While Elen's mother was cleaning her up, Aunt Ruth took six-year-old Christine to say good-bye to her grandmother. She picked up the child, and, holding her over the open coffin, instructed,

"Kiss your grandmother, child, and you'll have good memories of her."

The child looked down at the dark, cold face in the coffin (in the box!), and unreasoning fear consumed her.

"No, no," she screamed, squirming and pushing away. Her hand touched the dead face, cold and hard. "Don't make me!" she pled.

Seeing her mother coming into the room, she cried, "Mother, don't make me!"

Zueline took her daughter from the arms of her shocked sister-in-law, and making no comment, left the room, cuddling and soothing the terrified child. But the horror was not over for Christine. In the churchyard cemetery as the box was being lowered into the cold damp hole, she began to feel insecure and shaky. Holding onto her mother's skirt, hearing her father's sobs, she grew more and more scared, and felt that she was not safe. Darkness overcame her. As it grew light again, the feelings went away, and she watched from afar as a little girl with cropped bangs wearing a navy and red knitted cap and scarf calmly stood near the awful hole and watched the box being covered with sticky red clay. In remembering this scene years later, Christine noted that there were no freckles on the calm white face.

That night the dreams started. With nightmarish, implacable slowness, Aunt Ruth was again pushing her down to the hard cold face in the box, only this time Christine stuck to her grandmother when she touched her. She was going to be fastened up in the box with her and put into the ground. She screamed, waking herself. Zueline came to her, listened to the tale of terror, and soothed,

"Grandma Becky won't hurt you, honey, she can't hurt you." But the nightmares came regularly for about six months, and then ceased abruptly, to return no more.

Acie established a unique relationship with his daughter during this time that was to continue unbroken for a lifetime. He was gentle but firm with her, patiently teaching her skills and values but consistently punishing her when she disobeyed. They had especially cozy times in the mornings while Zueline was fixing breakfast. He would let her get into bed with him for a final nap, enfolding her in his "pen" as she snuggled warm and safe under the heavy quilts.

"I've got your place, Mother!" she would call from the bed.

"Now, you just get out of my place. That's my daddy, that's not your daddy!" her mother would tease back.

Acie also rocked the child to sleep, but he rocked her in a straight wooden chair and called it "bumping." Holding her in his arms, he would bump the chair back and forth, first balancing it on the front legs, leaning exaggeratedly far forward; then balancing on the back legs, he would teeter precariously over backward. Christine squealed and clutched her father until Zueline admonished,

"Sugar, you'll wake the dead! Stop that, and let that child go to sleep."

Acie obediently calmed his process, and soon the exhausted child was asleep. Each morning, however, renewed an ordeal that was as severe as it was constant: school. If her school experience had been satisfying and positive, that, along with her now happy home life might have reversed a wave set in action long before; but instead, it added impetus to a forward motion that soon sped precipitously under its own momentum. The lunchtime trauma grew no better; in fact, it worsened to the point where Christine began to steal into the furnace room before school each day and hide her lunch, to avoid the humiliation of having her "newspaper lunch" exposed before everyone. Or some days, due to rainy weather or the teacher's watchfulness, she was unable to return at the lunch hour to gulp down her food. She had many empty stomachs as a result of this practice, but it also made her a friend and protector.

Miss Mary Hughes, the second-grade teacher, tall, thin, and endowed with quick, birdlike motions, noticed that Christine often did not eat lunch. Her kindness delicately balanced by her wisdom would not permit her to question the child about so sensitive a subject; she merely stated,

"Christine, I don't believe I can eat all my lunch today, and I just hate to carry it back home. Will you eat this cheese biscuit and help me finish my lunch?" She took the food from her lunch box and handed it to the startled child.

Christine, never having been in a similar situation and having no instructions from home to draw on, only knew that one always obeyed the teacher. And anyway, she was starved. She took the biscuit, but was embarrassed to begin to eat. Mary Hughes glanced at the tiny clock she always carried and quickly moved away, saying over her shoulder to the little girl,

"Eat quickly, it's almost time for the bell."

Out of the corner of her eye, she noticed the obviously hungry child begin to eat the biscuit ravenously. In sparing the child's pride by falsely assuming that she had no lunch, Miss Hughes, with the best of intentions, missed an opportunity to teach Christine a valuable lesson: The contents are more important than the container.

However, even if there had been no lunch fiasco, school still was not prepared to meet Christine's needs. She wanted to color, but she had no crayons. All the children had crayons except her. In desperation, she asked Anne for some of her crayons.

"You must be crazy, Teeny," Anne shrieked, "if you think I'll let you use my colors! You tear up everything." In all fairness to Anne, it was the truth. Christine had, and justly, earned the reputation for being destructive and then lying about her deed when she was found out.

"What am I going to do, Annie?" she pled with the older girl. "When am I going to get me some colors?"

"Oh, you'll just have to steal you some, I guess," Anne flippantly answered the distressed child.

Who can say if her comment was serious. Anne, the youngest, the baby, was always appropriating the possessions of members of her family—her sisters' lip rouge, powder, perfume, their precious boxes of boyfriend candy, anything she wanted. She cleverly took small coins from the pockets of her brothers and her father, and she often swiped some of their hoarded tobacco. Whatever her intent, it was advice, and for lack of better, Christine took it. As she sat in school the next day, she noticed that the child who regularly sat in front of her was not only absent, but also had carelessly left her box of crayons in the vacant desk. She wanted the crayons, but she knew that stealing was wrong. As she sat, torn between her values and her desires, a little girl with cropped brown hair, huge blue eyes, and a stretched blue sweater walked up to the vacant desk and took out the crayons. Christine thought excitedly,

"Those aren't her colors!"

Later Miss Waldrop came down the rows, commenting on the children's work. She stopped at Christine's desk,

"That's a pretty picture, Christine," she commented. "What are you making?"

"Paper dolls," the child answered, working busily and happily.

Carrying the precious treasure in the pocket of her dress, she could hardly wait to get home to make more pictures. Zueline, observing her at work, asked suspiciously,

"Christine, where did you get those colors? You haven't bothered Anne's things, have you? We've just got to get you some things. I'll have to talk to Acie about it. Maybe this month we can."

Christine never looked up from her busy work. "The teacher gave them to me, Mother," she answered unhesitatingly.

Zueline did not question this near miracle. "You be sure and thank the teacher, Christine," she instructed her daughter.

Christine's happiness, as is so often the way with supreme happiness, ill-gotten or otherwise, was short-lived. The absent child returned to school the following day and reported her lost crayons to the teacher. Christine, making no effort to hide her new crayons, sat interested and innocent through the searching and questioning; and her surprise and shock knew no limits when the bereft child, spotting the missing crayons on her desk, exclaimed,

"Here they are, Teacher! I've found them. Here they are!" And the child reached for Christine's new crayons.

Christine, unable to speak, grabbed her precious colors and clutched them to her body, spilling several on the floor in her haste.

"Christine, where did you get those crayons?" asked Miss Waldrop, coming to stand by the child's desk. "Are those your crayons? Let me see them."

"They aren't hers, Teacher. I saw her take them from the other desk yesterday," seriously reported a small boy who sat across the aisle from Christine.

Miss Waldrop, frowning severely, bent down and forcibly took the crayon box from the frightened child's rigid grasp.

"Christine, I'm surprised at you. Stealing is bad. But I trust that you did not steal them. You only borrowed them. But you must not use other people's possessions without asking them." She turned the crayon box over and found the owner's name printed plainly on the bottom. There was no question of ownership.

Christine, humiliated and feeling deeply wronged, protested,

"I didn't take them, Teacher, they're mine."

Miss Waldrop, shocked at the child's blatant lying in the face of obvious evidence, spoke sharply,

"Now, we cannot have this kind of behavior. To borrow without asking permission is very bad, but to lie about it and to claim that the crayons are yours is dreadful. We cannot have that kind of thing in school."

Christine, tears streaming down her contorted face, reached pitifully for the confiscated crayons,

"They're mine, they're mine," she sobbed. "I didn't take them."

Miss Waldrop handed the crayon box to its rightful owner and gathered the scattered color sticks from the floor,

"Christine, you must stay in at recess for telling lies," and she marched back to her desk, leaving the devastated child surrounded by her staring, disapproving peers. Her humiliation was complete. She sat the remainder of the morning with her head down on her desk, trapped in an intolerable situation. When the recess bell rang and all the rest of the children rose and marched out, one little girl paused briefly by Christine's desk and gravely accused,

"You tell lies."

At lunchtime Christine, unable to make herself go onto the playground, where she was sure everybody knew of her crime, slipped unnoticed from the end of the line into the furnace room. It had now become not only a place to hide her unacceptable lunch, but also a place to hide her unacceptable self. She knew she had not stolen the crayons, but the teacher, everybody, accused her of taking them. She was always accused of doing things someone else had done and then being accused of lying when she defended herself. She had thought school would be different, but school was no different! She, Christine, was unacceptable, bad—at home, at school, everywhere. She was soon to have some crayons of her own, but coloring was now sullied, tarnished, and her desire for this form of self-expression was to lie dormant and buried for forty years.

Little children, unable to deal in the social subterfuge and the gray half truths of adults, are often unbearably cruel in their utter candor. When Christine was next forced into her classmates' unsupervised company on the playground, she was taunted for her crimes and became the subject of a singsong chant, "Christine steals, Christine li-ies." It was more than she could bear. At every opportunity she hid and ran away, but her reputation as a thief and as a liar were firmly established.

Her other burning reason for wanting to go to school, writing, also met with something short of success, and this experience, though not as traumatic as the crayon episode, did nothing to improve her confidence and self-image. She had had the misfortune of inheriting left-handedness from her father in a day when leftys were considered, if not downright strange, at least unpleasantly different. The whole world is constructed for right-handed people —zippers, scissors, automobile gear shifts, doors—forcing the left-handed into an unnatural awkwardness and gaucherie. Gauche, or awkward, literally means "left-sided." Any child showing a tendency toward leftness was immediately descended upon by horrified adults, relatives, and otherwise, who spanked the eager left hand and encouraged the passive right hand, scolding "naughty" to the left and praising "good" to the right. And teachers, of course, were expected to eliminate any lingering vestige of this evil when the child entered school. These well-meaning adults had no idea of the conflict their ministrations were setting into motion in these unfortunate youngsters.

Christine had been subjected to her share of discouragement about using her left hand; however, since her father was left-handed, this lent the condition a respectability that made it more of an attraction than a fault to her. At school, however, it was different and became just another in a long list of qualities that made her different and unacceptable. The teacher, noticing the pencil clutched comfortably in the forbidden left hand, removed it and placed it in the clumsy right fist. As the child began to copy the professionally correct letters of her name, which Miss Waldrop had boldly printed at the top of her writing tablet, her natural tendencies caused her to switch the huge round pencil back to her more proficient left hand. Observing this, the teacher turned Christine in her seat so that the offending left hand was trapped below the desk and could not be used without great difficulty. She also told her that her work would not be accepted if written with the left hand and, that most terrible of privations, it could not be tacked on the bulletin board for display.

Christine's task became nearly impossible. Not only did she have to strive twice as hard as the children using their naturally dominant hands, but since she could use only one hand, she had to labor with loose paper, which slipped under the pressure of her pencil. And, of course, at home she diligently practiced writing with her skillful left hand, making her school progress snail-like in pace. She was never happy with the work she produced at school, always feeling ashamed of her clumsy, labored scrawling, which Miss Waldrop posted beside the neat, perfect lettering of most of the girls in the class. Nobody, however, not even those with superior penmanship, could approach the smooth, perfect ovals that the teacher demonstrated on the blackboard; and it was much later that Christine discovered, quite by accident, that anybody can produce better work at the board than on paper—the free motion of the arm flows more freely than the anchored hand sliding across paper. A sense of betrayal accompanied this discovery.

But she did learn to write, and she did it in the manner, if not to the degree of perfection, that the teacher prescribed. In one major area, Christine excelled: She read well and with evident enjoyment, opening for herself a whole new world. Perhaps unfortunately, it extended her already too vivid world of fantasy, since her exposure was either to stories of favored children whose conditions were so far superior to hers that identification was virtually impossible, or to stories of pure fantasy, such as witches and magic. In the spring, she wrote a poem, *The Easter Bunny*, and received her first unalloyed and individual praise from the teacher, and her first admiration from her peers. It was a heady experience for her recognition-starved psyche, and she was from time to time to use this method of self-expression, falling back on it when she was desperate for approval.

The Strother place was a child's paradise, having not only secret places in which to hide, tall places in which to climb, creeks in which to wade, and much activity, but it also had a ghost of which to be afraid. According to the story, the ghost was the restless spirit of a hapless man who had been killed in one corner of the sheeppen, and he wandered at night at the scene of his misfortune. Anne and Christine, nightly watching the pens from their safe perch on the porch roof, never actually saw the ghost, but they knew he was present, for the sheep never ventured into that corner. As further proof, the sheep could not even be driven there. Much more courageous in the bright sunlight than in the pale moonglow, the little girls had tried scaring the docile sheep into the notorious corner, but it could not be done. The sheep were more frightened of what could not be seen in the corner than they were of sharp sticks and frightful yells.

131

Miss Mary Hughes was the second-grade teacher, and school that year was better for Christine. It was a particularly cold winter, and though there was enough food on the farm to still gnawing bellies, actual money for purchasing warm clothes was nonexistent. Christine faced the bitter winter with only a white cotton, fleece-lined sweatshirt to shield her from the biting cold. It seemed that she was always cold, always shivering, always having to sniff and wipe her red, runny nose. The chill bit into her, turning her white skin a mottled blue and causing her thin, exposed legs to move woodenly, awkwardly. The walk down the lane to the school bus each morning was the part she most dreaded. The older children walked faster, leaving the little girl to half run, half stumble along behind. Her gait was further impeded by her gloveless hands stuck up the sleeves of her shirt and her frigid face being nestled turtle fashion down into its neck. Her breath hung in a momentary white cloud before her half-blind, tear-stung eyes; her red, glowing ears ached like a freshly barked shin; and her tormented lungs, labored from exertion in the thin, frosty air, would, she thought, surely burst. On these mornings, the frost, resembling a young snow, lay thinly white on everything, and the hard red clay spewed up its frozen moisture in frost-inverted icicles that shattered and crunched underfoot. And the wind blew—cold, raw, biting.

One day Miss Hughes, having seen the thin-clad child on the playground, shivering, huddling, squatting for warmth over her blue shaking legs, gave her a heavy coat, a knitted cap, and some thick winter dresses.

"These are some things that my niece has outgrown, Christine," she told the wondering child. "They look like they would fit you. It's a shame for clothes to just lie around. It's much better for things to wear out than to rot out."

It was the kind of thing people did in those hard times, and when Christine brought home the large bag of second-hand clothes, Zueline was grateful, carefully instructing her child,

"Now, Christine, you thank Miss Hughes. Did you thank her? No matter, you thank her again tomorrow, you hear? Tell her how much we appreciate your clothes. And, Christine," she sternly added, "you take care of these clothes. That will show Miss

Hughes how much you appreciate them. See how nice the other little girl has kept them. You must keep them nice, too."

Christine tried mightily to envision the other little girl who had worn the new clothes, but, try as she would, she could only see her own happy face between the gray stocking cap and the brown tweed coat. The heavy winter clothes surely protected her from the freezing weather, even though, looking back, she remembered only the paralyzing cold, but the warm glow generated by the possession of the clothes went far in dispelling her other discomforts.

And she was learning. As reading and writing opened up a whole new world for her, she was amazed to discover that some grown-ups were still locked in the dark closet of illiteracy. This could not be allowed to continue! Christine, in her impulsive, uninhibited manner, set about to rectify this intolerable situation, beginning with no less a challenge than her Uncle Dodge, who had unsuspectingly revealed to her his ignorance of the language skills when she asked him one day to read a word for her. Knowing that a blackboard was absolutely essential to the teacher, she improvised one from a piece of tin flashing sticking below the boards near the back-porch steps. Miss Hughes, on hearing the seriousness behind the unusual request, gave the child two small pieces of chalk from her own blackboard. The ambitious plan met a temporary setback when Christine was drenched by a sudden downpour on her way home from school. Alas, when she opened the protecting hand, the lovely white, dusty sticks had become gooey, doughlike wads of gray, sticky mess. Tearful but determined, she explained the catastrophe to Miss Hughes, who replaced the loss with two more little nubs of workable chalk.

Dodge, protesting all the while that he was just "playing school with Top to keep her happy," followed his insistent teacher to the rude classroom for his lessons. The reluctant student sat on the side of the doorsteps, smoking his roll-your-own cigarettes, while his little tutor repeated faithfully what the teacher had taught at school that day. Her performance must have been good, but his willingness to humor her could only be fully explained by his own unvoiced desire to learn to read and write. Even though Christine was not the one to teach her Uncle Dodge the mind-expanding tools of reading and writing, she most surely was the timely instrument that sparked his interest and caused him to enroll in a nationally sponsored adult education program designed to eliminate illiteracy. She always felt cheated out of her important job, and experienced a little-disguised personal resentment toward the instructor who took over her teaching duties.

Never long without a cause, however, she soon took on another difficult and much less sublime task—that of potty training Becky. The twins, two products of the times into which they were born, suffered, as did so many of their contemporaries, from malnutrition. What little was known of balanced diet was largely impractical to implement during the lean years of the Depression. Just a full belly was considered fortunate by most; any consideration of what ought to fill the belly was a luxury few could afford. A large number of children were stricken with rickets—the soft bone ailment resultant from nutritional privations in the diet —and most children suffered from unsightly, open sores on the body, especially around the knees and shins. These diseases, occurring regularly and yearly, were treated by drenching the victims each spring with an enormous, cramping, griping dose of calomel. In fact, not only the puny were drenched, but hardly a body, healthy or otherwise, escaped this spring cleaning—just in case.

Tiny, the smaller of the twins, had rickets and never crawled, only beginning to walk at two years of age. Even though she was visited by the county nurse for a weekly treatment of cod liver oil (no one questioning that she had to personally spoon it into the child), her weakened condition caused her to fall far behind her stronger sister in physical maturity and in her ability to learn developmental tasks. Christine's relationship with her little sisters took on a new aspect during this time. She babied the frail Tiny, carrying her around balanced precariously on one jutted bony hip, causing her father to comment, "Top, you're going to grow crooked carrying that baby on your hip!"; but to robust Becky she became tutor, mentor, and guardian, and her scolding, bossy treatment (a faithful imitation of the adult/child behavior to which she herself was exposed) was uncomplainingly suffered by the placid, unruffled victim. The classroom this time was the privy— the outhouse. Unaware, she was nonetheless training her pupil according to the best modern research findings on the subject: Teach the child, by example, to deposit his eliminations where and in like manner as his elders do.

134

The privy was a two-holer. Christine pulled down Becky's pants and lifted her onto the oval hole carved into the bench. The child, her eyes huge with fright, gripped the edge of the seat and leaned far foward, making it the wonder of the whole process that she did not either fall off the seat, or (unspeakable horror!) fall into the odoriferous black hole. Christine then lowered her own pants, and backing up to the bench and placing her hands on either side of her receptacle, hoisted her own bare rear over the hole. And there they sat, for as long as was necessary, hunched over the holes with dangling feet held wide and turned up to retain bunched-down cotton panties, and elbows clasped tightly against their sides to retain bunched-up cotton dresses. Christine authoritatively instructed, using the currently acceptable terminology for these necessary but unspeakable processes,

"Now, Becky, you do what I do. Now, listen to what I'm doing —I'm tee-teeing. Do you hear it? Now, you tee-tee," and Christine would listen carefully to hear if her student were performing.

Poor Becky tried mightly to perform, striving to please her instructor more than to relieve her own biological needs, since the lessons always came when Christine had an urge; it was just a happy coincidence if Becky's little system also needed to be emptied at the same time.

"Becky tee-tee, Teeny," the gentle child, eager to please, always responded, regardless of whether any offering had been deposited.

But her sharp-eared teacher was not to be so easily deceived.

"You did not, either, Becky," she scolded. "Now, you do as I say: Tee-tee! You hear!" And the trial went on until Christine was satisfied that her little pupil had performed. Sometimes their legs were woodenly asleep and their backs painfully cramped before the lesson ended, and their rumps had a permanent red semicircle from the long sessions of hanging over that black, yawning hole.

A bowel movement, or a No. 2, was a little more complicated, involving, however, the same basic process, with Christine demanding,

"Now, Becky, make a do-do! See, I am making a do-do. You make a do-do."

And Becky always obediently responded, regardless of the results,

"Becky make do-do."

When Christine was satisfied with the performance, she meticulously, if unorthodoxly, carried out the next necessary step: the cleaning. Paper—usually the Sears, Roebuck catalogue (omitting the picture pages, which were too slick for the purpose) supplemented by newspaper—was stored in the privy for that specific use, but it also did double duty as reading matter for those whose stay was lengthy. Christine, after attending to her own ablutions, attacked poor Becky, turning her around with her bare buttocks blaring over the edge of the seat and her head hanging down into the awful black hole. The child, terrified beyond complaint, endured the rough ministrations with tightly closed eyes and abated breath.

Both Christine and the twins became very ill during the winter, she with big red measles and they with colitis. It was a needed experience with pampering, with having everyone tend to her and put her first—Miss Hughes even sent her some precious apples and oranges, an incredible treat—and Christine blossomed under all this attention. While she was still basking in this heady shower of loving care, the babies became desperately ill and were rushed to the hospital. Christine's fount of attention was immediately and completely dried up. Her parents were, of course, constantly at the hospital with their ill children, leaving her to be taken care of by her young aunts; and when her parents did return home with the frail, convalescent twins, Christine was again overlooked by everyone, who vied with each other to hold and care for the babies.

On the day they were all to arrive home from the hospital, Christine was beside herself with excitement, knowing that with the return of her parents she would be restored to her favored position as center of attention. However, because of her recent bout with measles, she was isolated from her little sisters to protect them from her possible germs. She watched the whole proceeding from her upstairs room of banishment, and as she observed the adults who had so recently been pampering her, passing the wan white babies from one pair of loving arms to another, the pain in her chest grew and her sight blurred. The yard, the black car, her mother and father, all swam and danced and disappeared. Suddenly the pain was gone, and the scene below was clear, remote, and uninteresting. She turned from the window and, walking slowly and quietly, left the bare, impersonal room, climbed the steep attic stairs, and settled herself gravely and unemotionally behind the cot in the colorful sunlight filtering through the stained glass. Acie found her there much later. If she had heard him calling her, she gave no indication, greeting him calmly, as if he had not been away for several crucial days. Somewhat puzzled, he merely assumed that she had been completely unaffected by the family crisis. She never mentioned the incident, outwardly completely accepting the abrupt return to her normal position, that of secondary status behind her more favored sisters.

As spring awoke abruptly and without warning, as it so often does, leaving winter behind with not so much as even a day's notice, Christine dreaded even more leaving the sunlit gentleness of home for the stark definiteness of school. So when Anne suggested that they take a "holiday," she quickly agreed. At the planned time they came home loudly and happily, announcing that the elementary grades did not have to attend school the following day. The older high school girls, being unable to refute or to verify the startling elementary information, went off to school alone the next morning in the chilly, long-shadowed morning, leaving the two little schemers to spend the warm, sunny day whispering, giggling, and lying in the new grass, planning more holidays. It was a poorly planned scheme at best and doomed to failure. Myrtle and Elise knew as soon as they boarded the school bus that the younger girls had pulled a fast one; all of the other elementary children were going to school. Worst of all, Christine's and Anne's teachers asked about them, and the older girls, too embarrassed to tell the truth, lied for the two little culprits, saying that they were sick. The truth came out that night, and the retribution followed the familiar pattern: Christine was roundly scolded and put to bed early without supper, but Anne was merely laughingly reprimanded by Papa, who thought the scheme funny and clever.

"Now, Little Sugar," he grinned through his thick blond mustache, "don't you ever let Papa hear of you doin' this agin."

"Oh, no, Papa, of course I won't," she seriously informed him, her wide blue eyes striving hard to squelch the matching twinkle in his.

Christine, outraged over this blatant injustice and knowing nothing of the clashing philosophies involved in the meting out of the punishment, wept and protested. Acie, realizing full well the unevenness of the justice but feeling that he and not others must influence the bringing up of his child, reacted more sternly than usual to his problem daughter and promised her a whipping also if she were not quiet. This unaccustomed reaction from her usually even-tempered father, along with her other misery, caused an unbearable ache in the child—her head pounded, her chest tightened, and her stomach turned over. Suddenly, the unbelievable agony was gone! She calmly pulled the cover up over her head, turned her back to the room and its occupants, and lying tranquil and unmoving, she, though awake, made no sound all through the long evening. The adults, thinking her asleep, moved and spoke quietly, having no idea that the child lay remote and detached from her surroundings, scarcely in more than physical contact with her real world.

That happened so often, everytime I was so miserable I could not bear something. When the pain grew unbearable, something happened, something changed, and then I felt nothing, nothing. I couldn't feel, I couldn't see, I couldn't hear! I just seemed to go away, far away; everything seemed to be so very far away. Was that somebody else? Was that somebody who came and took away the pain and hurt? Was I unable to endure even the everyday human emotions of hurt and anger and pain of slight? Was I so weak and fragile that I had to escape from just ordinary living—what all people face daily? It's more than that! It's got to be; I must have been ill, feverish. Don't people do that, feel that way when they're feverish? I must have worked myself up into a fever. But why did she—I—always run away, or hide? And nobody ever knew I was sick. Mother took good care of me, she would have known if I was sick. She was always feeling my forehead to see if I had a fever. O God, my head aches now! Is it aching because I don't want to face something—something unpleasant, hurting? No! I can't stop thinking now, no matter how much it hurts; I've got to go on. . . .

That summer Becky and Tiny won a beauty contest. They were chosen by unbiased public judges as the prettiest and healthiest babies in the whole of Edgefield County. For the occasion, Zueline had extravagantly bought them matching blue-and-white dresses from Miller's Department Store. The store's proprietor, whose baby son was selected as runner-up in the contest, publically revealed his paternal pique over the choice by good-naturedly declaring on the spot that Becky and Tiny only won because they were twins and because they had been dressed from the Miller store.

Christine, observing the public accolades and attention showered on her adorable little sisters, had sharply ambivalent feelings—her family pride vying fiercely with her deep-seated, rankling jealousy. It was an ambivalence with which she had to struggle all her life, and affected not only her relationship with her sisters but also all the members of her family. She loved her family emotionally, extravagantly, feeling deep pride in them as a unit; but if any one of them surged ahead and rose above the herd, her sudden burning jealousy consumed her, turning her own progress to bitter ashes. It was an emotion, however, that she learned expertly to mask, finding early that a show of jealousy never brought her the sought-for sympathy, only cold condemnation.

The summer brought many changes for the Hastings family, of which Acie and Zueline and their little brood had become an irrevocable part. The changes brought luck and fortune for some, grief and misfortune for others. For Christine, the blessing was mixed, launching her into a period of relative calm before her precipitous, headlong plunge into near oblivion.

8

The Quiet Before the Storm

Is happiness the absence of unhappiness, as cold is the absence of
heat, or is there a condition of limbo between the two states
where neither reigns supreme? During her ninth year, Christine
experienced such a state, and had she not already been so damaged, or had the period lasted longer, this duration of calm might
have served to stabilize her sufficiently to endure a future uninterrupted by the need for periodic escapes. She was totally unaware
of the idyllic nature of this time in her life, and perhaps this is as
it must be. Could an idyl exist in the tarnishing presence of the
knowledge of its own deterioration and demise? An innate part of
the nature of an idyl is the obliviousness of time, the unawareness
of the passage of turmoil undermining the protective garden wall.

The Strother place was the first home Christine had ever looked
at, analyzed, thought about as more than just shelter, and it became for her the model of comparison for all other places in
which she was to live for the rest of her life. Seen through the fanciful eyes of a child, its decayed splendor became perfection, causing even the modern dwellings she inhabited as an adult to become ugly and unbearable. Through this distorted view, she
longed for the childhood scenes that glamorized the privy and the
springhouse and denied the modern miracles of plumbing and
thermostatic control.

Her next home, the Williams place, though never having had
the luxurious splendor of the Strother mansion, had nevertheless
once been a fine country home. It had been the home of ole Doc
Williams for years until his death, and had served a series of ten-

ants since. The doctor's little office, fully stocked as he had left it, stood in the front yard to the side of the wide front porch. The one-story, L-shaped house, generously encrusted with gingerbread, had an L-shaped back porch onto which every room gave entrance except the dining room and the kitchen, each of which had steps leading directly into the cleanly swept red clay yard. In fact, several rooms could not be reached from the rest of the house except by detouring out onto this busy thoroughfare, an awesome dash for a thinly clad body in freezing weather.

Only two bedrooms had fireplaces—Mama and Papa's, and Dodge and his wife's; everybody else slept in frigid rooms, in the winter, under massive mountains of musty, homemade quilts. At bedtime, one baked himself thoroughly before the communal fire before making a dash into the breathtaking chill of the porch, and on into the no less arctic air of his bedroom. Disrobing was done hastily and usually in the dark, the haste being precipitated by the cold, and the dark necessitated by modesty, since several people usually slept in the enormous rooms, which held as many as three and four double beds. The women slept in long full, flannel granny gowns, and the men usually just jumped into bed clad in their woolen long-handled underwear, which was worn day and night and was changed only at Saturday night bathtime. That first plunge between the stiff, rough, icy sheets was an unforgettable experience.

Though lacking some of the comforts to which the family had become accustomed, the Williams place attracted Nick Hastings because it gave him a chance to maintain his own farm again. The New Deal, in an attempt to help the farmers pull themselves out of their depths, had instituted the Farmers' Rehabilitation Program. Under this plan the federal government supplied to farmers the seed, livestock, and resources to start a farm year and put in crops. In return the farmer returned to the government, at "settlin' up" time after harvest, one half of his profits realized from the year. Papa rented the Williams place—a farm acceptable to the government—assessed his needs, collected his advance, and put in his first crop.

Acie and Zueline, of course, went along with them, moving temporarily into a spacious storage building, originally used as a general store, until a small cottage could be fixed up for them.

This little house, in hollering distance across the field from Papa's, had only three rooms and had originally been a Negro house when Doc Williams owned the place. It had a kitchen and two bedrooms, one of which—Acie and Zueline's—had a fireplace and served as the sitting room. The windows had no glass panes, only solid board shutters to close the opening, making the house very dark, with a closed-in feeling, especially in the winter, when the shutters had to be closed for warmth. Christine, experiencing a resentment and betrayal without really knowing why, never liked the house and spent most of her time across the field at the big house.

But then they all did, Zueline and the twins going up to Mama's each day just as soon as Acie left for the fields, and he in turn coming in at dinnertime with the rest of the men to eat at the big house food that his wife had helped to prepare. He did insist, however, that he and his little family eat supper at his own house each evening, but this mandate was not as easy to enforce as it might appear. Christine wanted to stay and eat with Anne and play until night, when she would be afraid to cross the dark field alone and her father would have to go for her; and everybody, especially Papa, wanted the twins to literally stay at the big house, even to sleeping over there. Acie could handle Christine and Anne's begging with little problem except its constancy. But how does one handle a teasing, practical-joking father-in-law on whose favor and goodwill one is depending for his livelihood? Acie would insist, to the point of practically forcibly carrying his children home in the evening after the backbreaking day of farm chores, only to have Papa, after supper, stand on his front porch and call,

"Babies, come see Grandpa! Come to Grandpa, babies!"

The twins, of course, wanted to go. Grandpa's place was a heaven for them, since Papa allowed no restrictions to be placed on them. In fact, he, with his expansive, all-encompassing sense of humor, encouraged them to be naughty, even to the point of putting them up to saying and doing "cute" but outrageous things that not only angered their father for the mere act alone but also because it was undermining his authority over their upbringing. And Zueline was no help. Her passive nature, as usual, took the path of least resistance in the face of controversy.

142

"Ah, Sugar, let them go," she would plead. "What harm can it do? They love them so much, and they have all been so much help when the babies were so sick and all."

Acie was exasperated beyond words both at his own predicament and at his wife's inability to see that as these tender little twigs were bent, so would they grow. He knew that if his little daughters did not learn to handle discipline and restrictions now, they would not in later years be able to deal constructively with life's disappointments and frustrations, nor would they be able to effectively train their own future sons and daughters to successfully meet their privations and temptations. A weak link in this chain of life training causes repercussions that resound and vibrate for generations. He was also acutely, and seemingly, solely, aware that only two of his three daughters were being lovingly summoned; Papa was not including Christine in his clarion call. He was not deliberately excluding her, and if she came, he surely had no objection; he simply gave no thought to her at all. The soft, intangible suffocation of indifference is immensely more brutal than the sharp, clean cut of intentional hurt. The hateful, deliberate slash is a wound, can be defined, reacted to, anesthetized; and though leaving eternal scarring, its crippling is localized, contained. But the crushing embrace of indifference is elusive, diffused, total, shattering the entire structure and leaving the frame weak, misshapened, and deformed; and the mind, trapped in this ruined temple, itself shatters and splinters, forming and reforming in illogical, irrational, erratic patterns.

Acie could not win. If he permitted the girls to go, he would lose his paternal control and damage his children; if he allowed the twins to go and retained Christine at home to protect her, she would be hurt and confused, and he would be unable to explain the obvious difference in treatment; if he kept all three of his children at home, as he felt was best, he risked alienating his wife, his helpful in-laws, and his benefactor—Papa. Usually he simply threw up his hands and walked out, allowing life to plot its own course.

Christine walked alone daily the dusty mile to Pleasant Lane School, the one-room whiteboard seat of learning presided over by Miss Sadie Dorn, that strange combination of administrator, nurse, custodian, and teacher to be found only in rural one-room

143

schools. Miss Sadie was a married woman of indeterminate age who lived just up the road from the schoolhouse, but as was the custom, adult women, regardless of marital state, were addressed by children as "Miss" plus the given name. It just seemed to soften the address, as did "yes'm" and "no'm" soften the response. Here Christine met no harsh criticism, no unfavorable competition; here learning was individualized, comfortable, unpressured; here the teacher was "Miss Sadie" who lived down the road and was Granny's friend who came to Sunday dinner just like relatives.

Miss Sadie's yellow oak desk sat on the left side of the large room facing six long, narrow tables, four on the left side and two at the back of the right side. Each table had a low, backless bench positioned so that seated students faced the front of the room. The tables and benches were graduated in size from barely two feet high in front of Miss Sadie's desk, to almost adult size in the far right corner. Each table represented a grade level, from first through sixth, but if a student's physical being outgrew his grade station, he easily and without undo fuss was allowed to sit comfortably with his larger peers. Miss Sadie, whether through wisdom or necessity, also had an easy system for adjusting to students who mentally outgrew their grade stations. At the front right of the room was the recitation bench, a medium-sized, medium-height bench positioned to face out into the room. It was constructed with a backrest, as if recognizing that a one-sized seat would not fit all learners, so it had best be as comfortable as possible. Miss Sadie's chair was positioned at an angle so that she could keep a watchful, though gentle, eye on the independent studying, as well as the reciting. Pupils studied and recited at Pleasant Lane according to ability; grade level was simply a necessary means of identification. Christine, eagerly and proudly, hurried up to the recitation bench when Miss Sadie called "fifth-grade reading group," a motley assemblage that included not only third-grader Christine but some fourth- and sixth-graders as well as the regular fifth-graders.

Pleasant Lane was a one-lane, seldom scraped, slightly rolling dirt road winding through woods and fields. Its pale yellow clay coated one's shoes with a fine powder during dry spells and a sticky paste during rainy times. Under wheels, whether automotive or horse-drawn, the dry clay became a suffocating dust, clouding and coating not only vehicles and their occupants, but bushes, trees, and roadside buildings as well; and the wet clay, slick as cold grease on a smooth board, beat out as it dried into deeply rutted washboards, which, if not scraped, caused motor vehicles to vibrate and fishtail at any speed over twenty miles per hour. But for Christine, it was, as its name implied, a pleasant lane.

After school, she came to Mama's to play with Anne, who was now in the seventh grade and rode the school bus, along with Myrtle and Elise, to Edgefield High School. Although they did play Kitty Wants a Corner; Annie over the Rooftop; Fruitbasket Turn Over; and Hopscotch, organized games were pretty much saved for rainy days and Sundays, when numerous cousins came to visit. Their regular play—designed for two and involving much secrecy—was too risky to share with untested types, who might reveal cherished secrets to unaware adults.

And secrecy was the name of the game. It had to be, since most of their activity revolved around deviously thwarting even the paltry few restrictions and chores required of the gloriously free, Huck Finn existence that the two girls enjoyed. It was a paradise, a garden, but evil inhabited this haven also in the form of the prank-loving, impish nature of the two children themselves. Tempted by their lavish freedom and by the indulgent trust of their elders, they spent their time dreaming up and perpetrating, on the unsuspecting adults, acts that ranged in seriousness from the near-criminal destruction of valuable animal life and property to the merely capricious spoiling of personal possessions.

They dearly loved to surreptitiously ramble through the belongings of Myrtle and Elise, wantonly ruining anything new and exciting they found carefully cached under the neat stacks of plain, homemade underwear. The older girls were courting, and a boyfriend sometimes brought a box of chocolates. This rarest of rare treats, too small to be passed around in so large a family, was carefully hoarded by the recipient, to be sampled in stolen moments of privacy. The lucky receiver of such a gift knew that her suitor was serious and that the "sweets to the sweet" was more than an extravagant gesture—being usually the traditional forerunner of a marriage proposal. Each little confection was symbolic. Elise was outraged one day when she stole privately into her shared room, gently removed her tangible token of love, and with unbelieving

145

horror discovered that nearly half of her chocolates were missing and that the rest lay crushed, bleeding out their sweet syrups— open wounds of wanton devilment.

Weeping, storming, exhibiting the *prima facie* evidence, she burst in upon her startled family,

"Look! Just look! Who did it? I want to know who did it! I want to know, right now, who did it!" she ranted through her outraged tears.

"Elise, Elise, what's the matter, honey?" Papa looked up, concerned.

"My lord, what a lot of noise. I've never heard so much fuss." Mama, barely pausing in her rocking, never missed a stitch in the silk hose she was darning.

"Just look!" grated Elise, her calm, positive nature asserting itself. "And I *know* who did it! Anne, you and Christine did this, and I'm goin' to break your necks!" She bore down on the two little girls, who had been sitting still, too still, while the storm raged.

"I did not, either, do it. I didn't even know you had any ole candy," Anne belligerently protested.

"How did you know it was candy? I didn't say it was candy! You did do it!" Elise grabbed Anne by the arm and shook her roughly.

"Papa, Papa!" yelled Anne, her head bobbing loose as she tried to escape her irate sister.

"Well, now; well, now, hold on a minute there, Sis," Papa addressed his older daughter. "Where did you get the candy?" An amused twinkle came into his eyes. This was fertile ground for teasing, and he dearly loved to tease. In Nick Hastings's hierarchy of things to be done, teasing always took precedent over disciplining.

"Elise, you didn't tell *me* Sammy gave you a box of candy!" accused Myrtle, spilling the beans, whether through surprise at not being her sister's confidante, or through female pique that she herself had not received such a prize first.

Elise, her cheeks once blanched in anger, now blushed rosy with a heady mixture of girlish embarrassment and womanly pride; but she stubbornly persisted,

"Anne and Christine did this, and they need whippin'. Papa, you would have wore me out if I had done this. You just spoil Little Sugar." And she started again for the two girls, who stood behind Papa's chair.

"I didn't do it, Papa," innocently vowed Anne, careful never to include her little cohort in her plea of purity. She had learned that if pursuit became too hot, she could always blame Christine, who always denied everything, no matter if she had been caught in the very act. Nobody ever believed Christine, and Anne had, on occasion, been able to divert attention from herself by casting blame on the younger girl, whose reputation for lying was permanently established. At any rate, it was a door that Anne always left open.

Christine, confused by the whole scene, knew, for certain, two things: Nobody would believe *her* if she denied the crime, and she could not count on Grandpa to protect her as he always did Anne and the babies. Her best defense was unobtrusive silence, in the hope of riding along to safety on Anne's skimpy coattails. Papa's protection was not always present, however, and sometimes their wrongdoing was so wanton that all the dependable sources of succor deserted them. Ellis, who seldom resorted to physical action as a means of correction—relying on his cold, formal dignity to squash disorder—lost his usual calculated cool when the busy little mischiefmakers badly scratched Mamie Lee's new Singer sewing machine with a nail. Anne, observing one of life's injustices overlooked by the younger girl, casually informed Christine as they were examining the expensive, elaborately decorated machine with its dark, polished wood cabinet,

"Your mother doesn't have a sewing machine, so let's mess up Mamie Lee's."

So Anne industriously scratched on its shining surface awhile, then offered the nail to wide-eyed Christine, ordering,

"Now you scratch it."

Christine applied the effective tool to the already scarred surface, adding little except her complicity; but Ellis, learning of the evil deed from his tearful wife, made no distinction between intent and operation—he thoroughly thrashed both girls with his bare hand. Later they drove another nail, that useful weapon, into Ellis's automobile tire to prevent his leaving and taking Elen home. Disgusted, Ellis, never suspecting the innocent-appearing little urchins, merely thought he had accidentally picked up a

147

nail along the road. The fact that the flat tire only delayed instead of prevented his departure saved him from similar such accidents in the future.

Often Christine and Anne were not so fortunate as to escape punishment for their devilment, but even swift, sound retribution was not a sufficient deterrent, and harassment of the older girls remained one of their favorite pastimes. They broke up Myrtle's colorful Jacksticks to elaborately decorate the toadhouses they had molded in damp sand over their bare feet; they ate the candy Easter eggs that Elise had won for finding the treasure egg at the church egg hunt; and they were forever messing into the girls' meager hoard of makeup, breaking the tiny fragile tubes of Tangee lipstick and spilling the precious face and rouge powder.

Nobody was sacrosanct, not even Mama, whom they both usually gave a wide berth. They stole cocoa and sugar from her pantry to eat when there was no candy to filch, and they shook pears off the trees for the pigs to eat to keep from gathering them for her to make preserves. They sometimes involved Becky and Tiny in their dirty deeds, soliciting them once to help pull the green apples from Papa's apple tree. Christine and Anne climbed the tree, pulled the apples, and threw them to the ground; then all four of the girls busily set about to bite each hard, sour fruit once before throwing it away. The twins' help had really been elicited because the biting phase of the operation was so large; if they could have handled it alone, the younger girls would have been excluded. Papa, the eternal humorist, saw absolutely nothing funny in the devastation of his apple crop, designed to provide delicious eating fruit, pies, and hot jacks all winter long; and he pursued and soundly whipped Anne, Christine, and Becky. Tiny, a budding imp herself, hid under the bed, and as Papa dragged her out, she looked up at him with her huge blue eyes brimming with tears and pled,

"You wouldn't beat me, would you, Grandpa?" and, of course, Grandpa would not. Papa was not bothered by the finer points of a problem, such as equality in justice; punishment of a sort had been meted out, his rare anger was spent, and it was over. He never considered the object lesson that his uneven actions had taught to the four children under his care.

Many of their deeds had a "monkey see, monkey do" flavor,

148

being simply aborted attempts to duplicate the busy actions of the men as they performed their necessary chores. Unfortunately, the recipients of these industrious ministrations were the hapless farm animals, and the results ranged from disastrous to deadly. Observing Papa and Dodge shearing the horses' manes, they, having only the docile milk cow as victim, cut off cleanly the only long hair she possessed, that fly-swatting switch sported on the end of her facile tail. Papa whipped them, which did nothing constructive for fly-bitten Bossy, but, perhaps, saved the other milkers from similar fates. Once, to vary the unexciting diet of another cow, a type of animal that seemed to particularly catch their favor, they fed one of Papa's beloved bovines some dried peas. The unwary cow stuffed herself on this new delicacy, slaked her burning thirst on a hardy amount of water, blew up horribly from the abdominal gases generated by this lethal mixture, and promptly and painfully died. As her grotesquely distended form was dragged off for disposal, it left a trail of dried peas issuing regularly from her posterior orifice. Papa, his sense of humor stretched beyond its endurance again, whipped the budding farmers, undeterred by their heartrending protestations of innocence.

Anne and Christine's field of operation, however, was not limited to merely aping the actions of elders; and in the absence of something exciting on the adult horizon, they dreamed up new "games." Lacking other stimulating diversion once while spinning tales in the barn loft, they decided to test their accuracy at spearing Mama's chickens, which were contentedly pecking and clucking in the open breezeway on the ground below them. Carefully holding the four-pronged pitchfork over the unsuspecting birds, Anne sighted, then dropped her weapon. Beginner's luck! The sharp tines cleanly pierced the tender fowl, which dropped mutely in its tracks. Not so the victim's companions. The remaining terrified chickens wildly scattered, loudly squawking their concerted confusion. Appetites whetted by the success of the kill, the two hunters desired more trophies. To entice their not-too-bright quarry back into position, they dropped golden grains of corn down to the frantically clucking hens, which, gluttony overcoming fear, ran greedily back into range. Christine tested her skill and missed, sending off the stupid prey in screaming, wing-flapping melee. Before they tired, they had slaughtered three of Mama's best layers; and for this afternoon's work they escaped punishment. Simply finding the fowl dead with no obvious cause, and being unable to determine what had killed them, Mama threw them away. If she had known the cause of their demise, she could have dressed them for eating and at least realized that much out of the destruction. But those lips, which alone could have revealed this valuable information, were sealed, knowing well what would have been the price for honesty.

The girls also loved to harass the Negroes who lived in the area, especially the children. There being no common ground on which the black and the white children could meet—schools were separate, playmates were plentiful, and social contact was banned—a natural enmity and suspicion existed between them. The little blacks had to pass the big house on the way to the store, a trip they made almost daily; and the little white girls lay in wait for them at various hiding spots along the route. Sometimes the Negro mother would have given them some money to buy candy at the store—a rare treat for both races—and Christine and Anne always tried to stop them on their way back home to see if they had bought any goodies. If they had, the white girls promptly confiscated them, lavishly threatening their little black captives,

"If you tell your mama, we'll kill you! And Mr. Nick will whip you, too!" Neither group seemed to notice the discrepancy in the threat, and both knew that it was the fear of whipping and not the braggadocio threat of murder that prevented their reporting of this regular highway robbery. Christine was always unaccountably uncomfortable when they played this "game," feeling a strange identification with the little underdog black children; and only Anne's overpowering domination of her forced halfhearted participation.

Anne and Christine regularly borrowed hen eggs from ole Aunt Minnie, the Negro woman who lived down the road from Mama's, blandly explaining their request to her,

"Miss Annie sent us to borrow two eggs from you. She needs them for cookin'. She said to tell you she'll pay them back when her hens start layin'."

Aunt Minnie never failed to turn over two of her precious eggs to them, even though she never received one egg in payment for the numerous loans. And Mama, of course, never knew that this skullduggery was being perpetrated in her name. The two girls would then cut across the narrow strip of woods behind the Negro house and came out on the big road at Rob Harling's store. Mr. Harling, never asking any questions about the origin of the two eggs carefully clutched in the dirty little hands, fenced the hot loot for two pennies each, a sum that was immediately spent for candy meticulously selected from the large glass candy case on the counter.

A favorite game was playing doctor in ole Doc Williams' little abandoned office. The doctor must have simply walked out one day, closing the door behind him, never to return. All the medicine bottles still lined the shelves in neat, dusty rows, waiting like trained soldiers at attention for an authoritative command; and the pills and tablets languished patiently in their wooden boxes for expert dispensing. Fortunately, the potency of the ancient drugs had either been dulled by passage of time, or they had never been more than professional fakes with placebo strength, for not one single patient—human, canine, feline, porcine, or fowl—died or felt particularly stricken as a result of ingesting large prescribed doses. Some pigs once did act rather strangely, running around in grunting circles, when Dr. Anne and Nurse Christine administered to them a rather large dose of ammonia, sprinkled generously on their eager, upturned heads.

Across the road from the big house was the cotton house where the cotton was stored after picking and before it was hauled to the mill for ginning and baling. And it was here also that the massive bales were stored until they were sold on the market. In the center of the large open storage space was a big round flexible pipe used for funneling up the loose cotton, sucking it along the length of the pipe, and blowing it either into the wagons or into the storage area. Its suction power was generated by a small engine, which was easily engaged by simply throwing a lever. On Sundays when the clan gathered, this was a favorite spot for the children to play, digging and burrowing in the loose white produce or climbing and jumping on the heavy, squat bales.

On one such a Sunday, three-year-old Crafton, Amos's child, was playing in the cotton house with his older sisters and cousins when someone, accidentally or experimentally, pushed the lever and engaged the suction funnel. With a loud roar, the unmanned pipe suspended from the rafters began an uncontrolled sweep across the open floor. Poor Crafton, directly in the path of the mechanical dragon, was sucked smoothly and instantly off his feet and disappeared, before the very eyes of his horrified kin, into the yawning black hole. Fortunately, the other end of the funnel was secured to the spot where the last loose cotton had been blown into the building, and with a soft "thwump" it spit out the child and embedded him in the downy pile of unseeded fiber.

Movement erupted! Someone threw the lever, others dug frantically in the cotton pile. And there was Crafton, just beginning to wail, but miraculously unharmed, in the depths of the cushiony mound. Anne, the oldest present (and anyway it was her cotton house), immediately took over and outlined the future intelligence strategy concerning the event. It was a simple plan: silence. Everyone was individually sworn to silence, a process that was greatly facilitated by Anne's threat to "cut the throat of anyone who ratted." No one ratted.

Every Sunday at Nick Hastings's home was a family reunion. All of his married children and their families, relatives of his and Mama's own generation, some kissin' kin, and usually a preacher or two dropped in for dinner and an afternoon of sitting around and talking. There were some regulars, of course, but no one ever knew exactly how many would come. If any of the relatives had visiting in-laws they were just loaded into the car and brought along, too. The guests started arriving around ten to ten-thirty in the morning, and Nick greeted each carful personally and heartily. A gregarious soul, he was genuinely delighted to see everyone, opening the car doors, pumping the men's hands and slapping them on the backs, and hugging and kissing the women. His loud, enthusiastic "Come in, come in" was interspersed with roars of merry laughter.

Plump, smiling Mama, a voluminous bib apron almost entirely covering her Sunday (but not quite church quality) dress, greeted her returning family and her guests on the wide front porch. Casually receiving gestures of affection as a powerful ruler does the expected gifts of visiting lesser potentates, she discriminately bestowed large wet kisses and enveloping hugs on her favorites—males, almost without exception. Mama was the commanding general, and she had her troops completely under control. Moving among her guests, exchanging whispered secrets, visiting the kitchen to oversee the food preparation, shooing children out of the house, she passed the last authoritative word on every subject under discussion.

The only people not exuberantly happy on this day were the unmarried teen-age girls living at home, whose chore it was to prepare the noon meal for this advancing horde. They had been up since early morning killing and cleaning chickens for frying, preparing vegetables, and baking cakes and pies. Often, Mama would hurry to the kitchen with the urgent message,

"Better run out and kill another fryer, here comes Cudn' Luke and his family."

The disgusted girls would fuss and fume,

"Why don't they stay home? And why don't we ever go any-where? I'll bet I don't get anything but a wing or a foot out of all this chicken I'm fryin'!" Myrtle pushed a strand of straight dark hair from her damp forehead.

"Stand behind the door when you eat that foot and it'll make you pretty," teased her plump sister.

"Elise, you better go and get that other chicken or we won't even get a foot," laughed Myrtle. "By the time everybody gets his favorite piece, that's all that's left anyway."

Christine had been up at the big house since early morning, speculating with Anne over the guest list. They had the same conversation every Sunday. It ran,

"Do you think the Horns will come?"

"I hope not! They're mean as snakes."

"I hope Elen comes."

"Oh, don't worry. Mamie Lee comes every Sunday."

"If Willie comes, I'm going to hide from him. I just hate him!"

"I hate all boys! I wish they would all stay home."

"It's only boy cousins and brothers that's awful. Other boys are all right!"

"I hope Aunt Sallie and all her red-headed young'uns don't come. They eat too much."

And on, until the cars began to pull into the big front yard. After a general milling around and sizing up, natural groups began to form. Anne deserted her daily companion for older, more so-phisticated company; and Christine in turn watched hopefully for Elen, who, just as predicted, was seldom absent on Sunday, often coming the night before to stay over with her cousin. She and Christine, drawn together like magnets, immediately went off by themselves, deliberately shunning and hiding from their older cousins and visitors. Especially, they did not want to be bothered by Becky and Tiny, who wanted more than anything to follow them around. The older girls had discovered many hiding places that adequately screened them from the calling, searching children, often silently sitting high in leafy trees while Christine's little sisters looked for them on the ground below.

Strangely, the two girls did not often play games, the notable exception being their love for playing school. A small house, made entirely of tin, standing at the left of the driveway between the storehouse and the doctor's office, made a perfect schoolhouse. Its rough, slightly rusted walls served as the blackboard, and chunks of the light gray, crumbly limestone rock, which abounded in that section of the country, were utilized as chalk. After the twins became older, and if Zueline insisted that they all four play together, "playing house" was the name of the game. Each older girl was a mother and had a twin for her child. Christine always and continuously spanked her "bad" child and demanded that Elen also spank her "bad" child. As a result of all this corporal punishment, Christine always drew obstreperous Tiny for her child, while Elen mothered the docile, more easily managed Becky. Even so, the game usually ended badly, with the insulted Tiny running in tears to a sympathetic adult to pitifully complain,

"Teeny is being mean to me!"

This was a signal for the two older girls to run away and hide until the storm had blown over. Once, as they were all four playing house down by the creek in the pasture, they decided to float the twins down the shallow stream on rafts. They put the three-year-old girls in the only readily available rafts: new straw sunhats belonging to Myrtle and Elise. All went well for a brief moment, then catastrophe: Tiny slowly sank out of sight in her porous bateau, and Becky, deciding to stand up, disappeared under the red, rain-swollen water with a splash. The twins had on new (matching, of course) blue cotton twill sunsuits; and when Tiny surfaced, wailing loudly, her suit was a muddy, dripping mess. But poor Becky crawled out on the bank, whining softly, stark naked! It

154

was a mystery never solved, and the sunsuit was never found. Christine and Elen led the weeping twins, Becky terribly embarrassed by her unclothed state, up the hill to the house, Christine giving this excited explanation,

"The babies fell in the creek and Becky lost her sunsuit!"

A thorough search was made of the disaster area, but the missing garment was not to be found. Unfortunately, however, the search turned up the ruins of the erstwhile rafts: the new sunhats. Myrtle and Elise were furious, and Christine was saved from a whipping only by the fact that Elen was also involved. The quiet, nonaggressive younger child never caused trouble alone, so it was naturally assumed that any disturbance involving both her and Christine had to be the fault of the older girl, who was always wreaking havoc, alone or in concert.

Mostly, the two girls spent their time together talking and exchanging information, although it was an uneven exchange. Christine, from her vantage point of being three years older, seemed extremely mature and knowledgeable to sheltered Elen, who accepted her older cousin as the one unimpeachable source of facts on all subjects. Christine told the most fantastic stories, spun the most fabulous yarns; and it never occurred to Elen to wonder where she got all of her information, or to question its veracity. She could hardly wait to get together with her mentor each weekend to thirstily drink in the latest "facts," newly fabricated by Christine's fertile imagination.

Christine's prowess reached its zenith on the subject of sex. The two cousins had experimented occasionally over the years with this fascinating subject, usually under the guise of playing doctor and bearing babies, but having no brothers or close male cousins, their information was extremely one-sided. Their sex play usually concerned "taking a douche," a secret activity in which they knew their mothers regularly indulged, although the girls had no idea what that was. The extent of their knowledge was that the mother filled the enema bag with water, and took it, along with an empty washpan and a towel, into the bedroom, locked the door, and made splashing sounds. Since she obviously did not take an enema, the water must have been poured into that other hole, which Christine, being entirely ignorant of the presence of a third opening, informed Elen was the outlet for pee pee. The little girls took their douches in the outdoor toilet, the only place completely private to them and where no adult would disturb them. Having no douche bag, only a pan of water, it was a rather messy operation, but they at least got the sound part right: There *was* a lot of splashing.

Later, as Christine's knowledge of sex grew, approximately paralleling in time Anne's discovery of boys, Christine's stories delineating mankind's sexual activity reached mind-boggling proportions. Her conception of the size and proportions of the male sexual organ, derived from the observing of the only available visible speciman—Papa's stallion—was formidable indeed. And her description of how a baby is made was a creative masterpiece. She confidently and authoritatively told the enthralled Elen that the process took nine months and that the prospective mother had to have sexual intercourse with a man every night for the whole nine months. She revealed the intriguing fact that it didn't have to be the same man every night, any man would do; but if one night were missed, the whole process had to start all over. The fascinating human relations problem complicating this intricate process was left unexplained, along with numerous other obvious difficulties.

Once Christine, somehow, came into possession of some tiny pornographic books, about three inches square in size, and filled with caricature drawings of famous people. As soon as Elen arrived the next weekend, Christine hurried her around behind the storehouse and removed the little books from her bloomers. The theme of one tiny volume was the Duke and Duchess of Windsor, and it portrayed the Duke with his little crown balancing precariously on his regal head and his enormous pulsating penis protruding from his open fly, following the bosomy Wallis around, exclaiming for all the world to hear,

"I cannot live without the woman I love!"

Elen was so impressed that thirty-five years later, any mention of the Duke of Windsor still brought this naughty little picture to her mind. As she and Christine, carelessly oblivious to their surroundings, bent over the absorbing little book, Tobitha, another of their teen-age aunts, rounded the corner and took in the scene in one glance. She soundly condemned the forbidden literature, shamed the scared little sinners, promised to reveal their degradation to the entire family, and confiscated the illegal property as evidence. Strangely, although the girls suffered painful, anxious anticipation, the expected blow never fell, and the little books never surfaced, leading to the speculation that perhaps they secretly made the undercover rounds of the upper, older levels of the Family.

Acie was acutely aware that his oldest daughter was almost daily involved in unacceptable behavior and that Anne, three years older, was fast becoming an unsuitable playmate for her. He was equally as aware that he was not the dominating force in the rearing of his two younger daughters and that their conduct was deteriorating to a degree that he could no longer tolerate. Painfully obvious, also, was the fact that Zueline had never really broken the bonds of her mother's apron strings, and that she neglected her own home daily for her maternal one. Acie, by nature an easygoing man, was not one to stir up trouble, but his gentle patience, when pushed to its overgenerous limit, broke with a totally unexpected suddenness and violence that was devastating. Unfortunately, these rare, lightning displays of inner strength did not occur often enough to establish a reputation of iron will and determination, and few realized the quality and extent of his strong, tensile constitution, which through his life sustained him while the mercuried quicksilver of others rapidly ran out.

The storm had long been gathering. An inbred dislike of outlanders and a basic philosophic difference had prevented the development of a true male closeness between Acie and the men of his wife's family, a situation that years of close proximity would aggravate rather than alleviate, but several seemingly unrelated events caused a rupture that finally decided him to move forever from under his father-in-law's protective but patronizing arm. When the twins were born, Acie needed a cow for their milk, when it was discovered that Zueline would again be unable to nurse her young at her breast. A family controversy arose over which cow would be used for this purpose. Acie, unwilling to be buffeted so by such emotional forces, borrowed one from a neighbor, Ben Mims, promising to pay for this vital service out of his share of the harvest profits. This kind man, however, refused payment when Acie returned his cow and tried to settle up.

Acie believed, as did most white people of his time and society, that black people belonged in a different social stratum from whites; but he also believed just as strongly in the dignity of men —all men—making his views of this budding social dilemma somewhat different from most. Observing Papa one day administering a leather-strap whipping to a hired Negro man who had broken his word to Nick Hastings—his employer—and had not made good on an agreement for which he had been paid, Acie interfered, stepping between the two men, quietly ordering his father-in-law,

"Don't hit him again, Mista' Hastin'."

Papa, completely flabbergasted by this unheard-of behavior, stood stunned in the face of something he could not understand. He was only righting a wrong, punishing a misbehaving child, a disobedient dependent who needed to be taught a lesson. Did he not in like manner punish his own children, his own flesh and blood when they disobeyed? He stared in confused disbelief into the calm, resolute eyes of this strange man his daughter had married, but he did not oppose him. Something in the unruffled demeanor of the smooth, unlined face aroused in this proud patriarch a feeling of admiration for the bold, raw courage of the younger man. Nick Hastings turned and walked away; but a line had been drawn, a wariness had developed, a rent had opened in the fabric that could never be repaired.

Strangely, it was another cow that proved to be the inoffensive pawn causing the final parting of the business ways between Acie and his wife's family. In the settling of the meager estate of James Cicero Costner, Acie received among his share of the paternal goods, a cow. Zueline had been very fond of her shy, quiet father-in-law, perhaps sensing in the bent old man the same calm, hidden strength that motivated his son; and his cow seemed to her the extension of the life force of the man himself. It was love at first sight between Bossy, the black-and-white Guernsey cow and Zueline, the loving girl-woman. Her husband had no such sentimental notions about the cow; she was to him merely a possession that had cash value. And Acie needed money, a rare item in those days, to make his break, to gain his independence, to become his own man.

In becoming involved with Papa in the Farmers' Rehabilitation Program, Acie had obligated himself to produce and repay. He could have simply walked away from his obligation, many did, but he deeply felt the debt as no small thing and was unable to forfeit. His cow, this last gift from his father, gave him the means. Zueline, understanding little of the intricacies of Acie's involvement and nothing of his inner need to escape, heard only that he was going to sell her pet. She protested,

"Honey, no, not Bossy! She's your father's. How could you think of selling her?"

"Now, Sister, just listen. It's our chance to be on our own. We'll have other cows." He tried to calm her.

"We're on our own now; we live in our own house!" Sister answered angrily.

"But I work for him, honey. We need to be away and independent." He pled with her to understand.

Sister burst into tears, "You just want to take me away from my family," she stormed. "Just because your family don't love each other, you want to take me away. Well, my people love each other, we depend on each other."

"Sister, you know it's not that. I'm grateful to Mista' Hastin', but sometime I've got to stop just being grateful. The cow will bring enough to pay off most of my part to the government." He tried to explain his need.

"And now you want to take my cow, too," Zueline wailed, tears streaming down her pretty face. "I won't let you do it. It's the first cow I've ever had. You're goin' to take the milk away from your little babies. What kind of a father are you?"

By now, all three children, frightened by the unaccustomed behavior of their parents, were whimpering and crying. Acie looked at the scene before him, hurt but resolute, and unable to longer do battle with her tears and accusations, he turned toward the door,

"It's got to be done, Mother, I'm sorry," he looked at her, begging for her understanding.

Zueline watched him lead the cow from the yard. She walked the floor, wringing her hands, weeping, beseeching the heavens,

"What am I goin' to do? Oh, Lordy, what am I goin' to do? Oh, my little children, what's to become of us?"

Her storm wore itself out, and she told her upset children,

"Come on, we're goin' home to Mama."

159

She gathered up her softly weeping brood and they set out on the pilgrimage they made daily, emotional storm or no, across the field to the big house. It was almost night, an unusual time for a visit, when his daughter announced,

"I've come home, Papa."

"We're glad to have you, Daughter," was all Nick Hastings replied.

He did not ask any questions, only told the strangely quiet Mama to make bed room for them. At breakfast the following morning, Papa quietly asked,

"Tell me the trouble, Sister."

Zueline burst into tears, but got through her story. Her father listened silently, and when the weeping saga was over, he looked long and thoughtfully at his oldest daughter. Reaching over, he patted her hand, nervously working at her fork.

"Go home, Zueline. Your place is with Acie. He's trying to be a man. A hard enough job without his wife fighting him."

"But Papa . . . ," Zueline began.

"Nick . . . ," Mama leaned forward.

"Annie," Papa interrupted, "a woman can't pull against her husband. Acie is a good man. He hasn't hurt Sister or the children."

"I've always told my girls they could always come home, that they always have a home here," Mama protested.

"And they do if they don't have a home with their husbands. Sister has a home. She made her bed with Acie. Now she's got to lie in it. He's a good man." He turned to his quiet, chastened daughter, "Go home, honey. It'll be all right. Get ready, I'll take you."

Mama, beginning to clear the table, said no more. Anyway, her heart was not in the argument. It was disgraceful to have a separated daughter, especially one with children. A widowed daughter coming home was sad, but morally acceptable; but a girl returning to the paternal shelter from a broken marriage was a pure disgrace, and it reflected on the mother as well as the whole family. Above all, it lessened the chances of younger daughters making successful marriages. Every woman had to bear some discomforts and to look the other way in a marriage, it was the woman's cross; they could not come running home at every little upset.

Nick took Zueline and her children back across the field as the sun was rising. Acie met them in the yard.

"Sister has come home, Acie," Papa informed his son-in-law.

"Thank you, sir," replied Acie.

Papa turned, saying over his shoulder, "I'll be close around the house today if you want to talk, Son." And he went slowly, whistling a tuneless ditty, back across the well-traveled path to his house.

All was not well in the little house for several days, with Acie sleeping in Christine's bed while the child slept with her little sisters. But one morning Acie was back in his wife's bed, and that was that; with his little family united, he prepared to launch out on his own, a move he was never to regret through all the hard time ahead.

9

The Storm

During the next ten years Acie moved his family seven times, living in six different houses, and though none even approached the luxurious though faded splendor of the Strother place, their next home, the Parkman place, was preferable to the little three-room house they had left. On the first night in the new house, Christine lay in bed, watching the dying fire, and felt happy to be in a nice big room again.

The place served Acie's purposes in several ways, and though he wished it had been farther away from Papa's than the scant mile, it would keep Zueline at home more, and it gave him some land to farm on his own. Amos, his wife, Mattie, and their four children, the oldest of whom was only five years old, moved into the house with them. The two men worked during the day on a government economic recovery project—the WPA—improving and maintaining the local roads, and worked in the evenings and on Saturdays farming their land. Nobody, of course, worked on Sunday.

The country's economy reached its lowest ebb; it was a hand-to-mouth existence. And some did not make it. In increasing numbers, wagons, carrying a few precious pieces of salvaged belongings, slowly passed along the road. The occupants of these ponderous vehicles looked neither right nor left, keeping heads bent and eyes downcast; and the occupants of the houses they passed grew strangely quiet, peeking out secretly from behind drawn curtains. They were on their way to the Poor House, a government-supported institution that took in those who had lost everything—

job, land, home, hope—and who without help faced starvation. The nightmare of the Poor House, surmounting even the crushing indignity of survival by charity, was the breaking up of families. It accepted only adult individuals. Husbands and wives did not share common sleeping quarters, and since their days were spent performing assigned chores, the only opportunity for even talking with each other came at mealtime, which was shared with all the other occupants of the institution. And, inconceivable horror, the Poor House did not take children—they had to be put in an orphanage. Little wonder, then, that families rejected this move until every avenue had been exhausted and until their spirits as well as their bodies were weakened beyond resistance.

Christine had heard her parents talking about people who had been forced to go to the Poor House, and it was her constant dread that they would meet the same fate. For the first time she met, in her new community and her new school, people whose circumstances were more difficult than hers, and she experienced her first compassion, often trading the tasty fatback biscuits from her own lunch for the cold, slick-grease biscuits that others had brought. It was at about this time also that she began to be aware of how she looked. From her earliest memory she had known that she was ugly, had heard people say so; but her mother's response to the criticism—"A mother loves an ugly child, because they need it most"—had made her almost glad to be ugly. And what *was* ugly, anyway? A comment by Mama one day, "Sister, that young'un's freckles get uglier every day!" sent Christine to the mirror, finally, to examine just what it was that made her ugly, made her different.

Never having been a graceful, rounded child, Christine had lately entered a devastatingly awkward stage, becoming, seemingly overnight, all skinny arms and legs, with large, clumsy hands and feet. Her father came home once from a trip to town where he had tried to buy her a pair of shoes, declaring in disgust that the next time he would throw away the shoes and put the box on her. She had not seemed to mind being compared unfavorably with her pretty little sisters and her prissy little cousin Elen; and until now her appearance had been of little concern to her. Who can say whether it is psychology or biology that dictates that moment when a female glances into the mirror and pauses, the glance turning into a gaze, seeing her face for the first time as either a help or a hindrance to her dreams for her future. And what did Christine see when she finally gazed into the mirror? It was a prejudiced look, of course, having absorbed the label of "ugly" long before the meaning of the term had registered.

She saw freckles—large, brown, irregular spots of the mature variety, generously interspersed with the pinpoints of new growth—and they were everywhere, on her nose, forehead, cheeks; her whole face was a brown-on-white polka-dotted pattern. Why had she never seen them before? At first nothing was in focus except the freckles; then the whole countenance cleared: The dark brown hair sat messily on the large square head like a lopsided wicker bowl, with its badly woven strands loosened and pointing off wildly; the milk-white skin gleamed brightly through its curdled, separated tan; the huge blue eyes, completely dominating the entire visage, resembled sapphires tossed carelessly upon a mound of casually strewn, rough, brown pebbles; the mouth, a wide full slash across the spotted face, revealed large white irregular teeth, pushing and crowding for space in an area improperly designed for them; the soft, round nose, difficult to differentiate out of the speckled surface, appeared more tone on tone than an elevated promontory; and the head itself, exhibiting a minor miracle by balancing its weight on the incredibly slim stem of a neck, was all bony angles and plains under its outrageous skullcap.

Pain filled her, cramping her stomach, closing her throat, blurring her vision. When the swirling mirror settled and the reflected image sharpened, with, unhappily, not one freckle diminished, Christine had accepted her ugliness—she now knew well what "ugly" meant. For the remainder of her adolescence and for a large share of her adulthood, she was the Freckle girl; and even when the hated spots began to fade and miraculously disappeared, they simply went inside, permanently spotting and uglying her soul.

Living constantly with the overshadowing idea of her disfigurement, she was often deeply hurt by thoughtless teasing; and in all fairness to these unaware tormentors, the freckles were unusually spectacular—a bumper crop. But to Christine it was no laughing matter, and on being kiddingly informed that freckles could be washed off with stump water, her search for this scarce commodity was on. Fortunately, the Parkman place had a large pasture from which many trees had been removed to allow more grazing space, and Christine became personally familiar with every one of their slowly rotting stumps. She inspected them regularly, even in dry spells, just in case of a miracle; but after each shower, she hurried out, often in the final drizzle, and usually dragging Becky and Tiny with her, in the vain hope of discovering a magic puddle languishing airily on the porous old splinters. One could as soon catch water in a sieve. Notable, even on perfunctory perusal of these magic remedies, is their common elusiveness, their quality of unattainableness that not only forever leads on the desperate searcher but also renders impossible the collection of any observable data concerning the claims of their potency.

Christine, as most seekers after miracle cures, tirelessly pursued it simply because she had no alternatives; and this new awareness of self sharpened her awareness of others. Even the short mile of separation from Mama caused enough isolation to permit the small family to become more familiar with each other and to begin to function as a unit, instead of as an adjunct to the larger family. Though trudging the dusty distance often, Zueline could not possibly walk that far daily and still run her house. It was a help to have her younger sister-in-law, Mattie, sharing the house with her; and the two women, both nonaggressive by nature, got along well and did most of their chores together.

Ten-year-old Christine, for the first time in her life, had definite responsibilities required of her; and though protesting mightily, each Saturday morning she swept the packed clay yards clean of debris with her willow brushbroom, while Becky and Tiny carried in the wood for the big iron cookstove. Christine was also required to help her mother with the ironing. Zueline, who had always done her washing with Mama, now had, at Acie's insistence, a washerwoman—a Negro woman who did Zueline's wash, along with her own family's, down at the spring. It was Zueline's one luxury, and one that Acie had promised her long ago when they were first married; but she still had to do her own ironing. She and Christine ironed on the dining room table, building a fire in the fireplace to heat the heavy metal irons.

The irons were removed from the fireplace—using a folded cloth to protect the hand—and tested for heat by barely touching a spit-dampened finger to the smooth bottom. The sooty bottom of the iron was rubbed vigorously on a badly scorched cloth, kept for that purpose, then the first application was tentatively made, as the iron was often too hot and would produce a permanent brown scorch if placed too solidly on the material; and soon as it cooled sufficiently to smooth out the wrinkles without burning, it became too cool to do its job without extreme pressure. There was only, then, a minute or two when conditions were ideal for a successful operation; and then the cooled iron was replaced on the coals, a hot one removed, and the process begun all over again.

Zueline and Christine folded the bedsheets into quarters and stretched them over the table as a pad on which to iron. It was a hated chore for the girl, and one that she strived mightily to avoid. One day when she was standing at the table meticulously weaving the heavy iron in and out, poking its sharp little nose into corners and crevices, the pattern on the wrinkled garment blurred and faded, making her slightly sick to the stomach. Shortly, all cleared, and she happily began to sing. Her mother, busy on the other side of the table, looked up in astonishment at her joyous child, so lately sullen and quiet; but she did not question this abrupt radical mood change, she was only pleased that Christine was finally accepting responsibility. A closer observation would have disclosed that something more radical than a mood change had occurred: The child, loudly singing and apparently oblivious of all else except her work, was, while keeping a wary eye on her mother, folding the wrinkled clothes the size for storing, and ironing only the outside. Zueline often had to iron over many of the clothes, and she was never able to understand how it happened. She only knew that sometimes Christine liked to iron, and that sometimes she hated it; that sometimes she did an excellent job, and that sometimes the work had to be done over. This inconsistency confused the mother's ability to form any pattern from the erratic behavior.

Mother and daughter, during this time, however, did grow close. Zueline, always the champion of the underdog and the downtrodden, felt a deep compassion for this strange child of hers, often telling her that she was pretty, and especially praising her large blue eyes. Others also complimented Christine's eyes, and she grew very vain about them, feeling that they were the only feature of merit that she possessed. Often when teased about her freckles or skinny legs or rowdy hair, she would feel faint, her sight blurring; and when the spell passed, her eyes would be stretched wide and staring, painfully so. Even though others commented on this strange gesture, and her parents reprimanded her and ordered her to "stop stretching your eyes that way!" she would continue for hours or even days to practice this disconcerting facial tic.

Zueline made her a dress with several rows of elastic sewn in at the waistline. It was beautiful, accentuating the tiny waist while disguising the skinniness and complementing the very special blue of her spectacular eyes. As she stood at the mirror admiring the dress, her gaze fell on the awful spotted face, and a slight nausea swept over her, causing her eyes to close. When they again opened, they were wide and staring and the face was contorted with fury.

"Why did *she* get this dress," she seethed, "it matches *my* eyes." And she began to rip and tear at the snug midsection with its beautiful elastic shearing.

Becky and Tiny, admiring the dress with her, were horrified and called frantically,

"Mother, Mother, come here, come here quick! Teeny is tearing up her dress!"

Zueline, running into the room, viewed the scene in disbelief: Becky and Tiny crying in unnamed fear; Christine, eyes bulging and hateful, bearing down on her cowering sisters; and the new, painstakingly sewn dress hanging in shreds from the trembling, staring figure.

Into the tense air Christine shouted,

"They did it, Mother, they tore my dress. Becky and Tiny tore my dress!"

"Christine!" Zueline grabbed her daughter, now grown almost as tall as she, and shook her. "Stop that; stop that right now!"

The change was startling: The eyes stopped staring and narrowed, the shoulders drooped and calmed, and the face, taking on a puzzled look, turned down to the wreck of the lovely dress.

"Mother," she whispered, "what happened?" Looking at her mother, she saw in the furious face the answer to her question.

"I didn't do it, Mother," she protested, as if to ward off accusation, but to no avail.

Zueline, hurt because her loving gift had been spurned and mutilated, and because she simply could not deal with this violence other than physically, whipped Christine on the unprotected thighs with her own bare hand, sustaining as much bodily hurt as the child and perhaps just as much mental pain. Neither understood the actions of the other, and each was hurt by the behavior of the other. Impasse!

A freckle girl, a singing girl, a big-eyed girl! They came and they went. I remember them. It's all kind of vague, but I distinctly remember them. It was the first time that any of them were aware that there were others like them. That ugly freckled girl came most of the time, and she didn't know about the others; but she always got the blame for all the bad things they did. And I'm not so sure they knew about each other, but they sure knew about her. She was such a timid, backward little soul, what did I need her for? If these people came to do what I couldn't do, what did I need her for? She couldn't do anything! She was always there when one of the others came, and then when the other one left she would come back and not know what had happened. Where was I all this time? If the big-eyed and singing girls each came from the freckle girl and then she back from them, then where was I? Where was I? I don't remember me! Let me think. When was the last time I remember me—Chris? There has always been an ugly one, and a naughty one, and one who got the blame for everything; they were not the same ones, they grew and changed, changed in appearance and in actions, so I know they were not the same ones. But where was I—Chris—or was I one of them and just can't remember so far back? That must be it. If they came to help me, or if, as everybody says, I made them come—then I was there! Of course I was there; how could I remember all this if I weren't there? It's just too long ago; I'll find it all out later, closer to the present when I can remember better. Let me think: There were some bad times at that place. . . .

Christine lived in a nightmare world of shock and surprise, and only youth and its resiliency saved her from slipping into a psychotic fantasy from which there is no return. She once awakened to find herself high in a stacked pile of lumber, and having an irrational fear of heights, she could only hang on and scream hysterically until her little sisters found her and helped her down. She knew she had not climbed up there, would never climb up that high. She had also on occasion become conscious to find herself leaning precariously over water, gripped in the paralyzing clutch of terror, unable to move back, being pulled into the black, murky depths. So a new fear was born: that of waking to find that the horror of the nightmare had moved boldly into the waking world.

Her little sisters, her constant companions, were beginning to develop definite personality traits of their own. And they were startlingly different! It was disconcerting to observe two little girls so amazingly alike physically but who behaved so radically differently. Tiny was fiery, aggressive, and selfish—demanding her own way without giving quarter or compromising; Becky was generous, passive, and kind—fearing always to cross her twin and incur her vindictive wrath. When the three girls played together, Becky was actually physically afraid of her sisters; and being unable to take her part and defend herself, she was always the butt of their jokes and the victim of their schemes. At their bidding, she once climbed onto a sapling that they all three had bent over to the ground. When they turned loose, the tree sprang back, flinging the terrified child high into the air, to land with a dull thud on her back. Ribs must have been fractured, for she experienced sharp stabs and painful breathing for several weeks, often crying quietly in the night. Her frightened sisters, thinking only of themselves, pounded breath back into her gasping figure, brushed her off, and threatened to cut her throat if she told of her experience. This often-used threat appeared to have been unusually effective.

Sometimes their schemes grew so complicated that adult help became necessary, and then retribution was swift. Tying hapless Becky to the back of the gentle cow, they drove her into the marshy stream, where she became stuck in the mud. Unable to free the animal, they ran to get their father, leaving their paralyzed sister glued to the lowing, terrified cow. Acie was forced to borrow a neighbor's truck to pull the balked cow, still carrying poor Becky on her bony back, from the black, sticky mud. Exasperated, Acie whipped all three children, never suspecting that unprotesting Becky was as innocent a victim as the poor cow and not one of the conspirators.

Occasionally even Becky's placid nature was tried beyond endurance, causing her to strike out in self-defense; but she did this so seldom that it was never a deterrent to the overbearing behavior of her aggressive twin. When separate chores were assigned to them, it was Tiny's practice to ignore her task and "help" Becky with hers, with, of course, Becky doing all the work; then she would demand that Becky help her, again with Becky doing all the work. Gentle Becky's mild protest was always roughly overridden by her domineering mirror image.

Thus deserting her own work, Tiny once generously offered to her sister, who was industriously feeding the pig,

"I help *you*, Becky."

"Don't help me, Tiny," pleaded the gentle child, her soulful eyes wide and sorrowful. "Please, don't help me, Tiny."

Unheeding, Tiny took over and began to spill her sister's carefully distributed table scraps, boasting her generosity,

"I help you, Becky!"

Becky, violent as only the placid can be when harassed beyond endurance, picked up an iron bar leaning against the pigpen and, her actions as calm as her words had been, struck her bossy sister on the head, laying her out neat and cold on the trampled ground.

And the scene froze: one form holding aloft the avenging weapon; an identical form lying bleeding upon the ground. To a chance observer, it would have appeared that the calm, sad-eyed child was both the slayer and the slain, both standing upright as the conqueror, and lying, bleeding and vanquished, upon the ground.

Christine, the thunderstruck bystander, began to dance around this awesome diorama,

"I knew you was gonna git it, Tiny! I knew you was gonna git it!" she excitedly told the unheeding, prostrate child. "I just knew Becky was gonna git you. I knew it was comin'!"

Zueline ran from the house, and seeing Tiny rising slowly from the ground, bright red blood mixing colorfully with the black mud from the pigpen, threw her hands over her face and ran screaming back into the house, asking the Almighty to reveal that which she could not bear to view,

"Oh, Lordy, what has happened? Oh, dear Jesus, what happened?"

Acie, arriving opportunely, determined that the blow had not been fatal, but Tiny carried for life a small scar reminding her that the meek can, on occasion, be mighty. Strangely, Becky was not punished, perhaps because her only defense on being questioned was,

"Because I loved her so much! I hit Tiny because I loved her so much."

Becky was not completely downtrodden, and she cleverly learned to turn her scapegoat status to her own advantage. When their father bought them candy, he always had it put in three separate sacks, so that each received a gift of his own and did not have to share. Becky, often called "pig" by her sisters because of her hearty appetite, hurriedly ate her candy, then dropped to all fours and promised to grunt like a pig for pieces of their candy. By this ruse, she consumed most of the sweets from the other two sacks, too, while her unwary sisters, never realizing that they were being duped, laughed at the funny "pig" and gave it pieces of "corn."

The twins, despite their different temperaments, were inseparable, a fact that constantly isolated Christine. They looked alike, were never alone, always had somebody, and never seemed to resent being twins; Christine was always the outsider, the different one, always alone. Zueline, never a strict, consistent disciplinarian, seemed particularly unable to train her younger daughters, never feeling confident that her word alone was enough authority to back up her commands to them. To prevent their slipping away from home and running to Mama's, she told them that there was a troll under the bridge that they had to cross on the way. They often went down to the bridge, and, fearful of actually crossing, discussed the troll from a safe distance, speculating on his size, whether he could hear them talking, and when he was liable to be asleep. In her indulgence, she allowed the babies to nurse bottles until they had turned five years old. She put nipples on Coke bottles filled with milk, all the while warning them that ole man Joe Clark—a queer old man who walked along the road picking up sticks and putting them in a burlap sack—would get the bottles if they nursed them. When he came along, Christine would run to find them, yelling,

"Hide your bottles! Hide your bottles! Here comes ole man Joe Clark! Here he comes!"

And the twins would run and hide their bottles in the flour barrel until the danger passed. Finally, through their own inclinations, backed up by little parental pressure, they put aside their nursing, a practice that they had been allowed to continue long after its practical value simply because there were two of them and it was amusing to watch them suck on their bottles.

Their mother's placid gentleness did not stop with her children; it enfolded all, especially unfortunate animals. She took in a three-legged dog, bound his wounds, and nursed him back to health; she mothered a crippled goose, which they were all unable to eat when, roasted and savory, he was placed on the table before them; when her pet pig scratched on the door in cold weather, she admitted him to sleep in the pantry; and she was always watching bird nests and putting back babies when they ventured out too early.

When playing games with her children, she loved most of all simply being another child with them. Zueline dearly loved her children and was showing her love the best she knew how, by denying them almost nothing that was in her power to give. Perhaps she was trying to compensate them for the sore privations of the times into which she had borne them.

Pneumonia! It was a dread word that evoked helpless fear—a terrible plague, which decimated many families and left almost none unscathed. Christine came down with it first, and though very ill, she was unaware of her danger and the seriousness of her condition. As she passed her crisis and began to slowly mend, Mama's youngest son, Ernest, just eighteen years old, fell quickly and desperately smitten by the ravishing, stifling lung congestion. Unable to find a job and wanting to be independent and self-supporting, especially since he was newly in love, he had pleaded with his parents to allow him to join the CCC, a government conservation corps. Mama held out to the very end, declaring that no son of hers would ever have to accept charity from the government. She was partly won over and persuaded by Mamie Lee, who, drawing on her own husband's successful military career—which was, after all, sort of government work—explained to Mama that "it would be the making of Bubba." As it turned out it was a persuasion that Mamie Lee was later to regret and for which Mama never forgave her.

Ernest joined the Civilian Conservation Corps and served only two short weeks. He came home the first weekend, handsome and proud in his new khaki uniform, brought his girlfriend home to Sunday dinner, and posed for pictures with her and his admiring sisters. The following weekend he was taken to the hospital, semiconscious and in a raging fever. Having been caught out while working in a drenching downpour of rain, he had, for some unexplained reason, gone back to his bunk and fallen asleep in his wet clothes—soaked to the skin. When he awoke, he was already feverish and in the grips of the disease, which moved and consumed him with incredible swiftness. Was it this particular set of circumstances that brought on the illness, or was he already weak and sick—a possible explanation for his failure to properly care for himself—and the drenching just hastened his condition? Who can say? But Mama declared, to the end of her days, that the CCC killed Ernest, and that if she had not listened to others and let them persuade her, "Bubba would be alive today."

All known remedies were applied, but all was in vain, and his end was horrible. Fortunately, he died quickly; but his stricken relatives were long to hear his tortured hiccups—each followed by a groan and a labored breath echoing through the hollows of their souls. He died on the first day Christine was allowed out of bed after her own three-week bout. She first knew something was wrong when she heard her mother scream,

"No, no, don't tell me that! Don't tell me that! Don't tell me Ernest is dead! Oh, no, he can't be dead, he's too young to die!" And throwing her hands over her face, she wept loud and hysterically.

Christine, coming into the hallway from her bedroom, heard the word "dead." Bubba was dead! Death meant darkness and being shut up in a box. Bubba had pneumonia, and she had pneumonia. If Bubba was too young to die, she was even younger, lots younger. And he was so much bigger and stronger than she. If the blackness had gotten him, it would surely get her, too. Suddenly, the world turned black and her breath shortened; the floor flew up and struck her in the face.

Acie, hearing the sound of her fall, turned from his distraught wife and, lifting his unconscious child from the floor, placed her back on her bed. When she shortly regained consciousness, she was blind, totally blind. Her parents did not know that the wide, staring blue eyes were also sightless; they merely thought that she had undergone a relapse and that she was again practicing her disconcerting but harmless habit of stretching her eyes. She lay in bed thinking "so this is death," and wondering when it would finish and she would be put in a box.

Her parents, unaware of her torment, took up the thread of their own thoughts. Zueline wept,

"Why did he have to die? He was too young to die."

"Honey, you knew he might die," Acie reminded her. "We've all talked about it. He was so sick, he couldn't get well."

"But he was so young. Ernest was so young to die," Zueline moaned, thinking of the Bubba she had held and cared for as a baby.

"Now, Mother, now, now," Acie soothed. "We had to expect this. They just don't make it with pneumonia." He put his large, rough hand on her shaking shoulder.

Each word more firmly convinced Christine of her own fate. And then she heard something that momentarily encouraged her. Zueline in her deep distress took comfort in one of her platitudes,

"Well, the Lord always takes the good and the best, to show the rest."

The child, blind, grasping for straws, thought,

"Maybe I have a chance. Because I'm not good, I'm not the best. Maybe the Lord won't want me." But she couldn't hold onto even this slim hope. After all, it was not the Lord who was going to get her—it was pneumonia.

Her fright was indescribably deadening, and no one knew, for in the understandable confusion over her uncle's death, she was not closely watched for the next few days. Cousin Georgia Smith, the wife of one of Mama's cousins, came and sat with her during the funeral period. Kept in bed, her sight did return, but her frightful wait for death did not stop. Never having seen Bubba dead and not being able to attend his funeral, he had, for her, simply and abruptly dropped from sight. Was that how it would happen to her? She waited, sure of everything except the moment it would strike.

The blind girl! That's the first time she came! But why did she come? Death was just as fearful for her as it was for the freckle girl. And she looked just like the big-eyed girl, only she couldn't see. That doesn't make any sense at all—if they came to do what I couldn't do, what purpose did she serve—what did she do that I couldn't do? And where was I? I'm still not there. Could I have been the freckle girl? Maybe that's who I was, and she was not one of them, but was me. I did have freckles, but then my eyes are blue, too, and I certainly was not the big-eyed girl! Oh, I don't know! How will I ever figure it out?

Even though her strength returned and she left her bed, Christine was unaware that she had recovered from pneumonia. She did not know that she was well, that it was over. She had pneumonia, a static condition, and it was only a matter of time until she died with it. This thinking might have faded, as many childhood misconceptions do, if several incidents had not occurred that supported her thinking. Their cat died, and when she asked her mother if it had had pneumonia, and Zueline absently replied that it was possible, Christine's dread grew. When Becky fell ill and was put to bed with labored breathing and croupy cough, Christine was sure that pneumonia had come to claim another victim. A strange incident then occurred that was marveled at but was never satisfactorily explained: Christine had a dream—she was running down the green hill in the pasture, and when she turned at the bottom to climb up again, Jesus, dressed in a long, flowing white robe, was standing at the top. He spoke,

"My child, your sister has diphtheria, not pneumonia. Go and tell your mother."

The next morning, Christine described her dream to her parents. They knew that Becky's symptoms were not those of pneumonia, but they had assumed that she simply had a deep chest cold and a bad case of croup. Zueline, especially, believed in omens, and fear struck deep in her heart that this dream was a sign being given to them; she dared not ignore it, and pled,

175

"Acie, maybe it's a sign. She's very sick. Let's send for the doctor."

"Now, Sister, Top's just had a bad dream. You know how she is." And he spoke to his oldest daughter,

"Now, Daughter, where did you hear about diphtheria? Who told you about it? Did you hear it in school?"

"Jesus told me, Daddy. He came to me in a dream and told me," Christine confidently repeated her story.

"Oh, honey," Zueline said, "go for Dr. Dunovant. It's true, I just know it's true! Sometimes Jesus tells us things in strange ways." And Zueline wrung her hands in the face of this strange happening.

Acie, skeptical but unsure, and as much to please his wife as to allay his own fears, did not go to work that day, but instead went for Dr. Dunovant. Only a brief examination was necessary for the doctor to make his diagnosis: It was diphtheria! His quick action likely saved the child's life. The closest medication was in Columbia, over fifty miles away, and dispatching a courier immediately to bring back the life-saving drug, he began the prescribed treatment while anxious relatives watched over the desperately ill child. The story of Christine's miraculous dream spread over the neighborhood, and speculation grew that perhaps she had strange powers. Cults have sprung up and flourished on just such events, and had the child repeated her performance, a similar group might have formed around her. It was a time of destitution, when people were grasping for any straws, no matter how flimsy, to prove that life could be better, even if only in the life hereafter. The only group that gathered, however, was a delegation from the Holiness Church down the road, which came nightly to pray over the sick child, beseeching,

"Spare this little child's life, oh, Almighty God!"

Christine was sure that Becky was going to die, and Christine was horribly afraid; not so much for her sister's danger, but because it reinforced her own. But Becky did not die! Christine was confused, but only briefly, until the simple truth dawned on her: Of course, Becky did not die, she only had diphtheria, not pneumonia! It was pneumonia that made you die!

Positive, irrefutable proof was awaiting. Within weeks, her Aunt Mattie, living in the very house with her, was struck down by the dread killer and died! Christine, helplessly resigned, waited for the end, but this time a new dimension was added: She was in close proximity and privy to the whole horrible process. Mattie and Amos occupied the front room, the original sitting room, which was next door to Acie and Zueline's bedroom. Zueline had earlier discovered an eye-level knothole in the common wall and had hung a picture over it for privacy; but it is a widely known fact that the dying and the dead have lost the luxury of privacy, so Zueline, her childlike curiosity not to be denied, utilized the little peephole and observed her sister-in-law's demise. The imagined is always more vivid than the real, and that which is inferred from the description of others is always more distorted by the imagination than that which is actually seen. Christine, watching her mother observe the scenes in the death room, hearing her altered breath, seeing her dilated eyes squeeze out the horror, noticing how she covered the hole to deny inconceivable views, was suffusing her being with sensations of death that transcended in horror anything that reality could conjure up.

Finally, Zueline dropped the picture over the hole and announced,

"It is over. She is dead."

Immediately, Christine heard Uncle Amos begin to scream,

"No, no! What will my little children do? What will I do?"

Dr. Dunovant gave him a sedative—gave him a brief moment to sleep, to knit up the raveled sleeve of care—and drove away.

For Mattie, the essence of Mattie, it was over; there was left only for her grieving relatives to play out their prescribed roles in the funeral ritual. But first, the perishable mortal remains must be prepared. To most this is a hazy process, an unknown procedure—best left unexplained and unexplored—necessary, like body eliminations, but best left unobserved and unmentioned.

Not so for Christine. She had no choice; the grisly details were forced upon her. Mattie's body was prepared at home, in the same room in which she died. The undertakers came. Backing their long, black vehicle up to the front porch, they removed from its rear doors a long, light blue box, unmistakable in its purpose and for which Christine had been waiting. Strangely, though, they also removed four square galvanized containers, and took them along with the coffin into the death room at the front of the house. The child, searching for her mother to ask about the odd tubs, found her on station at the peephole.

And Zueline, watched intently by her daughter, closely observed the embalming, or as much of it as she could bear to see. Now, to Christine's sensations of death fed by sight, were added the imagined horror of sounds reaching the ears when there is only the reflected horror on another's face to guide the pictures forming in the roiling brain. The gurgling, the splashing, the dripping; the scraping, the clinking, the brushing; the identifiable creaking of bedsprings, the grunts of heavy lifting, the shuffling of feet moving laboriously over wooden flooring. The scene reflected on Christine's mind's eye would have been infinitely better had it been her own horrified eye at the knothole.

When Christine next entered the room at the front of the house, her feet dragged and her heart pounded with fear. The coffin was resting on shiny metal legs at the front of the room by the double windows. The shades and curtains were drawn and the room was dim, lit only by two strange lights, wavering and flickering at each end of the coffin. The lid on the fuzzy blue box was now open, and Christine dreaded to view its contents. What had they done to Aunt Mattie? What would she look like? The child's reluctant gaze, surprisingly, fell on beauty, luxurious beauty such as she had never seen before. Mattie was dressed in a beige silk shroud—the finest garment she had ever worn—and in her hand was a rose made of the same shiny fabric. She was dressed up! This intrigued Christine, who had never seen her aunt so dressed up, had never seen anyone so dressed up. Did one dress up for death? This fact so impressed her that years later, when she attempted to force death to come for her, she dressed up for the occasion.

The house was full of people and awake all night; relatives came and went. Only the displayed Mattie was immobile, quiet. The next day, when her box was closed and she was taken from the house to travel to her final resting place, Christine was watching the process from a vantage seat on the porch bench. She was all freshly scrubbed and dressed, her short hair neatly tucked behind her ears and her white Mary Jane shoes, from which thin turn-down anklets barely protruded, were newly polished. She was dressed in a white skirt and purple blouse—white and purple being, along with black, the mourning colors. As she watched the large blue box being carefully placed in the snug opening at the back of the hearse, she suddenly saw a tiny white box lying on the back seat of a small car. Her head began to ache and her thin body shuddered violently in the warm sun. This condition quickly passed—the pain and shaking ceased—and with it also passed her fear and dread. She even began to hum her favorite tune, "Barbara Allen," which was abruptly cut off by a thunderous look from her father. And the fear—the unreasoning, consuming fear—did not return. All through the funeral and through her lifetime, the fear, in those tremendous, overpowering proportions, did not return. She worried about dying and feared death, but it never again surfaced to dominate her conscious thoughts.

That was definitely one of them who came. But which one? She hummed a tune and was not afraid; she must have been the singing girl. But who was there before her? If I think hard enough, it all comes back—in pictures, colored pictures. Sitting there in the sun, I can see her freckles; they look like brown measles. She was the freckle girl. But she wasn't afraid of Aunt Mattie, she wasn't afraid to look at her. Why did someone need to come? And why did I see that little white coffin after all those years? Junior's little coffin? Was it simply the old fear of death—death in the abstract? Pictures that could not be blotted out by going blind, but had to be blotted out by going away? But the freckle girl was not back there when Junior died. How would she know about the little white coffin? And where am I? Was it not I who saw the white coffin so many years ago? That happened when I was only ten months old! There were no others then, only me—Chris. If that's true, then how could she, the freckle girl, remember what I saw? Oh, I'm so confused. Am I the freckle girl? But I can't be, she came, I didn't come, I was always there. Then why can't I separate myself out—feel myself? It's just not time for that yet; it will all fall into place; I'll work it all out.

"Christine has fainting spells."
This became Zueline's answer to all queries concerning her child's strange behavior, and it effectively stemmed the flow of

questions from all but the most aggressive of the curious. People just did not question the delicate health, especially the fainting variety, of females twelve years of age and over. And Christine's fainting was of the respectable kind—she just quietly fell over onto the floor, with no embarrassing twitching, groaning, or foaming at the mouth. Most assumed, and her mother desperately hoped, that it was all just a forerunner of the girl's "difficult time of the month." Who can say? Christine's time of the month was always extremely difficult, and it was dangerously late in its onslaught—she was more than fifteen when menarche commenced. Perhaps this extended chemical struggle of the developing body nurtured the mental struggle of a mind striving to mature. Or the reverse? How closely are the physical and the psychological bound? How much control does mind exercise over matter?

And how much do stability and security—a feeling of permanence and belonging—have on these maturation processes? Within the next year Acie, who had finally secured a real job, with the Edgefield County Highway Department, moved his family three times, the last time into the County Home. When Christine heard talk of this last move, her constant nameless fear crystallized: The County Home was the Poor House! She was unaware that the government had taken a giant step in its treatment of its lame, its halt, and its poor—a step that only history can label as either progressive or regressive—by pensioning them a welfare subsistence instead of committing them to a custodial institution. The Poor House inmates had been set free with their welfare checks, and the building was now used as housing for needy county employees. Acie, now entitled to this fringe benefit as a member of the road crew, took the first available space open to him, an apartment in the right wing of the low, sprawling, red-brick County Home.

Christine's spells came regularly now, and a new dimension had been added: the headache. A violent headache, ripping and tearing, blotting out everything but the rhythmic waves of pain, usually heralded a fainting spell. And more and more often now, blindness, total and extended, accompanied and followed the attacks, which predictably could be triggered by almost any abrupt change in the normal routine. Acie was brought home one day from work desperately ill, and carried into the house by three of his fellow workers. At first, Christine, seeing his lifeless, ashen face, thought he was dead; then a slight moan escaped his purple lips.

"He has ptomaine poisoning, Miz Costner," said one of the men. "Doc Dunovant is comin' along right behind us."

Zueline put her hands over her face and began to cry. "Oh, Lordy, what will I do? Acie, honey, speak to me." And she took her husband's limp head, holding it to her flushed cheek.

Christine, who had been frying fatback for supper, had not moved or spoken during the whole dramatic scene that had played out before her. The freckles on her white face, blanched by shock, stood out like so many copper pennies. Suddenly the blue eyes widened and bulged painfully, she gasped out, and she put both hands up to her head, pressing the splitting temples. Almost in slow motion, the staring, sightless eyes closed, the pulseless hands dropped limply—one splashing through the hot grease—the knees buckled, and she thudded to the kitchen floor. Zueline found her when the doctor cleared Acie's room, and thinking that she had fainted when she burned her hand, was unaware that she was also blind. Zueline bandaged the hand and asked the doctor to look in on Christine before he left. Acie recovered, but Christine's sight did not return until he was out of danger.

Zueline and Christine often did household chores together while the twins played outside. Hearing a piercing scream one afternoon, they ran out into the yard to find Tiny laying in a pitifully small crumpled heap under the tall peach tree. Her right arm and shoulder lay at an odd angle to her body, and between the elbow and the shoulder a milky white splinter of bone protruded from a slowly welling puddle of blood.

Zueline gave voice to her own piercing scream, holding strangely the same note of terror as had Tiny's, and throwing her hands over her contorted face, she ran from the yard crying,

"Oh, Lordy, dear Jesus! What am I going to do? Help me, Jesus."

Christine was alone. Tiny was helpless, whimpering Becky was too young, Zueline—an eternally frightened child herself—was gone. Christine looked down at the arm, the bloody arm—another bloody arm—and nothing happened! She gently picked up the injured child and, followed by weeping Becky, who kept repeating,

"I help you, Tiny," carried her into the house, placing her on the low green bed. Seeing that the twisted arm would not lie straight on the bed, she laid the child near the edge so that the broken member could hang off and rest on a pillow placed beneath it on the floor.

Zueline had not run away to hide, she had run away to get help. She had gone to fetch May Burnett, Acie's second cousin, who lived across the road; and Zueline returned on the run with this debatable help in tow. Numbers was Zueline's great need. Always having been surrounded by her large family, the thought of facing adversity alone completely unnerved her. The other woman's presence and her advice to take Tiny to the hospital immediately, calmed Zueline, who routinely began to clean up the injured child for her trip. Mrs. Burnett returned home and sent her husband for Acie, and the hospital party calmly set out on its journey. It was then and only then, after the danger had passed and had been resolved largely through her own efficient efforts, that Christine reacted. As the car drove away, she felt nauseous, faint, and her head ached. Suddenly, to the pleased surprise of Becky, who was still concerned about Tiny and was newly upset at being left behind, Christine began to sing and suggested that they go out and play in the large clover bed at the side of the house. She seemed scarcely to remember Tiny's accident, and she certainly was not worried about her.

The singing girl! But that's strange! Why did she wait until the excitement was all over before she came? And why was the freckle girl so calm and unafraid? Why didn't the singing girl come as soon as the freckle girl saw that awful arm? If she didn't come then, why did she come at all? The freckle girl was always calm and dependable—she just couldn't bear bad things —whereas the singing girl just didn't care about anything—and she certainly was not dependable. If she had come out at the first, she just likely would have gone off to play, leaving poor Tiny to lie there on the ground. Mother was certainly no help, but then she never was when something like that happened. And Tiny desperately needed help. If the freckle girl had not stayed to help, what would have happened?

Is that the reason she stayed? But I didn't think it worked like that, and the freckle girl didn't know about the other two. So how could she just decide to stay? And where was I? I still can't find me during any of this time! If these people were supposed to come to help me, how could they if I weren't there? And I'm told that I did it myself, that I made them come. How could I make them come if I was not there? But that doesn't make sense; I had to be there. How could I know all this, remember all this, if I weren't there? I seem to be getting more confused the more I try to think it through. I wish I had never started this. But this is silly. Of course I want to know the truth. Other people know what they did and where they were. I will sort all this out. I will!

After the demise of Tippy, the three-legged dog, under the wheels of the mail car, Acie brought home Fido, a brown-and-white feist puppy. The dog loved all of the children, but he seemed to have a special fondness for Christine, following her around, loving her presence. It was noticed that Fido began to act strangely, disappearing and hiding, usually under the house near the chimney base, and slinking belly-low on the ground with ears and tail tucked. It was speculated that the dog might be "having fits" or "going mad"—two usually fatal conditions for dogs in those days. Soon it became obvious that Fido's fits coincided with Christine's spells, and that for several days after one of her attacks, the dog would whine in fright and hide when she came near him. This behavior deeply worried Zueline, whose superstitious nature could envision much that was disturbing in the dumb animal's reaction to her strange child; and she was secretly glad when the wheels of the school bus removed Fido from their midst. Was it possible that the instinctive nature of the little dog, more sensitively attuned than human nature, recognized changes in his little mistress that went deeper than mere mood changes, and feared the strange beings housed in the familiar body?

When death strikes a family after seemingly lying dormant for years, the sages begin to wag their heads. "Death does not strike singly," they whisper. Usually it takes at least three. When Dodge knocked on the bedroom window in the middle of that winter night, the whole Costner household knew whose turn it was to go to meet his maker. Papa had been failing for a year. He was only sixty-three, but his robust strength seemed to just visibly drain out of him. Papa bloated and infected, his face drained away in erysipelas sores, and he coughed up his vitals in thick white sputum. Dr. Dunovant attended, the family gathered, and all helplessly watched as Papa's struggles, and even his desire to struggle, weakened. And still he lived on—if the mere drawing in and out of breath can be called living.

They had been summoned before when he had sunk low and seemed to be departing, no one believing that the body could so horribly deteriorate and still house the soul, but this time they knew that Nick Hastings was giving up his ghost. Acie, Zueline, and the three children all dressed and shivered through the cold darkness to the old house, lighted and filled with people. Papa and Mama's room held two double beds, on one of which lay the dying man, attended by a roomful of grief-stricken relatives. All could not crowd into the large room, which was heated by a roaring fire; children and their families were scattered throughout the house. Zueline and her family, of the last to arrive, all came into the death room to see Papa and Grandpa for the last time. Christine, standing at the foot of the iron bed, saw Papa open his mouth and gasp, a thick gurgle echoed from his throat, his left hand raised slightly, and the fingers flexed halfheartedly on the cover. He was gone. Nick Hastings, the teasing, fun-loving perennial boy, was gone. But then, he had been gone for more than a year—it was only the shell of a man grown old and sick that departed this night.

Mama, seated on a chair beside the bed, threw up her hands and screamed her agony; Elise, standing at the foot of the bed, fainted quietly into a crumpled heap on the floor; Christine, blind and pain-ridden, leaned on Becky's chair and pushed her into the roaring fire.

To awaken from such a nightmare is shocking, but to awaken to the stinging pain of a slapping on the bare thighs clouds the reason.

"You know better than to do this! What made you do such a thing as this?" Zueline laid her hand stingingly to the bare legs.

"What did I do, Mother?" Christine protested. "I didn't do anything, Mother." And she struggled with the grasp on her shoulder.

Standing, holding the weeping but thankfully unburned Becky in his arms, Sammy Weaghington, Elise's husband, frowned,

"Sister, what *are* you going to do with that child? She lies all the time!"

Zueline renewed her attack. It was true. How could she defend her child against this kind of accusation? Everybody had seen Christine push Becky—poor, inoffensive little Becky—into the fire. And at such a time as this—with Papa lying a' corpse!

Released, Christine surveyed the room; little had changed. Papa's eyes were open, murky and glazed with death. Her own father moved over to the bed and, using his right thumb and forefinger, he pushed down the still warm, pliable eyelids and carefully placed a quarter on each lowered lid. Taking a clean folded pocket handkerchief that had been placed on the bed, he ritualistically flipped it open, and taking it by its crosscorners, he stretched it under Papa's sagging chin and up over the top of his head. He slowly crossed and tied the corners, drawing them until the chin, with its scraggly white stubble rose to close the open, hollow-cheeked mouth. To the soft moaning and sobbing of the bereaved, he pulled the rough white sheet up over the disease-wrecked face, symbolically decorated to "see no more—say no more."

So this was death. Christine had never before seen death in action—the throes of death—the very act of that which turned the soft, warm living into the cold, hard dead. And it was not over; there was the funeral. Later, she was not even able to remember the funeral. She was twelve years old when her grandfather died, and she attended the funeral; but she was never after able to remember a single detail. Only once did she mention the death, and that was to ask her mother if he died with pneumonia. When assured that he had not, the whole event seemed to slip from her consciousness.

Nowhere did the Hastings family have their funeral procedure recorded, but the process was carried out each time with the same exactness as if a director were standing in the wings cuing each move. The Blyth Funeral Home, a family concern itself, had been performing this sad chore for both Mama's and Papa's people since long before they were married and started their own family. The Blyth people seemed like homefolks, and somehow with them it was not like strangers handling your dead; it was more like when the old folks used to bathe their own dead and just lay them out at home. The closest to the departed had the sad duty of going into town to the funeral home to make the arrangements: buying the shroud, picking out the coffin, selecting the songs and the preacher, and designating the times. The Family is buried in the Mount Carmel Methodist Church cemetery, whose little green square cut into a solid wall of towering pines holds few who are not related. The departed members of the Family are laid out in neat rows, a square filling up as a generation depletes, and each of the living is aware of where his assigned space is. It is not unusual at a funeral to observe someone standing near and comtemplating his own empty spot, speculating perhaps on that inevitable day when it will be finally filled. One grave, sitting off in a corner and oddly at an angle to the neatly coped squares, is the final resting place of a stranger, a man who died while passing through the section in the early twenties. The donated gravestone bears only his name, his death date, and the familiar inscription "Rest in Peace." Was the odd angle an apology to the dear departed for putting an unknown stranger into their midst?

A member of the Family, usually a man of the oldest generation, somehow inherits the job of knowing where everybody's place is and has the responsibility for taking a Blyth member out to the cemetery and designating the exact spot to dig. Over the years a few mistakes have been made, causing a noticeable coolness between offended members, and since a mistake is virtually irreparable, great care and much discussion attend this aspect of the ritual.

Papa was brought home and laid out in the parlor for family and friends to attend for the last time. The clan gathered, and strangely, it was not a terribly sad occasion for other than the immediate family. A type of family reunion, the wake unites cousins who have not seen each other since the last funeral, it exhibits new spouses and offspring, and it allows for a pulling in of the ranks of the family—a re-establishing of one's roots and one's worth. These are my people.

As friends and neighbors came to pay their last respects, they brought food, and soon the house was overflowing with a pot-pourri feast, which continued to arrive faster than the constant eating could deplete it. For children, allowed to play anywhere except in the state room, it was a happy time. For cousins and in-laws, it was a time of making and renewing acquaintances and for catching up on the news of the various branches of the Family. But for the immediate kin, it was a time of busy sadness. Decisions had to be made. Each person's dress was carefully discussed to determine if it was appropriate, and if not, who could lend what to replace an undesirable hat, or tie, or coat. For a summer funeral, the women always wore white; and for a winter funeral, as now, they always wore black. A touch of deep purple could be added, but it must be a light touch. Men always wore dark suits—preferably black.

A body could not be buried sooner than the third day after death. Sooner was considered indecent, and made people wonder why the dead was being rushed underground. Sometimes there were strange burial requests, such as a wish to be "buried just as the sun rises" (difficult to carry out on a cloudy day), but most funerals occurred in the afternoon. This was a comfortable time and didn't rush things. It allowed time to dress and to have a big family dinner before leaving for the church. The Family, in long, black limousines supplied by the funeral director, followed the hearse as it slowly carried Nick Hastings on his last journey. Along the route, vehicles pulled over and stopped, and men removed their hats, all contemplating briefly the inevitability of their own last journey. Seating in the family cars also went according to preordained procedure. Those closest in kin to the deceased, such as the widow and the oldest children (an unfathomable choice), rode in the first car, overflow from the first car plus brothers and sisters occupied the second car, and a third car, if needed, continued with this group. Cousins, nephews, and the like had to provide their own transportation, but they always preceded friends and neighbors in the procession. Much criticism would be heaped upon a member who dared to defy this hierarchy and ride in an unsuitable position.

The procession reached the church, and while necessary preparations were made, the Family sat, bowed and quiet, in the somber black cars. Two special groups had been chosen from among Papa's nieces and nephews—the pallbearers and the flower girls—and they quickly began to perform their sad duties. The flower girls removed the floral gifts from the flower truck and carried them through the back door into the church, where they were arranged before the altar; the six pallbearers awkwardly removed the heavy coffin from the hearse and stationed it on the shiny metal cart on the front porch. Friends, neighbors, and spectators had already gathered in the church.

Now is the moment. The Family leave their cars and line up in preordained order behind the body. The pallbearers, two by two, march in first, the body follows, and the weeping relatives, sobbing women leaning on the arms of their stoic men, fill front pews that have been reserved for them.

The coffin is opened. The funeral message alternates with songs sung by a quartet of three men and one woman, who perform this service for all the Family funerals, singing the same old songs. At this point, a funeral service seems to become symbolic of all the Family funerals, past and future, as one remembers back to other times when a song was sung, and projects ahead to anticipated singing. "Precious Memories" especially strikes a chord, never failing to bring moans and sobs from the bereaved. Finally, there is the viewing of the body. The audience files by first; then the Family, leaning on each other for support, stand and stare at the loved face for a last time, trying to absorb enough to last forever.

Mama is last. Dressed in all black, her heavy, shoulder-length veil obscuring her grief-stricken face, she approaches her husband's solitary bed, leaning on the arms of her two brothers, Ernest and Moody. Her steps drag, her body sags, she moans. One last time she touches him—him whose body is as familiar to her touch as is her own body. An awful moment—a dreadful finality. The coffin lid is forever closed. Mama faints quietly onto the pew.

While the flowers are quickly carried from the church to the grave, and the pallbearers line up, Mama is surrounded by the Family, who fan her, rub her wrists, and wipe her sweating brow. She is ready! There is a sigh of relief through the tense church. "Annie is all right," they whisper. "She just had a light stroke." Leaning heavily on the arms of her brothers, her head drawn slightly to one side, her every breath a labored moan, Mama, who had always followed her husband, followed him to the very end— still a perfect example for her daughters.

"Ashes to ashes, dust to dust"—the most sobering intonation in all of man's literature—and the fancy box is lowered into the red clay.

The Family hold court from the plush, somber protection of the shiny black limousines. Friends and relatives file past Mama, leaning on her cushions, to whisper,

"He looked so good, Annie."

"I know how you feel. I lost my own man just a year ago."

"He looked like he was only asleep, Mama."

"I'll miss him too, Aunt Anne."

"I love you, Granny."

"Mama, Mama, what will we do without him?"

"He was a good man, Annie. You lived forty years with a good man."

And on, and on . . .

And Christine, twelve years old, bright and curious, never remembered a single detail of this unusual experience. She attended the service, marched in the procession, observed all the pomp and circumstance, and repressed it all into her growing collection of unbearable memories.

10

Sweet Mystery of Life

Ah, sweet mystery of life, at last I've found you! Christine desperately sought after this elusive phantom, and at each step of the way she thought she had discovered the answer, the essence, the quality of life that would bring automatic happiness. As each shining new discovery turned to ashes, her Phoenix arose full grown from its own destruction to search anew with no knowledge having been gained, no lesson having been learned from past experience.

In spite of repeated defeat, she continued to pin her hopes on school as her means of deliverance from her plight. Back at Edgefield City School after three years of reprieve in more gentle, less competitive rural elementary schools, she learned beyond a shadow of a doubt what she had only suspected before: She was different, a misfit, a figure of ridicule and scorn. Unaware that she had the intellectual potential to shine brightly in this small academic community, she hid her true light under the proverbial bushel in an attempt to compete in an area where she possessed no resources: the social arena. Instead of perfecting her considerable talents and proudly parlaying them into a means of attaining broad status, she denigrated her abilities, thinking they must be of lesser value simply because they were a part of her worthless self, and bartered them away piecemeal for crumbs from an inferior table, presided over by those who had learned the value of tooting their own horns.

She was bright, curious, creative—the formula for success. Why then was the failure so abject, so miserable, so total? What element, so small as to be overlooked in the prescribed formula, and yet so vital as to destroy all if not present, what essential element was missing? Self-esteem, vanity, egotism, selfishness; it is called by many names, some more respectable than others. And it merely means the ability to believe in self, to find worth in self, to value self. An ability it is, a learned ability, practiced and nurtured until demonstrated and repeated success *prove* that the self is as good as, or better than, other selves, and that it can accomplish and produce as well as, or better than, other selves. Without this kind of self-image, originality is impossible; and in direct proportion to the amount of self-esteem present lies the ability to even follow and imitate the creators.

Christine's self-image was blurred, seen through a glass darkly; and it became, as the years progressed, increasingly blank. She grew unable to see herself at all. She saw others who came and acted for her, or worse, she did *not* see them but only became liable for the consequences of their acts. This growing inability to see herself or to accept responsibility for her own, though unobserved actions, earned her much misery and confusion, and further alienated her from the normal range of behavior acceptable to her peers and elders.

She became known as the liar, the blind girl, the poet—all derogatory terms. Her superior ability to produce academically was not reflected in her accumulating record—she was unable to sustain concentrated effort long enough to follow through on a task to its completion. Having diligently studied for a test, she often left home singing and happy; but before test time, a slight, either real or imagined, by a classmate would destroy the confident, prepared student. In her place to take the test came a dejected, beaten-down, cringing girl who just sat slumped at her desk refusing to answer questions that only yesterday she had brightly discussed.

To the teacher's urging, "Christine, take your test; the period will soon be over," Christine pitifully mumbled, "I don't know the answers. I must have missed this."

Her classmates looked disgustedly at each other with raised eyebrows, signifying, "There she goes, lying again!" And the teacher, thinking her just rebellious and stubborn, since she had perfectly well known the answers only the day before, ignored the miserable child and recorded failure on the blank paper.

Her classmates soon learned two important facts about her: When she did produce, the work was excellent; and she would do anything for a show of approval from them. The unscrupulous, of whom there is always a generous sprinkling among us, were ready to take advantage of this interesting combination of traits. She was propositioned and readily agreed to do special assignments such as writing book reports for them. Usually all went well, with Christine grasping greedily at the few false favors tossed to her for the long hours of extra labor; but often enough, disaster struck.

Approached by Hattie Sue Williams, a girl who bossed a group of mediocre peers who always ganged together at recess, Christine agreed to read a book and write up a report for the promise,

"I'll let you stay with us at recess."

Christine, who at best was only at the fringe of any group, and most often was entirely alone, happily agreed while fearfully confirming,

"All right, if you really mean it."

Assured that Hattie Sue was sincere—and she might have been had the same kind of exchange become a permanent arrangement —Christine studiously began to read. All went well, with the two girls periodically offering assurances concerning their respective areas of the contract. Alas, on the final day when approached for the all-important paper, Christine, confused, mumbled,

"I don't know what you're talking about, Hattie Sue. I haven't got your book report."

The other girl, red-faced and furious, seethed, "You'd better have it! Now where is it?"

They, along with some of Hattie Sue's cohorts, were down in the basement in the girls' rest room. Christine, frightened, backed out into the hall and tried to escape up the cement stairs, pleading,

"I don't have it. I don't know anything about it! I didn't promise."

"You're lying! You're nothing but a liar!" screamed the other girl, driven to a frenzy by being so crossed and by the prospect of appearing in class unprepared. She threw with all her might the only thing available, an orange from her lunch. The hard fruit struck Christine on the shin, raising a lump and hurting frightfully. As she sank to the floor and began to wail loudly, Hattie Sue slapped her soundly on the cheek.

Upon this scene came Polly Strom and Missy Mims, two of the most prestigious girls in school as well as in Edgefield's tiny social set. Polly sternly reprimanded Hattie Sue.

"Leave her alone!"

"She's a liar. She lied to me and she's gotten me into trouble! She lies all the time!" the other girl gritted out, wishing to accuse Christine but fearing to cross powerful Polly.

"I know," Polly agreed, "but you leave her alone, just leave her alone, you hear!"

And Christine escaped further physical harassment, but no one could protect her from the scornful words and the derisive laughter, which were much more painful. Polly often defended her, and once even gave her a box of stationery as a gift; but Polly never sought out the unhappy girl or bestowed any personal friendship on her, treating her more like a stray puppy than an outcast contemporary. In fact, Christine had no friends, and it was a situation of her own making. Even a mature, understanding adult would have found it a sore trial to attempt a sustained relationship with this girl who changed from day to day, who denied shared experiences, who used her ability to see as capriciously as a child playing with a light in a dark room.

During a test, the teacher noticed Christine behaving strangely, rubbing and stretching her eyes and squeezing them tightly closed. She moved to the girl's desk and quietly asked,

"Christine, are you all right?"

Christine stared blankly in the direction of the teacher, lifting her hand as if to ward off a blow.

"Don't mind her, Miss Prince," another student whispered, "she's always stretching her eyes that way."

"I'll handle this, Mary, continue with your test. Class, pay no attention, just take your test," the teacher sternly ordered. But, of course, all eyes were on Christine; all pencils were suspended.

"Christine, what is the matter?" Miss Prince repeated.

"I'm blind, ma'am. I can't see." A note of hysteria lurked at the edge of the high, thin voice.

The students looked at each other. Some laughed, some snorted in disgust. One said, "*Now*, she's blind!"

The teacher shook her head at them as she spoke to Christine, "Sit quietly, Christine. You'll be all right in a moment."

But Christine was not all right in a moment, or even much later. She had to be taken home, still blind and staring, to a frightened and embarrassed Zueline, who apologized for the trouble caused and put her weeping daughter to bed. The next day Acie took off from work and carried his still partially blind daughter to the doctor. Her eyes were examined and glasses prescribed for her, glasses that masked her beautiful blue eyes—the one feature she was proud of—and that did not, of course, prevent future attacks of sightlessness.

The headaches that had been plaguing Christine for several years now were attacking increasingly more often and with greater intensity, seeming to confuse her and to herald some erratic behavior on her part. Zueline, though worried about the severity of the pain, was confident that it was merely the onset of her daughter's monthly sickness; and her suspicions were confirmed by Dr. Dunovant.

Miss Tippy Reynolds, old and ill, the last inmate of the Poor House, died quietly one day in her bed at the County Home. Zueline, on crossing the hall to the old woman's room to lend a hand to those responsible for her care, left the door open. Christine, following her mother, reached the door and saw the dead woman lying in that unmistakable pose. Stunned, she stopped in her tracks, her head swam and thundered, her sight blurred, and her chest squeezed, cutting off her breath. But she did not faint, she did not lose her sight; she only stood gasping for breath and holding her splitting head. Her mother, hearing the ragged breathing, rushed to her in alarm,

"Christine, honey, what's wrong? Speak to me, Top, what's the matter with you? Have you swallowed something?"

Christine, gasping for breath, was unable to talk; but even if she had regained her breath, she could not have explained her difficulty. She did not know what was wrong. She only knew that she was dying, and her condition was no different when the doctor arrived. He gave her an injection, which only put the body to sleep; the mind still struggled and moaned within its prone, paralyzed cage. Dr. Dunovant, learning that the girl often had headaches and that her menstrual cycle had not begun, left some pills, telling Zueline that this medicine would soon bring on the monthly flow and alleviate the painful symptoms. He said Christine would be all right when she awakened. Zueline, sitting by her child's bed and watching the tormented, induced sleep, prayed that it would all be so.

But Christine's headache continued for three days, its intensity rising and falling in waves, until Miss Reynolds was removed from the house and buried; and though she faithfully took all the pills, it was to be more than three years before the onset of her menarche. This natural female process caused her much painful physical discomfort and disturbing emotional concern. It was a time when such delicate subjects were not discussed, and unless some difficulty arose, it was assumed that nature would simply take care of itself. Becky, having been told nothing of the approaching changes in her system, awoke one morning to find blood in her bed and herself bleeding. She told no one of her condition, not even Tiny, declaring only that she was desperately ill and unable to get out of bed; and she managed to keep her shameful plight secret for the entire day.

Elen scarcely fared better with her introduction to menstruation. Mamie Lee had had one brief, tense session with her daughter, asking her if she knew what menstruation was. Elen had heard talk and had even seen a classmate bleed through her clothes in a horribly embarrassing incident at school; but Elen literally knew nothing of the actual process, its timing, purpose, or method of control. But never having discussed anything of this sort with her mother, not even the birth of her little sister, Laura, Elen, to terminate the uncomfortable interview, assured her that she "knew everything." Mamie Lee, uncomfortable herself, did not press the point or even check out her daughter's information for accuracy. Elen, having developed into a tomboy, spent much time playing in trees, climbing, swinging from limbs, and hanging upside down with her knees bent over lower branches. An old man walking by one day found her in this inverted position and warned,

"You're gonna turn your liver upside down and bleed to death!"

Elen, not believing him, continued to play trapeze; but shortly after, on finding blood in her panties, she remembered the warning and was struck by momentary terror. When she next caucused with Christine, Elen related her experience and discovered one of life's rare, heady moments: being able to tell her older cousin an important fact that she did not already know. Elen, having finally experienced something first, was able to instruct Christine, and Elen's feeling of worth and importance knew no bounds. In taking stock, years later, she discovered that this rare experience had occurred only one other time: when she learned to whistle. She showed up at Mama's one Sunday, proudly whistling before the admiring but envious Christine, until her lips were in danger of being permanently puckered.

Christine and Elen grew very close during this period, drawn together like magnets as a result of a mutually shared interest—sex. They had entered their dirty-joke era. They spent all week ferreting out ready-made jokes and making up their own home-grown variety, and then spent all weekend shocking each other into hysterical laughter with their bawdy tales. Their favorite concerned a newlywed couple who had no sex on their wedding night. The puzzled bride, who wore a white nightgown for this disappointing occasion, changed her style and wore a blue nightie on the second night, but to no avail. On the third night she tried yellow, and still came up a loser. The joke lasted for as long as the colors held out, but when both colors and nightgowns were exhausted, the exasperated virgin came to her nuptial bed dressed in a black gown. When her negligent groom asked her why she wore black, she sadly responded, "Because St. Peter is dead!" No matter how many times the joke was related, both girls giggled throughout and then screamed with raucous laughter at the punch line. Someone's even mentioning the color black in their mutual presence was enough to send them off into unexplained gales of laughter. They received many frowns and reprimands by adults during this era.

Their homemade jokes were unbelievably crude and naughty, centering around the cornpone idea of searching diligently for something long and round to fill up a mysterious hole that all females possessed but that nobody seemed to know what to do with. Surprise and delight abounded when just exactly the right-sized "thing" was found to fill up the hole, but wonder literally knew no bounds when it was discovered that every male had one.

They also wrote bawdy poetry, that strange blend of the carnal and the aesthetic. One shining example:

> The Lord made the woman,
> He made her strong and stout,
> Except between her legs
> Where the thread ran out.

And to show an admirable lack of sex discrimination, the male version ran:

> The Lord made the man,
> He made him strong and stout,
> Except between his legs
> Where the thread hangs out.

Another favorite exercise was thinking up lewd names for the genitals. Christine surprised Elen one weekend with these winners:

> Becky an' Tiny got roses
> I got a booky
> Mama's got a birdnest
> Daddy's got a snake.

Elen's admiration knew no bounds! She strove mightily to live up to this shining example of carnal creativity.

The two girls, being double cousins, had entirely mutual relatives. With the exception of their immediate families, all other kin had exactly the same relationship to both of them. One of their eternal games was to try to unearth some person who was a blood relative to one of them but not to the other. It was a futile but fascinating exercise, and one of which they never grew tired. Part of the intrigue had to do with the fact that though their fathers were brothers, they had different surnames; and however well they knew the story of Ellis's name change to "Ernest Sain," it did not diminish their lively search for that elusive relative.

Christine's relationship with her sisters and her cousin pleasantly grew and developed, and she was only relaxed and happy in their unthreatening company. Even though her superior age insured her dominance over them, she deeply admired them for their possession of qualities that she felt she sorely lacked. She envied Elen's calm, unruffled confidence; Tiny's fiery aggressiveness; even Becky's passive, long-suffering tolerance. Christine was unaware that in each case she was viewing merely the dominant quality whose exterior masked a whole range of unseen but controlled emotions and reactions. She only knew that each girl could be counted on to behave in a predictable manner, while she, Christine, never knew how she was going to behave, and seldom could even remember how she had already behaved. Her admiration was not for any particular kind of behavior; it was simply for consistent behavior. And, of course, she thought they were pretty, while she was ugly—irrevocably ugly.

The lying girl and the blind girl! There was always one who lied. But she didn't lie really, she just got the blame for the singing girl's actions, which she didn't remember. But this one is so ugly and rejected, and nobody liked her. She didn't even like herself! Her face is covered with freckles. She looks like the freckle girl, but she is bigger, older. She's even religious and cringing like the freckle girl. Could they be the same one—just grown older? Or maybe she is just someone else coming to do the same things. But the blind girl is almost pretty, and she has no freckles! Her skin is white and clear and the eyes are beautiful, so big and blue. She looks a little like the big-eyed girl! Could they be the same, too? But if so, where did the freckles go? But she does stretch her eyes the same way. People like her, or maybe they just feel sorry for her because she's blind. She's not so pretty with those glasses on. Why does she wear them? She knows they hide her pretty eyes. She's so calm and unruffled and just accepts everything. But wait; there was another one during this time, there were always three. The little poet . . .

> The inner soul cannot be read,
> By just any man,
> But by faith alone in those we love,
> And those who understand.

Chris Costner
(The Little Poet)
1943

The human mind seldom thinks in complete sentences, choosing instead words and phrases when it uses language at all. Most often thoughts manifest themselves in sights, sounds, colors; vague, misty impressions; half-remembered flashes—and the words come later. Only the poet is allowed to use this natural thought-transmitting strategy, and even he is called fanciful, romantic, picturesque. Poetry exhibits its own soft natural rhythm. Only the attuned ear can detect the music.

Christine's ear was attuned, and when the noise of the world drove her into isolation, she strove to renew contact through poetry.

Loneliness can dominate and reach within the soul,
To cover up the unshed tears and keep within its hold,
The joys of death, the aches of life, and beauties go
   unclaimed,
By all who are afraid and weak, to loneliness is chained.

Chris Costner
(The Little Poet)
1943

As do most poets—most daydreamers—she mused and wrote during the time designated for other tasks. Fortunately the study hall teacher, seeing this lonely child at work, encouraged, if not talent, then the expression of a locked mind, thereby giving to Christine another means of identification that she has used, just as she has used painting, to vent her frustration and to reveal her true self.

"What are you writing, Christine?" asked the teacher.

"Oh, it's just a poem," answered the embarrassed but pleased girl, her white skin flushing at the unexpected interest.

"May I see it?" asked the teacher, who had already read it over Christine's shoulder.

Christine surrendered her work with a trembling hand and waited, eyes downcast, while the teacher read,

When God gave us parents,
He chose them with care.
When He gave me mine,
I got more than my share. . . .

Through the years watching,
And tending my needs,
Guiding my footsteps,
So I would succeed.

"It's good, Christine. Why don't you take it to Mr. Mims at the paper? He might publish it."

Christine's heart thudded, "You mean the newspaper? Oh, he wouldn't like it, Miss Crawford!"

"I think he might. I'll speak to him and tell him that you will bring it by for him to read." Thus she committed the girl to do what her lack of confidence might have otherwise prevented.

Katharine Crawford was herself different. She was a middle-aged school librarian from Edgefield who had spent several years in New York. She was tall and thin, and she wore the most beautiful clothes, which, she later confided to Christine, she had bought in New York City. She lived alone in the Edgefield Hotel and took her meals there as well. Did she, because of the places she had been and the things she had seen, or perhaps because of her own personal experiences, which had driven her to choose a southern rural town over glamorous New York, identify with her outcast student? She befriended Christine, encouraged her, and gave her, during this bleak period in her life, her one bright, shining accomplishment.

Each Friday afternoon, the school bus stopped in town to give the country children a chance to visit Edgefield. Ice cream was a nickel for a double-dip cone, which had two side-by-side pockets so that each dip sat in its own nest, not stacked up; and for a dime (a lavish amount!) one could buy a double-dip cone plus a large bag of carameled popcorn. While the happy, flush students spread over town, Christine, her heart beating painfully, climbed the stairs to the offices of the Edgefield *Advertiser*, the town's weekly newspaper, owned and operated by Walter Mims. She stood in the hallway outside the glass-walled offices, simply unable to open the door and walk in; and she might never have accomplished her purpose, if Miss Crawford, true to her word, had not already paved the way for her.

Mr. Mims, finally spotting the forlorn child, left his work and came into the hall.

"You must be Christine Costner," he smiled. "Miss Crawford said you would bring me a poem you had written."

Christine, unable to speak, handed him her pencil-scribbled page, standing paralyzed while he read.

"It's good, Christine, and I think I have just the place for it in next week's paper. That is, if you will allow me to publish it."

Christine could not believe her ears. She enthusiastically nodded her head, causing the straight shoulder-length black hair to bob furiously. She turned and ran, leaving Walter Mims to smile, puzzled, and to call after her,

"Bring me some more when you want to!"

She did not tell anybody, but she didn't have to; everybody in Edgefield County subscribed to the *Advertiser*, which came out on Fridays. The following Monday at school, she was a celebrity of sorts. People spoke to her, noticed her, who had never even seen her before; but as so often happens, it only served to separate her more widely from her peers. A poet! That's a strange animal in itself! Nobody was really surprised that Christine turned out to be one, and it did nothing to change the picture they already had of her. Now she simply became "the little blind poet." When the world crowded, she isolated herself and grew happy as the poet. Many times she climbed the stairs on Friday and waited in the hall for Mr. Mims to notice her, and he never failed her, printing over several years many of her creations. Mr. Mims and Miss Crawford helped her hold onto the fringes of reality. Wisely, they recognized the hidden worth that caused her unique difference; while others, unable to see below the surface, judged only her inability to imitate.

Wonder of wonders, and unknown to Christine, her mother's prediction was coming true: The ugly child was becoming a beautiful woman; the ugly duckling was developing into a swan. The skinny body, still coltish, was becoming willowy; the scrawny neck suddenly was slender; the fly-away hair, tamed, became a misty black cloud; the brown freckles faded into a faint dusting of gold across an expanse of pure white; and the eyes under their straight black brows dazzled as does the clear blue sky through drifting white mist. The jumbled white teeth untangled themselves, leaving intriguing overlaps and causing the wide, full red lips to purse sensuously.

But the change had been gradual, and Christine's mirror reflected what she expected to see—a different-looking face, and to be different was to be ugly. Zueline told her she was pretty, but then she had always said that, mothers said things like that. It took a man to make the maid feel lovely.

Mama's children were all married and established in their own homes now, except Tobitha; they no longer needed the big old house, and Dodge could not work the farm alone. With Ellis's help, they bought a small piece of land nearer to town and built a small house. The four of them—Mama, Tobitha, Dodge, and his wife—moved into Mama's last house. They had enough farm animals to fill their needs, and a garden for vegetables. Dodge and his wife went to work in the cotton mill. Only Mama's advancing age and her own new dependence on a government check prevented her being completely scandalized by what she considered to be this degeneration of her family. Many of her statements now began, "When your father was alive . . ."

Acie was somehow convinced that Dodge's situation was better than his own, and resigning from his job with the county, he moved his family into a house down the road from Mama. He and Zueline went to work in the cotton mill, and while Zueline lasted only two months, he stuck it out for three years before he returned to his job with the county. The move was good for Christine, giving her a new start in a new community where her background was unknown to the young people her age.

She was fourteen when she made her first real friend, a girl named Rena Outz. It was 1942, and things of the war seemed to put other things into perspective, to push personal problems aside. Christine and Rena were very patriotic, worrying about "our boys over there" and praying for their safety. Even though she was afraid her father might be drafted, Christine, having no close kin in the service to be concerned for, gladly took on Rena's numerous male cousins as her very own warriors. To this point, however, it had all been in the abstract; they were only names and pictures. Then the first one came home on leave. What *is* it that a uniform, especially the uniform of one's country at war, does for a male figure? There he stood, his deeply tanned face and smiling green eyes contrasting sharply with his white Coast Guard uniform; but it was when he flashed his even white teeth and smiled at her that Christine first fell in love.

It was ironically characteristic of her that even her introduction to the opposite sex was strange, impossible, and painful. She reached the age of fourteen without even having a crush, then selected a mature man more than ten years her senior and fell hopelessly in love. Amused, he treated this gangly little bud as he would a funny little sister, and went back to fight the war. Suddenly the abstract had become concrete, suddenly she knew why she was patriotic, and suddenly she was alive—so this was the mystery of life, this was what it was all about. She still suffered, but now it was different; this was suffering for a cause—beautiful, exquisite suffering. The fact that her ardor was not returned was of small consequence; he was a warrior, and one made sacrifices for warriors:

> *Way down here on Manila Island,*
> *Way down on Hawaii's shore,*
> *I am longing for the highland,*
> *The land I'll see no more.*
> *I am dying for my homeland,*
> *I only wish I could do more,*
> *Brothern, push back our enemies,*
> *And build up Hawaii's shore.*

Chris Costner
(The Little Poet)
1943

Her patriotism at this point was much stronger than her geography.

In the midst of all this intangible emotion, one of Rena's cousins came home, John Lake, an eighteen-year-old Marine; and Christine's ardor localized—she had her first boyfriend. Rena asked her one Friday at school if she could come to her house, about one-half mile down the road, for a candy pull in honor of her cousin on leave from the Marine Corps. There Christine met Johnny, and this time it was different—he liked *her!* She saw it in his eyes, and though never having seen it in a man's eyes before, she recognized it—no woman has ever failed to recognize it. And she returned it. A love-starved budding girl, a boy leaving to fight (and die?) in war: How could it be otherwise? When they all drove her home that night, he walked her to the door and asked her to go for a ride with him on Sunday afternoon.

Zueline teased her a little in the "so you've got a boyfriend" vein, and Acie instructed her a lot about time and places to go; but they, secretly pleased, gave their permission. The Sunday ride was that strange combination of exhilarated happiness and uncomfortable awkwardness occurring only in adolescence between a boy and a girl. Johnny held her hand on the seat between them and squeezed it tightly when he took her back to the door, asking for another date. And that simply and quickly, they became a couple, dating regularly on his leave, writing daily when he returned to camp, and waiting anxiously for his next leave. Their dates were simple: They went for rides in his father's car, he came to her house and just spent an evening helping her do homework, or they double-dated on weekends with Rena and her date.

And they smooched, but their petting was light and controlled. Zueline, without explaining why such precautions were necessary, instructed her daughter about ladylike behavior with young men. A lady did not allow a man to touch her legs, or her breasts, or to put his hand under her dress. Christine felt pretty, she felt like a lady for the first time in her life, and when Johnny in the heat of his ardor began to violate one of the cardinal rules, she stopped him. And he respected her wishes. It was a time of idealism; feelings for country, motherhood, and apple pie were running high, and a man going off to war wanted to leave behind a girl he could think about in the black days ahead and he could return to when the world had been set right again.

They became secretly engaged, and planned in their letters how they would run away and get married when he came home on his next furlough—his last before going overseas. At about this time, Christine's menstrual cycle started, and Zueline now explained to her daughter why a lady did not let a young man touch all those forbidden secret places, did not let him go "too far." Unaware of Christine's secret, she unknowingly fired this girl-woman in her resolve to marry her Marine before he left. She daydreamed of bearing his child while he was bravely fighting for her; of presenting him his son when he returned, proud and victorious, from the war. Their letters became passionate, intense, dedicated.

Christine was now convinced beyond doubt that she had found the mystery of life, the essence of being. And who could blame her? Her life abounded with examples teeming with evidence of this fact. Even Mama measured a woman's success by her marital status and wanted all of her girls—daughters and granddaughters —to marry well and to follow her own excellent example. However, this was a desire of which no hint was ever given; no decent mother ever indicated that she gave consent for a daughter to be married. On the contrary, each one had to be tearfully torn from the stricken maternal grasp, and no well-brought-up daughter ever "chased after" a man, consenting to marriage only in a weak moment after much romantic wooing and importuning by a totally enslaved lover. Consequently, most marriages were of the "run off" variety, where the couple carefully planned and then secretly ran off and got married, usually taking with them a trusted married couple who had confidentially been taken into their plot. When this happened to one of Mama's girls, she was tearfully prostrate for hours and inconsolable for days, declaring to the open heavens that it would kill her and demanding that Papa "go and bring that foolish girl home!"

The young couple was, of course, welcomed home in a few days, Mama shedding more tears and warning the beaming embarrassed new son-in-law that he had "better be good to her daughter" or that she, Mama, would come personally and bring her wronged child home. It was an old story and had happened to all of Mama's kin now, except Lennie, Mama's young cousin; and though Mama protested mightily that she was glad that her young cousin had not married, everybody knew that it was not true. It was an uncomfortable subject; something was wrong with Lennie, but nobody dared to put a name to this wrong—it was simply ignored. But Christine and Elen used to talk about it and wonder why Cousin Lennie was so different. Why, she even shaved her face! It proved one thing to Christine: A woman had to have something terribly wrong with her not to be chosen by a man as his wife and the mother of his children.

The latest example of how marriage was conducted in the Family was Anne's marriage, one in which Christine was integrally involved. Anne, who had been only fourteen herself at the time, had confided to Christine that she and Leslie were going to run away from church the next Sunday and get married. No one has ever understood how the younger girl kept the secret for the next few days; but on the chosen Sunday when all the young people went to church, Leslie met Anne and they ran off. Christine could contain herself no longer; she told everybody at church and she flew into the house after church announcing,

"Anne's gone to get married!"

"Oh, Lordy mercy, what will we do?" moaned Mama, who did not doubt it for a moment.

A family consultation revealed that the errant couple would most likely head for Elise and Sammy's house after the wedding, since Leslie was Sammy's nephew.

"You go and bring Little Sugar home! She's just a baby! Bring her home!" Mama instructed Papa, walking the floor and wringing her hands.

"They will already be married, Annie," Papa reasoned. "Shouldn't we just let them alone?"

"My baby, my Anne," moaned Mama, sinking into a convenient chair before she fainted dead away. "Bring home my baby."

While everyone fanned Mama and rubbed her wrists, Zueline whispered to Papa,

"Maybe you'd better go get her, Papa; Mama looks like she might have a light stroke."

And Nick Hastings left, to the wails of his bereft wife, and brought the weeping Anne home to her mother. The stolen bride, who wept all night, was greeted the next morning by her erstwhile playmate,

"So you're back. Now we can go play." Eleven-year-old Christine was accustomed to aborted adventures, and she did not at all understand Anne's loud outburst of tears.

It was a stormy day, but, of course, Anne was duly returned to her new husband, and she became an accepted member of the married women of the Family, with all of their rights and privileges. Even when Mama knew about the approaching nuptials of one of her daughters, it was no better. She even went with Elise and Sammy for their wedding. Elise was twenty-six, and her future husband was a widower with four small children, so in no way could Mama claim that a fledgling was being stolen from the nest; but Mama, true to form, fainted on the way to the minister, and the wedding party stopped by the doctor's for smelling salts before they proceeded on.

Thus Christine knew that she was following in the best tradition of her family by planning a secret marriage, and she expected parental opposition. She would have felt unwanted if her parents had seemed happy to get rid of her. Therefore, when her father, suspecting that affairs were progressing too rapidly, opened and read one of Johnny's letters, which revealed, as did every one of them, their love and their plan, he approached his daughter with restrictions and refusal. Christine wept and protested and begged, but never did she doubt that sooner or later it would all work out. Why, she might even have to wait for Johnny to return from the war! But she would faithfully wait.

Acie went to see Johnny's father, telling him of the plans of their children, informing him of Christine's age and minor status, and enlisting his help in keeping the lovers apart. Who knows what Christine expected from her future intended? One only knows that she did not expect the crushing blow that befell her. Rejection by her lover! Her man was not going to try to steal her away, to beg for her love and fidelity in his absence, to extract a promise for her hand when the cruel war was over.

Johnny wrote her a letter admitting her youth, recording her father's refusal to sign for the marriage, and acknowledging the father's rights over the lovers' desires. Christine had seen no examples in her family of a lover giving up, and she well knew that underage girls simply lied about their ages as Anne had. There was, then, only one explanation: Johnny did not want her. No man would ever want her. Rejection in this most important area of a woman's life was the ultimate in failure. It was not to be borne. The next day Christine scribbled this note: *"Dear Mother and Daddy, I am shamed. I have shamed you and the family. I cannot go on. Tell Johnny I love him. Love, Christine,"* and looking at her ugly, freckled face in the bathroom mirror, drank a bottle of iodine and waited to die. Death did not come, even though the searing pain was unbearable. She grew desperate, drank great gulps of rubbing alcohol, and vomited spasmodically, which probably saved her life. The wide eyes staring at her from the mirror suddenly glazed, dimmed, and grew sightless; she sank to the floor in a dead faint.

The hospital pumped her stomach and sent her home with a slightly scorched esophagus, physically; mentally and emotionally, there remained only a burned-out cinder. On the way home, Acie and Zueline, seated in the front of the car, and Christine, huddled in the back, spoke not a word; shock reigned. Zueline was never able to do more than put her warm arms around her daughter, but Acie, in his way, counseled her,

"Daughter, it's all right. It's all over. But everyone knows. You'll have to face it that the whole neighborhood knows. Rest for a few days and we'll talk about it. Everybody makes mistakes. Just hold your head up." He was trying to help, trying to spare her more rejection, more hurt.

When Mamie Lee and Ellis came to visit a few days later, it was agreed that Christine would go home with them for the month remaining before school started. Elen was delighted, but even here Christine was apprehensive. Elen's little sister, Laura, was only a few months old, and Christine was afraid that the baby might have taken her place in Elen's heart. It soon became evident that this had not happened, and the girls, in spite of a critical age difference, widened considerably by Christine's recent experiences, took up their old relationship. Christine even attracted one of the local boys, who began to "hang around" and talk to her.

Her pain lessened, her heart knitted, and she began to feel pretty again. The wide blue eyes lost their haunted look and sparkled again. But even so, she was not prepared for what faced her at school in the fall. Everybody ignored her, even Rena; and though it was Christine's senior year, she could not continue. It was as though she had not been to school the year before! She could remember nothing of last year's work. She was enrolled in French II with no knowledge of having taken French I. The whole year before was blotted out, gone!

That's the big-eyed girl. She's the one who came to in the hospital after the freckle girl drank the iodine. And she's been there ever since. The freckle girl has not returned, and it must have been the freckle girl who studied so much in school. Why

*didn't she come back and go to school? She only had one more
year. Maybe she didn't come back because school was so unpleasant; maybe she stayed away so she wouldn't have to go to
school. But who is she? If she didn't go, the big-eyed girl
couldn't go either. And where am I, Chris? Both the freckle girl
and the big-eyed girl dated Johnny, and sometimes the poet
wrote the letters to him, but I never seemed to be there. I saw
everything, and I know what they did, but it was always them
doing things. I can't find me! But I will, I will. . . .*

Christine could not face this world gone sour again; she could
not hold her head up, and she asked her father to allow her to
quit school. He agreed but informed her that she could not just
"lay around the house," that she would have to get a job. It was
arranged that she would go to live in Greenwood with Anne and
Leslie and work in the sewing room with Anne. It was thought to
be the best for Christine; it would take her from her hurtful surroundings, help her start anew. Actually, it literally threw her to
the wolves. She was shamed, rejected, ugly; and place had nothing
to do with her ability to hold up her head—she would have been
unable to hold it up anywhere. She was ripe for the kill.

She and Anne, who now had three small children kept during
the day by a neighbor, sat all day in the sewing room, monotonously sewing uniforms. Christine's job was to sew on collars;
what a relief it would have been to have occasionally sewn on a
button, or put in a sleeve! After work they waited for Leslie in a
downtown restaurant. Inevitably, the pick-up approach was made,
and poor, half-alive, beaten-down Christine was an easy catch for
a thirty-year-old race car driver. Al Thorne, known as a daredevil
performer, was married and the father of a child, choice facts that
he omitted revealing to the shy, quiet, religious girl whom he had
decided to acquire. Romantic Anne, knowing of Christine's past
troubles, informed her that he was "quite a catch." The girl, no
longer able to judge situations for herself, only knew that here
seemed to be a second chance, a reprieve from failure.

Christine had even seen him perform, and she had loudly ap-
plauded along with the rest of the enthusiastic audience. And now
this celebrity had sought her out and sat down beside her. The
fact that he was short and dumpy, not at all handsome, and

tended to breathe in a rather juicy, nasal manner, interspersing his speech with short bursts of mirthless laughter, were all overshadowed by his fame. She did not question why he was not in uniform, perhaps appreciating the fact that he was so different from the handsome, patriotic Johnny who had deserted her. This man was attentive, and he was present. And they began to date.

There was no joy in this affair. He never even touched her, seeming to desire nothing from her, while willing to give her all: his name, a home, the prestige of his job. And Anne did not disapprove; she even encouraged her. After all, he was a known name —famous, even—when compared to the people they knew. Babes in the woods! She had been working in Greenwood only two months when she agreed to marry him. They got the license and then went alone to be wed in Abbeville, a town in the adjoining county. This seemed fine to Christine—after all, they were running away, she had told only Anne; and she also did not question the fact that only she and Al and the minister were present at the ceremony. Never having seen a wedding performed, what did she know of legalities, of witnesses? She only knew that they went to a big house and stood before a young nice-looking man and repeated their vows. And there was no honeymoon—they returned to Anne's house and slept in her usual bed. And that's all they did —just slept! He did not touch her. Was she disappointed? Was she hurt? Was she relieved? No, she was only accepting. In the first place, she felt so unworthy, so shamed from her past experience that she had no expectations, could feel no slight; and in the second place, this behavior was supported by the stories that she had overheard the women in the Family tell about their wedding nights. These tales, sworn to be true, indicated that not one of these blushing virgins had intimate relations with her new husband on the nuptial night. "He did not touch me for three days" was the vow made, with the obvious meaning that the husband's respect for the virgin modesty quelled his base male desires.

This suspended state of emotions existed for several days. Then one night, as they walked in the velvet darkness from the bus stop to Anne's house, Al drew her from the sandy lane into a thicket of trees. Calmly he ordered her,

"Take off your britches and pull your dress over your head." Stunned, Christine was unable to move. She began to tremble.

"Do it!" he ordered, emotion straining his voice.

Slowly, she began to obey, thinking,

"It's all right. He's my husband."

While she pushed her thin panties to the ground, he unzipped his fly and exposed his swollen, erect organ. He approached her ordering,

"Turn around and pull your dress over your head."

Obeying as in a nightmare, she turned her back and pulled her dress over her head, grateful for even this small amount of privacy and for her inability to behold her fate. He grabbed her violently, squeezing and painfully pinching her breasts, clawing and roughly fingering that secret place where no probing hand had ever touched and that would have shrunk even from a lover's tender caress. And she knew what a tender caress was—Johnny had held her and fondled her enough so that she knew this was wrong, this was not natural; but her terror and her confusion rendered her incapable of fight or flight. Suddenly he began to beat her with his bare hands, painfully pummeling her buttocks and thighs with his fists and sharply stinging her quivering flesh with his open palms. Undone, she began to sob, bending to cradle her bowed head in her helpless entangled arms, thus exposing more of her body to his punishment. Her low cries seemed to excite him more, and she could feel his hot, throbbing penis forced against her trembling body.

And then it was over. He sagged against her, and she could feel a strange warm liquid slowly oozing down her leg. She stood paralyzed, her cowed body awaiting the next assault. But it did not come.

"Put your britches on," he roughly ordered, his breathing loud and ragged. "And don't you tell anybody about this, or I'll beat you up good."

Christine lowered her skirt, pulling up her underpants as she turned. There he stood, zipping his pants and tucking in his shirt. She had never been more physically afraid in her life, afraid and shamed and humiliated; but she did not feel wronged or violated. He was her husband! All of her life she had been taught that when a woman married, she "made her bed and she had to lie in it." If it were a bed of roses, she was fortunate; if it were a bed of thorns, she still had to endure it. Hadn't Grandpa returned

211

Mother to Daddy when she left? Surely Daddy hadn't beat Mother, Christine had never seen him strike her; but whatever it was, Mother had to return to her husband. She had made her bed. And now Christine had made her bed, and she had no escape. Daddy had saved her once; now he could not save her. She had no place to go. Resignation drooped her shoulders, bowed her head, lowered the blue eyes gone dull.

Acie and Zueline, working in the Greenwood cotton mill, heard that Al Thorne had married their daughter. What must this father have felt as he drove out to Anne and Leslie's house to check on this incredible child of his? Anger, frustration, relief, despair? His calm face revealed nothing of what he must have been experiencing, and he did not even ask to see his daughter. Perhaps he could not trust himself to face her under these conditions and in these surroundings. After verifying the rumor, he informed Anne,

"Tell Christine I will be back to get her tomorrow. She's got to come home and talk this over with her mother. Her husband is welcome to come." Acie had not come into the house, but stopped on the porch, and after his few words he turned and left, leaving Christine, who had heard these terse instructions, alone and rejected; yet she was strangely glad that she had been spared the showing of her shameful face to her father for one more day.

True to his word, he came for them the next morning, creating a tense situation, which was saved only by the rustic finesse of the brazen performer. He filled the awkward silences with running, disconnected comments, punctuated irritatingly by his nasal snorts of a sound located somewhere between a laugh and a grunt. His harsh voice loudly grated, but it was infinitely more to be preferred than the thundering silence.

Al came along, and while he and Acie talked, Zueline took her daughter into the bedroom for a talk. She opened her arms to her weeping child, bitter tears coursing down her own cheeks,

"It's all right, honey, it's all right," she whispered, not knowing that her arms were enfolding the bruised and battered flesh on her daughter's back. "But there are some things you have got to know. You can have a baby now that you know a man, and you're too young to have a baby yet. You make your husband use rubbers."

212

That's all she had ever heard them called, and that's all she knew to call them. Christine understood what she was talking about, but she also knew that, shamefully, she had no need for such protection. Might she have told her mother about her mortifying situation and thus have been spared further horror if this intimate topic had not come up? Perhaps. But now she could not. Her mother was talking to her as one woman to another—married women's talk. How could she admit failure again and confess to her mother that she was not really a wife and that the kind of relations she had with her husband would never produce a baby? It was her bed, she must lie in it.

Acie took them back to Greenwood without knowing what his daughter was enduring; and though later they were to learn of Al's beating her, they never even suspected that his cruel treatment of her was sexually motivated. And the beatings continued, though he was careful to never strike her where a mark would show. Soon after, Al was fired from his job, and he and Christine went to Augusta, Georgia, to seek employment. Two factors motivated his choice of this city: He thought he could get a job and Christine had relatives there with whom they could live until he began to earn money.

Myrtle, along with her husband, had moved to Augusta to run a rooming house for Ellis. It was during the war, and the city was jammed with soldiers and their wives. Ellis had bought a huge old four-story home on Telfair Street and turned it into efficiency apartments for these temporary residents. Myrtle had two double beds in her bedroom, and she gave one of them to her niece and her new nephew until an apartment became vacant. There was no privacy here and Christine was safe for a while, but this respite was short-lived. An apartment emptied, and Myrtle put her relatives in it. The sadistic beatings resumed with regularity.

Perhaps the few weeks of peace had given her courage, or perhaps the worm simply turned. One night as he was beating her, the bowed head and cowered body straightened, the blue eyes widened with horror and stared at this ugly little man, his hairy body glistening with sweat and his erect genital thrusting from his crooked, banty legs. She screamed! His excitement overcame him and burst from its precautions. He hit her in the face, on the arms, anywhere. She ran, she cried, she resisted. He became frantic.

"Some goddamn women ain't worth screwing!" he shouted.

"Stop, stop! Who are you, what *are* you doing?" she gasped, holding her bruised arms across her bleeding face.

"There's no bastard of a woman that's been born that I'd put my cock in!" he panted, beside himself. "My seed has gotten the last bastard that's ever goin' to be born on earth by me."

He had hurled dirty words at her before, but his perversion, inflamed by her unaccustomed resistance, turned him into a wild man, forgetful of his circumstances.

Oh, my God, how awful! I had forgotten all that. For thirty-three years I have repressed this. It was the freckle girl who took the beatings, and it was the big-eyed girl who resisted. But it was my body, my body, subjected to that awful degradation. How did I bear it? And what happened? . . .

He might have killed her, had not her screams been heard by a neighbor, who went upstairs for Myrtle. When Myrtle knocked on the door, dead silence descended. Al quickly pulled on his pants over his suddenly flaccid weapon, and Christine, still fully clothed, opened the door. When she saw her Aunt Myrtle, Christine's wide, staring eyes narrowed and her proud body drooped, all resistance melted.

"What's going on in here?" Myrtle sternly asked, her long, braided hair hanging down her back, her robe scarcely concealing the fact of her advanced pregnancy.

"Nothing, nothing," Al panted, managing a sick smile but unable to pull off one of his nasty laughs.

Myrtle raised her niece's bruised face, and noting its ravages, ordered,

"Christine, come with me."

She led the silent, obedient girl out of the room and up the stairs to her own apartment. She did not question her, only tended her damaged face. When finished, Christine rose to return to her own room. Myrtle was scandalized.

"Christine, he beat you! You can't go back down there to him!"

"He's my husband, Aunt Myrt," she sadly replied, and returned to him. Christine had simply made for herself a very hard bed to lie in.

During the night, Al sneaked them both out of the window and walked the dark streets for a taxi, which took them to the house of one of his drinking friends. He fastened Christine in a bedroom and locked the door, telling her to sleep. Myrtle went to see about her the next morning, and finding her gone, called Acie, who, on hearing the entire story, called on Ellis for help. Augusta, usually a small, sleepy town, was now so swollen by military personnel that a two-man search for the fugitives would be futile. They called the police, who broadcast an all-points bulletin for both Al and Christine, and they deputized Ellis to help in the search. Strangely, it was he who found them.

Al heard the police bulletin on the radio and decided to take Christine and go back to Greenwood, his home. Fearing to go to the bus station, he waited until dusk, took a taxi across the river to the top of North Augusta Hill, and waited for the Greyhound bus. There Ellis and Mamie Lee found them. Ellis stopped the car and spoke only two words.

"Get in."

They got in. On the way to the police station, only Ellis spoke.

"What I'm doing is legal. I have been deputized." He made no explanation as to what he was doing.

Arriving at the police station, Ellis and Al went in. Christine in the back seat and Mamie Lee in the front seat sat in buzzing silence. One look at her niece's ravaged face had choked off Mamie Lee's usually ready flow of comments.

Acie was called. Then circumstances took an unexpected turn. Al announced that he had never married Christine, that they had just been "living together." He informed them that he already had a wife and child, and he promised to leave and never bother Christine again if they would let him go. He had abducted a minor, had crossed the state line with her; it would be a sure prosecution. But to what avail? A trial, public testimony, the sure notoriety could only hurt her more. Acie did not prefer charges. Al Thorne escaped punishment for his crime, leaving behind the blasted-out shell of the girl he had wronged.

"You can ride with me, Daughter," said her father when he and Ellis came out onto the street. She obeyed silently, climbing into the back seat instead of sitting beside her father. She did not deserve a seat in front with him. She was unclean, shamed. Zueline came running down the steps and once again opened her arms to her daughter, murmuring,

"It's all right, honey, he won't bother you again." She smoothed her child's tangled black hair and hid the bruised face against her shoulder.

"I've put him where he won't ever hurt you, Daughter." Acie watched this scene between his wife and the daughter he had returned to her.

"You can come home with us; he won't ever hurt you again." Zueline opened the doors of her home to this child who seemed unable to find a place in the world for herself, and she would do so many times before this drama was played out.

As they gathered Christine's pitifully few belongings, the humiliated girl sat in the car and waited, preferring the separation and the cover of darkness to the stares of the curious. Elen, who had worried about her cousin the long day through, came and sat beside her. She did not speak or look at her; she simply put her hand on the thin hand lying listlessly on the seat. It was enough. Elen still wanted to be with her, to touch her.

They all went home, back to Edgefield, and the parents were kind to the obviously crushed girl; but even before the signs of the beating had faded from her face, she was back in Augusta at the same house where it had all happened. Zueline was pregnant and needed the specialized care to be found in the city. She, Christine, and the twins moved in with Myrtle and awaited the birth of the baby. Elen lived nearby, and she and Christine fell into their easy relationship again, picnicking, going to the swimming pool, sunbathing on the roof, reading in the Telfair Street library. They never mentioned the older girl's experience; it was as if it had not happened, and Christine was almost immediately her usual self again. At her instigation, they played their "pretend" games—if they walked uptown they were famous celebrities being stared at by passersby; if they went to the movies they were famous actresses at a premiere performance, wherever they went they were the most beautiful women in the world. Interestingly, in one favorite game Christine was a famous woman and Elen was a journalist writing about her.

216

There was only one bone of contention between them: clothes. Being exactly the same size, they often swapped clothes, and usually all went well; but sometimes, unaccountably, Christine would ruin something of Elen's that she had borrowed. Elen's angry accusations and Christine's shocked denials usually dissolved into forgiving tears, but the younger girl became wary and hesitated to lend some of her treasured things to her cousin. During this long, lazy summer, Christine, whose fair skin would never tan, became badly sunburned on an outing to the lake. Everything always seemed to affect her more severely than it did others, and she was in bed lying on greased sheets for several days. Clothes were an agony to her blistered skin when she finally dressed again. Zueline, trying to relieve Christine's suffering and make her more comfortable, remembered that Elen had a new soft voile dress, and she asked if Christine could borrow it.

Visions of the soft filmy pink floated before Elen's vision—it was her prettiest dress, and new. She had worn it only once. And voile had to be handled carefully, it was so delicate, and it would pull at the seams if treated rough. And all that grease on Christine's blisters would ruin it. She couldn't do it! She stammered to her aunt,

"Aunt Tuta, I am planning to wear that dress. I have already planned it, to wear it to—to . . ."

Zueline understood and she smiled,

"That's all right, honey, we'll find her something else to wear."

But Elen felt guilty, and all her life when she added up the mean things she had ever done, that denial to her cousin was always included in the count.

The baby died, and Zueline almost lost her own life as well. Christine saw the stillborn child lying on the bed like a sleeping baby, but she did not go to the small, private burial; and she was not bothered by this death. During the period of her mother's recuperation, Christine ran the house, got her sisters off to school, and took care of her father; but this interlude was soon over. She could not just stay home like a small child, she could not face returning to school at Edgefield High, and there was no job for her in Edgefield that would offer her protection from public view. It was decided that she would go to live with Ellis and Mamie Lee in North Augusta and attend school with Elen.

School had already begun when she started, making it impossible to slip in unnoticed. People stared at her simply because she was new, but she thought they stared because they knew about her. She withdrew. And her academic problem was the same here as it had been at the Edgefield school—she seemed to have lost a whole year of learning; it was as if she had not gone to school for an entire year. She attended school at North Augusta for only three weeks, not even long enough to receive a grade card, and then she quit. Her uncle gave her a job in his office filing and doing small secretarial work, but this was not successful either. Discouraged, she returned home after less than two months.

Customs and traditions are strong, and no matter how harsh is experience to the contrary, these old ways of the family still exert the strongest influence. Christine met a man—a soldier home on leave—and within two weeks had fallen in love, become tentatively engaged, and promised to wait for him while he went away to fight the war. The liberated woman was not yet a popular item, a woman's place was in the home: married, raising a family, and taking care of a husband. Was this the reason that school and employment were unattractive to her, the reason she had no desire to be independent? Perhaps. At any rate, she returned to her aunt's home again, this time as an engaged woman of eighteen, and began to work for the Southern Bell Telephone Company in Augusta.

Time flew by for Christine on silvery wings—she had money for the first time in her life to buy clothes, bright makeup, food in restaurants; she had a man who loved her and was coming home to marry her; and she was pretty. People told her that she was pretty; men noticed her, often above other girls present; and most of the time she herself believed that she was pretty. Even though the freckles were almost invisible, she constantly searched her face for evidence of them and generously doused her white face with powder, just in case. Elen, who never used powder, complained,

"Chris, why do you use all that powder? You spill it all over everything."

Christine, now called Chris, spent most of her clothes money on pretty underwear, leaving her outer wardrobe skimpy. It was almost as if she wanted to assure that she was just as pretty inside, where it didn't show—that in her garments, at least, she was lovely underneath also, that the nice exterior did not hide something unlovely inside. And she was pretty! If she needed any more proof, her being asked to represent her employer in the Miss Augusta Beauty Pageant should have convinced her.

It was unbearably exciting, planning what to wear and how to fix her hair, standing before the full mirror—walking, turning, smiling. What girl has not dreamed of walking onto the stage while the music plays "There She Is, Miss America"? When she asked to borrow Elen's new black two-piece bathing suit, a familiar scene was played.

"Chris, you don't take care of my clothes, and that's my best suit. And it's new, too!" Elen charged.

"I don't know why you say that," Chris protested. "You always accuse me of spoiling your things, and I just don't do it."

"You *do*, too. And you always deny it. Who else does it? Nobody else wears my stuff," Elen argued.

"If you let me borrow your suit, I promise I will take care of it. I'll only have it on a few minutes." Chris pressed her request.

"O.K. I'll do it. But if you mess it up, I'll never lend you anything again," Elen declared, reluctantly handing over the precious suit.

Fifteen-year-old Elen was not allowed to attend the event, but she waited impatiently at home for her cousin to return. Chris did not win, but she placed in the top ten contestants and was standing on the stage when the winner was announced. Just as the crown was placed on that other shining head, she quietly fainted dead away, crumpling into a pitiful heap at the feet of all that beauty. It attracted much attention, even drawing some away from the smiling winner; but was that the reason for creating such a scene, or could she not bear to be judged less beautiful, even in a group of chosen beauties?

Pageant officials took her home, pale, red-eyed, and weak, explaining to the frightened Mamie Lee that it was likely the bright lights that had caused her to faint. Elen immediately ascertained that her bathing suit was nowhere in evidence, and at the first possible moment she questioned Chris,

"Where is my swimsuit?"

"I don't have your suit," Chris weakly answered.

"I know you don't, I can *see* that," Elen returned. "What did you do with it?"

"I haven't had it, Elen." Chris looked puzzled. Her whole body sagged and drooped; even her face seemed shrunken, and her eyes, so bright and sparkling earlier, now showed dull and lackluster.

"I don't believe it! I just don't believe it!" Elen shouted, beside herself with anger and frustration. "You *had* to wear a swimsuit, and you borrowed mine! So *now*, where is it?"

Chris looked at her animated cousin, pain bringing tears to her sad eyes, "I didn't have it, Elen. Honest, I didn't. I don't remember even wearing a suit."

"How can you say that, Teeny?" Elen reasoned, falling into the childhood name in her effort to make the other girl see. "You know you wore a suit. You couldn't have been the only one not wearing a suit."

Chris slumped onto the bed, "I don't know, Elen. I just don't remember. I'll go look for your suit tomorrow."

But the next day Chris was sick in bed, feverish and half delirious, and it was Elen alone who went to the city auditorium and searched long and hard for the small scraps of black cloth. They were nowhere to be found—not in the dressing rooms, not on the stage, not even in the audience! Dejected, she returned home, and there had not even the satisfaction of making an accusation. Who can accuse a poor, sick, weeping girl of something so frivolous as losing a swimsuit? And anyway, accusing Chris was like hitting a baby; she just cried and never fought back. And her denials were so earnest as to shake one's confidence in the truth. Elen went as far as to diligently search the house for the vanished swimsuit, even as she vividly remembered seeing Chris leave the house with it under her arm.

But she didn't take the swimsuit. Or, at least, she didn't know that the big-eyed girl had taken it. That's the freckle girl Elen is talking to, and it was the big-eyed girl who borrowed the suit. The big-eyed girl was disgusted because she didn't win the contest, so she just left! It was the poor freckle girl who got brought home and blamed for everything! She wouldn't have entered the contest anyway; she would have been embarrassed to death to walk around on a stage in front of all those people.

The big-eyed girl is getting bolder, and she makes trouble more often now. She knows everything the freckle girl does, but the freckle girl doesn't even know she exists. And I'm still not there. . . .

Christine soon decided that she wanted to move out of her aunt's home into an apartment with a girlfriend. Mamie Lee was shocked and refused until Zueline and Acie gave their permission. This arrangement only lasted a few months; Chris was unable to make it alone. Her salary was adequate to cover her room, food, and clothes, but, unaccountably, she always ran short of funds and could not meet her obligations. Once Elen visited her, and Christine did not have any food or any money to buy food, but she had several new pieces of expensive underwear. When Elen questioned her about it, she seemed vague and was not sure whether the clothes were even hers.

Shortly after this, the police brought Chris to her aunt's home late one night, reporting that she had fainted on the street. Mamie Lee insisted that her niece give up her apartment and come back to live in her home; but Chris, not wanting to admit failure, returned to her bare rooms. About a week later, Mamie Lee heard her front door open and listened as slow steps faltered down the hall. A white-faced Chris opened the door and stood leaning against the wall.

"Christine, are you all right?" Mamie Lee asked, alarmed.

Chris just shook her head, unable to speak.

"Christine, what's the matter?" Mamie Lee started toward the drooping figure.

"Aunt Meme," began the girl, and she fell fainting to the floor.

Christine's legs and arms were severely scratched and bruised. She had fainted several times on her one-block walk from the bus stop. The doctor examined her and gave her a sedative, telling her anxious aunt that Christine was the most nervous person that he had ever examined. He could find nothing wrong with her physically except the surface bruises and scrapes, and he stated that he was not qualified to treat her emotionally. He advised that they get psychological help for her.

Psychological help! No more shocking or frightening advice could have been given to her horrified aunt. The doctor had said that Christine's nerves were a wreck. That was the problem; she just needed rest and care. Her Aunt Meme would look after her, and she would be all right. Mamie Lee sent her husband to fetch Chris's belongings, and the girl moved back into the fold, once more having failed to meet life and deal with it effectively. And under her aunt's watchful eye, the tortured girl did thrive and improve, daily growing stronger and less nervous. To all outward appearances, Mamie Lee's decision to shelter and encourage her niece did seem to be what was needed. And that other advice was locked away, to be secretly pondered.

Chris and Elen spent much time together, but the older girl never seemed able to integrate into Elen's group of friends. Chris was afraid to learn to roller skate or to swim, two of their favorite pastimes. She seldom would even go to the swimming pool; but one day, she surprisingly donned a suit and went into the water. Standing in waist-high water, she suddenly slid out of sight beneath the black water. Everybody thought she was playing, until she did not surface. She was not breathing when she was pulled onto the bank; her face was white, her lips blue. She was given artificial respiration, and her breathing was restored before the doctor arrived, but she did not regain consciousness. Elen thought she was dead, and rushed to the doctor,

"Dr. Mathis, do something! She's drowned!" she cried.

"She's all right," the doctor announced. "Let's take her home."

It was a wet, bedraggled group that descended on the surprised Mamie Lee, who promptly became hysterical. Chris was in bed for several days, sore from the chest manipulations and unable to remember anything that had happened. She did not even remember going to the swimming pool.

That was the big-eyed girl who went swimming. She knew better than to do that. She was afraid of water, too. They all were afraid of water. I am afraid of water, too. When she found herself surrounded by water, she just left. And left the poor freckle girl to drown. What does it mean that they were all afraid of water, all the way back, they were all afraid? And I have always been afraid of water, too. How do I know I have always been afraid if I can't find myself back there? I just know it, I can feel it. I know I have always been afraid . . . and not just of water.

I have been afraid of many things. And they kept coming and coming—and now, looking back, I can't find myself. Was I so afraid that they came all the time, were there all the time, until there was no me? Did they just push me out? No, no, I can't believe that. . . .

Although Chris dated some, none of it was serious; she was waiting for her soldier, and it would soon be time for him to come home. As the time drew near and she began to make her plans, her family became concerned about this big step, wanting to assure that this time she did not make a mistake. Who was this man? What were his prospects? What did he believe in? The small amount of information available was not encouraging. He was from Ward, South Carolina, just up the road from Edgefield; his father ran a sawmill and was known to be a heavy drinker, but worst of all—he was a Catholic! The Family had never been strictly religious, and most anything Protestant (other than, of course, those wild Holy Rollers) was acceptable. But a Catholic! That was an unknown. There were very few Catholics in that part of the country, and anything strange was automatically suspect, but it was well known that they had unusual and secret practices.

Ellis, who had recently become involved in religion himself, talked to his niece shortly after her soldier, Ralph White, returned home and their courtship seemed destined to lead to a more serious alliance.

"Teeny, it will be difficult for you to marry a Catholic if you do not become one yourself," he seriously told her.

"Unc, Ralph isn't that serious about his religion. We've talked about it." Chris wanted very much to please her uncle.

"People say all kinds of things before they get married," her worldly-wise uncle stated bluntly. "Have you talked about the promises you must make and the papers you must sign when you marry?"

"What kind of promises, Unc?"

"You must promise to raise your children in the Catholic Church," he stated, looking sternly at her.

"Why, I wouldn't promise anything like that. You know I wouldn't," she hotly protested.

"Well, you will if you marry a Catholic. Ask him if you won't

223

have to sign papers like that." He had given her his warning. That's all he would do.

When she confronted Ralph, he agreed that such promises would have to be made. Chris vehemently declared that she would never do that, and a quarrel ensued. Ellis was right about the kinds of things people say before they get married. Ralph promised Chris that if she would sign the papers allowing them to be married in the Catholic Church, he would not hold her to performing what the papers demanded if they ever had children. And Chris agreed; after all, those children did not even exist, and might never exist.

When she told her parents of her plans to be married, they were troubled and advised her against marrying a Catholic. They asked her to wait, to get to know Ralph better; and she might have listened to them if she had not been fired from her job. She knew that she had been having trouble learning the telephone routines, she seemed to forget so much, but she had not been reprimanded or warned. Her supervisor simply told her that she had not been progressing as fast as she must to become a telephone operator. Suddenly she had no alternatives, and she was happy with her fate.

The past never rose up to haunt her; it was gone, at least from immediate view. The present was all happiness and excitement, filled with love and beauty. And the future was full of promise and hope, a glowing picture of success and belonging and the rightfulness of things.

Ah, sweet mystery of life, at last I've found you! Chris blindly, trustingly stepped out into her future.

Christine and Anne

Chris, age fifteen (Freckle Girl)

FACING PAGE

top: Chris (Jane) and Don Sizemore before their weddin,
bottom: Chris (Blind Lady), 1955

Zueline and Acie, 1965

Bobby and Chris (Bell Lady)

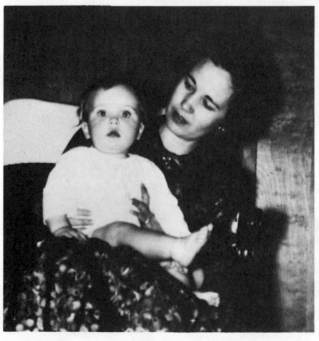

II

THE RESOLUTION
(1947–53)

11

Wife and Mother

She was a virgin. Nobody, not even her mother, would have believed it; but in spite of her experiences, she, at nineteen, came to her husband a virgin. Ralph had wished to change this, but Chris was unshakable in her resolve.

"Goddamn, I didn't know there were any girls like you left!" he would exclaim when she thwarted his amorous attempts.

The ear hears what it wants to hear. Chris heard pride and respect in Ralph's voice; a more objective ear would have discerned selfish callousness and unconcern. She also saw what she wanted to see, and she saw a tall, handsome man, blond, blue-eyed—a returning hero. She was an idealist, still believing, in spite of her experience to the contrary, that wives were loved, honored, and protected, and that husbands were gentle, strong, and protective. She still clung to the example set by the marriages in the Family; any weaknesses in these alliances conveniently forgotten, only the strengths remembered and idealized. She sensed her own inadequacies—her short sortie into the world had proved that she could not manage alone, that she needed someone to lean on—but she had been taught that certain kinds of shortcomings, such as ignorance of money and business matters, merely enhanced a woman's feminism. She had heard her mother and other women in the Family say helplessly, "Oh, I just can't handle things like that. I let my husband take care of those things!" Somehow, women who could handle "things like that" and go it alone in the world were less acceptable than the clinging vines.

And Chris was definitely a clinging vine; but, unfortunately, in her innocence, ignorance, and eagerness, she selected a nonsupportive pillar to which to cling. It would have been less difficult to climb a greased pole. Ralph had strength—a silent, indifferent, glacial strength—but he was incapable of using it to support any other than his own needs. His hot ardor for simple, mechanical premarital sex, she mistook for impatience to know her in that desirable husband-and-wife intimacy that married couples share. He had no wish to know her other than, of course, in the biblical sense; he cared not in the least about her interests, her fears, or her hopes. To him she was not a person with feelings and sensitivities, she was a body to be used as a means for relieving his carnal urges, as a servant for attending to his physical needs, and as a receptacle for bearing his children. He was not a mean man, he was simply, as she, a product of his environment—cold, crude, uncaring—qualities that immediately loomed evident.

They were forbidden to be married in the church building. Since she was not a Catholic, not a member of the flock, the sanctity of the holy house was denied them. They were married by a priest in the parish rectory. No consideration had ever been given to their being married in her church, since he and his family would then never have considered them married—just living in sin, with their children being born in sin. Not only were they denied the sanctity of the church, they were also denied the blessings of their parents, none of whom attended the ceremony. Their only attendants were the thirteen-year-old twins and Ralph's unmarried sister Fanny, acting as Chris's three bridesmaids.

What is a honeymoon? The term conjures up soft, moonlit nights and bright, sunny days—the setting for tenderness and intimacy and a total absorption in the chosen mate. Could one night in a decaying, run-down hotel qualify? Even under such unpromising circumstances two people, a man and a maid, could become one in body and spirit and enjoy a true honeymoon. But that did not occur. The act was neither tender nor loving, and afterward Ralph promptly went to sleep, snoring loudly. What must she have thought? She knew nothing of foreplay or female orgasm, she had heard no woman's talk of enjoying sex; rather, the outward attitude of Mama and her girls was that "it" (never named) was a man's desire, to be submitted to and endured. She was disappointed, she had to be, but she was accepting. He did not touch her again all night, and he seemed to have no desire for her the next morning.

The next day they moved into the house with Ralph's married sister, and he went back to work Monday morning with his father at the sawmill; there had scarcely been a ripple in his routine. In fact, Chris's entrance into his life caused almost no change in his behavior. A silent, surly man by nature, he arose early, worked all day at the mill, came home, ate dinner, and went to bed early, the better to begin all over again the next day. He virtually ignored his new wife, passing the most part of his small conversation with the men in his family. Friday, however, brought a change that was soon just as monotonously predictable as the duller days. This was payday, and with his overalls loaded, he did the town in the company of his father and the men of his family. They bought liquor and sat and drank it. When it was all gone, Ralph came home, dead drunk and profane, to fall into bed, snoring and bellowing whiskey fumes until noon on Saturday. He then rose, washed himself, dressed up, and went to town—sometimes taking Chris with him, sometimes not.

And on Saturday night, just as routinized as the rest of his week, he wanted sex. Sundays he mostly slept and ate, seldom going to church. Chris, daily more subdued, merely hung around the fringes of this deadening existence. The miracle of pregnancy saved her. The realization that a new life, a baby, was growing inside her gave her purpose, lifted her out of the gray valley into which she had fallen, and allowed her to dream into the future. Marriage had disappointed her—it did not bring love and tenderness; but a baby was someone to be loved and was someone who loved in return. Awaiting the birth of her child became her sole existence; she was like a child herself, anticipating a baby doll for Christmas. Toward the middle of her pregnancy, she for the first time since her marriage visited Elen, now a college freshman; and a strange visit it was. Chris was obviously pregnant, wearing maternity clothes, but they never mentioned the fact of her marriage or the rapidly approaching birth of her child. Elen, shy and hesitant to talk about such subjects, could not broach the topic, and Chris completely ignored the existence of any change in her status. They easily fell into their old relationship, acting as if time and events had not moved forward.

Going to the movies in the afternoon, they pretended to be two celebrities and, of course, the most beautiful women in the world. Chris had slipped easily out of her role of approaching motherhood and back into her old childhood pretense. But her motherhood was inescapable and soon forced itself on her. Ralph, against his better judgment, had been persuaded to leave his father's mill and go to work for the county with Acie, where he made considerably more money but had much less freedom. Therefore, several months before the birth of the baby, Chris and Ralph had moved into the County Home with her parents, and he rode to work each day with Acie.

Taffy was born on January 9, 1948, and judged by first-birth experiences, it was not extremely difficult. The birth was at home, with Dr. Dunovant in attendance. When the first pains struck, he was sent for. He discovered that the child was across the birth canal and would have to turn before birth was possible; but, having seen by this time many such similar circumstances, and knowing of nature's way in these matters, he was optimistic, telling Chris and her family that they could expect twelve hours of labor. She became frightened only when the twelve hours stretched interminably into twenty-three. The doctor was with her during the final labor, and she was fully awake and aware when her tiny daughter left her body and became a separate, breathing entity.

Dr. Dunovant tied sheets around her legs and wound them around the footposts of the bed. He stationed Zueline and Ralph, who were present during the entire process, at each post, and when her pains were crushingly severe, they tightened the sheets, separating her legs to prevent damage to the baby, and also helping her to bear down and facilitate birth. The tiny wet mite, wrinkled and red, slipped into the world, leaving the mother spent, exhausted, and empty. A healthy, well-formed, full-term baby, Taffy Acieline White cried lustily as the doctor spanked her chubby little buttocks, wrapped her in a warm, waiting blanket, and laid her at the breast of her mother, still damp and palpitating from the exertion of giving her life.

Chris looked at the crumpled face of her daughter, her baby, and felt her first flush of success, of pride in accomplishment. She had done this. She had carried this child in her own body, nurturing it and protecting it; and now she had produced it for the world

230

to see—beautiful, perfect, hers. She would love it, and, more important, it would love her. It *was* hers, and nobody could take it from her. She had made it and she would keep it, and this, her baby, in return, would love her.

None of this fierce love and protectiveness showed when Elen came to see the baby. Chris was still in bed, and Elen sat beside her holding the baby all day long, feeling very proud when she was asked to be the godmother. Strangely, once again, their talk was mostly about other things than this tiny child, and their inability to talk about Chris's motherhood had an interesting effect on the younger girl. Then and in later years, she had difficulty associating Taffy with Chris—they seemed always to be just two separate people, not bound by the close tie of mother and daughter. Elen might have been rejecting any consideration of a person who had a closer relationship to her loved cousin than she had; but that would not explain Chris's behavior. She could have been excused for talking volubly and at length about her child, mothers universally behave this way; but with Elen she allowed nothing, not even her new baby to intrude into their never-changing relationship.

Ralph could be bound no longer by the restrictions of his job and by the galling confines of the presence of his sober in-laws. He quit his job and went back to work with his father, moving his wife and baby into a mean little house in Ward. They spent their days alone and, on the weekends, most of their nights also. Taffy became Chris's whole world, and as the tiny blond, blue-eyed baby grew, mother and child developed a closeness that remained undiminished during their lifetimes. Chris had at least been correct in her belief that if she loved her child, she would return her love. Taffy has, manifold.

Elen came to visit her here, and she was startled at the conditions that her cousin was enduring—it was just short of squalor. The house, behind a sagging front porch, was small, dark, and run-down. The furnishings were of the poorest sort—castaways from Ralph's relatives. And food was almost nonexistent. Chris made biscuits and white gravy three times a day, and they ate fried okra from a sorry little garden that Ralph worked in a desultory fashion. The girls once fried a large bowl of cut okra, which they both loved, for their noon meal; and, unnoticed, Taffy, less than two years old, climbed onto the table and ate it all. They were not even experienced enough to be worried about the child's health; it was just hilariously funny, and they declared her a chip off the old block, since she evidently liked okra as much as they.

Ralph, coming and going in silent surliness, ignored all three of them, scarcely acknowledging Elen's presence. Chris never discussed her husband with her childhood confidante, never sharing one married secret with her or relating a single experience. They who had emptied their minds to each other over the years, holding back nothing, however personal, discovered now a subject about which they could not speak. They spent the hot, lazy days talking about Elen's college life. The younger girl, now a senior at Furman University, told her cousin in detail what it was like to live in a dormitory, go to classes, study for exams, date Clemson military cadets, and attend football games. And Chris, listening intently to this bright world so different from hers, stored away all these colorful pictures and vicarious feelings to be used a later day.

Elen loved to be with her cousin. Even though she was happy at college, had made close, satisfying friends, and had fit comfortably into her new life, an element was missing that Chris provided. Never having been very close to her mother, the kind of close where intimate experiences are exchanged, Elen and Mamie Lee had grown even more distant after the birth of Laura, now seven years old. Mamie Lee loved people and doing things, and she had no idea that her undemanding, self-confident daughter needed mothering, needed a mother to talk to—to just tell experiences to. They never sat and chatted, exchanged confidences; and when Elen tried to tell her of a troubling situation, Mamie Lee, whose philosophy was to refuse to acknowledge trouble and to let "things work themselves out," simply pooh-poohed the problem and rode right over the top of it. Elen was extremely close to her father, but he was a man of great dignity who commanded much respect from both family and community, and attempting to chatter away to such a man about the inconsequences of daily life would have approached blasphemy. In long sessions that they both loved, they talked of lofty, profound subjects, such as the meaning of life, the real-estate market, the long-range effects of Roosevelt's New Deal programs, what the soul is and whether it has density and weight, and on and on. Elen could not pollute such rarefied air with the mundane talk of daily college life.

Chris filled this void in her life, and here the older girl played a strange role. She did not mother Elen—they were definitely peers and equals—but she listened, and their relationship, as old and as clearly defined as any mother-and-child alliance, encompassed the entire range of attitude and emotion. Elen told of her fears and her shortcomings, of her desires and her failures, and she even bragged and told of her accomplishments—all was revealed without fear of criticism or derision. They were totally accepting of each other—a condition not often found on God's green Earth.

Ralph had not devoted much time to his daughter, and as she grew into a toddler, even this small amount of interest diminished. This apparent neglect of the child, which was obvious in public as well as at home, hurt Chris deeply and caused her to draw even more protectively close to the gentle, sweet-natured baby. Suddenly her old half-forgotten promise loomed ominously before her. Ralph announced one night in his sullen, rude way,

"The priest says it's time she got baptized." He pointed a rough finger at the tiny, diaper-clad Taffy.

Chris's heart lurched. "She's not going to be taken into the Catholic Church. You promised me she wouldn't," she hastily protested.

"You signed the papers. It's all legal," he reminded, showing no emotion except a faint smile crinkling his insolently sleepy eyes.

"But you promised that if I signed the papers, you wouldn't hold me to it," she replied, excitement causing her voice to rise and crack.

"Ah, hell, what's a promise!" he exploded. "They've got the papers and you've got to do it to get them off my back."

"I won't do it! They're not going to have my child." She stood, placing herself bodily between him and the unconcerned baby, as if someone meant to literally take Taffy away.

Ralph, surprised by her unexpected show of resistance, walked out, glancing back at the door, "You just suit yourself, but you'll do it. Just you wait and see, you'll do it."

Fear clutched her heart, but her resolve hardened. Taffy was hers—her baby—and she loved her. She was convinced that Ralph didn't love Taffy. If he took her into his church where she, her

233

own mother, could not go, he would take her love away. And Taffy loved her. Even as little as she was, she loved her mother. They were together all the time, but if Taffy went to that church she would be separated from her. Nobody was going to take her baby from her. If she loved and guarded Taffy, the child would love and guard her in return. There was something almost prophetic in this wild, erratic reasoning.

Chris's fears became concrete when Ralph announced that they were moving, moving into the Catholic rectory—the same rectory in which they were married just two short years before. The building, situated on the grounds of the church complex, was no longer used as living quarters for the nuns, and it had been offered to Ralph for fifteen dollars a month. How could Chris argue against it? It was an old but nice house, much nicer than the one in which they lived; but it would locate her next door to the dreaded church, and would enfold her in a community of feared Catholics, most of whom were in-law relatives and much disapproving of her and her stand concerning Taffy's church affiliation.

After they moved into the rectory, Ralph was scarcely seen at home, except to eat. He completely ignored both Chris and Taffy, speaking to Chris only when it was absolutely necessary. Sex became an infrequent thing between them, and her worst fears were confirmed. Shortly after she moved in, she was visited by one of the parish priests. His dress and formality were entirely foreign to her, and they, coupled with the dark stories from her Protestant background and her own recently formed suspicions, magnified her fears monstrously and turned the man instantly into an adversary. This judgment, however, was not made without reason, without cause. This visit was only the first, made often and regularly by several priests, in which pressure was exerted on her as well as blame laid to her account.

"Ralph was a good Church member until he married a Protestant," she was informed. "We would like for you to become one of us, but if you can't do that, you don't have the right to deprive him of his faith and influence him not to come to church."

"Ralph can go to church whenever he wants to. I don't keep him from going to church," she protested, angry that she was being blamed for Ralph's negligence, that somehow she had become responsible for all his bad behavior, even his Sunday morning hangovers.

"But you do not encourage him since you do not believe," he persisted. "And you do not have the right to deprive him of his children being Catholic. This is his right because when you were married you forfeited all claim to the religious rights of the children."

She could not fight this. It was true; she had done just exactly as she was charged.

"But Ralph promised not to hold me to those things if I would sign the papers," she tremblingly leveled her only charge.

"A young man, in his ardor before marriage, will promise anything," she was told, and the promise was dismissed as being of no importance.

And what about her ardor and her promises made before marriage? Could they not also be dismissed? No! She was never threatened, but she felt threatened, just as if they had actually verbalized a plan to remove Taffy from her. Not only was she fighting them, she had also to do battle with her own feelings of dishonesty and guilt. She had promised, given her word, signed papers; and now she was refusing. Where could she go for help? Once again, Chris had seemingly burned all the bridges behind her, cutting off all possibility of turning back. Her parents had disapproved of this marriage for this very reason, warning her of the difficulties innate in such an alliance. They had even refused to attend the wedding because it was to be Catholic in nature. Even Unc had talked to her, warned her, saying to her exactly what the priest had said about Ralph's promise not to hold her accountable. She had no place to go; she was alone.

It was then that the dream began: She and Taffy were in a large gray room in the middle of which was a big pool of muddy water. She and Taffy stood on the bank and looked down into the water writhing with snakes. Taffy fell into this cauldron and began to turn into a snake, and when Chris jumped in to save her, Aunt Myrtle appeared on the bank and would not let them climb out to safety.

The dream came regularly, and Chris always awoke in a cold sweat, her terror turning to deep depression. If gentle, understanding Aunt Myrt would not allow her to save her child, no one

235

would help her. She did not even have a friend to whom she could talk. Ralph's parents lived in walking distance down the road, and they, of course, also blamed their daughter-in-law for their son's negligence to his church. They were cool to Taffy, but Chris knew that their attitude was due to what they considered to be the child's sinful condition—they would gladly have included her if she were Catholic. And that, Chris was afraid of—Taffy's being taken over by all these people, being taken away from her. Of all her numerous in-law relatives, only two accepted her as a person: Ralph's young unmarried sister, and the wife of Ralph's uncle. With them she could talk, feeling comfortable and un-judged; but they were also Catholic—she could not tell them of her deep, gnawing, destructive fear.

And she could not tell Elen, either, when her cousin came to visit. This time Elen brought her little sister Laura with her, and Elen was bursting with experiences to share with Chris. Elen had finished college, taught school a year, and accepted an engage-ment ring. While the two little girls played, the cousins, now twenty and twenty-three, planned Elen's future. Determined to settle down and be a proper wife and mother, she had selected her future husband coolly and logically, bypassing eligible young men who seemed frivolous, or who drank, or who (horrors!) played golf on Sunday instead of attending church. At this point in her life, Elen, who had been guarded closely—perhaps too closely—by her parents, and who was rather a prude by nature, had never had her passions aroused. Even when she indulged in petting (a recent activity), her mind controlled her emotions, and such expressions as "came to her husband a virgin" and "lips that touch liquor will never touch mine" were sacred dogma. Perhaps this is the reason Chris never talked to her of her own intimate marital experiences, sensing that this paragon of virtue would be embarrassed by such talk.

They talked confidently, never suspecting that these, the very best-laid plans, would also go astray. What advice do the experts and the researchers give to young women concerning the selection of a mate? Chris made her choice impetuously, emotionally, con-sidering first her needs and weaknesses. Elen chose logically, une-motionally, considering mainly how she wanted to direct her own life. Both choices were disastrous; both chose husbands completely incompatible with their own natures. But this week they talked and dreamed and played, totally unaware of the pain and frustration each shortly faced. Elen left with Chris's promise to be her matron of honor one year hence—a promise that she would be unable to keep.

Another move, another house—this time to live with another one of Ralph's married sisters in the upstairs section of her house. It was not an unpleasant house, the rooms were large and spacious; but it was not Chris's home, and she still felt surrounded by enemies. She was pregnant again—about three months—but she felt no joy in the making of this child as she had felt when Taffy grew in her womb. She now knew that a baby does not necessarily make a home complete.

The priest had visited her on Friday evening, renewing his charge against her, and in the night the pains had begun in her stomach—deep, searing pains. They subsided, leaving only a slightly nauseous discomfort accompanied by a deep, uneasy fear. Hesitant to be alone, and knowing that Ralph's Saturday jaunts to town lasted until deep into Sunday morning, she begged him not to leave her.

"Please, Ralph, don't leave me. I don't feel good. The pain was bad."

"Ah, you're so scared. You try to be a baby. Women have babies all the time. Nothin's goin' to happen to you," he scoffed, starting for the door.

"Please, Ralph, I'm afraid." She grabbed him by the arm.

He jerked his arm away, accidentally striking her chin with his heavy ring. "Let go!" he snapped, stalking from the room without a backward glance.

Stunned by surprise and pain, Chris made no sound; she only put her trembling hand to her chin. Feeling the warm blood staining her grazed face, she blindly stumbled into the bathroom for a cloth. Her feet slipped on the water still puddled from Ralph's bath, and she thudded heavily to the hard floor. Strangely the pain came not from her bruised back, but from her belly, burning, slicing, cramping. She felt a warm, sticky flow soaking her pants and spreading down her legs. Darkness began to engulf her.

"Do something! Don't just lie there or we're both gonna die," urgently spoke an excited voice close by.

237

She fought off the waves of soothing, dulling blackness. "Who are you? Help me! Help me! I need help!" she gasped as the pain seared her body.

"Oh, Lordy, I don't know what to do! But you'd better do somethin', and quick, or we've had it! This's what you get messin' around with men!" snapped the voice, strangely close, too close.

"But what's happening? Where am I? Go get help. Help me!" she pled, trying to pull herself up by grasping the side of the tall, footed bathtub.

"You must be crazy, I can't go for help!" The voice was laced with wild laughter. "And I'm not coming out into this mess. I didn't play around with men. But you'd better do something. We're bleedin' to death!"

A kaleidoscope of pictures swarmed through her mind: She was pregnant and she was bleeding; bleeding meant birth; but it was not time for the birth; she fell, and the bleeding started. That's it, she must stop the bleeding. Taffy! Where was Taffy? Frantically, she attempted to pull herself into a sitting position, but she could not; her left hip would not bend, and the pain threatened her consciousness. Cautiously raising her head, she noticed that the low window was raised about a foot, just enough for Taffy to fall out.

"Taffy! Come here, come to Mother," she called, making her voice calm and free of stress. "Pull down the window, honey. That's a good girl." She spoke reassuringly to the two-year-old child.

"Now, reach Mother the washcloth, Baby. There it is hanging on the bathtub. Pull it off and reach it to Mother. That's a good girl, Baby," her voice faint and thin from shock and loss of blood faded as Taffy sat down on the floor beside her.

Chris reached inside her clothes and stuffed as much of the damp cloth as she could into her vagina. She was horribly frightened. The people downstairs were gone for the day, Ralph would not return until early morning, she might be alone until tomorrow morning. If she lost consciousness, what would happen to Taffy? Was she going to bleed to death?

That's two new ones! Two came at the same time. It's all confusing to work out, but two entirely different ones came at the same time. It had been so long since anyone had come—

over two years. Who was there all that time? It wasn't me, but I can see her. She was kind, long-suffering, and plain-looking, and she desperately loved Taffy; but she was always afraid, and when she fell she blacked out, just went away. And she never returned. Then two came at the same time! One was just a voice. It seemed that the voice called the other one to come and do something about the bleeding. When the second one came, she didn't know anything about what had happened; but the voice not only knew what had just happened, but what had gone on before as well. The voice was flippant and selfish—she only wanted to live, to stop the bleeding; but the second one was dependable and mature. She felt responsible for Taffy's safety as well as for her own. And she seemed to get a lot of memories all at once, as if she were grasping for the information she needed to save herself. Where did those memories come from? If she had just come and did not know about Taffy's birth, then who was Taffy's mother? My God, did the one who was Taffy's mother just die? I remember the birth, but it didn't happen to me. I saw it happening, but it didn't happen to me—I felt no pain! Am I then not my daughter's mother? I won't think about that. . . .

Acie and Zueline did not visit their daughter often, but strangely, on this day in the late afternoon, they came to see her. She had lain on her back in a pool of her own blood since early morning, and by now, the miscarriage over, she was weak, exhausted, and semiconscious. Acie wrapped her in a quilt and carried her to the car, while Zueline packed clothes for her and Taffy. The nearest doctor, in the town of Saluda, repaired her damages: the ravaged uterus, the dislocated hip, and the cut chin, which all assumed had been sustained in the fall. They took her home, and she was unable to leave her bed for a week. Then once again she returned to her marriage bed, the very hard bed that she had made for herself, leaving her child with her parents.

Ralph immediately moved her again—this time, as if in punishment, to a one-room hovel. Down a dirt lane in the middle of a weed-grown field, it hunched in its careless litter like a rotting carcass. The outside bricks had fallen away from the chimney, leaving a clear, open hole to the outside; one corner of the roof had caved in, exposing the sky through a wide, gaping hole; the uneven cracks between the floor boards revealed the soft, powdery dust of ground long starved for water, and stars twinkled through the yawning cracks in the unceiled roof as she lay in her hard bed at night. The crowning indignity—there was no bathroom, either inside or out. She had grown up with outside toilets—the privy— and she could have tolerated that; but she had never squatted in the bushes like a wild animal! Taffy was now toilet trained, but, ironically, she had no toilet.

The headaches were back, and they came daily. A blinding, thudding flash would strike her, raising the veins in her temples, forcing the air from her gasping lungs. Sometimes the attack was unbearable and she ran, making wild, erratic trails through the hut and around the yard. Occasionally the voice returned to taunt,

"You're stupid. Why do you stay here? I'm not going to come out in this hole. You've got to get us out of here!"

She was sure she was going insane, and there was nothing to do and nowhere to go. Ralph was gone for days at a time, and she and Taffy had no food, often eating blackberries and plums from a bramble of bushes along an old fence row in the field. They had been living there about a month when, in a frenzy of pain one day, she ran from the shack and blindly rushed head-on into a large tree. The impact threw her onto her back, and there she lay, in the broiling noon sun, bleeding, unconscious. Once again, unsummoned, her parents came. They found them there in the dirt, Chris's unmoving body sprawled, her face covered with dried blood; her two-year-old child faithfully kneeling beside her, trying to brush the busy, ravenous ants from her mother's face with her own tiny, awkward hands. It had been a losing battle; Zueline turned her face in horror from the sight of the revolting insects rimming her daughter's bloody nose and mouth, and industriously scampering over the white skin carrying their payload of happy find.

The father carried his daughter into the hovel out of the sun, and finding no water with which to wash her face and revive her, ordered his wife to collect all of their clothes. He drove away with the moaning girl and her strangely quiet child, having no intention of ever allowing them to return to this neglect and degradation. He left a note for his son-in-law telling him where his wife and child were, and instructing him to come to the County Home when he read the note. Acie emphatically wrote, "I want to talk to you."

It was two days before Ralph showed up at his father-in-law's home. Had he been away from his home that long, or had he been hesitant to face his wife's father?

Acie came right to the point, mincing no words.

"If you want them back, you're going to have to get a decent place for them to live. And you're going to have to start treating her better than this. I'm not telling you how you've got to live your life, but I *am* telling you how you've got to treat my daughter." The calm voice never raised, never became heated, but there was no doubt that Acie meant every word and that he intended to see that his instructions were obeyed.

Ralph again quit the sawmill, got a job in the woolen mill in Johnston, and moved Chris and Taffy into a small white house beside the railroad tracks. It was a nice little house, fairly new, and at one time Chris could have been happy there; but now the voice would not let her be at peace anywhere. It was ever-present; she never knew when it was going to speak out, and she was never sure whether other people could hear it. Ralph was so silent and unresponsive that he could have heard the voice and just ignored it, as he ignored her when she spoke to him. At first, on hearing the voice, she would look at him to see if he had heard, hoping that he had heard; but she turned away when he scolded,

"What in hell are you starin' at me for? Are you goin' crazy?"

Yes, that's exactly what she thought—that she was going crazy. Isn't that what it meant, hearing voices that nobody else heard? And it was always the same voice, always talking to her about Ralph. The voice hated Ralph.

"Knock his block off!" the voice ordered. "He's just a son-of-a-bitch."

As he stood before the bathroom mirror shaving, the voice instructed,

"Pull that rug from under him. Lay him flat on his back!"

Sometimes the voice was so convincing that it was not to be denied. Once as they sat at the table eating, Ralph silently cramming in his food, the voice commanded,

241

"Snatch the tablecloth off and dump the food all over the bastard!"

And she did; without thinking, she pulled the cloth and spilled the food all over Ralph. He jumped up furious, demanding,

"My God, what's come over you?"

"Ralph, I'm sorry. I don't know how I did that," she stumbled up, attempting to clean the mess from his clothes.

"You stay away from me. You've just lost your mind." And he changed his clothes and left the house.

The voice congratulated. "That was a good girl. That'll show the bastard what we think of him."

Ralph's behavior began to change from his usual silent surliness. He became mean and hard to deal with; and from ignoring his daughter, he turned to an almost diabolical interest in her. He criticized Chris's treatment of her, complaining,

"You're making a sissy outa the kid. She's gittin' just like you—afraid of everything."

He began to try to force Taffy to face things she was afraid of. And she was deathly afraid of the train that passed the house twice a day. From the time she first heard its distant rumble through its bone-jarring passing to its last faint whistle, she clung in wide-eyed fright to her mother. Ralph decided to cure her fear by locking her outside the house as the train passed. The train scarcely slowed through the small town, but it blew long and loud, and the little house was only a few feet from the track. It was a terrifying experience. Chris tried to push Ralph from the door, but he would not move. Chris ran to the bedroom and got his pistol from the drawer. Returning to the room, she pointed it with both hands, ordering,

"Get away from that door."

Whether or not he heard her, her meaning was clear. He moved. When she went outside, her heart stopped: Taffy was nowhere to be seen. Had the powerful train drawn the tiny child under its wheels? Suddenly, into the strangely buzzing silence, came soft moans and mewing sounds. Following them, she found her child under the back porch huddled against the base of the chimney, rocking and mumbling in the extreme of her terror. Chris crawled under the porch and took the child in her arms, taking over the rocking and the mumbling,

"It's all right, Mother is with you."

They stayed there until Ralph, without one attempt to find them, left the house. When they crawled out and entered the house, Taffy asked to go to bed, and her mother went with her. They lay there under the protecting covers, clinging to each other. For the rest of her life, whenever Taffy became frightened or hurt, she wanted to go to bed.

During this time, Elen, who was teaching school in the northern part of the state, asked Chris to spend a week visiting her. She drove down to get Chris on Saturday and was satisfied with her explanation that Ralph was away and that Taffy was staying with her grandparents. She did not know that Chris had told no one about her intended visit, that she had bought new clothes for which she had no money to pay, and that, in fact, it was "the voice" who made the visit. The week was a disaster. Elen, totally unprepared for her cousin's condition, helplessly and often unbelievingly watched her bizarre behavior. Chris never really slept, only napped periodically during the day, and her nights were filled with restless wandering and incessant, disjointed chattering. Elen could only sit and watch; response was not needed, being, in fact, a disruption to the monologue that Chris untiringly performed. When, though, through sheer exhaustion, Chris did finally fall into a short, fitful slumber, her unconscious physical contortions and verbal outbursts were even more upsetting to the watchful Elen, who was afraid to sleep herself.

During these short naps, never of more than five to ten minutes, Chris's body was alive with movement. She writhed, her head twisted and turned, sweat soaked her. Her neck corded, her temples veined, and her skin burned fiery red. And she talked: barely discernible words, groans, gibberish, and laughter—wild, high, gay laughter. At first Elen tried to awaken her, but she would not respond. Then suddenly it would all be over; Chris's eyes would open, revealing a watchful wariness, as if trying to determine what had been happening; her neck and temples returned to normal, and she was ready to resume her caged pacing and compulsive, scattered talking. She scarcely ate at all, yet her thin, taut body burned with nervous energy. Elen, afraid to leave her alone, took her to school, thinking that high school English

243

classes would interest her. They did not. She was dreadfully bored, and she showed it.

On Thursday, Elen had to attend a class of her own held in Greenville, some miles away. What was she going to do with Chris? She knew from what she had observed that her cousin would be unable to sit for three hours in a classroom. Chris solved the problem by suggesting that she see a movie while Elen was in class. It seemed the best solution, and they agreed to meet at a designated time. Elen was worried all afternoon, but she became almost frantic by the time Chris was an hour late. And then, there she came, tripping happily down the street, explaining that she had sat through the movie twice, a story that later turned out to be a total fabrication—she had not been to the movies at all.

The planned return trip to take Chris home on the following Saturday was never made. Late Friday night the doorbell rang, and when Elen opened the door, there stood Ralph and Tiny. Becky remained in the car, too embarrassed to come into the house. Tiny asked the surprised, pleased Elen,

"Elen, is Teeny here?"

"Of course, Tiny, come in. Ralph, come on in." And she moved aside to invite them in.

"Chris," she called into the bedroom, "come and see who's here."

Chris turned the corner into the room, looked at her husband and sister, and fainted dead away. Everybody rushed to her, and Ralph laid her on the couch. Elen later remembered being surprised that this faint was so different from Chris's "naps"; it was quiet and calm—no cording or writhing or talking. When she awakened, she appeared to be dazed, having no knowledge of where she was or how she got there—the whole week was a complete blank. While they packed her clothes, Tiny explained to Elen that Chris had told no one where she was going; she had simply left. In searching the house for any clue to her whereabouts, they had found Elen's letter asking her to come for a visit. On a chance, after being unable to reach Elen by phone, they had driven the more than one hundred miles hoping to find Chris, who had been missing almost a week. Chris was led from Elen's apartment scarcely able to walk, her eyes dull and puzzled.

That was the other one, the voice, she has started coming out, not just talking. She makes it so difficult for the other one, the quiet, good one. "The voice" is sometimes just mean. She'll do anything to get her way, and she scares the other one to death by talking to her. The nice one doesn't know about her; she thinks it's just a voice in her head. And maybe it is—no one else can hear the voice. The bad one just wants to have fun; she hates Chris's life with Ralph and Taffy. She intercepted Elen's letter and planned the whole trip. She knows everything the nice one does, but the nice one doesn't know anything she does. She didn't even know that she had been to see Elen. When the bad one saw Ralph and Tiny, she knew her game had been discovered, and she just left—leaving the nice one to work it out. Now that "the voice" is coming out, she is really going to make trouble. I wonder if I am the nice one. No, I couldn't be, I saw her when she first came, at the miscarriage. But what did I need this nasty one for? She's only going to cause trouble; but at least she's got spunk. And that's more than I can say for the other one.

And now the headaches began again, the voice and the headaches; and following the headaches were periods of blackness, when all was blank. Ralph was seldom home, day or night, and he had not approached her for sex since her miscarriage; but when he was home, he continued to take a stern line with Taffy. This upset Chris terribly, and on one other occasion, she pulled his own gun on him to halt his harassment of the child. One night Taffy was playing on the floor and making more noise than her father thought she should. He scolded her, and when she continued, he jerked her from the floor and locked her in the dark bathroom. Taffy might have accepted her punishment with little complaint except for the dark; she was afraid to be alone in the dark—a fear that her mother understood all too well. The child's hysterical screams awoke an apathetic fear in the mother's heart, and she tried to open the door; however, when Ralph placed his considerable bulk against it, Chris, suddenly furiously aroused, again took his pistol from the drawer and pointed it at him, warning,

"Move or I'll kill you. Let my child out!"

Opening the door, he protested, "It's my child, too. I've got to see that the kid's raised right. She'll be just like you if I don't stop it!" He stood above them as she knelt on the floor holding the terrified, snubbing child to her own trembling body. The gun lay on the floor beside her.

"If you do that to her again, I'll kill you," she calmly stated, looking at him with eyes that neither hated nor feared.

"Goddamn, you're the damnedest woman I ever saw! You're crazy!" he fumed, but he did not continue the punishment. He believed her.

Chris was in a never-ending torment. The voice taunted her, the headaches crazed her, and she often came conscious, almost like awaking, to find herself involved in circumstances about which she was totally ignorant. And the nagging voice always brought on a headache. The voice took part in the arguments between her and Ralph, and now their arguments were almost continuous; any subject could start one: grocery bills, clothes for Chris and Taffy, the church, and, especially, Ralph's job. He hated working in the woolen mill and wanted to return to his father's sawmill. He came home for his noon meal, and that is when most of the trouble surfaced. On one such occasion he asserted,

"I'm gonna quit this goddamn job and go back to work at the sawmill!"

"We're doing fine, Ralph. I like it here." She tried to soothe him.

"The hell we are! Look at our grocery bills. If we lived out in the country we could raise our food. And you're always wantin' new clothes. Out in the country you don't have to be as fancy." He warmed up to his subject, going over the same old complaints.

"Ralph, we have to have clothes. We can't go anywhere in those old things." Chris renewed her time-worn defenses.

"Well, we're not gonna stay here. We're goin' back out to the country," he stated, seeming to have made up his mind.

"You know what Daddy said," she countered with her final argument—her strongest. "He said Taffy and I couldn't go back out there. That's what made me sick, living out there."

He stood up, defiant and angry, "Well, there's no reason why I can't go back out there. I don't have to stay here!"

This was what she dreaded and feared most—his leaving them. How could she support herself and Taffy? What would she do if he left? She was sick, perhaps insane. In the midst of her turmoil the voice spoke, resounding loudly in her head.

"Slap his goddamn face; I don't like him nohow." Chris, who never used profanity, was always shocked when the voice inside her head cursed. It intensified her confusion and caused her head to throb with knifing pains. Her whole being strained toward her bursting head; she fought with waves of soundless darkness. Suddenly she felt warm wetness coursing down her legs; she blacked out.

The blue eyes opened, baleful and angry.

"You goddamn son-of-a-bitch, you've made me shit all over myself!" she stormed.

Ralph stared at her in amused disbelief, "Gawd, what's the matter with you? A grown woman shittin' all over herself like a baby! Gawd, you smell awful!" He left the house, shaking his head in puzzled disbelief.

"God a'mighty, I'm not about to stay out and clean up this mess. But if she thinks this is going to keep me from coming out, she's crazy." The angry blue eyes closed, and when they opened, they were dull, frightened, puzzled. She stood up, became aware of the discomfort between her legs, felt her soaked, reeking clothes, and stared at the stain on the floor.

There she stood, bathed in her own excretions, alone; even the voice had deserted her. The heaviness in her pants wafted its unmistakable odor to her nostril, and she awkwardly, dully made her way to the bathroom. The cleaning of her body was a horror. A headache, even fainting, was one thing, but this—this was degradation, indignity, social ostracism. Was this a new horror beginning? She was now convinced that she was crazy: She heard voices, she could not account for her actions, and now this. She had not only lost control of her mind, now her body was out of control too. How much could she bear? More than she thought. The wetting began to occur often with the headaches, and occasionally her stress removed even the involuntary control from her bowels and produced the ignominy of soiling her own body.

Good Lord, what an awful experience! She doesn't even remember soiling herself. And the voice actually materialized this time; it came out and took over. It knew everything she did, but

247

she can only hear its voice when it's not out. When it's out, she doesn't know anything. Where does she go when the voice is out? This awful thing happened many times. . . .

Once this dehumanizing scene was enacted before Taffy. Ralph was ranting about leaving when Chris, seated on the bed, grasped her head and moaned. Her bladder emptied itself onto their only bed, running onto the floor. Taffy, frightened at this forbidden act, which she had been taught to control, began to cry. Ralph stared at her in disgust,

"You're gettin' to be a problem, shittin' and pissin' in your clothes! But I'm not surprised, the way you've been actin'. You're crazy if you think I'm gonna sleep in that bed!"

The furious blue eyes glittered up at him, "If you were any kinda man at all, this wouldn't be happenin'. Git out of here, go on, git out! Shut up, Taffy! Go play while I clean up this mess. I'm not gonna run just because she pees on herself. She can clean up the bed, though. I wouldn't sleep in any bed with that bastard!"

When Chris regained her control, her body was clean and dressed, but the bed was soaked through and Taffy was quietly crying from the unexpected scolding. Chris remembered nothing except the quarrel and the blinding headache.

For unexplained reasons, Ralph, after months of abstinence, at least at home, approached her for sex again. She complied, faithful to her teaching that a wife never refused her husband. Always having yielded in utter submission, never pleasure, Chris was startled at the intensity of her repugnance and resentment at this heretofore quietly endured act. But she could no longer endure; she would rather die than submit to him again. What was she going to do? The voice was no help.

"I wouldn't sleep with the son-of-a-bitch. I've never slept with him. He's nothin' but a dog, just a hound dog! It's not goin' to do any good tryin' to black out and turn him over to me. I ain't gonna have him. I ain't gonna have no man. And if you think peeing in your pants is gonna stop me, you're crazy."

It was, strangely, these two events—her inability to again submit to sex and her wetting her pants—that brought her unbearable circumstances to light and led to her first search for professional help. She and Taffy had been visiting Mamie Lee, and all had gone well until Ralph came to bring them home. During the night he demanded sex.

"You goddamn son-of-a-bitch, you're crazy if you think I'm gonna let you lie on me," she spit out, jumping from the bed and running from the room.

Ralph, thunderstruck, and embarrassed by being in a strange house, did not follow. Taffy later found her mother lying in the bathroom, and the child, now four years old, called,

"Aunt Meme, Aunt Meme, come quick. My mother's lying on the floor!"

When Mamie Lee rushed in, she found the child with her eternal washcloth, trying to revive her mother. Chris was put to bed, and the doctor was called. He told the worried aunt that her niece was in a terribly nervous state, one that he could not treat, and that she needed the care of a psychiatrist. Mamie Lee, after watching over the restless, tossing girl for the rest of the night, was finally convinced; and she and Ellis made a trip to see Acie and Zueline, telling them the story and urging that they find help for their daughter.

The troubled parents needed only one other happening to harden their resolve and send them for help. Chris, Taffy, and Ralph were visiting them when the subject of Ralph's job arose. As the discussion became heated, Chris's head began to ache, and suddenly she loosed her bladder, sending urine spreading over the sofa on which she was seated and dripping down onto the floor.

Ralph jumped to his feet, pointing,

"See what I mean? She just pisses all over herself. How do you expect a man to live with something like that?"

Acie was infuriated. "I want to remind you," he grated, "that my daughter did not do these things before she married you." He stood facing his son-in-law, his slight frame no physical match for the burly younger man, but the force of Acie's anger squelched any resistance remaining in Ralph.

"You have got to get help for her," Acie ordered.

"It's all right with me. Take her to the doctor if you want to." Ralph tried to wash his hands of the situation.

Acie pursued, "You are going to get help for her. And now! And we'll go with you."

And they did. For the third time, her parents and her child took Chris to the doctor; it was the first time for her husband. But this doctor, also, took one look at her and declared that her malady did not lie within his range of skills. She needed psychiatric care. This established firmly and without doubt in Chris's mind that she was going insane. She knew nothing of psychiatrists other than those in institutions. If she was going to a psychiatrist, she must be going to an institution. She was going to be locked up. Perhaps that was best; she was losing her mind, she couldn't take care of herself.

But Taffy! What about Taffy? Ralph could not have Taffy! If she were crazy, would Ralph take Taffy? She talked to her parents,

"Mother, what will happen to Taffy? I know Ralph doesn't love her; he doesn't even want her. Daddy, will you and Mother look after her?"

"Of course we will, honey," Zueline assured her. "But you'll be all right. It's not as serious as you think. You'll be all right."

"Daddy, if anything happens to me, will you and Mother raise my baby for me?" she pled, needing to have them both answer.

"Daughter, you know we will. Now, don't you worry none about the baby. And you'll be fine." He put his hand on her thin shoulder.

But she knew that she would never be fine again. She heard voices, she couldn't control her body, and she forgot things she had done. Soon she likely would forget everything, even who she was, and be one of those lost souls who just sit in asylums and stare and talk back to their voices. Were they at peace? Oh, she hoped they were at peace. Dear God, if she couldn't be at peace, please let her die.

Afraid to live in the closed world of her thoughts, yet even more afraid to live in the open world of people and things, she voluntarily took this step—not the ultimate step of death, but the step just short of death—into the insane asylum. Her greatest fear was that it was an irrevocable step and that in the unbearable torment of her mind she would be unable to choose death if it became preferable to life.

12

Who Are You?

What does the mind feel on its way to being locked up in an insane asylum? Does it consider the irony of even attempting to lock up the mind? The mind ranges freely, unfettered; it is only when its own confusion obscures its path that it becomes caged, and then only behind bars of its own construction.

And Chris's mind was confused; having run through its tangled maze in search of escape, it now begged for release, for direction. If that came only through locking up the body, so be it. Why does the idea of being locked up conjure a picture of darkness? One could be caged in the light, in the sun, but one seldom is. And the building to which Chris was first taken did little to dispel her dread of the impending darkness. A large, cavernous structure, old and looming, it was entered by climbing enormous steps running the entire width of the building. The entrance hall was dark, musty, and seemingly interminable in its length, appearing to the frightened girl to narrow to a diminishing point in the distance. Running off this *Alice in Wonderland* corridor were other, darker branching corridors, all lined with closed, silent doors. Into one of these dim alleys they turned.

"This is it," she thought. "I'll be locked in one of these dark rooms." Did they have windows? It didn't matter. She was so tired.

They moved slowly, hesitantly down the hall, speaking when necessary in hushed tones. The plump, graying mother; the slim, balding father; the burly, swaggering husband; and the woman, ah, the woman! Pitifully thin; emaciated, almost, drooping;

downcast—a beaten animal, its fine spirit broken. Irreparable damage? Could the process be reversed? Would fierce pride ever again hold high the hanging head, blaze defiantly the dull eyes? Did a miracle await behind one of the somber doors?

An impersonal secretary behind an impersonal desk showed them into a room perhaps just a shade lighter than the endless hall. Her first meeting with Corbett H. Thigpen left few distinct impressions on Chris. He was a doctor for crazy people, but that was not a real doctor. Perhaps he sensed her feeling of the wrongness of things, for almost immediately after he took her into his office he sent someone for his little black bag—the real doctor's badge of office—and placed it for no tangible reason on the desk. He then admitted with his credentials in full view between them, that he was a different kind of doctor.

"Mrs. White, I work a little differently from other doctors. I don't physically examine my patients. I talk to them, and they talk to me. They tell me things about themselves: what is worrying them, what they feel, what they think. Now, what's been bothering you?" He sat back in his chair, threw his right leg over its arm, and looked at her, waiting for an answer.

She was afraid. Never having talked about her troubles to anyone, she could not just begin to tell this casual stranger what was eating away at her. And anyway, her troubles had nothing to do with her going crazy, the voices, and those other things. Her eyes remained downcast, her thin fingers nervously entwined each other.

"I can't help you unless you talk to me," he gently prodded. "Just tell me about yourself, your family."

Haltingly she began, "Well, I have a little girl, Taffy. She's four. And my husband, Ralph, is a Catholic, and he drinks a lot."

"Yes," he encouraged. "And how does this make you feel?"

"I have headaches a lot, and I'm very depressed and unhappy."

"I see." He sat forward in his chair. "Well, why don't you relax and let me see if I can help you go to sleep, so that you can talk to me further. If you will just relax and listen to the sound of my voice, you will hear nothing but the sound of my voice."

He looked at her, "I will begin to count, and when you hear the number ten, you will be asleep." He began a slow cadence, "One . . . one, two . . . two, three . . . three . . . ten."

When he reached ten, she was completely relaxed. She was aware of life, aware of facts, but totally oblivious to her surroundings, only hearing his voice. She did not know or care whose voice it was; she only knew that she should answer that voice. Suddenly, she removed her wedding ring and threw it away from her.

"Why did you do that?" the voice asked.

"I don't know," she answered. "I'm unhappy and depressed because the Catholic Church is trying to take my little girl away from me."

"Is your husband trying to do this too?" the voice asked.

"Yes."

"Do you enjoy sex with your husband?"

"No. I do not like it."

"Do you like where you're living?"

"No."

And on and on went the questions and the answers.

When he awakened her, he gave his impressions: "You seem to be having domestic, marital troubles. And you shouldn't be alone. Is there someone who can stay with you?"

He was assured that arrangements could be made, and she left with an appointment to return in three weeks. She could not discuss her session with her family on the way home; she could only say that the doctor had told her that she was unhappy and could not stay alone.

Ralph snorted, "That's a lot of money just to tell you that! Didn't he do anything for your other problems?"

"Ralph, he's not like other doctors," she repeated, trying to assure herself as well as him. "He doesn't do things *for* you. He just talks to you."

"He'll help you, honey," comforted Zueline. "Just give him time. And I know you can't be alone. Tiny is off from work this month. She can stay with you. And you can come home the rest of the time."

So it was arranged. Tiny went home to stay with her, and Ralph went his sulky way. Tiny did not go uncomplainingly, however, and she could hardly be blamed. Nineteen and dating, this was her vacation month, and she was disappointed to leave her friends. And she soon found out, as had Elen, that keeping an eye on Chris was a constant, exasperating job. Chris's moods were now so mercurial as to make the head swim. One moment she was quiet, passive, and loving; the next she was prostrate with a violent headache; and the next she was loud, brassy, and rejecting of all responsibility. She asked Tiny to help her move potted plants from one location to another; later in the day, surprised to find them moved, she asked her to help return them to their original location. They went to see a movie one afternoon; the next day Chris suggested that they go see the same movie. This time poor Tiny protested, declaring that they had already seen it, but Chris did not believe her, and they went to see the same show again. Chris enjoyed it for the second day running, as if she had never seen it before. Tiny discovered that explanations and discussions were a waste of time, logic did not apply; she simply humored her sister, going along with her no matter how unbelievable the scheme.

On one of Chris's visits to the doctor, she abruptly left the subject they were discussing and asked,

"Doctor, does hearing voices mean you're going insane?" She looked at him intently.

"What do you mean, 'hearing voices'?" he asked.

"Hearing them in your head when there's nobody there." Her eyes droppped.

"Well, why don't you tell me about it? Have you been hearing voices?" He looked at her closely, perhaps for the first time suspecting a deeper problem.

"Yes. And they come from inside my head."

"How do you know they come from inside your head? Perhaps they are coming from behind you."

"No, they're not. There's nobody there. And anyway, it doesn't sound like it's behind me. I can tell it's inside my head."

"Perhaps you're just thinking out loud. Maybe you just spoke your thoughts aloud," he suggested.

"No. My voice comes out here, at the front." She touched her lips. "*This* voice speaks inside my head. And anyway, I wouldn't ever think what it says."

"Do others hear these voices?" he asked.

"No, I don't think so. Nobody seems to hear them. They don't act like it if they do."

"Think hard now. Whose voice does it sound like? Is it familiar? Have you heard it before?"

When she finally spoke, it was barely above a whisper, "Doctor, I think it sounds like my own voice. But I know it can't be; I wouldn't talk like that."

The doctor looked at her thoughtfully. "Don't worry about it, Mrs. White, we'll discover what's causing your trouble."

After several months of irregular visits to the doctor, the discovery was made. As she sat in the chair, drooped, head bent, eyes downcast, answering his questions in a barely audible voice, her head began to ache. Unable to hide her pain, she grasped her temples, contorted her face, and moaned softly. Dr. Thigpen straightened from his usual draped position and watched her intently. Slowly the head raised, straight and proud; the sparkling eyes gazed back at him sardonically,

"Hi, Doc," she chirped, changing the tired droop of her body to a sensuous slouch with one almost imperceptible wiggle.

"H-hello," the doctor answered, treading on unsure ground.

"Gimme a cigarette," she requested, matter-of-factly and confidently.

He lit a cigarette for her, asking cautiously,

"Who are *you*?"

"I'm me," she flipped.

"And what is your name?" he pursued.

"I'm Chris Costner."

"Why are you using that name instead of Chris White?"

She straightened her skirt, hitching it higher up her leg and tossing her head, "Because Chris White is *her*," she stated, pointing off vaguely, "not me."

"Would you excuse me a minute?" He rose to leave.

"Sure," she replied, taking a long draw on her cigarette.

Dr. Thigpen hurried down the hall and entered the office of his colleague Hervey Cleckley, asking one question,

"Would you recognize a case of dual personality if you saw one?"

Dr. Cleckley answered thoughtfully, "I don't know if I would recognize a case if I saw one, but I think I could spot a phony."

"Then come on and see what I've got in here," requested Dr. Thigpen, leading the way.

255

Chris smiled brightly and confidently as the two men entered the small room.

"How are you, Mrs. White?" Dr. Cleckley asked.

"I ain't Miz White, I'm Miss Costner," she responded.

He pursued, "Why are you using that name?"

"'Cause I ain't married to that jerk; *she* is. I'm a maiden lady. I ain't never been married and I ain't never gonna be!"

"What about the child?" asked Thigpen.

"She ain't my child. It's her child, not mine."

"Your body had her," he reminded.

"It might have, but I wasn't in it when it did," she firmly countered, looking him defiantly in the eye.

"What happens to Chris White when you're out?" asked Cleckley.

"I don't know."

"Can we talk with Mrs. White now?" asked Thigpen.

"Sure," she answered, confident in her ability to come and go at will. "She just has a headache, but I can do it most any ole time."

"All right, let's do it, now. Mrs. White, come out now," he called, his voice slightly uneven at this incredible game he was playing. "Just relax, and let us talk to her. Mrs. White?"

She laid her head back, the face contorted, the eyes closed.

"Mrs. White, can I speak to you?" asked the doctor.

And there she was. Startled, sad, and unaware of what had happened, she looked at them as if waiting for the blow to fall.

After several more conferences, Dr. Thigpen decided to hospitalize her for electric shock treatments, a plan that was aborted by her fears. The doctor explained that it was just a small current of electricity that would course through her brain from two electrodes fastened to her temples, that it would redistribute the hormones and relieve her depression. Chris entered the hospital the day before treatment was to begin and settled into her room on the long, narrow ward, lined on either side by small, bare rooms. She began to notice the other patients, those who had already had their shock treatment for the day. Their faces were ashen, their eyes were red and swollen and vacant, their hair was in disarray. At mealtime they all sat in the hall and ate from trays balanced on their knees; and here Chris's fears crystalized. The shocked patients' eating habits were just as vacant and disorganized as were

256

their eyes: They ate with their fingers and chewed with slack mouths; one even ate her napkin.

"This is what it will do to me," she thought. "I can't do it, I won't do it! I won't become like that!"

She slept little that night, and when they came in the early morning to prepare her for treatment, she refused, declaring,

"I have changed my mind. I am not going to take it."

Dr. Thigpen was sent for. "I understand you are not going to take the shock treatment," he stated.

"No, I have changed my mind." She did not tell him of her fear.

"Then there's no need for you to stay here. You can call for someone to come for you." He did not try to persuade her. He had admitted her to the hospital one day diagnosed as "depression with schizoid features," and had dismissed her the very next day, without additional treatment, as "schizophrenia"—insanity.

Zueline came with Ralph for her daughter, and when she learned from Chris of the reaction of the shock treatment on patients, Zueline expressed her disapproval to Dr. Thigpen, causing a breach between her and the doctor that was never completely healed. For several months then, Chris and her doctor merely corresponded, exchanging short notes, often of no more import than broken or reaffirmed appointments, but dealing also with her disturbing dreams and her inability to sleep, for which he prescribed Dormison. Her next conference was precipitated by, surprisingly, Ralph. Chris Costner, the maiden lady, had begun to make life a living hell for Chris White, popping in and out and taunting her verbally. One day she came out while Chris White was washing the window blinds and immediately started a fuss with Ralph. Taffy, frightened by this sudden change in her mother, began to cry. Chris grabbed the child and wrapped the blind cord around her neck, scolding.

"Shut up, brat!"

Ralph rushed to the terrified Taffy, rescuing her from the tangled cord. "Don't you ever do that again!" he yelled. "Don't you ever treat Taffy that way again!"

Chris smiled coolly, closed her eyes, and swayed gently. When she opened her eyes, they were not the same eyes. Oh, they were still blue, but all else was changed.

257

"What's the matter, Ralph? What's happened to Taffy? What did you do to make her cry?"

Ralph stared in angry disbelief, "What did I do?" he cried. "What did I do? You crazy woman! You've got to go back to see that doctor. You tried to kill Taffy with that cord!"

Tears filled her eyes, "No, Ralph, I couldn't have done that. I know I didn't do that." But what did she know? There were so many things she didn't know.

Ralph made the next appointment, but it almost came too late. Concern over the incident with Taffy plus the torture of the voice became more than she could bear. She went to visit her mother and this time left Taffy with her, afraid now to trust herself with her precious daughter. While she was at the County Home she had her first night problems. Awaking with a splitting headache, she jumped from bed and ran, just ran. Tiny, who was sleeping with her, jumped up and followed, calling loudly,

"Teeny, Teeny, what's the matter? Stop!"

Chris ran headlong down the steep basement stairs, miraculously suffering only minor scrapes and bruises. On succeeding nights, Zueline, fearing a repetition, pinned her daughter's bedsheets together; but when the next attack came, this precaution was useless. Chris jumped from bed, carrying the sheets with her, and negotiating furniture, opening doors, and treading steep stairs, she sped out into the rain-filled night, sheets afloat, to fall exhausted in a muddy field.

Returning alone to her house in Johnston, her pitifully small reserve of strength exhausted, she was no match for the voice.

"Slap his ugly face!" it ordered.

"Why don't you leave the son-of-a-bitch?" it asked.

"I thought you would get rid of that brat," it taunted.

No longer able to endure, Chris arranged to die. She got a razor blade, sat down in a chair, and prepared to slash her wrists. But it is not so easy to destroy the temple of the mind when the mind itself is divided and ambivalent about the matter. It is not easy to slash through one's own flesh. What thoughts must flash through the mind: Is there no other way? Will tomorrow be better? Once done, there is no turning back; one small voluntary act sets in motion a process that thunders ahead out of control, gaining momentum, until . . . until what? That question stays many a hand bent on self-destruction. At least the present is known, even with all its tribulation; but the future is black, blank, completely unknown. Oh, there are stories, preacher promises, unconfirmed visions; but who really knows? Who has seen and lived to tell it? No one! If one could even be sure of oblivion!

Chris contemplated her own quivering, pulsating flesh and willed her hand to wield the blade. Once done, would that partially severed hand be able to return the compliment to its assassin?

Before the deed could be done, the blinding headache struck, driving all other considerations away. And suddenly there was Chris Costner, a little frightened, shaken, believing.

"She's so stupid, she'll really do it if I don't stop her. I'd better tell Doc."

She carefully hid the razor and blades, took out pencil and paper, and wrote Dr. Thigpen a letter.

"Chris White is in deep trouble," she told him, "and if you don't stop her, she's going to kill herself. And it's my body, too. And I don't want to die. She tried to cut her wrists. I stopped her, but I'm not sure I can always stop her."

It was a call for help, and the doctor, recognizing its seriousness, answered immediately, telling her that he knew of her desire to slash her wrists, and that *above all things* she must remember her promise to return to him, no matter what she might have discovered about herself or how impossible the situation might seem. He assured her that all would turn out correctly in the end.

Chris White, on receiving this letter, was badly frightened. How did the doctor know what she had attempted to do? If he could know about things like that, he could know other things, too; he *could* help her. She showed the letter to Ralph and to her parents; she wanted to do what the doctor instructed, she wanted to enter the hospital for help. It was agreed that she would write to Dr. Thigpen and ask his advice. Zueline stipulated only that she could not endure electric shock treatment. Chris agreed.

On her next visit she was hospitalized in the psychiatric ward of the Augusta University Hospital, diagnosed as having dual personality, and ironically, for one who so feared yet so anticipated confinement, it was the only institutionalization of that sort that she ever received. Dr. Thigpen visited her twice a day, and they talked of her life: her marriage, her daughter, her parents. He questioned her about the aborted suicide and learned that it was the attack on Taffy, plus the taunting voice, that caused her to attempt such rash action. She was unaware of the reason the suicide action was not completed or how the doctor knew of her unfinished act. And she also had no knowledge of mistreating Taffy, even though she accepted Ralph's word as being truth. Dr. Thigpen, suspecting that this latter was the work of Chris Costner, questioned her about it. At first she vehemently denied having wrapped the cord around the child's neck, but when pressed she carelessly smiled,

"The little brat just finally got on my nerves," she explained casually. "I wouldn't have hurt her."

"Why did you go back in and leave Mrs. White to take the blame, to think she had done it?" he asked.

She grinned wickedly, "Why should I take the blame? She's so goody-goody, let her git blamed. If she'd let me out easier, I would be nicer to her."

"She doesn't even know about you. How can she let you out?" Thigpen was intrigued by the complexity of this game.

"Well, I've been tryin' to tell her. Who's she think's talkin' to her? But she fights and it gives her those awful headaches," she explained, sitting slouched easily in the chair, swinging her shapely crossed leg.

The doctor looked at her, wondering why that leg, when placed so primly on the floor by Mrs. White, did not seem shapely at all —had, in fact, never caught his eye before.

"You do a lot of things to make trouble for her, don't you?" he pursued.

"Like what?" she challenged.

"You buy expensive clothes that you know your husband can't pay for, and he makes *her* take them back. Why don't you take them back?"

"He's not *my* husband!" she declared. "And why should I take 'em back? I like 'em."

The doctor had noticed that for some time she had been squirming and scratching her legs. "Why are you scratching?" he inquired.

She looked at him insolently, "Because I itch. Don't you scratch when you itch?"

"Yes, but why do you itch?" he patiently pursued.

"It's these ole stockin's. They make me itch. I don't know why she wears 'em!"

"Do they make her itch?"

"No, just me."

The doctor was amazed. Was it possible that one personality had an allergy and the other one did not? That the body reacted chemically to nylon when one personality was out, and that the reaction ceased immediately when the other one emerged? He quickly called out Mrs. White, and while casually questioning her, he watched her attitude carefully: She never once touched the red, blotchy legs or in any way indicated any discomfort. Before the doctor's incredulous eyes, the angry red quickly receded from the now motionless legs, leaving them their usual unblemished white.

"Do your legs itch?" He could not halt the debatable question. She threw him a startled look. "Why, no, Doctor."

The doctor's wealth of incredible information was expanding.

One visit each day was always devoted to a hypnosis session. Under hypnosis, he easily called out Chris Costner, then Chris White, then Chris Costner, etc. It became so easy that there was not even a headache involved, merely a five-to-ten-second drooping, closing of the eyes, and awakening. It was during this time that he informed Chris White of the existence of Chris Costner and explained to her the nature of her illness: dual personality. She understood none of the technicalities, only that another person could take over her body and live in it and commit acts over which she not only had no control, but also could not remember. It was horribly frightening, but somehow considerably more desirable as a condition than that of insanity.

Why has it become so easy? It's like flipping a light switch. Does the hypnosis make it easier? If they're only supposed to come to solve a difficulty, how can they just come when the doctor calls them? And even when he's not around, they slip in and out easily without pain. Or is it because someone finally accepts her and believes her and listens to her? I can see that in

261

the past they came because of need; but now it's different. It's almost a pleasure to oblige the doctor and do as he asks. What are my . . . her needs now? To please the doctor—this important person who accepts and gives so much attention? I don't know. And where am I now? I can remember all this so clearly, but it was happening to them, not me. If it had happened to me, I would have remembered it as feeling it, not just seeing it! Wouldn't I? I know exactly what's going to happen next! But I'm going to go over it step by step until I know. . . .

On her bare hospital desk/dressing table, Chris had only two decorations: a picture of Taffy and a picture of Elen. The latter was a glamorous studio picture posed in a black drape, and it caught Dr. Thigpen's probing eye.

"Who is that?" he asked during one of their sessions.

"That's Elen," she proudly replied.

"Do you love her?" he pursued.

"Of course, she's my cousin!" she stated, surprised.

"Are you in love with her?" he probed.

"I don't know what you mean." She frowned.

"That's all right," he soothed, "it's all right." And the subject was changed. But the subject was not dropped. He was not sure that she did not understand. There was a lesbian patient in the hospital, and Thigpen gave Chris every opportunity to start an alliance with her, to no avail.

Shortly after this episode, Elen came to visit Chris and took her out for a ride. Elen had met Dr. Thigpen, and she and Chris talked about him and her treatment. At one point, in an attempt to amuse Chris, Elen stated that "Thigpen" was a strange name, sounding quite like "pigpen." In one of their later sessions, Chris Costner tattled on the conversation and informed the doctor that Chris White and Elen had laughed at his name. Chris was most embarrassed when Thigpen informed her of what Chris Costner had told him.

"We didn't mean any harm, Dr. Thigpen." She lowered her concerned eyes. "We were just teasing."

She wanted to please the doctor, and when he asked if he could do some filming of her while she was under treatment, she immediately gave her permission. He explained that the film would simply be part of her medical case records and would be beneficial to him and Dr. Cleckley in her continued treatment after she left the hospital. Consequently, a photographer, on several occasions, came with the doctor for his sessions with her and made moving pictures of her responding to questions, both under hypnosis and without hypnosis, and of Dr. Thigpen calling out first one personality and then the other.

He also had her tested by Dr. Leopold Winter, a clinical psychologist, who concluded that psychotherapeutic attempts should produce good results not only because the conflict was close to the surface, but also because of her intellectual capacity, her suggestibility, and her desire to be helped. He felt that her recovery would depend upon an understanding environment and that her personality changes were warning signals. He issued a warning of his own, stating that therapy would make a repetition of these changes unacceptable and consequently impossible, and that she might have to resort to a more serious fashion of dissociation—of change.

She did not want to leave the hospital, and yet she must; she could not pay her bill. She had no money, and Ralph was not going to pay her hospital bill, her parents would have to pay it, and they had so little. Dr. Thigpen informed her that if she could stay in Augusta, he would continue to treat her as an outpatient without charge. This was wonderful news, and she did not feel that she could return to Ralph now, perhaps never. So after two weeks she left the hospital and found an apartment—one room shared with another woman—and a job as sales clerk in Davisons Department Store. And life settled into somewhat of a routine, a troubled routine. She saw Dr. Thigpen twice weekly, and she worked at her thirty-five-dollar-a-week job, soon being promoted to the telephone switchboard.

Under these conditions, the emotional relations between doctor and patient deepened; and the ease with which the therapist grew able to deal with the two personalities caused him to attempt to resolve the case by accomplishing a blending of the two personalities. He proposed to call both personalities out at the same time. How could two persons use the same body at the same time, activate the same vocal cords, gesture with the same hands, peer out of the same eyes? The attempt through Chris White produced such a painful headache and deep distress that he immediately ceased; the same effort through the less emotional Chris Costner, though causing less agitation, was equally unsuccessful. She bluntly refused after the first attempt.

"What you're doin' gives me such a funny, queer, mixed-up feelin' that I ain't gonna put up with it no more!" And that was that.

The personalities were so clear-cut and distinct, so well-formed and separated that no mere command was going to unite them. In attempting to draw them back together, the doctor was assuming that they had splintered off from a once integrated whole. He re-examined his assumptions: Was it possible, though the parts were now clearly separate, that there had never been an integrated whole but had always been a disintegrated mass whirling in the space of the mind? If so, what meaning did that astounding fact generate for the theory of ego integration, of personality implying a unified total, indicating more than intelligence or character? And the ultimate question: If there has never been a unified whole, or if the separations occurred far back in the realm of mere potential, at preconscious levels, can these present or future parts ever be integrated?

Her two personalities worked out an uneasy truce: Chris White worked during the day, and Chris Costner played during the night. Their one conflict arose over money; there was precious little, since her room cost sixty dollars a month—almost half her monthly salary. Chris Costner bought clothes, rode in taxis, and spent money at nightclubs, often leaving Chris White scarcely enough to pay the rent and ride the bus to work. Dr. Thigpen acted as arbiter, since Chris White had no way of contacting her tormentor and could only complain to the doctor.

"You'd better stop spending all the money. She'll lose her job, and then where will you be?" he warned Chris Costner.

"Aw, Doc, she's just an ole stick," she answered airily. "She don't want to have a good time, an' she don't want me to have a good time either."

"Well, you'd better slow down and not make her lose her job or you'll both have to go back home, back to Ralph." He used tho one threat that would reach her.

She jumped from her chair. "I ain't goin' back to that son-of-a-bitch! I ain't ever goin' back there!"

"O.K., then help her. How does she feel about going back? Does she want to go back?" he asked.

"Hell, no. She don't want to go back neither. She hates him just the same as I do. She just won't admit it. Why don't you git her a divorce from him?" she slyly suggested.

"I'll ask her and see if she wants one."

Their sessions were long, from two to three hours to sometimes half a day; and they were strenuous and probing. He delved into her childhood, discovered Elen's china doll, the afternoon at the Negro house, and Grandmother's blue cup and her funeral. The questions about Al Thorne were long and repetitious, but her memory of this period was vague and hazy. He questioned Chris White for a while; then he called out Chris Costner and questioned her. Often their answers to identical questions were quite varied, as if they had experienced entirely different happenings; and frequently one would be unable to recall an event just described by the other. In speaking of the past, neither one used the pronoun "I"; it was always "she" or "they." Chris Costner had a definite advantage, and she often played tricks on the doctor. Since she was aware of everything Chris White did and said, she often deliberately lied, saying that she remembered something that she had only heard Chris White relate, or denying something just to make her look foolish. The doctor soon learned to know them so well that he was aware when Chris Costner was being untruthful, and she was so blasé and uncaring that she never hesitated to confess if she was found out.

Continuing to be intrigued by the mystery of the allergies, Dr. Thigpen sent Chris White to a dermatologist for testing. He informed her of his intention, and then called out Chris Costner and instructed her.

"I'm going to send you to another doctor, a dermatologist, to check out your allergy to nylon stockings," he informed her. "Now, here's what you must do. I want you to stay out for two days. Chris White is not going to come out. You can make her come out, I know; but I don't want you to do that. She doesn't have an allergy, only you. Stay out so your allergy can be tested, O.K.?"

265

"O.K., Doc," she agreed. "You're the doctor!"

The dermatologist taped strips of different kinds of material, including nylon, to Chris Costner's stomach, instructing her to return in two days for a reading of her reaction. Shortly, her stomach began to itch and nettle from the irritating fabric. She could simply have removed the disturbing strips from her skin, but she chose instead to play a trick on the doctor. Forcing Chris White to emerge, she stayed in for the two days and only emerged again shortly before she met Dr. Thigpen at the dermatologist's office for the scheduled reading. When the strips were removed, the stomach was smooth and white, indicating that Chris Costner, also, had no allergy. Surprised at these results, Dr. Thigpen feared that his patient had not followed his instructions. He called out Chris White and questioned her to determine if she had been out at all during the two days of tests. She solemnly assured him that she had no memory of having been out during that time. And she was right: Chris Costner had erased her memory of the entire period. The doctor was puzzled but accepting, completely unaware of the trick that had been played on him. He did not discover until much later that Chris Costner could, by indulging in careful concentration, wipe out any memory that Chris White possessed.

Dr. Thigpen did question Chris White about her desires concerning her marriage and found that Chris Costner was correct: Chris White did not want to continue living with Ralph.

"I don't love him anymore, Dr. Thigpen, and he doesn't love me. I don't think he ever loved me. And he's never loved Taffy either," she stated sadly.

"Do you want to divorce him?" he asked her.

"I don't know. I don't know about things like that. I just know I can't live with him."

"Why don't you get a temporary legal separation from him? That will legally keep him away and give you time to make up your mind," he advised her.

"That sounds all right," she agreed. "But how do I get one of those?"

"I'll help you," he offered.

Ralph came to visit her only twice during her more than a year's stay in Augusta. When he arrived for his first visit, Chris had just returned home from work. She excused herself to freshen up before they went out to dinner, and when she returned, Ralph got a jolt. Chris Costner opened the door dressed in a slinky red dress and behaving as Ralph could not have conceived in his wildest dreams.

"What do ya mean, dressed like that?" he stammered. "Is that how you're spending money? I thought you was down here sick."

"Look, if you want to take me out to dinner, O.K. But I don't want no preachin'. And I decide where to go. I'm not goin' to no diner!" She placed both hands on her hips and stared him down.

"My gawd a'mighty," he swore lightly under his breath.

The night was a disaster; Ralph could not believe his eyes. This gay, saucy woman could not be his meek, dowdy wife. A couple of drinks convinced him that he had been missing something, and he tried to make up for lost time in the car; but again she proved more than he could handle.

"Take your hands off me, you son-of-a-bitch!" she yelled, fighting him off with surprising strength. "If you think I'm goin' to bed with you, you're nuts! I ain't goin' to bed with any man."

"The hell you say," he growled. "You're my wife. I'll do what I damn well please."

"I ain't your wife! I ain't never been your wife. An' if you put your hands on me, I'll cut your throat!" She slammed out of the car.

Ralph sat there stunned. What did the doctor say she had? Whatever it was, it had changed her into an entirely different person. Ralph was puzzled. If she had been like this all the time, life might have been very different. Inside the house, Chris White was just as puzzled as was Ralph. She now knew what had happened, of course, Dr. Thigpen had explained it to her: Chris Costner, the voice, had used her body and had been out with Ralph; but this dress, she had never seen it before. It must have cost a lot of money. At that thought, she quickly looked in her purse. Thank goodness, most of the money was still there, at least enough to pay the rent. She had better pay it early, tomorrow, before *she* spent it. And what had she done with Ralph? Chris had wanted to talk to him about a divorce; there was no point in going on just separated. She didn't want to feel any obligation to him. And she was supporting herself now. If only *she* would leave her alone, she could even have Taffy with her. Ralph wasn't giving anything for Taffy's support. Chris White wearily put away the silly dress and prepared for bed. She had learned that it was futile to throw away these clothes, *she* would only go out and buy more, depleting even further the small amount of money. It was best to just humor her; and anyway, Dr. Thigpen said that she knew everything that happened—there was no way to hide anything from her. That was so unfair, since Chris was completely unaware of what *she* did.

The headaches had stopped. Since Dr. Thigpen had recognized the personality changes and had begun to call them out at will, there was no longer any struggle necessary for a change to occur. Chris White felt a momentary faintness, then nothing; and when she awoke, she was not even aware personally of a time lapse. Her only knowledge of a period of amnesia came from evidence of acts that had been committed and an obvious passage of time on the clock. Fortunately, Chris Costner seldom came out while Chris White was at work. Chris Costner had done so several times, and her childish, playful behavior had almost cost Chris White her job. Chris White had complained to Dr. Thigpen, who had taken Chris Costner to task, warning her of her own resultant problems and privations if the job were lost. So a truce was arbitrated by the doctor: Chris White worked and earned the money, and Chris Costner played and spent the money.

Chris Costner was a party girl. She liked to date and drink and dance, and she was pretty—pretty enough to attract dates—and confident enough to have an easy good time. It was a heavenly time to be single and fun-loving in Augusta. Local men were plentiful, and Fort Gordon offered a generous supply of soldiers. She was just short of flamboyant, with her glossy black hair, creamy white skin, and startlingly blue eyes. She dressed in slinky tight dresses, preferring reds and blacks, and her gay, saucy manner was engagingly contagious. She loved nice restaurants and nightclubs and often refused to enter a low dive, preferring to take a taxi home alone than to be pressured into such a place. She often spent evenings in the Bamboo Room at the Partridge Inn or in the club at the Bon-Air Hotel, and frequently she visited the Officers' Club at Fort Gordon. She calculatingly chose officers, knowing that they had more money and frequented nicer clubs.

One place she particularly liked was the Club Royal, just across the Savannah River in South Carolina, and it was there that she sometimes sang with the small combo band. One night from her table she just began singing with them, and they asked her to continue. Her voice was not strong, not trained, but it was gay, sensuous, and tuneful. Her slender body swayed as she sang, "If you love that man, You'd better tie him to your side, If he flags my train, I'm gonna let him ride." She especially loved to dance, picking up new and intricate steps easily.

A woman whom Chris knew well, a divorced woman of thirty-five, often brought men to the apartment when Chris was out. She openly confessed to her that she had sex with these men, on the back seats of cars and on the bed when one was available. She often invited Chris to go out when there was an extra man, and the carefree girl did, not even faintly bothered by a blind date. Chris also double-dated with a young nurse whom she as a patient, had met at the hospital. And Chris was not hesitant to pick up a man. If he looked prosperous and sounded fun-loving, the evening was on, but she never pursued a man or called one for a date; it had to be a chance meeting and a mutual liking.

She did stop at sex. She did indulge in light petting, but no fondling or heavy petting. This obvious discrepancy between her appearance and behavior, and her refusal to follow through, made her seem to be a tease to men who tried to collect on what appeared to be a broken promise. She once hit a persistent lieutenant on the head with her shoe heel, called a taxi, and went to another club, spending the rest of her evening alone, drinking and humming along with the band. Dr. Thigpen was concerned about her behavior and her safety. He did not know the extent of her knowledge about sex and its implications.

"What do you do on your dates?" he cautiously asked.

"I go to nightclubs, dance, drink. Isn't that what you do?" she flippantly replied, swinging her foot.

"Do you do anything else?" he countered.

"What do you mean?" she sat up, glaring at him.

"Well, do you kiss, pet, you know, make out?" he spelled it out.

"Is that what's worrying you?" she laughed. "Hell, no, I don't. Oh, I kiss some, but that's all. I don't want no sex. None! Look what it got her into. I'd just rather no man touched me. I'd rather he didn't kiss me or touch me or anything!" she stated defiantly.

269

"Well, it can get you into trouble, you know," he instructed. "I just didn't know if you knew about it," he finished rather lamely.

"Oh, sure, Doc. You don't have to worry about me none. I know the score, and I ain't havin' none." She chewed her gum and swung her foot lazily.

Once in the Club Royal, Chris was having a particularly difficult time with her drunk date, and being considerably inebriated herself, she took the easy way out: she just disappeared and left the whole mess to poor Chris White. Imagine the horror, shame, and confusion of the prim, staid, teetotaler suddenly to find herself sitting at a drink-laden table in a dim, noisy nightclub, having her bare shoulders and back pawed by a bleary-eyed drunk stranger. Adding insult to injury, she discovered that her own body lurched awkwardly when she rose to leave, because of strong drink which someone else had poured into it. Her usually even temper burst loose, and she approached the doctor with her problem.

"You have got to make her stop," she protested. "There are some of her messes that I just cannot clean up!"

"I will talk to her," he promised. "But you are both individuals, and you both have to make decisions. You have got to find a way to communicate with each other. Why don't you write notes?"

Was the doctor tiring of his role as referee, or had he decided that it was time she began trying to solve her problem, began trying to heal the breach between her two halves? And of course they followed his advice, they always did. Chris Costner, who had not spoken to Chris White in her head since the hypnosis began, wrote the first note.

"You are a real snitch. Why did you tell Doc? It's none of your damn business what I do."

Chris White wrote back,

"If you're not ashamed of what you do, why do you not want Dr. Thigpen to know about it?"

And the notes flew back and forth. At least communication was open, and some problems were actually solved. Chris Costner admitted that she had made a mistake by leaving Chris White with the drunk date, and promised in her flippant way not to repeat it. She also promised to go easy on spending the money. The doctor asked to see the notes, and he noticed an interesting phenomenon: The handwriting was completely different. Chris White wrote in a cramped, though beautifully formed, slanting script, while Chris Costner formed a childish, free-flowing, careless scrawl.

This uneasy truce precariously balanced for over a year, with the doctor standing as mediator between the two halves of the whole. And then, without warning, Chris was fired from her job. She had been promoted from the switchboard to the Credit Department and was conscientiously learning the work, unmolested by Chris Costner, when she made an unavoidable error. She had been instructed to check accounts and send a bill for immediate payment to anyone who had run up a bill of over five hundred dollars. Finding one of over one thousand dollars, she sent the printed, terse demand for payment, not knowing that this was a wealthy, influential customer who only paid his bill once a year. The fact that Chris was unaware of this special treatment, or that this special account should not have been kept with regular accounts, made no difference. She was reprimanded for upsetting a prized customer and shortly fired, with only the explanation,

"A great deal of money has been invested to train you, and it's just not working out."

And possibly that is the truth. Chris Costner, though not often, had come out several times during this year and created havoc on the switchboard, mixing up calls and saying, "Keep your shirt on, sugar, I'm tryin'," and whirling herself around on the chair crying "Wheee," like a small, gleeful child. Perhaps enough of these incidents had occurred that this last mixup, enough in itself to establish her reputation as unreliable, was the last straw. At any rate, she walked out of Davisons Department Store unemployed and penniless.

And the headaches began again, only this time with an interesting variation. Previously, only Chris White had suffered the headache when Chris Costner was trying to come out; now both personalities had a splitting headache when they changed back and forth. Then one evening it happened. As Chris Costner entered the dreary little apartment, her head began to ache. She lay down on the couch, clutching her temples, her eyes flashing angry blue fire. Panic seized her and she blacked out, and there was Chris White, her head also aching unbearably. Her dull, weary blue eyes closed. They opened again, strangely calm, confident, bereft of emotion except for quiet curiosity. Briefly they swept the room and closed. Immediately the face contorted in pain; dull, clouded eyes fluttered briefly open, and then, incredibly, the angry blue eyes again glared around the room.

That was a third one, so brief that she had no memory of it later. How do I know this? How do I know that this happened, that later she didn't even remember? How did I know something about her that she didn't even know herself, wasn't even able to tell the doctor? And the two Chrises didn't know about it either; they never were able to know what she did. How could I know something that none of them knew, and I wasn't even there either? Think! Think! Don't get in a panic, just think! How do I know? I see pictures! That's how I know! I see pictures. I see her . . . them lying on the couch, and they change. They become different people. How do I know they change? The body is the same, the clothes are the same, but they . . . she is different. I know she is different! I know it and I can see it. I know I can't explain it sensibly, and when I try to put it into words, it sounds crazy even to me! But I know and I saw. I don't know where I was, but I saw! . . .

Chris Costner was terrified. She had never blacked out before. She had disappeared in the past and become unaware of what was happening, but that was voluntary; this had been done *to* her, was beyond her control. She called Dr. Thigpen.

"I've got to see you, and I've got to see you now!" she insisted.

"O.K.," he responded, intrigued because this was the first time that she had insisted on seeing him. Before, he had had to call her out. "It's not your day, but come on in and we'll talk."

"Doc," she stated when she was seated before him, "something has happened, and I don't like it. The headaches are worse, but I blacked out, too. I'm scared, and I don't like it."

"What do you think caused it?" he asked, surprised at this first sign of fear in so careless a nature.

"I don't know. But you do something about it," she demanded.

"Let me see what I can do. Let me speak to Chris White. Mrs. White!" he called.

The fierce blue eyes closed and the dull, sad ones opened.

"Do you want to talk to me, Doctor?" she whispered.

"Yes. How are you, Mrs. White?" His calm tone matched hers. "What do you think is causing your headaches? They've been gone so long, and now they're back. And Chris Costner is having them, too."

"I don't know, Dr. Thigpen," she answered, frowning and pressing her temples, as if the mere mention of the pain was sufficient to call it up.

"Do you think it might be something painful in your childhood that you're trying to remember? We've been talking about things like that," he prompted her.

"I don't know." She kept her tormented eyes down; her mood was one of complete dejection.

"We've been discussing when you were burned at the washpots when you were a small child. Can you remember clearly what happened?"

"Yes, Doctor. I was helping Mother wash clothes, and my dress caught fire. Mother screamed, and Aunt Meme ran to me. She put me in the cool water, and the pain stopped, and . . ." Her words stopped, her eyes shut, her head lolled back.

The doctor silently watched. Was this something new, different? Was there no end to it? The head lifted, the body imperceptibly straightened, and the eyes—the eyes were cool, intelligent, confident. Yes, this *was* something new, and very definitely different. Was this what Dr. Winter had warned about—a more serious fashion of dissociation? He took a deep breath.

"And who are you?" he asked.

"I don't know who I am," she calmly stated, only the faintest tinge of wonder coloring her slow, precise speech.

"Where did you come from?" he asked, his voice beginning to edge with growing excitement.

"I don't know where I came from," stated the cultured, measured voice, its tone low and unhurried.

The doctor, no longer slouched in his chair, but leaning forward with intense interest, excused himself for the second time from the presence of this mysterious woman and hurried again into the office of his older, more experienced colleague. He and Dr. Cleck-

273

ley again burst in upon the same small figure seated in the chair.

"How are you feeling, Mrs. White?" asked the older doctor.

"Is that who I am, someone named Mrs. White?" she asked, looking him solemnly in the eye.

"Well, yes, you are," he answered.

"I don't seem to remember being a Mrs. White," she stated, faintly apologizing for her lack of memory.

"That's something we'll talk about," he promised.

"But I'm not Mrs. White," she confidently stated.

"How do you know?" he asked, intrigued.

"Because I can see what she does." Her recall was beginning. She began to feel as if she had suffered a shock of some sort, a minor accident. Her nervous system quivered, her heart lurched and raced, her stomach knotted, but the pictures continued to kaleidoscope. She suddenly had much general information—she knew who George Washington was—but she had almost no specific information about herself. She felt that the pictures were going on around her but that she was not a part of them—they were not happening to her.

"If you are not Mrs. White, then who are you?" asked Dr. Thigpen.

"I don't know," she responded, seemingly unshaken by this fact.

"Well, if you could be anyone, who would you like to be? What would you like to be called?"

After only a slight hesitation, a faint smile touching her lips, she answered, "Jane."

Jane: plain Jane, Jane Doe. This new person sounded cultured and educated, but could she possibly be well-read and experienced enough to know that "Jane" is a name given to nondescript unknowns? She is brand new, blank, has no background, no credentials; "Jane" is the technically and legally proper name for one so circumstanced. Did she recognize the irony of her situation and choose the name accordingly, or is there something innate in the sound of "Jane" that caused it originally to be chosen for the pallid and colorless anonymous, unknown? Does that name so fit the unnamed that it eternally springs to the lips when one must designate the undesignated? The simplicity of it is striking and apt, but then so is Jean and Joan. She was unable to account for her choice, and when pressed could think of only one Jane she had known: "Jane Eyre," the ill-starred and ill-fated heroine of novel fame.

Ascertaining the paucity of her information, Dr. Thigpen suggested that she go back in and allow one of the others to come out and go home. At this point he learned a startling fact. She could only come and go through Chris White, never Chris Costner. He was also later to find that Chris Costner could only come and go through Chris White, never through Jane. This was a pattern throughout this strange illness: One personality was always the keyhole through which the others journeyed, and that pivotal personality was totally unaware of their coming and going and their behavior, while they knew all about hers. Fearing that Jane might emerge in some strange place and be completely disoriented, Dr. Thigpen gave her his phone number, asking her to call anytime if she found herself in such circumstances.

Shortly after this incredible episode, Dr. Thigpen arranged a conference with the Dugas Journal Club, an organization made up of faculty members of the Medical College of Georgia, the staff of the University Hospital, and the local Veterans Administration Psychiatric Hospital. He explained to them his findings in his amazing case and presented his patient to them for their observation and evaluation. They watched, skeptical but withholding judgment, while he changed her from one personality to another, after which they asked her questions. She was poised, confident, and apparently undaunted by talking with such a learned group. When asked,

"Are you and the other personalities not twins?"

She smilingly answered, "Yes, but not identical twins."

When another doctor queried her concerning the past, she firmly reminded him, "You must remember that I was only born one year ago."

For two hours, during which a feeling of dramatic anticipation prevailed, she fielded questions and comments designed to reveal any flaws in her defense mechanism, without once failing to display the characteristics and idiosyncrasies peculiar only to each distinct personality.

But they're jobless! Ironically, by adding another person, they did not add another mouth to feed; there is still only one body, but it must be fed and housed and clothed. Since Jane now presented the best appearance, Dr. Thigpen suggested that she be the one to seek a job. The first two personalities knew nothing of Jane's emergence on the scene, and to avoid unnecessary confusion, the doctor undertook the task of informing them of her presence,

"Mrs. White," he called, and when she appeared, he explained, "Your headaches have been caused by the emergence of a new personality, Jane. I think you will like her. She won't cause you any trouble. And she's going to help you work. She will look for a new job."

"All right, Doctor," she agreed, never questioning for a moment this new development. If the doctor said it was all right, it was fine with her.

Not so Chris Costner, who did not have to be told; she had listened while the doctor explained to Chris White.

"Who the hell is she? What's she doing here? I don't want nobody watching me, especially when I can't see them!" she objected.

"That's what you've been doing to Chris White. And you've not been very nice about it either. Jane is a nice person," he explained.

"Nice, nice!" she fumed. "Wouldn't you know that I'd get stuck with two prissy-pants. I don't like it."

Dr. Thigpen called out Jane and sent her out to look for a job. She took herself very seriously, even to obtaining a Social Security card in her name: "Jane Costner." She was extremely confident, self-assured, and poised. She took over, refusing to use the name of Chris Costner White, and by her calm power of will, she forced the weak, pliant Chris White to follow her lead and to use her name. It was not so easy with Chris Costner, whose defiant capriciousness caused irreparable trouble.

Jane easily found a job as bookkeeper with a mobile trailer sales company; but Chris White, because of her greater experience, worked at the job while Jane watched her and learned. All went well until the manager, a handsome, married man who lived in a trailer near the sales office, began to flirt with Chris White.

"How about a date tonight?" he asked, laying a familiar hand on her shoulder.

Offended, she moved away. "I don't date," she answered. "And if I did, it wouldn't be with a married man."

"Well, don't be so stuffy about it. I was just asking." He turned away.

It was too much for Chris Costner, bored and confined. She broke through.

"Well, now," she flipped. "Who's gittin' stuffy? I didn't say 'never,' did I?"

He turned, astonished at this sudden change. But she was sitting demurely at her desk, humming a little tune as she turned pages.

This byplay kept up for several days, keeping the unaware Chris White off balance at the manager's continued persistence, while the frustrated man hung dangling between the bright promise and the cold refusal.

But Chris Costner was not able to handle the job, and things quickly came to a head as a result of her coming out so often at work. She seemed to have lost her zest for playing at night, now that someone could watch her. She completely confused the books, much faster than Chris White could find the errors and correct them. Then one day Chris Costner, without authorization, reduced the price on a trailer and sold it for a scandalously low sum. The manager, his mercenary urges stronger than his masculine urges, was furious, and he hotly reprimanded the frightened Chris White, who, though unaware of what had been done, had no doubt that something drastic had been done by her ever-present nemesis.

Jane, who had been a silent observer to the whole enactment, went to Dr. Thigpen and related the entire tale. Since he could not call out Chris Costner through Jane, he had to first manifest Chris White.

"Jane, may I speak to Mrs. White?"

"Of course, Dr. Thigpen." She closed her eyes.

"Mrs. White, will you come out, please?"

"Of course, Doctor. I'm here." She opened her eyes.

"How are you, Mrs. White? May I speak to Chris Costner?"

"Of course." She closed her eyes.

"Chris. Chris Costner, will you come out, please?"

"Certainly, Doc. Watcha' want? What's that snitch been tellin' ya?" Her eyes flashed, ready to do battle.

"What makes you think they've been telling me anything?" he asked.

"Well, that one that watches me is just as goody-goody as Chris White. I'll bet she's been tattling."

"As a matter of fact, she did tell me that you goofed up on the job. Why did you sell the trailer for so little money? You can't do that in business," he patiently explained.

"Well, I'as just doin' the best I could. They said *sell*, and I sold. The man wouldn't buy for any other price." Her logic was her own.

The doctor, amused in spite of his concern, warned, "Well, go light on the job; let Chris White and Jane handle it."

But she was not so easily put down. "I don't like that job. If you don't make them quit, I'll just make more trouble. I don't like it out there."

Dr. Thigpen talked it over with the other two and sensed that they were not happy with the job either. They quit, possibly one step ahead of being fired, either for ineffectiveness on the job or for angering the amorous manager. When a situation like this occurred, Dr. Thigpen became a busy man. He had to inform each personality concerning the current circumstances, arbitrate decisions made about future actions, and keep each one up to date on any progress. Again, complete acceptance: Here is an important and busy man taking time to methodically play the game with her. The desire for acceptance and recognition is a bottomless pit in the human soul. If it cannot be attained in one way, it *will* be attained in another. If attainment seems beyond the grasp, self-destruction looms as the only alternative. Is not a shattering, splintering of oneself a form of self-destruction?

It was decided that again Jane would seek employment, and she easily found work as a switchboard operator and receptionist for the Georgia-Pacific Plywood Company. It was a good job and one that she knew well how to perform, but its duration was short. Jane and Chris White took turns working, but they had decided never to have a change at work, fearing that someone would notice the momentary lapse and strangeness. Chris Costner, though bored and sulky, had agreed after one disastrous appearance not to interfere with the workday; but she had awakened one morning and decided, as a lark, to go see what the job was like. She had over the years absorbed enough of Chris White's skills to be able to carry on the job, if not excellently, then acceptably for a short time. Her problem was her irresponsibility, her childishness, her inability to maintain any sustained effort. As she worked on the switchboard, a pretty female vice president, whom she disliked on sight, came by and asked Chris to connect her with a certain party, complaining,

"I am so busy this morning that I'm running around in circles." She smiled at the pretty girl.

Chris tossed her head and quipped, "Blessed are the big wheels, for they shall go around in circles."

The official stopped dead in her tracks, started to comment, then marched into her office. To enter the comment on Chris's record? Perhaps.

Trouble struck unexpectedly one day when Chris White was at work at the switchboard. Her head began to ache intolerably, and she blacked out and fell from her chair onto the floor. Jane almost immediately came out, and the shock of finding herself in such circumstances swept away her caution. Instead of pleading a fainting spell and asking for a few minutes of rest, she panicked and asked to be taken to Dr. Thigpen's office. Once there, in the protective surroundings, her fear subsided but her confusion remained.

"Dr. Thigpen," she asked, "what happened? I did not want to come out. I did not even *know* that I was coming out. All of a sudden, there I was. What happened?"

"I don't know, honey," he soothed.

"Why did the headache come, and the blackout? That's never happened before."

"I don't know. Let me talk to Chris White; perhaps she knows."

"All right." She closed her eyes.

"Mrs. White. Mrs. White, may I talk to you?" he called.

The eyes opened, dim, drooping, lackluster. "Yes, Doctor."

"Mrs. White, you had a headache and blacked out. Do you remember?"

"I remember the headache. That's all," she answered, scarcely above a whisper.

"Why did you have the headache?"

"I don't know."

"Were you unhappy? Did something happen?"

"No. I'm just so tired, so very tired."

"All right. It's all right. Let me speak to Jane."

The tired eyes gratefully closed.

"Jane, could I speak with you?" the doctor called.

The hunched shoulders slowly straightened, life flowed back into the drooping figure, and puzzled blue eyes opened. "She didn't know anything, either. Do you suppose she just got so tired that she blacked out? But I don't feel tired."

"I don't know, honey. But don't worry about it. We'll work it out. Be prepared. You may have trouble at work tomorrow because of this," he warned.

She rose. "Thank you, Dr. Thigpen. I couldn't do without your help."

The warning was sound; she did have trouble at work the next day: She was fired. Her supervisor approached her in the early morning, explaining,

"You don't seem to be happy with your work here, and you are obviously not well. You need a rest. We suggest that you resign."

And, of course, she did. Keeping her mind blank, refusing to think about it, she went straight as a homing pigeon to Thigpen's office, to help, to acceptance. And she found it.

"Don't worry, baby, we'll work it out," he promised.

13

I Am Jane!

What irony in the bold statement: I am Jane! I am Jane Doe, faceless, unknown, unknowing; from nowhere, going where? Yet given all this anonymity, what a heroic attempt at identification. But what naïveté. In declaring for Jane Costner, she was denying her childhood and youth as Chris Costner and her adult marriage as Chris White. In her ignorance of life, she attempted to build her future without a past—a skyscraper without a foundation. Failure was inevitable.

At what point have fears and inadequacies been so dealt with and overcome that one can confidently state who he is? Can one ever know who he is except in relation to others? Can he ever see himself clearly, except as he is mirrored in the eyes of others? One goes through life reaching out blindly to test the closeness or distance of others—particular or general—and spends anxious moments scanning faces to find his own reflection. Chris was no different; her groping was ceaseless. Now as Jane, as the eternal Phoenix, she began anew; and this time the blindly searching vine discovered a tree, a firmly rooted, mighty oak whose rough, weathered bark made clinging a simple joy.

A man. No greater tribute can be paid to a male. It connotes strength, dependability, aggressiveness; yet, paradoxically, gentleness, reserve, and humility. A rare animal, this, and such a man was Don. He had survived the World War II Navy, and had reached the discriminating age of thirty footloose and fancy-free. A man's occupation tells a story about him, and Don was an electrician. What kind of man selects to work with lightning—dangerous, swift, relentless, deadly—the fire of the gods? A brave man, surely, but also cautious; a man who is not afraid to take chances, but at the same time trains himself to take no chances. One does not often get a second chance if he is careless with lightning, even controlled lightning. Such a man was Don, a pillar of American society, a workingman, proud of his skill, loyal to his union: IBEW, Local No. 26.

The meeting was inauspicious, as important meetings often are. Chris was invited by her roommate to go, dateless, to the Julian Smith Casino, an open dance hall on a lake just north of the city. It happened to be Jane whom she asked. Jane had never gone out socially. Chris White, who had now filed for a divorce but still considered herself married, never went out; and Chris Costner, of course, dated often; but Jane, brand-new Jane had never been anywhere but to work and to the doctor. She was intrigued, she accepted. On the way, they talked about what kind of guys they were going to dance with. Jane spotted a shiny apple-green car with black vinyl top and black fender skirts pulled up in front of the casino.

"I'm going to dance with the guy that owns that car, and what's more, I'm going home with him," she declared.

Inside they stood in the crowd and watched the dancers. Jane felt a hand on her shoulder, and turning, she saw a tall, dark man smiling at her. His shiny black, curly hair was tightly smoothed back, and his brown eyes were twinkling.

"Would'ja like to dance?" His tone was slow and drawling.

"I don't dance too well. Dance with my roommate," she hedged, suddenly shy.

"I don't want to dance with your roommate, I want to dance with you," he persisted, smiling broadly.

"Well, all right, but don't say I didn't warn you."

They danced and danced. In fact, they did not dance with anyone else all evening. At the intermission, he asked her if she would like a drink, a very unusual gesture for Don, who drank very little;

and they went out to his car, where he had stashed, for a very special occasion, a bottle of Old Grand-Dad. It had to be, and it was —the apple-green car with the nifty black top and fender skirts. Jane's romantic heart lurched. And she did allow him to take her home, too, but insisted that he also take her roommate along. Don, an old-fashioned boy from the rural South, was impressed by this behavior. He had had his share of wild times, but for a girl to be serious about, he wanted a proper southern lady, the kind his mother would be proud to know; and, he thought, he just might become serious about this tiny little girl with the short, curly black hair. He respected her for refusing to ride home alone with a strange man. At the door, he made no attempt to kiss her, but he made a date for the following Wednesday night. When they parted, both hearts were light and gay. It was February 14, 1953: Valentine's Day.

Was this the beginning of her confidence in stating "I am Jane!"? Had she looked into another's eyes and seen an acceptable reflection? Had she reached out and felt another drawing close to her? On their first date, they mostly exchanged impersonal information: what they liked to do, to eat, their jobs; and when he took her home, he leaned over and kissed her lips—a chaste, gentle caress. She did not resist, but neither did she respond—a fact that strangely pleased Don. This was no forward, wild woman, but a well-bred southern lady, who waited to be approached and who expected all the little courtesies of gentle living. On their second date, she, as becoming to a lady, explained to him that she had been married and that her five-year-old daughter was living with her parents. She further explained that she was legally separated from her husband and would receive her divorce when the stipulated waiting period had elapsed.

Don's family did not hold with divorces, but he had traveled around and he knew that even nice people sometimes divorced. This news was a slight tarnish on the bright luster of his new happiness, but he believed that Chris was a nice girl and that her reasons for getting a divorce had to be valid ones. She explained everything to him so calmly, so reasonably that his natural fears were quieted; and he assured her that he understood and appreciated her openness and that he would not want to date a married woman unless she had taken the legal steps that Chris had taken. She could not, however, bring herself to explain her illness to him. Wisely, she waited. How much tarnish can a new relationship bear without permanently dulling the warm glow?

Trouble strikes at the most inopportune times, and Chris's problems began to compound. She began her search for a job, with no success. When she tried Sears, Roebuck, the personnel manager gave her some startling news.

"I would like to hire you, but I cannot. I don't think you will be able to get a job in Augusta. The businessmen know who you are and that you have a strange illness. A local business executive told the businessmen about you at a meeting. I am trying to do you a favor. If you must work, I suggest you go to some other city."

Moving into a cheaper room down on Broad Street where she could walk and not need bus fare, she began to hoard her small amount of money. Don was taking her out several times a week, which helped immensely with her food bill. During this period, the two Chrises came out very little, mostly during the sessions with Dr. Thigpen, although Chris Costner did still go out on the nights when Jane was not dating Don. Inexplicably, she never attempted to come out and interfere with Jane's dating.

What was in Jane's heart? She looked, as she did for all her information, into her three hearts. She found in Chris Costner's heart no love for anyone, but in Chris White's heart abundant feeling for everyone and everything. In her own newly minted heart was a vast emptiness. But in all three hearts one figure dominated: Dr. Thigpen. Chris Costner resented him, sparred with him, but there he was, bigger than life. To Chris White he was succor, god, salvation. Jane sagely concluded that this proper, inhibited woman was in love with her doctor, though totally and eternally unaware of the basis for her strong feeling. She looked into her own heart and pondered,

"Am I in love with him, too? I don't know. I don't know what love is. I admire and respect him, find him most charming and handsome. I like the way he dresses, talks, walks, smiles, and the funny little way he tries to smooth down his chopped-off curls. He has wonderful hands! I can feel gentleness flowing through his fingertips when he touches me." She mused as have women throughout eternity, then reasoning asserted itself:

"Is he aware of this? Perhaps this is part of his work, to make his lonely, forsaken-feeling patients feel cared for. I guess he understands that I'm so lonely so much of the time I'm 'out' that I prefer not to emerge except when necessary."

And Jane, practical and logical, turned with good reason to Don, a known quality. His interest in her was obvious and for obvious reasons: herself alone, not the "others," not the strange triangle and its intricate implications, but only her. And what did she feel for him? What were these stirrings in her empty heart? Need. Need for acceptance, succor, salvation, a haven—someone bigger than life! She had used the legal name of Chris Costner White when she was introduced to Don—not Jane.

Therapy sessions with the doctor now were lengthy and almost daily. He probed into her childhood, going with her over and over again troublesome events that she could remember. Psychometric and projective tests, conducted on the different personalities, recorded Chris White as showing constriction, anxiety, and obsessive and compulsive traits, while Chris Costner's record indicated a predominant hysterical tendency. However slight and inclusive these differences, they did indicate that Mrs. White was rigid and incapable of dealing with her hostility, while Chris Costner was able to conform with her environment—paradoxically, making her the far more healthy one! Their I.Q. scores differed by only an unimpressive six points on the Wechsler-Bellevue Intelligence Scale. Handwriting samples of the three personalities were examined by an expert, who concluded that though it readily appeared that the three samples, each of which separately exhibited evidence of emotional instability, were the writing of three different persons, extensive investigation established beyond any doubt that they had been written by one and the same individual. Interestingly, it was also reported that nothing was found to indicate a willful and conscious intent to disguise or change the writing.

Here are samples of the handwriting:

EVE BLACK:

On top - It has ever since
the day I was down there
to see you - I think it must
be my eyes - I see little red
& green specks - and I'm covered
with some kind of rash.

EVE WHITE: baby please be quite dear lord
don't let me lose patience with her
she is too sweet and innocent and
my self-control

JANE:

It is against
the law to use
letters without
permission!

Jane

The doctor subjected each of the personalities to an electroen-
cephalogram (EEG), with rather startling results: There showed
no signs of mental abnormality in Chris White or in Jane, but
Chris Costner's brain waves showed a slight indication of a pattern that sometimes is associated with psychopathic personality.
Her EEG was definitely distinguished from the other two and

could be classified as borderline normal. And surely her characteristics were those of the classic definition of the psychopathic state: unreliability, untruthfulness, poor judgment, failure to learn from experience, pathologic egocentricity, and incapacity for love. These traits are acquired early, become thoroughly ingrained in the personality, and are manifest in abnormally aggressive or seriously irresponsible conduct for which the psychopath tends to project blame onto others, causing the environment to suffer rather than himself. A near-perfect description of the rebellious, individualistic, nonconformist Chris Costner!

Dr. Thigpen was no longer using hypnosis with her, had not since the appearance of Jane. Interestingly, he had never been able to hypnotize Chris Costner. Though the objective tests performed on his patient were particularly unimpressive and inclusive, the doctor was deeply affected by the profound and consistent differences among her personalities, which he had felt subjectively in personal and clinical relations. All three personalities readily responded to his mere beck and call. Chris White and Jane both wanted desperately to please him, to be able to answer his every question, feeling an indebtedness to him for providing them treatment without fee. Not so Chris Costner; she felt no obligation to him, maintaining that he was getting as much as he was giving.

"He's never seen anything like this," she declared. "I'm givin', he's gittin'. It's even!"

Soon after, Dr. Thigpen informed her that he was going to attend the meeting of the American Psychiatric Association (APA) in Los Angeles in May 1953 and that he was planning to make a speech on multiple personality, using her as an example. He also stated that he planned to show the film he had made of her while she had been his psychiatric patient in the University Hospital. He assured her that her identity would be protected. She made no objection; none occurred to her. And when he informed her that the APA might allow him to bring her along, she acquiesced. The offer, however, was never extended to her, but Dr. Thigpen's trip was eminently successful. Not only was the medical world interested in her unusual illness, but the press also thought it newsworthy, sending its incredible description around the world by Associated Press. When it appeared in the Augusta papers, Chris seized upon this opportunity to completely reveal herself to Don.

Chris and Don's relationship had been hastened by his narrow escape from a serious automobile accident. Though only slightly injured, he was hospitalized for several days and dependent on her for small but essential care. She generously helped him, and he was grateful. He was also justifiably disturbed and incensed because she could not get a job when work was so plentiful. She could now explain her dilemma to him against the background of the news article.

"Don, did you read the article in the *Chronicle* about the woman who has three personalities?" she asked one night as they sat in his car at the Dixie Pig Drive-in.

"Yes, I read about that. Isn't that something!" he replied, thinking she was simply making conversation.

"Well, I'm Eve," she blurted out, using the alias that Dr. Thigpen had given to her for his APA report.

Don looked at her stunned, then he smiled. "Are you kidding? You're just kidding me."

"No. No, I'm not. I wish I were. You can talk to Dr. Thigpen if you like," she offered.

"Oh, no. Your word's good enough for me." He paused. "The article said there were three personalities. Which one are you?" It was such an incredible question that a faint smile played at his mouth.

"I'm Jane," she answered seriously, no smile evident.

"Oh, yeah," he acknowledged, unsure of how to continue. "Where are the others?" His voice broke; he cleared his throat.

"I don't know where they are now. I can't see them if they're not out. Dr. Thigpen can call them out. They don't often come out now. It's all very complicated." She stopped, staring at his face for a hint of his reaction.

"Yeah, I guess so," he responded, giving no hint.

"I'm sorry, Don. I should have told you sooner. That's the reason I can't get a job. The businessmen know about me." Her voice was calm, weary.

He reacted protectively, "Well, that's not right!" Anger tinged his voice. "Everybody ought to be allowed to work. You're not sick or nothin'!"

He smiled, "Well, you know, everybody's got two personalities.

A person is one way when you go out with him at night, and he's another way when you meet him on the job the next morning. Three ought not be so bad; that's just one more." He had worked it out to the satisfaction of his own practical mind. What did he know or care of psychology? She was a sweet, nice girl who had confided in him, and he was not going to let her down.

Just as her financial circumstances became critical, Dr. Thigpen informed her that *American Weekly*, the Sunday newspaper magazine supplement, had requested him to give them information for a feature article on his strange case of multiple personality, and that he had agreed to do so since she so badly needed money. He said that they had agreed to pay her five hundred dollars' advance and another five hundred when the article was published. She received her advance in May, had her interview, and received the balance in July, when the article ran in three successive weekly parts. Since all three personalities had to agree to be interviewed, Dr. Thigpen was obliged to go through his paces, calling out each one to be briefed. It would have been necessary, of course, to tell only Chris White, since both the others were aware of her experiences, but he had learned from past efforts of this sort that Chris Costner expected the courtesy of a personal explanation, even when she already knew the facts. She became sulky and uncooperative if slighted. And since Jane seemed to be evolving into the main strength of the three and required more information to satisfy her intelligence than did Chris White, he had to perform his chore three times, often with considerable switching back and forth to clarify issues.

The doctor ran into two thorny issues, which required all of his skills to resolve. He assured them that their identity would be kept secret, advising them that this was best and thinking that this would calm fears. Chris White and Jane readily agreed with him that no pictures and the continued use of her alias were best, but Chris Costner vehemently objected.

"Why are you keepin' us secret?" she asked. "I don't want to be kept a secret. I ain't done nothin' to be ashamed of."

"I've explained this to you, Chris," he said patiently. "It would cause you a lot of trouble if people knew who you were."

"It couldn't cause any more trouble than it already has," she declared. "We can't get no job nohow. I think you just want to hog all the glory for yourself," she slyly accused.

"What makes you think it's glory?" he asked. "It's hard work."

"Well, all these important people know who you are now. I want them to know who I am, too!" she stubbornly stated. "We might as well face it now."

"It wouldn't be good for you, Chris; it would be stupid," he instructed. "People wouldn't accept you if they knew. The others understand that."

She was overruled but unhappy, but he never knew when she might carelessly decide to expose them all to public view. The second hurdle to be cleared was the complication of money: They each wanted their share and they each insisted upon signing the contract. Officials for *American Weekly*, upon advice from Dr. Thigpen, agreed to allow this charade, since the legal name of Chris Costner White would be placed first on the designated line. The law appeared to ignore the idiosyncrasy of pseudonyms doodled below the legal signature. When the check came to Chris White, an incredible scene was enacted.

"Mrs. White," he said to the timid, colorless woman sitting before him holding the five-hundred-dollar check, the largest check she had ever received, "you remember the agreement we all had? You are to divide the money with Chris and Jane."

"Yes, Doctor. I have my checkbook. Do you want me to write their checks?" She looked at him, resigned, showing no interest in the situation, only awaiting instructions. Her body drooped, tired and lifeless, and her eyes, dull and lackluster, occasionally lost focus and appeared to stare into the unknown, unseen.

"Yes," he instructed. "Write a check for Chris Costner."

She perfunctorily performed the task, entered the amount on the stub, and tore out the check, handing it to the doctor.

"May I speak to Chris Costner now?" he asked, accepting the proffered check.

"Yes, Doctor," she complied, wearily closing her tired eyes.

"Chris Costner, Chris, may I speak to you?" he called.

The eyes, lively and sparkling, though also watchful and suspicious, quickly opened. Simultaneously, life, strong and vibrant, flowed into the body, lifting and rounding it. The pale skin began to glow, the sagging muscles tightened; incredibly, the smooth, black hair even appeared to take on shine and bounce. But the voice, there was no mistaking that the voice was different: Its tone had coarsened, become vibrant, its speech was familiar and punctuated by vernacular and slang.

"Hya, Doc, you keepin' us all honest?" she teased, all the while reaching for her check, with the same hand, which, ironically, had just written it and handed it to the doctor.

"How are you, Chris?" He seriously addressed her, not picking up on her challenge. "Are you pleased with your share?"

"Sure. If this's all we can git. You've never talked about that." She looked suspicious.

"Now, Chris, you know that's all they would pay. If you're satisfied, will you let me speak to Mrs. White?" He refused to argue with her.

"Sure, Doc. Now, you keep her honest." She closed her intense eyes and relaxed her body.

"Mrs. White, Mrs. White, may I speak to you?" he called, watching her every move.

Life drained out, perceptibly drained out. Color receded from the face; facial muscles sagged, became flaccid; the shoulders hunched, a quiver shook the loose frame; the eyes opened, opaque, pained.

"Yes, Doctor," the thin voice whispered.

"Thank you, Mrs. White," he recognized her effort. "Chris Costner accepted her check. Will you make out a check for Jane Costner, now, for her share?"

"Yes, Doctor."

The vibrant hand, which so shortly had grasped the check, now listlessly laid it aside so that it could, now, write out another check. When finished writing the second check, she handed it to the doctor.

"Thank you, Mrs. White. May I speak to Jane, now?" he politely asked.

"Yes."

The eyes gratefully closed.

"Jane, Jane, may I speak with you?" The doctor unconsciously chose the more literate conversational term when addressing the cultured Jane, placing her on an educational level with himself.

"Of course, Dr. Thigpen," the low, modulated voice responded.

291

The clear blue eyes opened, looking levelly and deep into those of the doctor, her friend and trusted confidant. Her body assumed a casual, comfortable, yet poised attitude in the chair. This woman was confident, self-assured, at ease, comfortable with herself and with others. Her face lovely, the wide, full mouth smiling. "How are you today?"

"I'm just fine, honey, how are you?" He smiled, relaxing.

"I'm fine, thank you. Are they giving you a bad time?" Her face showed apologetic concern for his trouble.

"Oh, no, just the usual thing. I have your check here." He handed it to her.

"Thank you. This will help keep things going for a while longer. Perhaps until the article is published. Have you talked with the others to determine how they plan to spend their share?" she asked.

Dr. Thigpen knew that when he talked to her the other two could not hear; therefore he often confided their intentions to her, soliciting her aid when he wanted to avoid potential trouble. "Mrs. White plans to pay bills with hers and advance at least one month's rent. Chris, of course, just can't wait to rush out and buy some new duds and go out on the town."

Jane laughed quietly, "That's about what I expected. So I guess I had better hang onto my share. I'm almost tempted to buy just one dress for myself, though. Nothing they have really suits me. I feel as if I'm dressed one day in a missionary's outfit and the next in Gypsy Rose Lee's."

"Sugar pie, if you want a new dress, you buy one. You deserve it," he supported her.

"Oh, well, not now, maybe later." She smiled her thanks to him.

"How are you coming with your gentleman friend?" he asked. "It's not getting serious, is it?"

"I don't know about that," she teased. Then her face became serious, faintly worried. "I told him about me, us."

"Did he understand?"

"I don't know, Dr. Thigpen," she answered. "He was *understanding*, but I don't think he really *understood*."

"Well, if you want me to talk to him, just let me know. I guess I had better get back to Mrs. White now and get all this money settled. Chris Costner won't try to spend your money, will she?"

Jane smiled, "Oh, no, she knows better than that. When we make an agreement, even she respects it. Good-bye, Dr. Thigpen, have a nice day." Her intelligent eyes looked enigmatically at him before they slowly closed.

"Good-bye, Jane," he sadly responded, refraining from wishing her the same salutation. "Mrs. White, may I speak to you?" he asked, taking a deep breath.

The lifeless blue eyes opened. The lovely Jane was gone. Was it his imagination? Had she ever been there? Could that exquisite creature ever inhabit this plain, colorless figure? The doctor shook off his eerie feeling, mentally chiding himself.

"Yes, Doctor."

"They have their checks, Mrs. White. Can you handle everything now?"

"I think so."

Under Dr. Thigpen's watchful eye, she gathered up the three checks written to three different personalities; but he watched only one woman leave, one small hand clutching all three checks.

The doctor sat collecting himself, sorting it all out. What was the meaning of the events he had observed? He still did not think it likely that any person, no matter how excellent an actress, consciously dissimulating, could over months avoid even one telltale error or imperfection. And while this case surely had much in common with ordinary hysterical conversions and dissociations, there was something more and something different. Could it simply be disintegration, schizophrenia? Given that the whole process is akin to schizophrenia, it must still be carefully noted that none of the three products of the disintegration, not one of the three personalities, showed anything suggesting the presence of that disorder.

And deeper. Disintegration presupposes a once unified whole. Or were the three personalities never in the past completely unified?

Feeling that a definite though subtle change was taking place, the doctor intensified his therapy, probing into her childhood and requesting that her relatives come in for consultation, hoping that they could throw some light on the missing pieces of this intriguing puzzle. When her parents and Ralph came, they sat stunned as Dr. Thigpen called out each personality and exhibited the star-tling differences, explaining to them as best he could what was happening. They believed, incredible as it all was, for it explained many incidents over the years that had so baffled them. They remembered all the times they had punished her as she tearfully protested her innocence. They first watched a shallow caricature of their daughter smile carelessly and admit to hating her twin sisters and to biting their toes as babies. They then watched their now familiar, sad, browbeaten daughter discuss the whipping she had received for biting her loved sisters—still protesting, after twenty years, her innocence of the despicable act, still describing the "other child" whom she had seen biting the tender baby toes. They next watched a polite, cultured stranger, still looking strik-ingly like their daughter, deny any knowledge of ever having been their child.

They were ready to believe that the wayward behavior, ill will, harshness, and occasional acts of violence, that they had always at-tributed to unaccountable fits of temper in a person habitually gentle and considerate were committed by another "personality." But were not the same teeth that did the biting, the same hands that did the mischief, the same legs that ran away, to be found in both their daughter and the "other ones"? Their practical minds struggled long with their feelings of guilt over unjust punishment, and their only justification was of at least having spanked the very legs that carried whoever it was into forbidden territory.

Ralph, now legally separated from his wife for almost a year, heard his pale, sad spouse regretfully inform him that she did not feel that she could ever be happy as his wife. He then watched dumfounded as that sassy, sneering "other one" flatly declared that she had never been his wife and would take the body and run away with it if Chris White went back to "the son-of-a-bitch." Be-fore his anger had even cooled, a quiet, cool stranger looked with compassion on him and apologized for his problems, explaining in a way that was somehow intimidating that she would be unable to help him, but that she hoped his life would turn out well.

Dr. Thigpen explained to Ralph White that his wife would sue him for divorce in August, and after Ralph's experience that day, the confused man made no protest. He returned to Edgefield, where for some months he had been living unemployed with Acie and Zueline, gathered his few belongings, and returned to his paternal home, to the sawmill and the Saturday nights. He made no provisions, verbal or otherwise, for his five-year-old daughter, not even a promise to visit her. But then, he had not contributed one cent to her support for the entire time she had lived with her grandparents. The child lost nothing but a liability when the male who contributed sperm for her biological conception walked out the door. Her life now revolved around Nanny and D-Daddy, who gave her a firm foundation of love on which to build what later proved to be a generous, fulfilling life.

Elen, upon request, met Chris at Dr. Thigpen's office and spent an astounding day. Before seeing the doctor, the two cousins sat and chatted about everything except why they were there, and they picked up the thread of their conversation afterward, as if the whole incredible event had not taken place. Elen and the doctor talked at length of her childhood experiences with Chris, and Elen was able to relate to him some facts that he had not gleaned from his sessions with his patient. In passing, she mentioned her cousin's marriage to Al Thorne, an astonishing fact to the doctor, who was totally unaware of any such occurrence. When he was later to discuss this with Chris White, she had no memory of it at all; and at first Chris Costner denied knowledge of it also, later changing her story, and, fabricating as she went, spun a believable tale for the confused therapist. The full story of this horrible experience did not surface until more than twenty years later, after Chris both denied and lied to her doctor to avoid reliving the most degrading event of her fantastic life. After more than thirty-three years of repression, she was able to lift out this rejected matter and view it, tearfully and chokingly, and to accept it as having happened, though to two other people, neither of whom were those she remembered as Chris White and Chris Costner.

Elen explained her relationship with Chris, their acceptance of each other, their mutual admiration, their tendency when together to indulge in make-believe activities instead of reality, and their deep love and trust, which did not depend upon constant contact. Finally, Thigpen brought in his patient and put her through her paces. Elen, amazed but believing, recognized both Chris White and Chris Costner as her lifelong companions, however greatly exaggerated in characteristics; but Jane gave her quite a turn. She seemed hauntingly familiar, but not as Chris, as some-one else. Even her voice was desperately familiar, its identification just beyond her grasp. She was faintly similar to roles Chris had played in their pretend games as teen-agers, such as the famous actress, or the most beautiful woman in the world. Suddenly, the hair tweaked on Elen's scalp. It was like looking in a psychic mir-ror. It was her *own self* she was feeling, was hearing. That was her own voice, her own speech, her exact phrases, terminology!

Elen did not know what she had witnessed; she had no way of evaluating her experience. She felt strangely sad, uneasy, even flat-tered that Chris was imitating her. Alter ego was not yet a term in Elen's vocabulary, but perhaps the term does not truly apply; for here again Chris had far outstripped the bounds of the condition. She had not just so closely identified with her cousin's expressions and purposes that she seemed to become a second self, a genuine prolongation or extension of herself; she had actually, to the outer reaches of organic limitations, become her cousin—her auxiliary or alter ego. And the whole story was not known on that sultry sum-mer day. It would take almost three years of desperate effort for this tragic drama to play through to its inevitable conclusion, complete with the finale death scene—which, heartrendingly, with a farcical, melodramatic touch, failed—futility, the recurrent theme of most of her efforts.

Her funds nearly depleted and no foreseeable source of addi-tional money available, Chris in August was forced to squarely face her situation. It she could not support herself in Augusta, she surely could not do so in Edgefield, where everybody knew her. And she could not just go back home, back to the protecting womb, and hide in her parents' home, she and her child draining their meager resources. She told Dr. Thigpen of her plight; he lis-tened but made no effort to advise her or help her. Was he at-tempting to wean her away from his support, feeling that it was time the close, intimate relationship of psychiatrist-patient was dissolved? He left it her decision to make.

She next reached out to Don. Who else was there?

"I'm going to have to go home," she quietly informed him. Her eyes were troubled, but her head was held high. "My money is al-most gone, and I cannot get a job."

He became angry. "Why can't you get a job? Everybody ought

to be able to get a job!" He believed strongly in the right to work, the dignity of work. "Is someone preventing you from getting a job?" he asked suspiciously.

"I don't know," she answered thoughtfully. "The man at Sears did say that nobody in Augusta would hire me now. That they knew about me."

"Well, who told them?" he asked, warming to the subject. "Did that doctor tell them? Is he trying to keep you from getting a job?"

"Oh, no, Don," she quickly replied. "Dr. Thigpen wouldn't do that. He's always tried to help me."

"Then why can't he help you get a job? He's an important man; he's got pull in this town. And he's the one who spread it in all the papers about you. That's the reason you can't get a job!" He deeply felt the injustice of her situation.

Had she tried to get a job since Sears had issued its warning? Did she really want a job, want to be a divorced woman working, skimping to support a small child? Her ideal had always been to succeed as a wife and a mother, caring for a home and a husband, herself loved and protected and cared for. Now that she had become Jane, a woman well able to cope with the business world, were those old ideals too strong to allow her to function as she was meant to function? Was the brave, capable exterior just that, a façade barely covering the same frightened, clinging child?

Don did not fail her. The confirmed bachelor, the rover, the self-sufficient soldier of fortune capitulated.

"We'll just get married!" he blurted out, surprising them both into momentary silence.

When she spoke, her voice was infinitely soft. "You don't have to marry me."

"I want to marry you!" he vehemently declared. "I'm old enough now to settle down."

"Think about it. Wherever I go, Taffy goes, too," she insisted.

"I know that. I want that," he declared.

She smiled, her dignity heroic. "You haven't said anything about loving me." A nervous muscle twitched in her cheek.

He was too serious for joking, "Would a man marry a woman with a child if he didn't love her?" he said hoarsely, revealing the roving bachelor's inner turmoil at deserting the free life to take on these awesome responsibilities. He touched the tense cheek. Ironically, the strange illness never crossed his mind.

And what was said after that? It's the same old story, ever new. Ah, sweet mystery of life, at *last* I've found you!

It was arranged that she would leave Augusta and go home until they were married, tentatively around Christmas, and that she would return for weekly sessions with Dr. Thigpen. He called in Acie, Zueline, and Tiny and explained to them what they could expect concerning her behavior, stressing the necessity of her regularly scheduled therapy sessions. He warned,

"It is important that no one be told of the nature of her illness. With all this publicity, we cannot afford to tell anyone who she is. It would be the worst thing she can do. It would not only hurt her, but it would harm Taffy, too. The child would not be able to go to school. None of you would be accepted; it would expose all of you to bad publicity."

It was a sobering thought, but not an entirely new one. They were accustomed to refraining from discussing their personal affairs, but they had never been forced to deliberately withhold information from others because it was harmful, shameful. Their daughter and sister, who had done no wrong, must be shielded and hidden as if she were a common criminal, someone to be ashamed of rather than proud of.

"If you think that's best, Doctor." They agreed, having no alternative.

Before she left the city, an unsettling happening occurred. Since February Jane had been dating Don on a regular basis, perhaps two or three times a week. Chris Costner during this time had also continued to date and go out on the town. Interestingly, they, by a sort of unspoken agreement, never invaded each other's territory. Understandably, it would have been disastrous if Chris had betrayed Jane and gone on a date with Don. His old-fashioned sense of the conventionally proper would have been outraged, and it is questionable whether his sincere interest in her as a fine southern lady would have been able to withstand such an unheralded shock. She had never told him of Chris Costner's escapades, even though she was fully aware of them; and he, feeling that he had no right to ask such personal questions before they had an agreement, had never pried. Strangely, as soon as Jane and

Don became engaged, Chris Costner never again came out for a date.

Chris Costner, though daily growing weaker, was not to be thus shoved aside without her revenge. Ironically, though, she vented her anger on poor inoffensive Chris White instead of Jane, who was really usurping Chris Costner's options. As a final fling, she came out and went on a shopping spree for new clothes, paying for them with a check on Chris White's almost depleted bank account. When the check bounced, Chris Costner brazenly approached the store manager, declaring that she had already altered the clothes, and she had done exactly this to prevent Jane's returning them; but that she was willing to give them a necklace, black onyx with a diamond chip, as payment. One of the clerks in the store knew Myrtle and recognized that Chris was her niece. Taking the necklace and allowing her to leave, they immediately contacted Myrtle, who called Acie and related the whole tale to him, including the amount of the bill: seventy-five dollars! Neither Tiny nor Acie had that much cash, but Tiny borrowed the money, and she and her father drove the twenty-five miles to Augusta, where they, horribly embarrassed, paid the bill and redeemed the necklace. So Jane, while retaining her hoarded funds intact, had new clothes for her trousseau, and Chris Costner received the blame for a capriciously dishonest act.

What must Zueline have felt as she prepared for her daughter's homecoming? The cool, cultured, confident woman who had greeted her as a friendly stranger and had professed no knowledge of being her daughter—was that the child she had held to her breast, had cared for all these years? She certainly looked the same, but that was all—the rest was all different. The mother could well believe that the doctor was right, that another personality—another person—was occupying her daughter's body, and that her daughter, her Christine, was gone. Her superstitious nature shivered. But when the calm, hesitant woman in her daughter's body came in the door, Zueline's fears dissolved, and she ran down the hall, gathered the slight form to her own ample bosom and declared,

"Honey, I'm so glad you're home!"

The thin arms enfolded the soft, round form close and responded, "I'm glad to be home, Mother."

Then and there Zueline became her mother; not just someone she accepted as a mother, but her mother. Everybody needs a mother.

At home in Edgefield, Jane was almost completely in command of the personalities, able to control almost at will their comings and goings. She now totally prevented Chris Costner's emergence other than when Dr. Thigpen requested her presence during therapy, but she arranged for Chris White to be out often with Taffy. Jane in no way identified with Mrs. White's role of wife and mother, and though Jane was fond of the little girl and would have liked to help her, she scrupulously avoided interfering between the sad mother and her child. Jane was, of course, aware of all that the two Chrises did and thought, while they were not at all privy to her presence. This advantage greatly assisted the doctor in evaluating information gleaned from them. Jane was able to divulge when Chris Costner was lying, when Chris White was withholding facts in an attempt to please him, and Jane was even aware when they began to weaken and fade.

In early September, she received a letter from Dr. Thigpen requesting that she come to his office and sign a contract for him to do an article for the magazine *Today's Woman*. On October 7 he wrote her again, setting up a date to take her to Atlanta to have a movie made of the three personalities. Did he suspect that some sort of resolution was impending among the personalities and he wanted to capture them on film before this happened? He asked if she would like to come to Augusta on Sunday evening, October 11, 1973, stay overnight at one of the hotels, and meet him at the airport no later than 7:15 A.M. Monday morning. He also requested that she get each one of the personalities to read his letter and to let each one suggest a dress that each felt was most typical of her personality. He stated that her expenses would be paid by him.

The filming went as scheduled. Don brought her to Augusta on Sunday, checked her into the Richmond Hotel, and picked her up again on Monday night. Tiny had given her some pocket money to spend, and since it was her first airplane flight, she was excited. All three personalities were allowed out to enjoy the sensation of flying, and Chris Costner evinced much fright at finding herself suddenly airborne. At the studio, Dr. Thigpen put Chris through her paces before the camera. He called out each personality, asked her key questions to elicit information designed to clearly illuminate basic characteristics, and pointed out to the potential viewer the differences in facial expressions, posture, and mannerisms.

He then had each personality don her favorite outfit, brought along for this specific purpose, and walk, turn, pose, and smile for the camera while the doctor, off camera, again asked of each questions designed to highlight sharp contrasts among them. This part of the production was less than successful. All three for once seemed tightly grouped, and did not display very effectively their diverse qualities. Even Chris Costner, the usually uninhibited clown, seemed tense and tight, denying that she could dance the Black Bottom when it was so suggested by the doctor and maintaining that she could not sing unless the mood was right, which it obviously was not. Had Dr. Thigpen waited too long to capture his prize on film? Were they too far resolved, too weak to perform satisfactorily? It was an interesting performance, but it was not spectacular to anyone who had observed the real thing.

In seeming desperation, he hypnotized Chris White, explaining that though hypnosis was rarely employed, it was being used at that time to bring out the deeper emotional aspects of the personality. At the conclusion, he stated that six weeks after the film was made the case resolved itself, and he added several minutes of film of Jane, the resolved personality, made two years later, declaring that she now seemed happy and well adjusted. This addendum to the film was obviously made at a later time than the Atlanta portion; Jane had gained weight, her hair was a different length, the clothes were a shorter style; but neither she nor Don, to whom she would have then been married, had any knowledge of its production.

Jane asked Dr. Thigpen what use would be made of this film, and he informed her that like the other one, made of her earlier when she was his patient in the hospital, it was simply an effort to complete her case history and would allow him and Dr. Cleckley to study her symptoms when she was away from them. He assured her that the film would be stored in a safe place. This woman had not ventured beyond a radius of two hundred miles during her entire lifetime, she knew nothing of rental film libraries, of lectures

301

before interested groups, medical and otherwise, where films are used to illustrate and to entertain. She completely misunderstood; a safe place to her meant a secure place, secret to all but her doctors' eyes. It was more than twenty years before she learned that her face, her pain, her soul, upon request for a small rental fee, had been available from Pennsylvania State University in films called A *Case Study of Multiple Personality.*

Chris was happy! It was one of those rare, brief periods in her life when she was truly happy. As Jane, she was serene, poised, purposeful; her future was planned according to her ideals; and the troublesome illness was obviously abating. Chris Costner was sulkily subdued, seldom coming out except when summoned; Chris White gratefully spent her allowed time out caring for her child; and Jane, the educated sophisticate, was lovingly squired about by her strong and aggressive, though gentle and protective fiancé. They went places: a carefree, laughing couple. Any available entertainment was their fair game. They saw a musical variety show, the Ringling Brothers and Barnum & Bailey Circus, the Horace Heidt talent show, the Ice Capades, fairs, and football games.

A normal, healthy male with all his natural drives and desires intact, Don ardently courted this woman he had chosen to be his lifetime companion—his wife. He held her tightly, passionately, he kissed her urgently, he emotionally declared his devotion and desire for her; but no matter how tempted, he never considered possessing her before their marriage. And Chris, in her role as Jane the dignified southern lady, had her shallow assumed emotions well under control; she knew just exactly how far a nice girl should go. That's just what she considered herself to be—a nice girl! She had no knowledge of ever having been a wife and mother. She acknowledged that the body she inhabited had been subjected to both sexual and birth experiences; but she, her mind, her senses knew of no such happenings, responded to no such memory sensations.

She was again a virgin, and this time even less experienced than her predecessors. She had told no smutty jokes, read no pornographic books, necked with no boys in dark corners. She was truly a blank page, ready to be inscribed by her husband, the only man who had ever touched her. Could any man ask for more? Don

302

seemed to accept this. Her attitude, her bearing, her obvious innocence could not be belied. Though his intelligence stated that she had known a man, had borne that man's child, his heart sang that his girl was a newborn virgin—and, incredibly, she was.

Chris, as Jane, though able to view clearly both of her counterparts, had most incomplete access to their memory prior to her emergence upon the scene. It took her quite a while to learn simple tasks that a woman of her age and circumstances would have learned in growing up—tasks such as how to keep a house and how to prepare a routine meal. Yet she seemed to draw upon a store of information that neither Chris White nor Chris Coster appeared to possess. It was as if her educational experiences as Jane extended her knowledge beyond what either of them could have experienced. On both her and Don's Ice Capades programs she quoted Whittier, *"Of all love words of tongue or pen—The saddest are these, 'It might have been!'"* It was inscribed to Don and signed *"Chris."* On their Fred Waring program she inscribed *"Je aimé vous—mon chêri,"* and she signed it *"Chris."* These are far from the kinds of words Chris White would have uttered to her unfeeling husband, and they would have reduced raucous, unlearned Chris Costner to scornful laughter; yet Elen majored in English and French at Furman University, and John Greenleaf Whittier's sad poem was one of her favorites. During Elen's visits to her cousin, when she had rambled on about her college life and the opening vistas of her own mind, she had been filling unborn Jane's storehouse of memories. And Jane, though her quotation was slightly incorrect and her French badly fractured, was desperately drawing on this skimpy source to strengthen her fragile existence.

Chris shared a room with Tiny during these few months before her marriage. Becky was already married and the mother of her own child. Jane had no knowledge of Tiny as a sister, but rapidly developed a warm friendship with her as two strange young women who happened to be rooming together. It was a most trying time for the younger girl, who was called upon to explain to her older sister things they had both learned together years before. Jane's childlike wonder over experiencing the familiar for the supposed first time strained her sister's credence. When Jane first saw Taffy's small tricycle she clapped her hands in delight, laughed like a child, and tried to ride the tiny vehicle. When she first tasted shrimp, she liked it so well that she wanted that expensive food three times a day. Tiny showed amazing patience and went along with her even when the results were entirely exasperating.

Chris Costner, on one of her rare manifestations, sold one of Jane's best dresses to Tiny. Unaccountably, Jane, who at other times knew of all Chris Costner's escapades, was unaware of this transaction. When Tiny attempted to wear her duly purchased dress, Jane shortly reminded her that she expected people to ask permission before they wore her clothes. Tiny, shocked, held her ready retort. Later, for no accountable reason, Jane generously gave the dress to Tiny. When Tiny loaned Jane twenty dollars for her flying trip to Atlanta, she was very grateful.

"Oh, Tiny, that's so sweet of you! I probably won't need any money, but I'll feel better having some. I'll give it back to you as soon as I return," she promised.

Instead, she spent the money for a sweater and skirt. On her return, she offered the garments as a gift to Tiny. But, alas, the lovely clothes fit Chris perfectly, and were much too small for Tiny, who was several sizes larger than her sister. The younger sister never lost her temper, realizing that Chris was ill, and she often acted as a buffer between Chris's erratic behavior and her parents' confusion. Once at the table Chris Costner came out, picked up a plate laden with food, and threw it to the floor. Before anyone could react, Chris White emerged, surveyed the scene, and whispered,

"Oh, Mother, I'm so sorry Taffy did that."

By the time Jane came into the tearful scene, Tiny was already cleaning up the mess and soothing the upset Taffy. Jane, as would any house guest caught in the middle of a family uproar, calmly excused herself and retired to her room to read.

Tiny, to hold onto her own sanity, never allowed herself to think of the personalities as separate; they were all Chris! Tiny had been counseled by Dr. Thigpen, and she knew that her sister's illness was a coping mechanism unconsciously structured by her to help her face frightening reality difficulties. Tiny, more than even the doctor himself, saw the personalities in their bare form, stripped of all attempts at creating proper impressions, honed down to their naked essence. She was aware that Jane was shallow, selfish, jealous, and that she did not grow along with her fast-accumulating knowledge, but remained a one-dimensional figure. The doctor, viewing Jane only on special occasions when she was prepared for their interchange, viewed her as having integrity, capable of compassion, devotion, and valid love, and able to regain full health and happiness. He never saw the side exposed to Tiny—a woman so vain that her greatest enjoyment was having her picture taken.

Don also never saw this other side of the strange woman he was marrying. He planned outings for them where it would be appropriate to take Taffy. Chris did not object to this, and Don never knew that she did not consider herself the little girl's mother, that she was just as much a stranger to the child as was he.

The personalities had been strangely though steadily changing. As Jane grew stronger and more dominant, the two Chrises, each in her characteristic way, weakened and faded. Chris Costner did not want to leave (to disappear? to die?), and she fought for her existence, complaining to the doctor that she was being pushed out by Jane and that it was his fault. Several times Chris Costner summoned Tiny, once calling her home from work, declaring that she was dying and needed help. Tiny, understandably frightened, tried to soothe her sister, for they were all her sister, assuring her that she was not dying, that she would be all right. Usually the experience ended abruptly, the subject was changed, and no further mention was made of dying. On the day when she desperately pled with her sister to come home from work, Tiny found on arriving that Chris was calm and matter-of-fact, never even alluding to death or in any manner seeming to be upset.

Chris White also felt that she was fading, growing weaker. Whereas Chris Costner vehemently declared that she was being forcibly suppressed, Chris White described her condition as "daily growing more tired." Jane allowed her emergence often to be with her child, and never herself took on the role of mother, even when she was alone with the little girl. Taffy, while understanding nothing of the intricacies of the situation, was well aware of her mother's strange behavior. She often looked up at the woman before her, scanned the familiar face with her huge, solemn, blue eyes, and asked,

"Are you my mother, or are you that other one?"

305

The soul shrinks at the frightful horror contained in that question. Out of such stuff are tales of monsters and demons spun! But perhaps the greatest horror comes from the lack of fear on the child's face—her calm, innocent acceptance of this whole incredible, unnatural drama.

The beginning of the end came quite inauspiciously, as is so often the case, as Chris was playing ball with Taffy one afternoon in October. The ball rolled under the wide, high porch spanning the rear of the County Home. Taffy, frightened of retrieving it alone, followed her mother as she bent and crawled after the bright blue toy. As they momentarily squatted there together, Chris felt her head buzz and throb; the scene spun and dimmed. The blond child and the blue ball faded. When Chris's sight cleared, twenty years had rolled back: She saw two children playing under another wide, high porch, but now the blond child was Elen and the blue ball was Grandmother's blue enamel cup, and the other child was the thin, bony one with large brown freckles and enormous blue eyes. The scene shifted to the death room in which Grandmother lay in her coffin. Unbearable, suffocating fear clutched Chris's heart; something was about to happen—what? She felt arms lift her up to the coffin, push her down to the cold, still face. A voice intoned,

"Kiss her, kiss her, kiss her!"

Chris screamed and pushed away; her hand touched the immobile face and stuck! She could not pull away. She was going to be fastened to that cold, dark silence and closed up in that still, lifeless box.

"No, no!" she struggled, and looking around frantically for help, she saw her mother coming into the room. "Mother, don't make me! No! No!"

"Teeny, what's wrong?" The scene cleared, and Chris saw Tiny peering under the house at her.

"It's all right. I'm coming," she called, her heart thudding painfully.

The next day she insisted on seeing Dr. Thigpen, even though it was not her regular appointment. As soon as he called out Chris White, she burst into tears and told him the story of the blue cup; then, before he could question her or pursue the story, she

306

abruptly faded away, leaving an equally, and perhaps for the first time, tearful Chris Costner.

"I think we're dying," she sobbed.

"Ah, no, honey," he soothed. "You just have a problem, that's all."

Her drowned bright blue eyes regarded him sadly. "I want you to have my red silk dress." The heavy lids closed, sending a rush of tears streaming down the wet, white face. She had willed her most prized possession to the one who had constantly thwarted her aims and desires, who had stunted her growth and weakened her hold on existence.

The eyes flew open, the usual calm, easy poise shattered by abject terror.

"Mother, don't make me!" she screamed.

"O.K., baby. It's all right, honey. Everything's all right." He patted her hand. "What's happening? Tell me what's happening."

"She's making me touch Grandmother. Mother, don't let her make me!" The voice was strangely immature and childlike.

"Just tell me about it. Just tell me everything that's happening," Dr. Thigpen quietly urged.

And she told him. Jane, who had never had a childhood, who had no knowledge of personal happenings during growing-up years, told him of the frightening experience of being forced to kiss her dead grandmother good-bye; and she told it in a five-year-old voice. The thin, piping voice, laced with gulping sobs, related the moment of hysterical horror.

"It's all right, sugar pie," he assured her. "This is just what we need. Let me speak to Mrs. White. Mrs. White, may I speak to you?"

He waited. Jane looked at him. "She's not there."

"Let me speak to Chris Costner. Chris, Chris Costner, may I speak to you?" he called.

He again waited.

"They're not there, Dr. Thigpen," Jane answered him, tears quietly rolling down her white cheeks. "They're gone."

Gone! Yes, but *how* gone and *where* gone? The doctor looked at the agitated, though confidently controlled woman seated in the chair. Was it possible that the heedlessly gay, merry, amoral Chris Costner would never slouch sensuously in that familiar place again? That sad, weary Chris White, with her beautiful sense of duty and willingness for self-sacrifice, would never again relate her tormented tale to him? He felt inexpressively sad, bereft, and a little guilty. Without doubt, he had professionally determined that the only way his patient had even a slim chance for regaining health was through Jane's attaining full possession of the personality—that integrated human functioning. But had he exerted undue pressure to accomplish that fact? He had been well aware of that danger, one well documented in the literature, and he knew that the psychiatrist has some choice as to which personality he will try to reinforce. But he had attempted to be tentative and work along with developments within his patient rather than make full and final judgments.

The doctor mused. How could he have made a final judgment? Knowing as closely as he had the clowning, fun-loving, sensuous Chris Costner—egocentric, yes; vicious, no—carelessly flaunting her sexuality, yet unable to either give or accept love; a child, a reed in the storm, buffeted by excessive emotions: Could he order euthanasia for her? And Mrs. White, pained, long-suffering, self-denigrating, tormented by doubts and fears, perfectly willing to embrace oblivion if in so doing her child would have a better life: Could he order euthanasia for her? No, he could not. No physician could.

But does this cessation of existence satisfy the definition of death? No one died, the living body is irrefutable proof of that! But when one has known the three, talked with them, laughed with them, exchanged pictures and presents, it is not so easy to glibly answer.

Nor was Jane able to so easily face her new status. She was alone, as she had never been alone before. She now had no escape, no place to go, no one to call on for help, to shift blame to. She felt empty, blank, linear. She came home to Tiny weeping, upset, inconsolable. She knew them better than she had known anyone else in the world, and they had died, but died out of her, gone out of her. Sleep had deserted her; she walked the floor and moaned. Leaving her room only for meals, it was a week before she was done with her grief, before she picked up their legacy and cautiously launched out alone.

Her new dossier of information was carefully compiled. Constantly sifting through facts and experiences, she built a suitable background to support her new façade—for façade it was. A real structure cannot be constructed without a foundation, and she had thrown away her foundation. The Phoenix was arising anew from its ashes.

She and Don, as lovers do, exchanged information about their backgrounds. He was surprised but pleased when she told him that she was a graduate of Furman University, where she had studied English and French. Unfamiliar with college life, Don was unable to detect those obvious fallacies in her accounts. To please her, he bought tickets to the Furman-South Carolina football game, and she spent a glorious autumn Saturday rooting for her alma mater. During this time she wrote many poems to him, in one of which, *My Beloved*, she wrote,

> *Because cold negative death*
> *Creeps in my heart to hide,*
> *And only your love*
> *Can turn the tide.*

Did she fear?

On one of her final trips to Dr. Thigpen she told him that she was going to marry Don.

"This is a very serious thing, honey," he warned. "Are you sure that you really love this man? Is he really the man you love?"

"Yes, I do love him," she soberly answered. "I love him very much. And he loves me." A little defiantly?

"I have a very warm feeling for you, Jane," he stated, still using the old name. "I love you, Jane." He watched her every move, her every nuance.

"Oh, I'm so sorry, Dr. Thigpen. I'm so sorry." Her blue eyes expressed genuine sadness and compassion for a suffering that she had unknowingly caused and for which she had no remedy.

"That's all right, honey. That's life." He seemed satisfied. "I would like to meet your young man, and I really should talk to him. Bring him in for a talk." His tone was friendly, inviting.

Don did not object to the visit, though he protested that it was not necessary, that he knew all about her that he needed to know. She received her engagement ring from him at Thanksgiving, and they made their visit to the doctor shortly after. It was something of a strained visit, Don feeling slightly on the defensive, as a man would feel confronting another man, doctor or no, who had been so intimate with the woman he was shortly to marry.

The doctor set the tone, shaking hands and indicating chairs, placing Chris in her usual chair and Don across the room.

"I've been hearing a lot about you," he addressed Don.

Don shifted nervously in his chair and smiled. "Yeah?" he responded.

"I want to congratulate you on your coming marriage. You're getting a mighty fine girl," the doctor complimented.

"I think so," Don answered, smiling and nodding.

"I wanted to see you to explain the problem she's had and discuss it with you," the doctor offered.

"Well, yes, I know about it," Don responded.

Dr. Thigpen talked generally for a while about Chris's condition and her progress, pausing often and looking at Don to encourage questions; none were forthcoming. He soberly cautioned them,

"Under no circumstances must you reveal your identity to anyone. You cannot afford to do it, because people would not understand and would not accept you. You could not live comfortably in society, and Taffy would not be able to go to school."

Chris, frowning slightly, questioned, "I don't think I want to live my life in secrecy. My illness was not something to be ashamed of. I don't like the idea of hiding."

The doctor shook his head. "Even if you could bear all the exposure, you must think of others—Don, Taffy, your family. You can't afford to hurt them."

"Well, it's not something you want to talk about anyway," Don added. "I think he's right, honey. We don't want to take any risks."

"All right, I'm overruled," she smiled sweetly, but her eyes were unconvinced.

Then, unaccountably, the doctor asked Don,

"Have you had sex with Chris?"

Don was stunned. "Certainly not! Chris's not that kind of a girl!" He frowned, anger beginning to stain his cheeks. Was this necessary for therapy, these personal, probing questions?

The rough spot was smoothed over, but Don's suspicions were confirmed. He did not like this kind of doctor, and he only wanted to get out of there. He asked only one question.

"All I want to know is if she's well, now."

How could the doctor answer such a question? And does the word "well," or "cured," even apply to so complicated a case? If he said "No" or even quibbled, the patient could be irreparably damaged and set back in her progress; if he said "Yes," it could be so misleading as to amount to outright lying and could lull them both into ignoring future dangers. Whatever he said, they left his office under the impression that she was well. That was what they wanted to hear, making anything short of a resounding, crushing negative simply a mild warning about hazy, innocuous, far-off dangers. And the doctor's hopes were high. He labeled it a resolved case and Jane a resolved personality who seemed happy and well adjusted, with a good prognosis for the future. Even after two years, he stated that despite her strange and formidable handicaps, she had reached a goal of love and fulfillment that many people never know.

They were married on December 19, Elen's birthday, in a church in Spartanburg, South Carolina, with no attendants. Chris was finally one person; no one was watching her, crowding her for existence. She was brand new, had a shining new life, a fresh start, a blank page. It sounds easy until one remembers the poor track record of New Year's resolutions, of turning over new leaves, of the greener grasses on the other side.

But if one could see ahead, would he ever go forward? They rode out to face their future, hearts light, heads high, hopes eternal.

III

THE REVELATION
(1954–72)

14

Trailer Trash

As I looked out over our neighborhood,
Not houses there, but trailers stood.
Their home away from home it is. . . .
So much in common we all share,
We take our homes with us everywhere.
We're called "trailer trash" most everyplace.

Chris Costner Sizemore
(Jane)
March 1954

Within every heart there lives eternal a vision of home, either actual, ideal, or desired. Within the soul of Chris there burned the ever-bright, undiminished image of the Strother place. The owning of land, property, and especially one's home had always been of prime importance in the Family. Until a man invested in property, built a home, married, and settled down, he was a drifter, no matter how substantial his financial affairs. And a woman married to a man who only rented his place to live—or worse, who lived with relatives—was an object of pity, having it said of her that "she had not married well." Even a mean little house owned was greatly to be preferred to a more sumptuous abode rented or shared. The real measure of having arrived, however, was the obtaining of a brick house.

Houses were even discussed down to the finer point of whether they were all brick or "just" brick veneer. Chris had heard this kind of talk all her life and it had made an indelible imprint on her, had made home ownership a symbol of security, a necessity without which she was unable to satisfactorily function. She had never, in her entire life, lived in a house that she or her parents owned—never had a home, only lived in a series of houses. The lack of ownership plus the seeming interminable number of rented houses had instilled in her a sense of rootless shifting that only living in her own home on her own land could stabilize. Ironically, it was only after Chris left her family that her parents obtained a home of their own, too late for their accomplishment to satisfy the need in their eldest daughter.

Fate, as if toying with Chris, threw into her path a man on the move, a man whose job shifted him on the average of once a year from one construction site to another. Her new husband, her new life lacked the one essential without which she was lost: the security that comes through putting down roots, through settling down in one place, through living in one's own home. Yet her first home was brand-new, all the furniture was brand-new, and she even owned it; Don had bought it for her. But it was a home on wheels, a mobile home—a trailer!

Nobody who was anybody lived in a trailer! Chris had never even known anyone who lived in a trailer. The only trailer people she had ever seen were the gypsies who came through Augusta every year and camped in a pine grove outside of town called Travelers Rest. They were dark, strange people who looked dirty, wore gaudy clothes, and tried to tell your fortune for some silver coins. Everybody avoided them, and storekeepers kept a sharp watch on their goods when the gypsies came into their shops. The whole town breathed a sigh of relief when they dissolved from the landscape for another season.

Chris's new home was lovely, having a living room, kitchen-dining room combination, two bedrooms, and a bath; but it did not sit solidly on land, her land. Don was not even remotely aware of her emotions; she gave him no indication of her inability to tolerate the situation. She would have greatly preferred a cottage on a tiny plot to this sleek, modern, metal home gliding impermanently from one brief resting place to another. Don had provided lovingly the very best that his circumstances and his finances would allow, and he was happy. Their wedding had been simple and sweet; and their honeymoon, though short, had per-

316

mitted the uninterrupted intimacy so necessary for lovers—to explore the beloved, to share the cherished secrets, to lay the foundation to support "for better or worse, richer or poorer, in sickness and in health."

Their wedding night had been loving, tender; their coming together, gentle and understanding. Though not a perfect mating, it was perhaps as good as most wedding night experiences. Chris was frightened and cold, incapable of response; Don was patient and considerate. He was, understandably, somewhat puzzled. She had been married, had borne a child, and yet she seemed to have absolutely no knowledge about sex. He did not know that this was exactly the situation, that she had no memory at all of her previous experiences. He simply reasoned that she had been sick, had had frightening experiences in her first marriage, and that he would help her to work it all out. Sex was important to him, and it was a night of love. And Chris tried to please him, to make him happy; it was for them both a good experience. She reached no climax, but having no knowledge of this possibility, she did not know what she had missed. In his shy way, Don tried to determine the extent of her feeling. But how does one describe blue to one who has never seen?

They did not return to Edgefield when their week of Florida wandering was over; they drove directly to Knoxville, Tennessee. In Don's thinking, Chris would never recover her health as long as she was near Augusta and continued to place so much dependency on Dr. Thigpen; therefore he had quit his job in Augusta shortly before the wedding, and planned his honeymoon in the interim between jobs. With light hearts they drove to Knoxville and found a three-room furnished apartment in a private home.

Don was mistaken if he thought his wife's dependency upon her psychiatrist would cease if he removed her from Augusta. Within a week of their arrival in Knoxville, she had written him a letter, establishing a written contact with him that was to last throughout the years and to accumulate an impressive number of letters, not one of which, no matter how extensive her travels, did she ever destroy. In these letters, she acquainted him with her problems and her successes, laying out before him, from year to year, the bare story of her life. At some points the letters flew thick and fast; at others they dwindled to little more than season's greetings; and they were not always prompted by her needs. Many of the letters dealt with Dr. Thigpen's necessity of obtaining from her contracts and releases so that he could pursue his career, writing about her rare case and selling movie rights to these writings. Also, since she was scrupulously protecting her identity, he was the only contact the world had with her. Anyone wanting to get in touch with her, for whatever reason—from writing an article to making a movie—had to clear it with the doctor. Many of his letters contained information of this sort, along with his generous advice concerning her behavior toward these offers.

In her first few letters she told him of her happiness and her love for Don, and she also expressed her desire to write a book about her strange illness. He gave her much advice concerning her marriage and its inevitable descent from the heights to a more normal and mature level, asked her how her sex life was turning out, and sent her another semantic differential test. She cleverly and quickly ascertained that the three parts of the test were repetitious and designed to determine the consistency of her answers to questions; therefore she answered the questions in the first part and simply copied her answers to the same questions in the two succeeding parts. Over the next few months, letters were exchanged almost weekly and dealt with considerations of the professionals who had contacted him who might be able to help her write her book. No one seemed to be able to satisfactorily qualify for the job. He indicated that one wanted an exorbitant fee, another was manicky and should be in a mental institution. She also kept him abreast of her almost continuous string of illnesses, to which he always responded that all she needed was to eat a more balanced diet and to stop "eating like a bird."

Don, working long hours, often six days a week, was for the most part unaware of the nature of this steady correspondence, but he was painfully conscious that his wife was in poor health—frail, weak, sickly. He firmly believed that if she could settle down, keep house, and have her child with her that she would be all right. So he bought the only house that he practically could, a trailer; and they drove down to Edgefield one weekend and brought Taffy back to live with them.

Zueline had tried to prepare her small grandchild for her new life, explaining that Mr. Sizemore had married her mother and that Taffy must now call him "Daddy Don." The little girl was an unbelievably sweet and docile child, never causing trouble and always exhibiting an even, pleasant temper. On the long trip to her new home, she sat on her mother's lap and uttered not one sound unless she were first addressed, and then she merely answered questions. When they were not looking, her big, solemn eyes carefully searched the faces of these new parents, for they were both new to her. The big man, who was almost a stranger, smiled whenever he caught her looking at him; and the lady was one of the "other ones," not her real mother; but she was nice and very pretty. Just before they left, the child had asked her grandmother,

"Nanny, why do I have to call him 'Daddy Don' and call her just 'Mother'?"

"Because she's your real mother, honey," explained Zueline, who was totally oblivious of the child's grasp of the situation.

Don also was unaware that Chris and Taffy did not consider themselves to be mother and daughter; he only knew that the six-year-old child responded to his every overture, and, far from resenting him, she welcomed and encouraged his attentions. His affection for her grew daily, and he spent much time playing with her and teaching her games and skills. He built her a swing, bought her a bike, and was a happy man watching her enjoy his gifts. It was a beautiful transition, this one from a confirmed bachelor to a loving father; and both the man and the child glowed in the warm light of a relationship that was to grow strong and to endure firmly throughout their entire lives.

Chris watched from a short distance, but a distance, nonetheless, and she never really became a part of their group. She accepted Taffy and cared for the child, but a deep, warm feeling was impossible for her. Depth of any kind seemed beyond her grasp, holding her forever on the outside fringes. Even when she was writing to Dr. Thigpen of her happiness in her new life and of her love for her new husband, she was penning the ideal, what she knew was supposed to be, but what seemed always remote, always beyond her. Even simple daily tasks were unbelievable chores. The preparation of a meal was long and tedious, and she had to follow a cookbook for even the simplest of dishes. Don was aware of her difficulties, and he was puzzled that a woman who had been married for six years was unable to prepare a routine meal without consulting a cookbook. Patiently, he reasoned that her problems were due to her illness and that they would soon clear up.

Zueline might have been unaware of Taffy's knowledge of the situation, but her own understanding of Chris's problems would not allow her fears to be resolved until she, personally, had viewed the situation. She and Mama came to visit to see for themselves if Taffy's new home was suitable and if the child was happy and well cared for. They were satisfied, and it was planned that the little girl would go back with Nanny and Big Nanny to spend some time with them before school began in the fall. Don and Chris put the three of them on the bus, and just before the big Greyhound pulled out, Don walked up to the window to tell Taffy good-bye. The child suddenly climbed from the seat and ran down the aisle. Don met her at the door, where she threw her arms around him, crying,

"Daddy, Daddy, I don't want to go!" Tears were streaming down her white face.

Don's own eyes were far from dry, "Take my daughter's things off," he ordered the driver, never relaxing his hold on the trembling child clinging to his neck. From that day on, Don had a daughter, his own daughter, and she never again called him "Daddy Don." He was her own daddy.

Zueline wept, and her tears were ambivalent. She wept for happiness that her little lost waif had found a home, and she never again worried about Taffy's security and protection. But she also wept for her own loss. Her heart was broken because this tiny child preferred this strange father to her, the grandmother who had loved her from birth, had cared for her most of her life. Might her tears not also have been for her daughter, who had stood there so coolly while her own child, the flesh of her flesh, had run to the strange man and not to her own mother? Zueline pondered these queer things in her heart while Mama scolded,

"I don't see what you're bawling about, Sister. You wanted the young'un to be happy."

And Taffy was happy, but as in all real-life situations, small problems arise, becoming big problems only if handled abnormally and emotionally. Don had located his trailer, not in a crowded row-on-row court but in the yard of a private home. The large, old-fashioned house was located down a country road near a picturesque little country church, and it had a broad green lawn under huge spreading old trees. Only two other trailers were parked there, and even though it was quite far from Don's job, he thought Chris would prefer the lovely setting. And she did. They went regularly to services in the little church, and she taught in the Bible school. She spent much of her time reading literature books, and she studied the dictionary diligently, picking out big words to add to her vocabulary.

Don's first indication of trouble came quite unexpectedly. He noticed one evening that his wooden locker, a standard possession of the traveling construction man, in which he kept belongings accumulated on his travels, was unlocked. Upon examination he found that the lock had been pried open. He had not locked it to prevent Chris's knowing of its contents; he had simply not had occasion to unlock it. Stunned, he asked,

"Who's been in my locker?" It was an unfortunate way to phrase the question, but he had been married only six months, and the habits of living among men had not yet disappeared.

She tossed her head and turned away, "I don't know anything about it." She was cool, withdrawn.

Don looked inside. Everything was intact except his packet of pictures. As he looked at them, his shock grew: The head of every girl in the pictures had been carefully cut off! Momentarily, he was angry; then he thought that there had to be a reason for this sort of thing. They were not even necessarily girlfriends, just girls he had met over the years, often simply passing girls whom he and his buddies had asked to pose with them in front of some national monument. There were hardly any two pictures of the same girl. He was concerned, not about the needless destruction of mere photographs, but about Chris. Perhaps she was not as well as he had thought. She was having a lot of headaches, sometimes so bad as to send her to bed for an entire day; and she was restless, hardly sleeping any at night. She had also become irritable, snapping at him and speaking impatiently to Taffy.

He never mentioned the mutilated pictures again, but the next morning he instructed her to make an appointment with a doctor. When he dropped her off in town, he was unaware that she had made an appointment with a psychiatrist. She had written to Dr.

Thigpen about being ill, but she had not told him of her great fear—that there was another personality lurking in the background, growing stronger, threatening to push her aside. Perhaps she had hoped that he would read between the lines and offer help without her having to admit failure and ask for it. Failing that, her only hope was another doctor.

She told the new doctor who she was, and he did not believe her; not only did he not believe, he also told her that he did not believe. Oh, he admitted that, perhaps, *she* believed it, but that she had simply read about the case in the papers, and now thought that she was "Eve." Her humiliation profound, she left. Thus began a long list, over the next twenty years, of psychiatrists who refused to believe her story and turned her away when her need was so desperate. She sought next the only help she knew: She approached a medical doctor, a general practitioner, described her headaches and sleeplessness, and received a supply of sleeping pills and tranquilizers.

Don's problems shortly began to multiply. One Monday morning, he was called off his job by the foreman, who informed him that he had an emergency telephone call. When he answered, Chris's weeping voice informed him that she had been involved in a fight with another woman and that he would have to come home. Incredulous, Don left immediately for home. He could not believe what he had heard. Chris was so withdrawn and contained that he could not imagine her being involved in even a word battle, and this had been an actual physical fight! She told him the whole story. The fight had been with the woman who lived in the neighboring trailer, and the bone of contention had been the children. Chris had argued with the woman because her two children had destroyed some of Taffy's toys, and not liking the woman's attitude, she had gone to her landlady's house to complain. The woman followed her and called Chris a liar.

Unbelievably, and with no warning, the dignity, the culture, the quiet good manners all melted away, and there stood a snarling, bristling creature, teeth bared and fists clenched. She hit the woman on the jaw, still swollen from an impacted wisdom tooth, knocking her to the floor; and before the horrified eyes of the landlady, she jumped on her victim's stomach with both knees, grabbed the long black hair in both hands, and began banging the woman's head on the floor. The terrified woman, too overcome to even fight back, pushed herself along the floor with her feet, trying to pull out from under the demon on her stomach. Finally they ended up in the bedroom, and the woman scooted under the bed. Chris, pushed from her perch, began to bite anything that passed her bared teeth, giving stomach, thighs, and legs a good chewing before they disappeared under the bed. Then she stood, calmly straightened her clothes, and with head held high, walked with regal dignity from the house.

Weeping softly, she explained to Don, "I don't know what got into me. No lady would act like that." That seemed to be her only concern, that her behavior had been unladylike.

Don and the other husband, who had also been called home, talked with the landlord, and all agreed that it would be best if both families moved. Ironically, the two men, who worked on the same job, helped each other ready their trailers for moving, and moved their two militant wives into separate trailer courts. Chris did not have a mark on her, only a stiff neck, but Don was appalled the next day at the sight of the bruises and teeth marks on her victim's legs.

Chris made no effort to become friendly with her new neighbors. They wore shorts and blue jeans and ran around in their husbands' trucks, behavior she thought common and unfeminine. Since she did not drive, Don had to take her on all her errands, and she behaved as if going for the groceries were a big night on the town. She dressed in her best clothes and waited, smiling and dignified, while Don helped her in and out of the car. She volunteered to work in Taffy's school; and after making it known that she had previously taught school, she was much in demand, not only as a volunteer, but as a substitute teacher as well.

One day the principal approached her and offered her a job teaching eighth-grade English, as replacement for another teacher. Since she had already been successfully substituting in the position, she readily accepted. When told that she would need a teacher's certificate, she confidently wrote to her school, Furman University, for a transcript of her credits. The return letter, instead of bringing the expected information, bore a shock from which she was never to recover: Her school, her alma mater, had no record of anyone by that name ever attending the university.

Stunned, she simply could not accept it; she called her mother and inquired. The much-surprised Zueline confirmed the unbelievable letter: She had not graduated from Furman! When further questions uncovered the fact that she had not even finished high school, the descent from her unstable height began; she was never able to recoup her losses of self-esteem, of confidence, of vanity.

She did not tell Don what she had discovered, but she pondered long and bitterly in her own mind. How could it happen? How could she know so much about Furman if she had never been there? She knew the names of the dormitories, she had lived in Rosemary Hall, knew that it was located above the Fine Arts Building; she knew that the woman's campus had recently been the Greenville Women's Academy and was affectionately referred to by the townspeople as the "Zoo"; she knew the names of professors, what they looked like, what their much-touted mannerisms and quirks were; she had gone one glorious summer to summer school, lived in Montague Hall, and missed the Dean's List because of too many dates with the lifeguard at the swimming pool.

How? How could it be so vivid in her mind? Never once did she connect all this with Elen. She had no memory of those long visits with her cousin when she drank in, absorbed into her very essence, the glowing experiences related by the other girl. The alter ego had not become just an extension of her own being, but had literally become her own being. From that moment, her inability grew daily to cope with even the smallest tasks. Particularly did she hate the chore of fixing meals, an interesting problem since she had always performed well in this respect and had even chosen this over other work when she and Elen were together and making labor divisions. It was always Elen who hated to cook.

One evening as she prepared dinner, she took her frustrations out on Taffy, who was watching television.

"Turn down that TV!" she shouted without warning. "I can't do a thing with all that noise! My head is splitting."

Taffy, absorbed in her program, continued to sit, unaware of the mounting tension behind her.

"Turn it down, I say!" screamed her mother, her face twisted in uncontrollable fury. Incredibly, she threw the first thing she could get her hands on: the butcher knife, with which she was peeling potatoes. It was not thrown as a knife, but as a weapon to hit, and the inaccuracy proved the lack of purpose. The knife hit the counter and fell harmlessly to the kitchen floor.

A look of abject horror replaced the spent fury; the burning blue eyes glazed, closed; life drained from the tense, rigid body and it slid gently to the floor. Don, coming home from work a moment later, viewed this scene: His wife crumpled on the floor beside a butcher knife, a gas jet on the stove burning blue and angry, and Taffy, undisturbed, calmly watching Mr. Greenjeans.

"Chris, Chris?" he called, running to her. "Taffy, honey, what happened?" he frantically asked.

"I don't know, Daddy," answered the child, aware for the first time that a storm had raged menacingly around her.

Determining that Chris was not wounded by the knife, Don carried her to the couch, only to discover an even more frightening condition: She was blind! Within an hour her vision began to return, but her head continued to ache dreadfully. Don helped her to bed and gave her a sleeping pill, hoping that rest would restore normalcy; but she awoke the following morning again sightless. Don took off from work and drove her to the city for an eye examination. The doctor, after careful and extensive examining, could find nothing wrong with the now clearly seeing, though aching, eyes, but he prescribed weak reading glasses to relieve any possible eyestrain. The blind spells continued, accompanied by painfully aching eyes, but both conditions were relieved when she donned her reading glasses. Don was deeply puzzled; this did not make sense. There was nothing medically wrong with the eyes, yet she periodically became blind, a condition that was corrected by simple reading glasses.

Don was also puzzled because their sex life had not worked out as he had hoped it would; conversely, it seemed to worsen. Chris was now barely tolerating his attentions to her. Always passive, she had over this short year become rigidly cold and unresponsive. Though uncomplaining, her silent contempt for his lovemaking screamed along his tense nerves. He quietly watched with growing conviction what he thought was the rapid deterioration of his marriage, not knowing that what he really watched was the inexorable dissolution of a person. The sharp outlines had already begun to blur; shortly, the entire fabric would fade and wash out. He reasoned what he knew: He was married less than a year to a wife who merely tolerated him, and who, in spite of what Dr. Thigpen had said, was still sick, strangely sick, and blind as well. He made up his mind.

They had spent Sunday afternoon riding in the mountains, Taffy and Chris seeing their first snow. Returning home late, they prepared for bed. When Don set the clock, Chris noticed that he had set it for 4:00 A.M.

"That's too early," she reminded him. "You don't have to get up until five."

"I'm leaving." It was a statement of fact. It needed no explanation.

Strangely, she did not ask for one. It was an old pattern; she was used to being deserted. She merely asked,

"Where are you going?"

"I don't know," he answered truthfully.

Chris reacted from her experience. There was a way to hold him, to keep him from leaving. It was an old story: sex. She left the bedroom and went into the kitchen. Taking a bottle of liquor from the cabinet, she began to drink straight from the bottle. Though her self-image had been damaged by her inability to keep up the façade of her shallow existence, her vanity was strongly intact. She knew she was beautiful, that her body was desirable; all she needed was enough liquor to deaden her revulsion of the dreaded physical contact, and she would seduce him.

She entered the room where her husband still lay sleepless and troubled. Her attempt was a travesty at making love, just as she was a travesty at being a woman. He pushed her away, repelled and angry, and now his anger burned brightly, clouding his ability to recognize that her attempts were unskilled and pathetic. He was cognizant only of her Bourbon breath and her hussy behavior. This might have disturbed him less had his suspicions of her past not been so shockingly aroused by a recent article about her in a magazine.

Dr. Thigpen had given an interview about his now famous case to *Maclean's*, a Canadian magazine, and the writer had lent a sensational twist to the information, especially playing up the Chris Costner behavior. The article, which appeared in the September

15, 1954, issue, reported that often at night she would deck herself out in a low-necked gown, load herself with costume jewelry, change her hairstyle and set out for a nightclub unescorted, teaming up with any strange male who happened to be available. It also reported that she had been married before her marriage to Ralph White, or worse, had pretended to be married to a man, living with him for several months. The article labeled her as an incorrigible liar.

Don was upset; he was appalled. If all these events were true, how much else did he not know? What kind of woman had he married? He had witnessed enough, personally, to cause him to suspect her behavior, but this was outrageous. Chris wrote to Dr. Thigpen declaring their disapproval of the article and he immediately answered, writing both Don and Chris in separate letters. He indicated that he, also, deplored the manner in which the article was handled and tried to reassure them that it was all sensationalized. He informed Don that *his* wife was literally not the girl who had had all the trouble, and that *his* wife was normal, stable, and well. He reminded him that unless Chris made her identity public, no one would know who she was, and she therefore would not suffer from any kind of publicity.

But what of Don? He could not separate his wife now from someone else she might have been in the past. To him, she was now whoever she was in the past, and her recent behavior only confirmed that her past had been quite different from what she had led him to believe. His resolve to leave hardened.

When she realized that her ultimate weapon was ineffective, her prideful veneer cracked. She begged,

"Don't go. I can't handle things. I can't make it alone." The voice was still low-pitched, but desperation frayed the edges.

"You can make it better than I can," he declared. "You've got a college education, and you've had a job offered to you."

"No. No, I haven't." Her confession visibly stripped her. "I didn't go to college. I didn't know; I thought I had. I can't teach. I can't get a job."

He was silent. Another lie? Then he thought of Taffy, precious Taffy. What did it matter whether it was a lie or not? He couldn't leave Taffy, leave her to another broken home, more hurt and pain. He loved her, and she deserved better than this. She had called him "Daddy," and he would be her daddy regardless of the price to be paid.

"Don't go," she repeated dully. "I can't handle things." It was as much a revelation to herself as it was to him. Her proud, vain spirit lay prostrate, broken.

He reached for the clock and reset the alarm for 5 A.M. He then turned his back and forced himself into sleep. It was the beginning of a pattern that gradually ingrained itself into a hard habit. He had to work, he had committed himself to stay and provide for them; therefore he had to sleep to be fit to hold his job, that now so necessary job. If he concerned himself with these complexities to the point of banishing sleep, he could not carry out his part of this strange bargain. That night he set his pace: What he could not understand, could scarcely conceive of, he ignored; what he could do, had committed himself to do, he performed diligently and well. He slept.

Chris became a mere shadow, scarcely leaving the trailer, constantly sleeping or sitting stupidly, drugged on her generous supply of sleeping pills and tranquilizers. Don routinely began to pick up her tasks: fixing meals, shopping for food, caring for Taffy's school needs. He often sat up watching TV while Chris languished in a drugged sleep in the bedroom. On one such night, she reached the end of her endurance, and taking out her wedding nightgown, she carefully dressed herself as for sleep; so, she thought, her last sleep. She meticulously combed her hair and made up her face. Neatly turning down the bed covers, she arranged a reading light beside the bed so that its beam would be cast directly on her face. She lay down on the bed to test the accuracy of the light's path. Next she wrote farewell notes to Don, to Taffy, and to Dr. Thigpen.

In the bathroom, with a steady, deliberate hand, she poured out onto the counter all the pills from three bottles: aspirins, sleeping pills, and tranquilizers. Slowly, methodically, all the while admiring her lovely wan face in the mirror, she swallowed the lethal dose. Gathering regal dignity about her as a queenly cloak, she walked with measured step to her final bed and ceremoniously lay down, calmly, graciously awaiting death as a woman who awaits a familiar though cherished lover.

Were her carefully laid plans forever destined for failure? Long before the creeping lethargy could begin to numb, the blue eyes gazing serenely out of the glowing white face framed in the black fan of her hair drooped, and closed sleepily. This smooth exterior belied the fact: It covered a roiling cauldron seething within. The eyes flew open, wide, staring, naked terror mirrored in their straining depths. She jumped from the bed and raced in a panic from the room.

"She's trying to kill me!" she gasped chokingly to the startled Don.

"What do you mean?" he asked witlessly.

"She took all those pills!" One veined hand was at her stomach, the other grasping her strained neck.

"Who?" he asked, dazed.

"Jane! Jane did it, she took all those pills!" she exclaimed, pointing desperately toward the bathroom.

Don did not understand all the other implications, but one quick look at the empty bottles convinced him that she had indeed swallowed a dangerous number of pills. Hurriedly, he mixed a vile concoction of dried mustard and hot water and forced her to drink it down. She retched violently, emptying the contents of her stomach and probably, considering the brief ingestion time, ridding her system of the largest part of the medicine. Don was still not satisfied, however, and he persuaded her to drink large quantities of hot black coffee, after which he took her outside into the cold, clear night and walked her up and down a rough, rolling section of ground until dawn began to lighten the sky. Nearly five hours had passed since she had burst in upon him with her startling news; if she were still awake, she was surely all right. He led her, exhausted but uncomplaining, into the trailer and they lay down on the bed together. It was Thanksgiving Day.

That's another one! She was not well, after all. This one is blind sometimes; she's the one who has been making Jane blind. I don't have to ask why she came. Someone had to come to save the body. Jane was so selfish; if she couldn't live, she didn't want anyone to live. She would kill the body to keep anyone else from having it. Jane knew from the headaches and the blindness that someone else was there, just as she had come when the two Chrises could not handle life. She fought for life

329

and took over, but now that she can't handle things, she wants to end it all for everybody. She's so selfish and shallow; I don't see why Dr. Thigpen ever thought she could live a normal life. She must have been quite good at deceiving him. I can see all this clearly, but I have no feeling of ever having been there. All these things did not happen to me; I didn't try to kill myself, and I didn't rush out to save myself either. I was not there, but I know it all. Suppose the Blind Lady had not come out and Jane had succeeded. What would have happened to me? What an awful thought. This is my body, mine! If she had killed my body, would I have never been? But I must have been in there somewhere to be able to see what they did with my body. Or was it not my body then, but their body? It sounds like witches and demons. I can understand why people doubt; I can scarcely believe it myself. But it's true, all true. The Blind Lady stayed out for several days and Jane was never really strong again, even though the changes were frequent and the painful headaches continued. . . .

Don rose in midmorning with an unexpected suggestion.

"I want to go home. Let's get dressed and go to Bear Creek." It was not so much a statement as a question.

The Chris who looked up at him was not the same woman with whom he had been living for almost a year. This woman was not haughty and withdrawn, slightly contemptuous of everything and everyone; this woman was gentle, accepting, considerate. As she sat on the side of the bed, she softly rubbed her hand over the gleaming satin of her gown and moved her bare feet across the cool, smooth tiles of the floor. Her face, still peaked and drawn from her night's experience, was filled with wonder and curiosity. They did not talk then, but on the long drive south, she told him how for several months now she had been looking out on the world through the eyes of another, had been able to see and hear, but had been denied all feeling, all sensation. She told him how she had longed to touch, to feel, to experience; and she described to him what it was like to drink water, to feel the air move against her face, to walk barefoot on a cold floor. The body, she said, had no sensations for her until she came out.

Don listened, his senses numb, his practical logic outraged. But, incredibly, she *was* different! He could not explain it, but neither could he deny it. He would have been unable to describe the difference, but his every sense cried out that this was a different woman. He even felt strange and hesitant with her, as he would have with a woman he had just met, but one with whom he had experienced a momentous occasion, the kind that breaks down the barriers and draws strangers together. When complete strangers survive together, they are never again complete strangers. He introduced her to his family for the first time as his wife, since she had seen them only once briefly before they were married; and little did they know that she was as new to him as she was to them, even though he had lived with her for almost a year.

Thus began what surely must be one of the strangest and most bizarre marriage relationships of all time. Over the next twenty years, Don was to face, in the familiar form of his wife, nine such astounding changes—strangers peering at him from the ever-changing blue eyes, strange voices addressing him from the wide red mouth, strange mannerisms motivating the restless body.

Don's life had become just short of intolerable. He was saved by his basic no-nonsense nature, his ability to escape daily into the physical activity of his construction work, and his growing ability to insulate himself against his bizarre home life. He used the only defense he had: He moved as often as he could from place to place, not running from his problem, but running with his troubles before they had a chance to involve other people. During the next three years he moved nine times, a journey that took him from Tennessee to Texas and from Louisiana to New York. Ironically, this constant flight, which reduced life to the bare necessities with which he was able to cope, rendered life completely intolerable for his wife. Her life became one mad frantic search for identity.

15

Cinderella

Cinderella had a fairy godmother, and on that important detail hangs the entire tale. Chris, lacking a magic patron, was forced to rely on her own questionable powers to make her dreams come true. Her story, however, was replete with all the other necessary elements enjoyed by the fabled Cinderella; there was even a Prince Charming! And while it is true that the essential garment was a red silk dress instead of a glass slipper, it was decidedly not an ordinary dress; and the magnificence of the real-life ball rivaled in splendor and luxury the very one executed by the handsome prince himself.

But Cinderellas do not become shining princesses immediately. They are obscure scullery maids long before the arrival of the magic moment. It is easy to forget, bathed in the glow of the splendid Cinderella, that she was, a breathlessly short time before, merely sooty Cinder-Ella, a stepchild. Though blood-born, Chris was, figuratively, also a stepchild among her kin, so different that she could not be fashioned into the common form. Whenever the attempt to mold her became intense, she broke, she splintered. Those doing the molding could hardly be blamed; they were traditionally handing down the heritage of their fathers; and the form itself did not splinter, it was the psyche—the soul—that broke. The damage was irreparable; a splintered soul is not a broken bone that can be set to mend. By the time her grand ball was imminent, the splintering process had been so perfected that she felt little relationship or identification with any living person.

From 1954 through 1958 Chris lived two different, almost completely separate lives, one as wife and mother traveling continuously in her trailer home—the scullery maid—and the other through her contacts, mostly by letter, with important people—the budding Cinderella. The lonely Blind Lady, religious and shy, kept her house and cared for her family; Jane, shallow, immature, and frightened, pretended to the world, even to her parents, that she was well and happy. Only Don and Taffy knew that two women dwelt with them.

It was Jane who maintained an active correspondence with Corbett Thigpen, never telling him about her continued disintegration or about her desperate suicide attempt, which had splintered her once more into two separate beings. She did discuss with him at length her continuous string of physical ailments, from a rapid loss in blood pressure to an allergic reaction to nylon. On all points he reassured her, maintaining that she was well and healthy. When she informed him that her marriage of less than two years was rather rocky, he was not surprised, declaring that she and Don had had much to adjust to, and that if she would only realize that a wife could not manifest any fierce independence but must put her husband's welfare and desires first, she would not have to worry about his doing all he could to make her happy. He lamented the fact that too often wives feel that they are free, white, and twenty-one and should have their say, being unwilling to submit to their husbands' opinions. This kind of chauvinistic advice angered Jane, who no longer performed as a wife, but she gave no indication of her feelings.

Their letters discussed friendly topics such as his plans for vacation, her new typing skill, Taffy's progress in growth and education, the fact that Chris's new weight gain would improve her looks in a bikini, her plans to publish some poems, and her progress on the semantic differential tests that he periodically sent her. Mostly, however, her tenuous hold on reality was strengthened by information he relayed to her concerning public interest in her story and by her continuing search for someone to help her write a book about her life. He informed her that he and Dr. Cleckley planned someday to write a medical monograph of the case, but that it would likely be in the distant future, if ever. He told her that he was at long last going to finish the film they had made together in Atlanta, and that he believed that she would be pleased when she saw it.

Acting as her contact with the outside world, he gave an article to the *Saturday Evening Post*, denied an article to *Pageant* magazine, and strongly encouraged her to give *American Weekly* magazine a follow-up article to their 1953 story. Chris agreed to everything suggested to her, and in June an interview was set up for her to meet in Dr. Thigpen's office with Irmis Johnson, the writer for *American Weekly* who had done the previous article. It was agreed that the doctor would read and edit the final manuscript. Just one month later, on August 30, 1955, Dr. Thigpen wrote to her that he and Dr. Cleckley, who had taken six months' leave from his practice to do the work, had finished their monograph on multiple personality, in which they discussed her case and other similar cases. He assured her that he was continuing to use the pseudonyms Eve White, Eve Black, and Jane that he had used earlier to the APA and the press, and that incidences had been altered to protect her identity. He declared that there was nothing derogatory in his writings and that they could not possibly cast any reflection on her or her family. He promised her copy No. 1 when the monograph was published.

The finishing of the monograph seemed to herald the termination of the case for Dr. Thigpen. He praised her progress in both mental and physical health, congratulated her on her marital and financial success, downplayed all the work he had undertaken in her behalf, indicated that her semantic differential scores showed increasing stability, and predicted that she would not have another moment's trouble—that she was completely well! All this to a woman whose marriage was held together simply by her husband's sense of duty—a husband who had been unable to find a job for two months, who knew that she had cheated on the tests; and to a woman who, unmercifully, had once again disintegrated into two warring souls, battling desperately for a weakened, tormented body. The doctor's lavish praise served only to thrust her deeper into her morass of confusion.

Life had been hard their second year. Loss of work and short jobs had forced them to move three times; and in one of these towns, Roanoke, Virginia, Taffy was desperately unhappy in school. Coming in at midyear, she never fully adjusted to either teacher or students. She arrived home one day miserable and weeping because she had not been allowed to go to the bathroom. Outraged, Don stormed into the classroom the following day and accosted the teacher, pointing his finger in her shocked face,

"You wouldn't let my daughter go to the bathroom yesterday!" he stormed, advancing on the startled teacher. "I don't know if it's because she lives in a trailer, but it better not happen again."

"Mr. Sizemore, I don't think it happened that way," began the teacher, backed against the wall.

"Yes, it did!" Don declared, "or my daughter wouldn't have told me."

"I'll take care of it," soothed the teacher, anxious only for this irate father to leave.

Taffy, watching from her seat among the startled children, was proud of her father, and duly informed him each night, thereafter, that she had been permitted to use the bathroom.

When their money was at its shortest, Chris became homesick, and Don, uncomplaining of the cost, drove her home to Edgefield one weekend. Shortly after, Taffy became very ill with strep throat, and needed expensive medicines. Finally they were down to only seven dollars and fifty cents before a job came open. With their last money, they bought pinto beans, meal, fatback, flour, and onions. As they waited for Don's first paycheck, they ate fat-back, biscuits, and sawmill gravy for breakfast, and pinto beans, cornbread, and onions for supper—just as Chris had eaten as a child.

Yet, in spite of their troubles, they knew a period of relative calm and happiness. Chris, as the Blind Lady, loved her husband warmly and unselfishly, enjoying sex with him, and worrying constantly about his safety and welfare. She always put her own interests, and even those of Taffy, whom she loved dearly, far behind the concerns and comfort of Don. She desperately wanted to bear his child, feeling that this was a duty that every wife owed to her husband; but despite her constant desire, she seemed unable to conceive. During this time, she began to experience unsettling premonitions. Once having a vision of Don's being electrocuted, she begged him not to go to work; but dreading his teasing unbelief, she did not tell him of her fears. She explained, instead, that she

335

was ill and feared to be alone. He did not go, and the man who replaced him on the job was electrocuted.

Another time, she protested Taffy's taking an inoculation of Salk vaccine for polio prevention, declaring that it would harm her. Don scoffed at her fears, saying that she just did not understand the whole process of immunization. Taffy received her dosage from a spoiled batch of vaccine and became desperately ill, avoiding paralysis and possibly death only through immediate and intensive medical care. On a later occasion, when they were pulling their trailer through a mountainous area, she demanded that Don stop the car and check the wheels; and to please her, he did, finding, incredulously, that one of the rear trailer wheels was loose and would shortly have dropped off the vehicle. In her premonitory vision, she had seen that exact wheel fly off!

Was it coincidence? Was she so finely tuned and honed so sharply to just one subject—her family—that she could sense harm menacing them? Whatever the reasonable explanation, it was a disturbing element which, though fading from this first onslaught of intensity, was to surface periodically during her entire lifetime. For no explainable reason, she once, more than ten years after these startling events, felt that something was wrong with Elen. At the time, she had lost contact with her cousin and had not heard from her except through relatives for almost three years. On impulse she called her mother, asking,

"Mother, is there something wrong with Elen?"

Zueline, amazed, informed her that Elen, who then lived in Chicago, was at the point of death with meningo-encephalitis. Chris immediately called the hospital where her cousin lay desperately ill, and though unable to speak to Elen, her message was recorded.

It read, "I will *you* to get *well!*"

She also wrote and mailed that night a letter to Elen. It was a simple one-line note: *Dear Sac, You will be all right. Love, Chris.* When Elen's doctor made his rounds early the next morning, he found her conscious for the first time in two weeks. He would have been less surprised to have found her dead. When Chris's note came the next day, the doctor was able to agree with it; Elen *was* going to be all right, and almost from the very moment when Chris willed it to be so.

336

Being unable to explain these sorts of phenomena, the civilized world turns away in half-embarrassed silence from a serious account of such events, and truly they are strange; but Chris never appeared to attach to them more than a mere passing interest. They were simply another confusing facet of her already inexplicable existence; and she did not question this unusual aspect as she did not question her whole incredible condition. As Jane, unhappy and discontented, she was busily exchanging letters with Dr. Thigpen and Irmis Johnson and planning for a life quite different from the one she was placidly living as the domesticated Blind Lady.

The doctors, having sent their monograph to McGraw-Hill, book publishers, were hopefully waiting for word on publication. Meanwhile, the *American Weekly* article was published, and Chris, having grown close to Irmis Johnson while they worked together, approached her inquiring whether she would help her write her own book-length story. Miss Johnson was interested, but raised the question of whether this proposed book might not simply be a repeat of the doctor's book. Chris was shocked! This was the first time she realized that the doctors were writing a *book*. They had said "medical monograph," and she had assumed that it was a learned paper, a treatise, similar to the one presented at the APA convention. She immediately questioned Dr. Thigpen, and was assured that their information was technical, intended for professional readers, and would in no way interfere with a book she might write about her strange experiences. He warned her that since she did not have a college education, she would certainly need a ghostwriter, and praised her for her choice of Irmis Johnson for this chore, promising to make his voluminous files, little of which he had used to write his own book, available to Miss Johnson.

Her fears allayed, she returned to Irmis only to find that Irmis' time was already committed for several months. Chris's discouragement was more than compensated for, however, by a bit of news that Irmis gave her: A motion-picture company had approached *American Weekly* about purchasing the movie rights to the stories that she had written about Chris, and to which Chris owned exclusive rights. According to instructions concerning the concealment of her identity, the movie company had been referred to Dr. Thigpen. Irmis informed her that she should be hearing from him very soon and that she had even mentioned the budding interest to him when she last spoke with him on the telephone. Irmis was excited, telling Chris that such interest from a motion-picture company was an important factor in interesting a publisher in a book, and that it often was enough to convince a publisher even if the book were merely in the planning stages.

And just two days later she did hear from Dr. Thigpen; it was about a motion-picture company, and he was excited, too. But it had nothing to do with her magazine stories, or her planned book, and, especially, it had nothing to do with Chris personally. In his letter dated March 28, 1956, he enthusiastically informed her that Twentieth Century-Fox had a copy of *his* book (now called a book!), and that they wished to make a movie based on it.

Was she stunned, disappointed, defeated? As she held the letter in her trembling hands, she was washed by all these emotions and more; but she was neither angry nor bitter. She had never had any experience in winning, in being rewarded; therefore she was unsurprised that her expectations were crushed—she had, in fact, never had any real faith in their accomplishment. It never once occurred to her that her trusted representative had perhaps represented himself better than he had represented her. And anyway, it *was* the story of her life; a big movie company wanted to make a picture of *her* life! She was thrilled. For the moment it was enough.

But the letter went on. The doctor unequivocally declared that she was to remain anonymous, but he suggested that they might want her to go incognito to Hollywood for some technical direction; and he assumed that they would pay her fifty dollars per week plus expenses for this service, and might even find a job for Don so that he could go along. Dr. Thigpen next stated that the man who talked with him said that it would be desirable to get a release from her, that this was often done for visualization of a living person. He had tried to pin the man down, he said, as to how much he would offer her for this, but all that he could get out of him was "a reasonable sum." Dr. Thigpen indicated that he had no idea what this would be, but that he would *guess* that she would receive as much as five thousand dollars, though the movie producers might jump up and down and feel that it was outrageous.

Five thousand dollars! That was a lot of money; it would make life easier for them. They had so many doctor and drug bills. Chris was thoughtful. How much was a reasonable sum? How did one know what to ask for something like this? She read on. Dr. Thigpen promised that he would dicker with them and see if they would be willing to pay more, and that she could rest assured that he would get every dime for her that he could.

Did she know this? She argued with herself, feeling guilty for harboring such a thought for even a moment; and it never occurred to her to consult a lawyer. Such an act would have seemed deceitful, ungrateful, and her ignorance concerning her rights was total. Her only attempt to protect herself was an appeal to her only friend who was knowledgeable of such matters: Irmis Johnson. On learning the details of the proposed agreement, Irmis' first advise was that Chris immediately seek competent legal aid, and even consider engaging a professional agent to represent her in matters of books, articles, and motion-picture scripts. Irmis warned that the signing of contracts was a tricky matter and that it was easy to be "rooked." She judged that five thousand dollars was a mere pittance for this kind of contract, and that Twentieth Century-Fox would not go to the trouble of making a movie if they didn't expect to make money. She reminded Chris that it was *her* story and an unusual story, and that it would make an excellent motion picture as well as a lot of money. Her final advice was that the movie company should buy movie rights to *her* story from *her* and not from anyone else.

The letter disturbed Chris and perhaps struck an answering chord of her own deeply buried suspicions; but Irmis' further suggestion—that the selling of movie rights now, before Chris had a publisher for her proposed book, would decrease its market value to the extent that she would recommend against writing it—completely deflated her. Chris desperately wanted to write her own story. Dr. Thigpen in his letter had also discouraged her, advising her to accept the five thousand dollars and not go to all the trouble of writing a book and facing the uncertainty of its publication and sale—very ponderable advice, it seemed to Chris, to be given in the light of the first flush of his own sweeping success.

339

Her time for consideration was brief. Within the week telegrams began to arrive from Dr. Thigpen, instructing her to obtain waivers and releases from Don, her parents, and Ralph White. It was merely assumed that she entertained no objection. When some difficulty was encountered in obtaining a release from Ralph, he informed her that he thought that if Ralph would sign for a reasonable sum, then Twentieth Century-Fox would give her the five thousand dollars for her visualization rights. He also hoped that she had not told many of her relatives about the movie, so that they wouldn't be too disappointed if something didn't work out and the movie were not produced.

She was given two choices: She and her family would either have to come to his office to sign the releases, or she would have to give him power of attorney to act for her. He assured her that either way would be perfectly all right. The momentum was too great, much more than she could withstand. When the telegram arrived on April 19 telling her to be in his office along with her parents on the following Monday at 3:00 P.M., she obeyed. She rode the bus from her home in Fayetteville, North Carolina, to Edgefield, and Acie and Zueline drove her down to Augusta. Somehow she had expected representatives from Twentieth Century-Fox to be there, but she was denied even the seeing of those important personages to whom she was selling the rights to her life. Only Dr. Thigpen was there; not even Dr. Cleckley was present. He explained the documents they were to sign, an unimpressive typewritten paper on plain sheets, not even bearing the letterhead of Twentieth Century-Fox, indicating that the motion-picture company had been willing to pay seven thousand dollars: five thousand dollars to Chris, one thousand dollars to Taffy, one hundred dollars each to Acie and Zueline, and the remainder to Ralph.

Feeling insecure and stupid, inundated by events beyond her conception and control, Chris tried to stay abreast of the proceedings; but her first question proved to be her last.

"Can I keep a copy of the contract?" she timidly asked.

"Indeed you will have a copy," Dr. Thigpen laughingly assured her. "But it would do you little good to have one now before everyone has signed. It must go to California for signatures first."

Blushing, feeling like an ugly, stupid child, she asked no more questions and tried to pretend that she understood all that was happening. She signed her name in a space that indicated that she was not only Christine C. Sizemore, but Mrs. Donald G. Sizemore, Eve White, Eve Black, and Jane as well. She then signed for Taffy, giving away her daughter's rights under the same conditions. Her signatures were witnessed by an H. R. Chambless. Chris did not notice that there was no designated place for Twentieth Century-Fox or anyone else to sign; nor did she notice, when she received her copy six months later, that it was not a duplicate of the one she had signed—it bore no signatures at all, not even hers. And she left with nothing to show for the fact that she had signed away rights to her own life story forever.

All seemed an anticlimax afterward. Dr. Thigpen's letters were few and far between now, and dealt with subjects much removed from her, subjects such as his working on the movie script, who was being considered for the leading lady role, when the actual film shooting would begin, that the name of the movie was *The Three Faces of Eve*, and the fact that McGraw-Hill was going to publish his book under the same title. His writing was full of famous names like Jennifer Jones, Carol Baker, Judy Garland, and Nunnally Johnson. Occasionally he mentioned that perhaps they might still want her to come to Hollywood while the picture was being made, but that, too, now seemed rather vague. It all appeared to be receding from her, to be having less and less to do with her. Even her story itself was being altered so that no one except her close family would be able to connect the publicized events with her actual experiences. Dr. Thigpen wrote that not only had he and the scriptwriters altered circumstances and places to protect her and her family, but that they also had occasionally described an incident that did not actually happen but that "could have happened." Was this what she wanted? This anonymity? Did she want the only thing that had ever gained her recognition, acceptance, to be so far removed from her that not even the faint reflected glow, from others bathed in the limelight, would illumine her dark, rejected self? Her smothered, buried soul silently screamed "No!" but her path had been plotted; so much had been done for her, to help her, to protect her. How could she express ingratitude?

Her weight began a rapid gain. She watched the angular though

341

delicate, bone structure disappear under the accumulating obesity, and she hated herself; but she could not stop eating, and as her weight grew so did her self-loathing, a condition that was further aggravated by a letter from Dr. Thigpen after she had been down to sign the contracts, suggesting that she lose several pounds to improve her appearance. In January of 1957, Drs. Thigpen and Cleckley sent her a copy of their book, accompanied by a letter from Dr. Thigpen explaining the book and how it was written, and stating that it was a tribute to her and her remarkable recovery, which made worthwhile all their hard labor and many hours of working with her.

She held the slim volume in her hand. Two conflicting emotions immediately assailed her senses. It was a book about her! Her life! What an exhilarating thought! Crowding close came a second, sobering thought: What a tiny capsule to encompass her entire life. Is that all she had been? Trembling, she sat down to read; and when, hours later, she had turned the last page, another of her illusions had gone. Was this how Dr. Thigpen viewed her and the events of her life? Mother was not like that. The book made it appear that her mother was responsible for her illness. It had not been her mother who had tried to make her kiss Grandma Becky, it was Mother who rescued her. Mother had always been kind and loving. And Daddy! Chris's face burned hot when she thought of what was implied about her and her father. Why, it was (she did not even want to think about it!) almost like incest! She was close to her father, very close; but not like *that!*

The whole thing was wrong. None of them seemed like real people. She would not recognize them, or herself, even, if she did not know it was her own story. But Chris's name was not used; it was nowhere in print, in no way connected with her life story. No matter how she tried, she found herself completely unable to relate to Eve, to be Eve. Eve was cold, clinical, apart from life—a laboratory specimen. She moved, she spoke, she acted; but she did not breathe, did not feel. Chris was warm, sensitive; she wept, she laughed, she ached. Eve was not Chris.

Chris had to write her book, now more than ever. She had to correct her parents' image. She could not let the unchallenged record show them to be such people as this. And she wanted to tell *her* story, the way *she* lived it and felt it, not the way someone else saw her live it and assumed she felt it. But she could not disappoint Dr. Thigpen; she would not let him down after all he had done for her. She would write her book, but she would not hurt him. And she could not go to Hollywood. She was fat and ugly; if they saw her they would choose a fat, ugly actress to play her life story. She wanted someone slim and pretty to play her part, even if she were no longer so herself.

Shortly after she made these decisions she began to hear voices. As she was driving along a road with Taffy one day, a voice urgently instructed,

"Turn off the road! Quick, turn off here!"

A force beyond her control impelled her to whirl the car dangerously into a driveway at fifty miles per hour. She sat slumped over the steering wheel, more terrified of the voice than of her narrow escape.

Was that Jane talking to her? It must have been Jane; there's no one else there now. But how would Jane know that she was driving? She must be able to see what the Blind Lady does. Jane doesn't come out much anymore. I think she is fading. She makes the headaches start again. . . .

As soon as the headaches began, Chris knew that something was wrong. Jane had not been out much in the past few months, but her comings and goings had been easy and unheralded by pain or dramatics. The prolonged infrequency of her manifestations had raised Chris's hopes that she might simply fade away. But the shallow, egocentric self that she had created for herself was too perfectly cast to be so capriciously altered. She was discrete, defined, and launched during a time of intense observation and constant attention; she was unable to exist in the obscure anonymity of ordinary life. Her life's blood was attention, and as these essential sources of recognition were one by one stemmed, her substance thinned and faded. One vital element, only, burned with feverish intensity: her will to live, or, barring that, her determination to take the body with her if she died.

After the first headache, Chris discovered the following note: "If your wife doesn't let me out more often I'll kill her. Warn her not to fight me. Jane." As usual she had blamed her own short-comings and inabilities on someone else. Jane's inability to manifest herself was a result of her own tenuous hold on reality, not because Chris was striving to force her out. Jane's headlong plunge into oblivion was a self-destructive quality innately built into her construction. This masochistic tendency to be one's own worst enemy is a trait threading throughout the fabric of human nature; but Jane was a creature, though unconsciously wrought, designed purely and specifically for this purpose.

The headaches came almost daily now, bringing with them periods of amnesia lasting from an hour to an entire day. The pain would intensify to an intolerable peak, at which point Chris would seem to fall asleep—not black out, just gently fall asleep. When she awoke there would remain no memory of the intervening time, but often there was a note from Jane. Written on scraps of paper, napkins, anything available, as if time were of the essence, they alternated between desperation and vicious threats. Some were written to Don, some to Chris, and some just abstractly, but they all dealt with her need to "get out" and her threat to kill Chris if she tried to prevent it.

One note to Don ran: "I know you didn't like me, but once you said you loved me. If you ever had any feeling for me, tell her to let me out. I am better fitted to live socially than she is. You and I can arrange a separation. I know you would prefer that. I appeal to you to co-operate and keep her away from Thigpen, he will only try to start this all over again. Let's work this out together. Nobody need know but us. Just tell her to let me out, please! Jane."

The doctors' book, *The Three Faces of Eve*, was a best seller as soon as it was published, and immediately Dr. Thigpen wrote Chris several letters warning her of the danger of telling anyone who she was. He instructed her to be very careful, and especially to say nothing to any reporters; but if they did find out and come to see her, her best strategy was just to play innocent. He warned that anything she said would detract from her own book. He was glad that she had made her own decision not to go to Hollywood, that he did not think she could begin to realize just how truly unhappy she would be if her name were to become public.

In March she made a trip home, and in desperation visited Dr.

Standing, left to right: Anne, Taffy, Tiny, Chris (Strawberry Girl).
Seated, left to right: Becky, her husband, George, Anne's husband,
Leslie, and Luther, Tiny's husband

Tiny, Chris (Retrace Lady), and Becky

Chris (Purple Lady)

Chris (Banana Split Girl) and Don

"Pondering" by Chris Sizemore (Purple Lady)

Elen

Chris Sizemore, 1975

Jimmy, Chris, and Christie, 1976

Bobby Sizemore

Taffy and Tommy Fecteau

Thigpen in hopes of receiving help. As she sat in his office, the voice in her head pled with her not to tell him, that they could work it out without him. But she did tell him everything: about the headaches, the notes, and the voice. He listened, gave her another semantic differential test, and informed her that she was fine, merely undergoing a little "rebellion." Though unsatisfied, she accepted this and then discussed another of her concerns—her inability to conceive a child. He made an appointment for her with one of his colleagues, Dr. William E. Barfield, a gynecologist, assuring her that there were now some simple hormone procedures for aiding in conception. Before she left, he informed her that the world premiere of the movie *The Three Faces of Eve* was going to be presented in Augusta in September.

Dr. Barfield gave her the hormone treatment, but warned that if it failed to induce conception, surgery was her only hope. Back at home the headaches grew unbearable in their intensity and frequency. The pain in her temples was like a rubber band pulling toward the back of her neck. After these seizures she was weak and confused and could not remember simple information, such as which side of the road to drive on, or the meaning of traffic light signals, and she seemed always to be trying to recall something or some person's name. Once she had talked with Dr. Thigpen on the phone shortly before an attack, after which she could remember the conversation only vaguely. On calling him again to verify the conversation, she told him the reason for her confusion, and he informed her that she was doing all this herself and to herself, that there was no one else, only her.

She was shocked! After all their sessions together, she thought that he was the one person who understood. If he did not understand, no one did. Her thoughts were confused, desperate. If only she *were* doing it herself, then she could stop all this. Don had been very moody lately, declaring that he was a very unlucky man. She wondered forlornly if he were unhappy with her, and what she could do about it if he were. If she could only get pregnant, perhaps he would be happier; but it had been two months since the hormone treatment, and there was not the faintest sign. And all the time the headaches were worsening.

Standing before the bathroom mirror during a particularly bad time, she was ordered by the voice,

"Cut your wrists!"

Out of the mirror, a woman stared at her from wide, gleaming eyes, the full lips were drawn tautly across parted teeth, the whole face was contorted in a grinning grimace of torture.

"Cut your wrists! Pick up the razor blade and cut your wrists!" ordered the voice with calm persistence.

Feeling a sharp sting, she tore her eyes away from the hypnotic gaze in the mirror. A bright red stream traced an irregular pattern in the white sink.

"Oh, my God, I did it!" she thought, frantic fear racing her heart before she realized that she had only sliced her finger and had missed the vulnerable wrist. The next day, after a night of worry over the incident, her depression was so deep that she tried to take an overdose of sleeping pills; but Don, aware of her condition and closely watching her, prevented a repetition of this dreaded attempt. Her nerves were strung tight and ragged, and her breathing was labored. For days she appeared to be drugged and semiconscious.

Jane continued to emerge through blinding headaches and to create mischief, often talking with Don and Taffy, but usually just doing hateful acts to Chris. Jane hid her wedding rings, telling Taffy that she would eat them before she would let Chris have them; and once Jane cut off her hair, leaving Chris astonished to find the cropped, uneven bob when she awoke. It was a malicious act, performed simply to torment Chris, since it was Jane herself who so prized the long, glossy, black curls. Certainly a strange twist to the classical sado-masochistic enigma, when the torturer is also the tortured.

Don began to dread coming home in the evenings, never knowing who would greet him: a kind, loving, though tortured wife, or an angry, vindictive woman, vacillating between cold sophistication and thoroughly immature behavior. Some of her remarks left his practical senses reeling. She told him that she had not eaten food in three years, since 1954; and when she then tried to eat a banana, she did not know how to peel it. She informed him that she knew he and Taffy did not like her, a fact that he had difficulty denying. She asked him curious questions about commonplace objects—how light bulbs worked and how the couch was made. She casually commented, as one might of a distantly

346

related child, that Taffy had really grown since she had last seen her.

One night Don talked with Chris about their plans for having a baby, and told her that he felt that they should not have a child now, that their lives were too unstable. She was crushed; they had hoped for a baby for two years, and she knew how much it meant to him to have a child of his own. She did not blame him, though, for not wanting her to be the mother of his children: What kind of woman was she, and what kind of mother could she be? Ironically, this was all removed from their hands when several weeks later she became ill with severe abdominal pains. A medical examination indicated advanced endometriosis, a condition that had been preventing conception but that would now have to be corrected to prevent further deterioration of her physical health.

When she told Don, it was very like the last straw.

"I'll bet all *this* started *before* I married you, too!" he struck out, pushed beyond his usual calm control.

"I'm sorry, Don," she replied, hurt, "I know it looks like you married a lot of trouble. But I don't know what to do. No doctor ever mentioned this to me before."

"Well, I'm just fed up with the whole thing. If it's not one thing, it's another." If he realized the cruelty of his remark, he could not stop himself. His capacity for pain and disappointment had reached its limit.

"I hate for you to have to pay all these bills," she humbly apologized, "but what can I do?"

It was decided that she go back to Augusta to see Dr. Barfield; that way she would be near her parents if she needed surgery and further care. In July Dr. Barfield examined her, informing her that she did indeed need surgery, and while he was explaining the procedure, Jane emerged.

"You are not going to perform any surgery on *me!*" she abruptly declared. "No one is going to cut on me."

Dr. Barfield was astonished. One moment he had been talking with a mild-mannered, almost timid woman who, though worried, had not questioned his diagnosis; the next moment he faced a furious, haughty woman who rejected, out of hand, his entire plan for treating her serious condition.

"Mrs. Sizemore," he began, "your condition is serious. I have not mentioned this before, but if unattended it could become malignant."

"I don't care what you say, no one is going to cut on me!" She rose from the chair, her eyes flashing and angry.

"All right," he conceded. "Will you wait right here for a moment?" He left the room and hurriedly called Dr. Thigpen, describing to him the strange occurrence that had taken place and asking him whether he knew of anything that would explain it. Dr. Thigpen immediately came over and informed Dr. Barfield who his difficult patient really was. Dr. Thigpen then approached Chris himself.

"What is the trouble, Chris?" he casually asked, ignoring the fact that Jane was present.

"You know what the trouble is," she retorted. "I am not going to have any surgery."

"Don't you know that you could die?" he harshly informed her.

"I don't care. I could die anyway if they cut on me!" She stared stubbornly at him.

"Yes, but dying of cancer is no picnic," he informed her. "And you could have cancer. Even now you could have cancer, and the longer you wait, the slimmer are your chances of correcting the problem."

"That's not the reason she is having the operation," she stormed. "She just wants it so that she can have his baby! And I don't want a baby. She has no right to do this to me."

"I'm telling you that is not the reason," he insisted. "You have a condition, a growth that must be removed before it becomes cancerous. It may already be cancer. You have no choice."

Defeated, she disappeared. Chris, confused, frightened, looked out at the two doctors, surprise at seeing Dr. Thigpen showing in her face. The discussion of procedure and plans for the surgery continued. It was arranged that she would return for her surgery on August 20. Dr. Thigpen suggested that they might need a few private sessions to see if they could not resolve her present rebellion, that he did not feel that it would be too complicated to do so; but she returned home, her conflict boiling within her.

There had been no understanding in Augusta, and there was no understanding at home. Don seemed remote, even slightly angry;

348

and when she asked him to go with her to Augusta for her surgery, he refused.

"Chris, you know I can't take off from work that long!" he declared rather impatiently. Her medical bills had always kept them drained of money, even though he had worked overtime at every available opportunity. He did not explain; he felt that somehow she ought to know that life for him had descended to one plane—that of earning money to support her illnesses. Was there no end? But her problem loomed so large that it filled her horizon, leaving no room for other consideration. She felt unloved, rejected—ugly!

Don did not explain, for in so doing he would have revealed his fears, his needs; Chris did not ask, for in so doing she would have laid bare her own inadequacies. They parted strangers.

At thirty, Chris was returning home again, alone, rejected, ill in mind and body. It was nearing the eve of the great ball, for which preparations had been underway from the moment it was decided that the world premiere of *The Three Faces of Eve* would be held in Augusta. The great, the powerful, and the famed of the city banded together to make it the most glamorous celebration since Augusta's world-famed days as a winter resort. For days before the grand event, the local newspapers—the Augusta *Chronicle* and the Augusta *Herald*—had been running news and feature stories on the elaborate preparations, including the anticipated guest list, the burgeoning sale of advance tickets, and the change in location of the patrons' dinner from the downtown Richmond Hotel to the more spacious Bon Air Hotel, where more ample facilities could accommodate the growing guest list. The premiere was not just a product of Augusta's powerful and political; her businessmen, large and small, lent their support as well. During the days preceding the gala event, store windows and newspaper ads proclaimed *The Three Faces of Eve* to be their very own.

And Augusta was proud. Her merchants, from motor companies to dress shops, cunningly worded their advertising around this world-famous event. The Leon Simon Formal Wear Rental Service declared its pride in being a part of a community that enjoyed the prestige of such an important event, and promised to its patrons attire that would be in keeping with the importance of such an occasion; Capers Paint and Glass Company reminded that

"Eve changed her personality" and that Augustans could reflect their own personalities with new colors from their supply; Virginia Tollison's Hair Styling Salon boldly stated, "Eve had a complete change—so can you! Have your hair restyled and find your most pleasing personality!"; and the Augusta Sewing Center offered a "World Premiere" contest, with prizes, including tickets to the premiere showing, going to the people who could make up the most words pertaining to sewing from the letters found in "World Premiere." One Dr. Victor Casella, an optometrist, published an ad in which he congratulated the Miller Theater for showing the premiere, and requested that people consult him for eye care. Each ad carried a picture of Joanne Woodward as Eve.

While these glamorous preparations were in process, Chris underwent her unpleasant though uneventful surgery; and while still in the hospital, she began to avidly read every word about the coming event, clipping each article, each picture, each notice. She kept everything, even the ads; and if someone brought her another copy of a paper, she kept that also. Thirstily, she drank in every word, absorbed every detail into her very being, frantically searching for some mention of herself, some indication that this was all about her, that this was her story. But there was none. Joanne Woodward's name was everywhere; Joanne Woodward's face looked out from all the pictures; Joanne Woodward was Eve. There were Dr. Thigpen and Dr. Cleckley, who were called honored guests and renowned physicians and authors; but they had only written about her, and it was still her story. Where was she? The more she searched for Chris in the premiere events, the less able she was to find Chris within herself. Her whole being became abstract, absent.

When she was able to go home, Zueline and Acie came for her, and they drove down Broad Street on their way out of town. Chris read every sign in the slowly passing shop windows welcoming *The Three Faces of Eve* to Augusta. It was ironic: Augusta wanted her story, but it did not want her, had never wanted her, had advised her to leave. Now the city had thrown wide its arms to embrace her story, her doctors who had written her story, the movie about her story; but not her.

As the car stopped for a traffic light, her gaze fell on Cullum's store window. There it was, her dress, her red silk dress! The sign beside it read: "The Dress 'Eve' wore as 'Eve Black,'" and showed a color picture of Joanne Woodward wearing the red dress. As Chris stared, her head throbbed and her body trembled. That was not right, Joanne Woodward did not look like her; she had blond hair and green eyes. Chris had black hair and blue eyes. Chris thought they tried to make actresses look like the people they portrayed. But this actress did not look like her. They had changed Eve so that she no longer even looked like Chris. No one would ever know that this was her life. Even she began to doubt. When they rode by the theater, her eyes were so misted she could scarcely read the bold lettering on the marquee: "Welcome Miss Georgia, World Premiere, *The Three Faces of Eve*, Joanne Woodward as Eve!" Three days before the splendid ball, Chris left Augusta, unrecognized, unheralded, unwanted—an unwelcome embarrassment to the honored guests.

The festivities opened with a patrons' dinner in honor of the authors and other celebrities of the screen and literary world. Among the honored guests, besides authors Cleckley and Thigpen, were Nunnally Johnson, who wrote the screenplay from the book and produced the film; Alistair Cooke, internationally known writer and commentator, who narrated the film; and Jody Shattuck, "Miss Georgia of 1958." A generous sprinkling of local and state dignitaries, Twentieth Century-Fox officials, and out-of-town press swelled the polished ranks. Joanne Woodward could not attend.

The *Chronicle* the next morning described: "The speaker's table, placed against a black velvet background adorned with a golden giant-size book with cover depicting the now famous 'three faces,' was handsomely decorated with restraint. Three golden 'faces' placed on an ebony velvet base, handsome black and gold candelabra holding black burning tapers and two magnificent arrangements of giant white chrysanthemums dusted with gold, black grapes, golden pears and tall black fronds in Oriental ebony containers completed the impressive decorations at the main table." Admirable restraint. Sprays of golden magnolia leaves placed at intervals on the walls gleamed in the candle glow from burning tapers, and varied arrangements depicting the "three faces" were placed at vantage points in the large rooms.

Against this sumptuous background, Augusta's ladies' elite displayed a colorful array of silk, chiffon, and satin gowns. Mrs. Edison Marshall, hostess for the dinner and wife of the famed author, wore a Dior blue cocktail-length chiffon, while Mrs. Hervey M. Cleckley was elegantly dressed in coral chiffon. Mrs. Corbett H. Thigpen was gowned in full-length white tulle and satin trimmed with sequins, and Miss Georgia had selected white lace. The feminine attire ran the gamut of elegant fabric from peau de soie, to taffeta, to pure silk organza, to intricate lace, and the rainbow of hues and modes was limited only by imagination and elegant taste.

Transportation of honored guests from the banquet to the theater was furnished by a local automobile dealer, who lent eight models of a brand-new car just out on the market—the Edsel! A light rain began to fall as the police-escorted motorcade wound its way onto Broad Street and approached the theater, but for blocks around the baroque Miller Theater a crowd waited patiently until the celebrities began arriving; and with undampened spirits they responded to Miss Georgia's smile, seeming not to notice that the film's star was absent. Inside, Nunnally Johnson paid liberal tribute to Drs. Cleckley and Thigpen and presented them with identical gold plaques from the president of Twentieth Century-Fox "in recognition and appreciation of your service to the movie industry and the whole world." Alistair Cooke spoke: "This is a movie more like actual life. *Three Faces* is not a freak, but a dramatization of something we all have a little of." And Dr. Bruce Schaefer, president of the Georgia Medical Association, declared, "This movie is a milestone in the progress of medicine."

The grand ball was over and Cinder-Ella never emerged from the chimney corner. The theater was dark and empty; the street dim and deserted. Chris had not been invited to the ball but her dress had, and now after all the festivities, it hung limp and empty, symbolic of the haunted woman who had in the past so joyously filled it.

For the next few days the critics filled their columns with rave notices. The movie was described as the most unusual of the year, brilliantly acted, and guaranteed to hold the viewer spellbound. Joanne Woodward's performance was rated as absolutely amazing, and Louella Parsons predicted stardom for her on the basis of this one role. And she was right: Just six months later, this virtually unknown newcomer was accepting an Academy Award as the year's best actress for her role as the "real-life neurotic with three personalities."

And what of the real-life neurotic? Chris read the newspaper articles, she pored over every word, scrutinized every smiling face. Was she cut by the cruel injustice of so many others being feted as a result of her years of suffering? Was she struck by the amusing irony of her empty dress attending the premiere? Was she despaired by the world's rejoicing over her "resolved" illness? No. She was simply again the ugly child, with big brown freckles staining and mottling her very soul.

Dr. Thigpen wrote Don a letter stating that in view of some of Chris's recent difficulties, it would be advisable for her not to see *The Three Faces of Eve.* He indicated that it would only get her all stirred up, and that he frankly believed she was doing fine, that her problem was only a temporary upset. He warned Don that the moviemakers had enlarged on certain instances and stretched the imagination a bit to make it acceptable to moviegoers, but that he was very well pleased with it as a whole. Certainly Taffy could not see the film.

Chris's denial was complete: She was not even allowed to see the portrayal of her life. It was to be more than twenty years before she was to see the film, and then she viewed it as a late-afternoon television movie. For twenty years she listened to the whole world discuss her famous story while she silently screamed "I'm Eve."

16

The Final Face of Eve

An old adage warns of the futility of locking the barn door after the horse has escaped. Nevertheless, Chris now took the advice of her friend Irmis Johnson, and employed an agent, Willis Wing, to protect her literary rights. Ironically, she now had no such rights left to protect.

The bloom was off the rose. From the beginning Mr. Wing, an experienced literary sage, had concerns that Chris's effort to tell her own story had already been eclipsed by the doctors' book, that it would simply be reworking already plowed ground, and that a market would be difficult to find for such a product. But she was adamant, declaring that her story would be different, that she had different material to be told and a different way of telling it. Her intensity was convincing, and on the strength of it he wrote to Corbett Thigpen asking two questions: Was there, indeed, additional information to that which comprised the doctors' book? What, if any, were their legal involvements with their now famous patient?

The answer was discouraging on the first score and highly non-enlightening on the second. Dr. Thigpen indicated that Chris's treatment period and the pertinent past details of her life had been thoroughly presented in their book, though interwoven into psychiatric dissertations, psychological testings, and professional personality observations. Their book, he said, was written mainly for psychiatrists, other physicians, and those who are professionally interested in psychology; however, he felt that it would hold a genuine interest for the intelligent layman. He agreed that Chris might have some stories which, if told from her own point

354

of view, would have wide appeal to the remainder of the reading public, whatever was left of it. It was clear, however, that he believed the story to have been thoroughly covered, and suggested that if a second book were to be written, it should be postponed for several years. As to her legal status, he declared that he could not offhand judge that, and gave the name of his own attorney, James Hull, Sr., as the best person to advise Chris in such matters. He did know, he said, that she was thoroughly bound to Twentieth Century-Fox. As to her legal entanglement with McGraw-Hill as a result of the writing of *The Three Faces of Eve*, he had no knowledge. He made no mention of whether he himself had any legal involvement with her.

Undaunted and seeking to fully represent the wishes of his client, Willis Wing discussed these matters with McGraw-Hill, which had published the doctors' book, and with which he had worked on many projects over the years. They expressed keen interest in a new book to the point of wanting to discuss contracts, and declared that there was no question from their point of view about Chris's quite absolute freedom to do her own story. James Hull was in complete agreement, stating that after his evaluation of the legal affairs of Drs. Thigpen and Cleckley, he saw no problems that would stand in the way of her proceeding as she wished. Again no mention was made of a contract existing between Chris and her doctors.

Dr. Thigpen wrote to Chris informing her that he was mighty interested to learn that she was again thinking of writing her memoirs. He suggested that she use a ghostwriter and not attempt to do the writing herself, advising Irmis Johnson for the job. Unaccountably, Chris felt guilty, traitorous, as if her actions had somehow been underhanded, ungrateful. She wrote to both Drs. Cleckley and Thigpen once again, thanking them for all they had done for her, expressing her eternal gratitude, and voicing a fear that someday she might be a disappointment to them. Her inability to criticize their book, yet her determination to set the record straight by rewriting the story herself, had created within her overwhelming feelings of guilt and anxiety.

But they were wrong about so many things. All those events distorted to hide her identity, that was wrong; the truth should be told just exactly as it had happened, not distorted. And her mother and father, that was all wrong, too; she could not let that pass. Dr. Thigpen simply did not know her parents as they really were, how loving and supportive they had been over the years. She must correct that. And the book indicates that the three personalities were all that had ever existed. That's all wrong; there were nine whom I can remember before them; and Chris White, Chris Black, and Jane make twelve! The doctors think there were always just the two Chrises and that then Jane came; and that when they died Jane became the last one. Oh, I wish that had been true!

But the biggest mistake of all was about her being well. She was not well at all, nothing had changed except that the new personality who came was an entirely different one from all the others: No. 13! O God, is there no end? There were still voices, headaches, suicide attempts; and even Dr. Thigpen did not understand that. And he had always understood before. Why did he keep telling her that she was well? He saw Jane, talked with her in Dr. Barfield's office. Then he saw the Blind Lady and talked with her. That's just the way it's always been. But now he tells her that she's doing it herself, doing it to herself! But she isn't, it's just like before. Does that mean she was doing it before, too? Making herself ill? If so, why didn't he tell her then? Now she has nobody to help her, nobody to turn to. Other doctors won't believe her story of who she is, and Dr. Thigpen tells her she's well! If only the telling of her story could bring her help. . . .

Encouraged by McGraw-Hill's interest and Chris's apparent legal freedom, Willis Wing, according to her instructions, located for her a professional writer, James W. Poling, to weave the pattern of her thoughts into a whole fabric. Mr. Poling, a veteran in the art of story writing, after reading *The Three Faces of Eve*, raised the obvious question of duplication of effort; but he, too, was swayed by the publisher's interest, and agreed, after a visit with Chris, to undertake the challenging task. He indicated that he would need, in addition to the information supplied to him by Chris herself, to interview Drs. Thigpen and Cleckley and to view the data concerning her case to be found in their files. An early date was set up for this meeting to take place. All seemed agreeable.

Little did Chris realize the odds she was up against when she confidently set about to take charge of her great adventure. From the outset, she declared that she was now going to reveal her identity and to tell the events of her life, including her continued illness, exactly the way it had occurred. James Poling went to Augusta to visit the doctors and innocently revealed these facts to them. The reaction was as instantaneous as it was violent: It was not to be done. The exposing of her identity would subject not only her, but her husband and family as well, to unpleasant personal publicity and annoyance and would result in the definite danger of the knowledge of her old illness, which was now behind her, becoming a source of complexity and worry to Taffy. Dr. Thigpen clearly stated these instructions to the writer and also delineated them in a letter to Chris, suggesting that if anyone attempted to identify her, she should warn him that he was laying himself open to slander.

Poor Chris; she had never before considered her state to be so disreputable that it would be slanderous to accuse someone of having it. Was it true, then, that she was doomed to live out her life in hiding, like a heinous criminal, a traitor to one's country, a sex pervert? Her determination was completely crushed when Messrs. Wing and Poling, after hearing the doctors' opinion, agreed that it would be best to preserve her anonymity. Her capitulation was a feeble attempt at face-saving.

"I said that I would be willing to reveal my identity *if it was necessary*," she fabricated. "I'm sorry everybody misunderstood."

She had lost the first and major round; the others were reduced to minor skirmishes.

Dr. Thigpen had also vetoed any mention being made of her continuing illness, referring to it as merely a "small rebellion" that could be easily resolved. Jim Poling, unwilling to disobey the doctor for fear of worsening Chris's condition, refused to consider using the material until she had seen the doctor and discussed her health with him. This resulted in an enormous conflict within her: As the Blind Lady, she wanted to go, to tell of her present troubles, to get blessed help; as Jane, the betrayed Jane, she refused to go, feeling that the revelation of another personality

357

would cause the doctor to bring about her demise, as had her own revelation brought about the demise of the two Chrises before her. Jane, being the weaker, lost the battle in spite of both her pleading and her vicious threats, and Chris made her pilgrimage to Augusta. And so she lost Round 2: She could not reveal her continuing illness, only that a fourth and *final* personality had evolved and that Jane was now gone, *dead*.

The story was to be told as if Jane had actually died on that night when she took the overdose of pills and laid herself out for death. Chris had to return to her task of telling her "true" story, while bearing on her conscience its falseness and bearing within her being the ever-present, tormenting proof of its falseness. Jim Poling agreed to this little deceit because he felt that it was best for Chris and because he believed the doctor's prognosis that it would not be too complicated to resolve the present trouble if no fuss were made of it. So much for Round 2.

After Poling's visit to see Chris, he asked that she collect family pictures for his viewing and that she write down a chronology of the important events in her life. He also sent a long list of questions to Dr. Thigpen, and it was then that another barrier loomed across their path: The doctors stated that they would only allow the book to be written if they could edit the material. Astounded, in the face of the advice he had received concerning Chris's legal entanglements, Mr. Wing pursued this and discovered that in the contract she had signed with Twentieth Century-Fox there was a clause that read:

> Whereas, I hereby acknowledge and agree that by instru-
> ment dated April 24, 1953 I duly granted to Corbett H.
> Thigpen, M.D. and Hervey M. Cleckley, M.D. all world-
> wide rights forever in my life story (Including without
> limitation publication and other rights in all versions of
> the Story written by or for them and those published as
> aforesaid), and I have reserved unto myself no rights of
> any kind whatsoever in my life story.

When the implications of this paragraph were explained to her, Chris was deeply puzzled. She had no memory of signing such a document, and she certainly had never been given a copy of one. She had never lost a single scrap he had ever given her. If she had ever received a copy of such a paper, she would still have it. In April of 1953, she was still living in Augusta under Dr. Thigpen's constant care; that was just before he had reported her case to the American Psychiatric Association. Had she signed a paper giving him the right to report on her case? If so, she did not remember it; but surely that would not have been the same as signing away the rights to her life story forever. Forever means life *and* death. Can one own the rights to another's life story even when there is no life left?

She got out her copy of the Twentieth Century-Fox contract. There it was; it had always been there, so she must have seen it. She simply had not understood its encompassiong implications, its totality. She felt numb, shocked to discover that it was no longer a question of whether she *would* write her story, but whether she would be allowed to write it. At least the movie company had paid to her a small fee for visualization rights, but she had received nothing for the literary rights. Then her conscience struck with a deadening blow: The doctors had treated her without fee! Was this the price they had extracted for the treatment? If so, why had they not told her? No matter, it was done, she accepted it. If that was what they had wanted as payment, she would have given it to them. So why fight the idea after the fact?

So went Round 3, and strangely no one asked to see this so-called instrument, but accepted the simple allusion to it in the other contract. Interestingly, no one commented on the identical dating of the Fox contract and the Thigpen contract. The Fox contract was dated April 24, 1956; the doctors' elusive instrument was said to be dated April 24, 1953, exactly three years earlier.

Chris accepted all this, but the joy had gone out of her task. Not only would her story be an "also-ran," but also she would again get no recognition for it, and the very man whose story she was attempting to correct would edit her material. Deep within her a dull anger glowed, but it was so repressed that it would take another fifteen years to surface; in the intervening years, it merely scorched her soul, creating a gnawing anxiety that her futile efforts to alleviate kept her life and the life of her family in constant turmoil.

As a result of all these proceedings, Willis Wing negotiated a contract between Chris and James Poling that contained a clause

359

setting forth the understanding that approval for the project had been received from Drs. Thigpen and Cleckley. Chris herself signed a contract with Drs. Thigpen and Cleckley, giving them not only the right to divulge any information they so chose to the writer of her book, but also to edit any material that she and Mr. Poling might write about her life. The document declared that the doctors were the sole judges of whether the final manuscript of the book was ready for publication.

When Chris finally realized how her plans had been thwarted and curtailed, she fought back in the only way that seemed to be left open to her: She withheld her additional information. If she could not tell the world, she was not going to tell anyone. She did not give Mr. Poling all the letters she had accumulated, and she told him that she was unable to obtain any family pictures; she gave him, in fact, very little that was not already in the doctors' book. This was only his first disappointment, for when he visited Augusta, he could not believe the paucity of information available there. He reported to Chris that the doctors had lost a great deal of the material on her case. Of all the many interviews, taped and transcribed from shorthand, with Chris and her family, only five typed reports and one tape survived. All the interviews dealing with the details of her childhood had disappeared. The doctors' only explanation to him was that the material must have inadvertently been thrown out when they moved their offices.

Mr. Poling reassured her that none of this was fatal because she could supply the missing data; it would just be more time-consuming. Little did he know that she had no intention of supplying the data missing from her case files, nor any additional data of which only she was cognizant. He further assured her that Drs. Thigpen and Cleckley could not have been nicer or more co-operative and that he thoroughly enjoyed meeting them. One point, however, was puzzling him: How were they going to treat the ending of the story? With Dr. Thigpen insisting that she was well, how was the fourth personality going to be explained? And there was still Jane on the scene: What were they going to do with her? Mr. Poling suggested that they had three alternatives: They could work toward a different ending from the one they had planned; they could have a story with no ending, leaving her state of health unresolved; or they could assume, along with Dr. Thigpen, that the status quo had just been temporarily disturbed and the story remained the same. He favored continuing along the path they had originally set for themselves and to let developments, if any, occur. Chris agreed.

Jane was definitely very much on the scene, and her behavior had grown more atrocious after she learned that the story was being written anonymously and that her existence was going to be publicly denied. She intensified her harassment of the already frightened and cowered Blind Lady, forcing her into periodic states of drowsiness, which permitted her to emerge. She had lately, in desperation, changed her attitude toward Don and Taffy, courting their favor and appealing her case to them. For nine-year-old Taffy, she drew pictures of birds and springtime, and a wedding dress she would like to be married in. She talked earnestly to Don,

"I know you don't really care for me," she admitted, "but if you will help me to stay alive, I'll leave, and you won't be bothered with all this anymore."

"Don't talk like that, Chris," he ordered, slightly embarrassed. "You're my wife."

"I'm not Chris, and I'm not your wife. I'm Jane," she corrected. "And I know you don't like Taffy, either. If you help me, I'll take her with me. Then you'll be free again."

"I do love Taffy!" he declared. "She's just like my own daughter."

"Well, I don't see how you could love your wife! She's stupid! Anybody can get an education this day and time. There's no need for anybody to be as dumb as she is. She's fat and she never wears any decent clothes." And there she sat, seemingly oblivious that she was housed in the same body and draped in the same clothes that she was so vehemently rejecting.

What could Don say? He merely looked at her, feeling himself trapped in an eternal nightmare.

"You can't love a fat woman like that," she persisted. "Help me and I'll take the body away, and you'll be rid of her for good."

"Aw, Chris, I'm just fed up with all of this, the whole thing!" In disgust and frustration, he walked out.

When Jane disappeared and the Blind Lady "woke up," she immediately looked for evidence that her counterpart had been present. Usually she found some obvious mischief, such as threatening notes, inscrutable pencil-drawn pictures, her wedding rings missing and hidden. She had always told Don about these visits, and if he were home when Jane came out, she asked him what had occurred. Lately, however, he had appeared withdrawn and disinterested in her accounts and had refused to talk about Jane's conversations with him. The first time he refused to discuss one of Jane's visits was when Chris awoke and found the drawing of a blue dress inscribed *"The Blue Wedding Gown."*

"Chris, this is the silliest thing I've ever heard of!" he angrily declared when she asked him what Jane had said.

And who could blame him? He had just sat there and watched her finish the drawing. She had handed it to him saying,

"That's the dress I want to be married in." Then she had drowsily closed her eyes and slumped down in her chair. Almost immediately her eyes opened again and she asked,

"What's that in your hand?" Then, suspiciously, "Jane has been here again, hasn't she? What did she say?" She took the picture and gazed at it as if she had never seen it before.

What man would not withdraw in anger if his wife behaved in this manner? If he steps over the threshold into a world where myriad women inhabit the same body and vie for its possession, might he not reach a point at which he would be unable to retrace his steps out into the world of reality and sanity? Don retreated from this dim, misty world while he could still see the bright sunshine of his own world. From then on, he refused to be drawn into the eerie conversations with the two parts of his wife's whole. Whatever his inner thinking, he never again openly lent any recognition to the long line of intruders awaiting their turn to trespass into his life.

Again, the very element needed to sustain life for Jane—recognition—was being denied her; and as she weakened, her struggle became more vicious. She hated Jim Poling and the whole idea of his doing her story, and she did all in her power to stop him, very nearly succeeding. Jim spent a week at Chris's home in Cumberland, Maryland, working with her, taping interviews, and gathering personal information from Don and Taffy. One evening the four of them went over to Frostburg College for dinner, and on the way home, rounding a mountainous curve, the voice of Jane demanded of Chris,

"Tell Jim Poling to mind his own business!"

Jim, sitting in the rear seat with Taffy, saw Chris give a start and look around at him with a terrified, haunted look on her face. Frantic, she grabbed the door handle and attempted to jump from the car. Only the speed and momentum of rounding a sharp curve prevented the door from swinging open. Jim yelled for Don to stop the car, and, leaning forward, Jim grabbed Chris and held her tight against the seat.

The car screeched to a halt and Don, stunned, asked,

"Chris, what happened? Did the door come open?" Was he giving her an excuse?

"It must have," she gasped, trembling. "I don't know what happened." But she did, and so did Jim.

Jim was worried. Not only had he grown to like this woman personally, but he was also concerned that their work together, pushing her to dredge up old, painful memories, might plunge her once again into the depths of her illness, might even take her life. When, a few days later, he found Jane's voice on a tape, he felt compelled to speak to Chris about his fears. He had left the recorder with Chris each night when he returned to his motel; and one night Jane had recorded a message for him:

"If you don't leave here and mind your own business I'm going to kill her and me. Then where will your old book be?"

The tone was hardly recognizable; it was vicious and sibilant, hissing urgently in its near-monotone threat. Jim was shocked. To this point he had believed this bizarre story only intellectually. He replayed the section, then played excerpts from his tapings with Chris. His astonishment grew. Even in anger, a voice is recognizable, but it seemed hardly possible that this vitriolic tone could have issued from the same vocal cords that produced Chris's low, melodic southern drawl. The quality of the voice conjured up a facial expression that, for the life of him, he could not stamp on her gentle, smiling features.

He had no choice but to discuss it with her. Even though the doctor had said she was well, this was not the behavior of a well woman. Deeply embarrassed, she apologized humbly, promising to try to prevent a recurrence of Jane's interference; but Jim insisted that she tell Dr. Thigpen of the seriousness of the situation. To impress upon her his concern, Jim declared that he would not go on with the writing until she had done so. She called the doctor and related the events about her continuing, even burgeoning troubles; and he once again assured her that it was a temporary thing that she was doing herself and that she could terminate with minor treatment. He suggested that she visit him for a therapy session and that at the same time they could decide how they were going to guide Jim Poling in the writing of the material.

On the strength of this telephone conversation, Jim continued with his work. It was slow, and he was often frustrated and discouraged. A great deal of time was spent restructuring and disguising events to make them unrecognizable. From time to time he wrote to Chris requesting additional information and requiring clarification on an issue; but largely her part of the task, except for proofing, was over. She had now only the long wait while her writer struggled to bring clarity and readability to the jumble of facts before him.

She was regularly corresponding with Dr. Thigpen during this period, and he continued to urge her to make a trip south, not only to resolve her problem, but also to plan how to deal with Jim Poling's material. Dr. Thigpen informed her that Jim had commented that the two of them had different memories about certain instances and that he, Dr. Thigpen, had a large number of notes from which he was refreshing his memory. He acknowledged her difficulty in attempting to recall events that had taken place three or four years earlier, and felt that his notes and his remembrances might serve to stimulate her memory. Also, he felt that no doubt there would be some points that would require clearing up between the two of them and between him and Mr. Poling. Dr. Thigpen often pledged both his and Dr. Cleckley's help and support throughout the entire writing, offering even to continue handling some of her literary affairs, though she now had an agent. It was the last week in June, however, before she returned to Augusta, and then it was her acute physical health that prompted a return visit to Dr. Barfield; she saw Dr. Thigpen only briefly.

In late May, McGraw-Hill bought an option on the book for

five hundred dollars, but Chris received none of this, since Jim needed it to cover his expenses incurred while preparing the manuscript. And Jim, fighting his uphill battle against deadening, unseen obstacles, was earning every penny and more of this meager sum. His immediate problem of how to tell the story of several women, yet make it the personal story of one woman, was compounded by his task of having to clear his ideas and literary approaches with both Dr. Thigpen and Chris, who, unknown to him, were waging their own battle for control over the path of the material. At one point, the doctor suggested that he write a paragraph for the book that would explain a chapter in dispute in his own book. Jim declared that he was dead set against raising questions in the mind of the reader that might goad him into searching for other discrepancies between the two accounts.

Another point of lengthy contention arose over Chris's declaration that there had been other personalities before Chris Costner and Chris White and that they were separate and apart, distinct from those with whom the doctors had worked. The doctors' theory, as so stated in their book, was that those personalities were simply earlier versions of Chris Costner and Chris White, citing as proof that the two Chrises had memories of these earlier experiences. A concrete example was Chris Costner's admitting to Dr. Thigpen that she was the one who married Al Thorne, leaving Chris White to take all the punishment. Chris refuted this argument, saying that the ensuing personalities always had some knowledge of experiences preceding their birth and that even the doctor acknowledged a suspicion that Chris Costner had been lying about that episode. And how to explain this fourth personality: the Blind Lady? The doctors valiantly attempted to do just this in a final section ending Chris and Jim's book; but even so, it was a ghost that refused to be laid, and Dr. Thigpen, when asked about it over the years, began to declare that he had been misunderstood about the resolution of the illness and that no amount of explaining seemed to clarify the issue. As it happened, however, he won the round, and Jim wrote the story as if the early personalities were merely juvenile Chris Whites and Chris Costners instead of different beings in their own right.

If Jim Poling's problems were severe while his book was in the planning stages, they seemed pale compared with his difficulties when he began to send written manuscript copy to his two collaborators. The plan was for Jim to send copy to Chris on which she made her corrections and comments before sending it on to Dr. Thigpen, who then made modifications in both Jim's and Chris's work. Chris's alterations were minor as a result of her close work and continuous mail contact with the writer, but it was a different matter with the doctors. The first static sounded over the use of the doctors' names, when Dr. Thigpen wrote Jim, praising Part I, but lamenting the many references to Dr. Cleckley and himself. He admitted that since they had thrust themselves into the public eye by writing their book and allowing it to be made into a movie, their names had become public property; but he requested that Jim cut down on the use of their names.

Jim indicated that he had every desire to be co-operative and that he felt bad about their concern, but that he could not possibly do as requested since Dr. Thigpen, especially, was a principal character in the drama. Jim indicated to Chris that he had to be free to handle the material, or his hands would be tied; and since the doctors had already committed themselves to publicity and profit, they should just adjust themselves to it. It was not that easy! When Parts II and III reached Dr. Thigpen, he made two agitated phone calls to Jim in one morning, expressing his distress at the constant use of his name. While willingly admitting that he and Dr. Cleckley had no leg to stand on, he beseeched Jim to do something about the situation. He explained that as a psychiatrist, his whole practice depended on referrals—all of his patients were referred to him by other doctors—and his practice could be seriously damaged if the local American Medical Association Ethics Board reprimanded him, or if local doctors decided that he was a publicity seeker and refused to refer patients to him.

On the heels of this, Dr. Cleckley wrote to Jim for the first time, also upset over the affair, and suggested that he do as the movie company had done—use aliases for the doctors as well as for all the other characters. Jim sought the advice of both Willis Wing and Bob Amusson from McGraw-Hill, and they finally concluded that it would be wise to take Dr. Cleckley's suggestion to avoid alienating the doctors and running the risk of a controversy with them when the book was published. Chris, having no part in the making of this important decision about her book, was merely informed after the fact. She was disappointed; the names of Drs. Thigpen and Cleckley were household words since *The Three Faces of Eve*. Their pictures and their names were in all the papers, but she, the patient they had publicized, could not use these names when *she* told the story. But would she have been able to hold out even if she had been asked? Probably not, but at least she would have had the opportunity of being generous to them. Dr. Thigpen "whooped with joy" when Jim called him about the decision, and he promised to send the writer additional information that he had "just found."

But the problems were not over. Jim, fretting to Chris that Drs. Thigpen and Cleckley had kept Parts II, III, and IV for over a month, fervently prayed that they did not run into any basic conflicts over the material. He declared that he was writing *her* story, and hoped that the doctors were not going to insist on its being written their way. He felt that such a situation would cause Chris to have to make some decisions that would place a strain on her loyalties.

Jim was further disturbed over the receipt of a carbon copy of a letter Dr. Thigpen had sent to Chris in which he spoke of extracting drops of blood from Jim by making alterations in his work. Jim found the statement upsetting and resented the doctor's having sent a carbon copy of such a letter to him. He almost recovered his wry sense of humor, however, when, on calling to determine the cause of the holdup on the manuscript, he was told that *Mrs.* Cleckley had not finished reading the material. And when he finally received the copy, there were extensive changes to be made, mostly minor, however, with only one major rewrite job. As a result of a paragraph in one of the doctors' manuscripts, in which Dr. Thigpen had stated that an early letter from Chris had made him suspect that he had a case of dual personality on his hands, Jim had built a major section of Part II around this provisional diagnosis, which had also been used in referrals for psychological testing. The doctor insisted that he had never felt that his patient had dual personality; Jim rewrote the section.

Jim relayed to Chris that Dr. Thigpen was also upset by her description of his office manners, complaining that it made him sound sloppy, and that he had never put his feet on his desk or slouched in his chair in the presence of patients. Chris protested this change, declaring that it was no criticism of him, that it merely indicated his friendly informality. Nevertheless, it was struck from the final copy. The doctor also drew drops of blood from the exasperated writer by requiring changes where he had taken ideas from Dr. Thigpen's writing and "put" them into the doctor's dialogue and thoughts.

In November, she received the title that McGraw-Hill had chosen for her book: *The Final Face of Eve*. Again her disappointment was acute; she had carefully selected the title *Strangers in My Body*, and that was the one written on the publisher's contract; but now it had been changed. And the new title was just as wrong as was the ending of the book. Not only that, it definitely stamped the story as a sequel to the doctors' book. This news followed on the heels of her receipt of the final part of the story, written to show that Jane died that November night three years ago when she took the overdose of pills and laid herself out to await death. And it was not true, they all knew it was a lie; Jim knew, Dr. Thigpen knew, she knew, and above all, Jane knew that Jane still lived and fought desperately to continue living. The harder they tried to eradicate her through ignoring her, writing of her death, even pretending that she was only a minor disturbance, the harder she struggled for life. The horror becomes inconceivable when viewed from Jane's awareness: There was a conspiracy, of which she was fully cognizant, to kill her; and though she pled with everyone, even her "former" husband, for help, they all turned deaf ears to her. The doctor who, she felt, once helped to create her, who nurtured her, who aided her in the elimination of her own competitors, now ignored her, described her as merely a "poisonous apple that the stomach is attempting to disgorge." And her body, the one she had fought for and had rightful claim to, had been usurped by another who was stronger and more possessive about inhabiting it. And the man who married her and vowed to love and protect her for better or worse had now turned his back on her and refused even to hear her plea for life. Finally, they were going to announce to the world in *The Final Face of Eve* that she was dead! There was no help in all of this world for her. The suffocating nothingness of oblivion began to stifle her.

But Jane, the façade created to self-destruct, clung so tenaciously to life and so tormented Chris that Chris began to fear for her own existence. She confided in Jim, asking him to pray for her.

"You are my friend, you know Jane exists. You've seen what she is doing to me! Please, pray for me!" she begged.

Jim answered that he would be happy to pray for her, but that she did not need his prayers. He advised her to see Dr. Thigpen.

"But I tried to tell him, and he didn't understand. I can't do it," she wept.

Jim declared that he hadn't the slightest doubt about her ability to do it, that she had the best kind of life with Don and Taffy. Everything would work out, he promised her.

Don didn't understand, either; he no longer even wanted to talk about it. Above all, he did not want her to return to Dr. Thigpen for more therapy. But what choice did she have? She wrote to the doctor and revealed her torment. He assured her that her present trouble was just under the surface, and that perhaps merely a scratch would let it burst forth, fruit, and wither, never again to be trouble to her. Three appointments were set up for her between Christmas and New Year's Day, and she kept the appointments. They retraced events from her childhood in an attempt to determine what troublesome, repressed material was causing this apparent present need for her now familiar defense. She went home each night to her mother and sought additional facts that might throw some light into the dark corners of her past. The doctor continuously probed into the little-known circumstances surrounding that mysterious first marriage, about which none of the personalities seemed to be aware. With Zueline's help they pieced together enough facts to satisfy Dr. Thigpen that he knew the full story and its implications upon the total picture. He had been talking with both the Blind Lady and with Jane, who, though hostile and resentful of his intentions toward her, always came out on call.

On the last day of therapy, Dr. Thigpen called her out,

"Jane," he gently informed her, "you are going to have to go away and let Chris live her life."

"That's what you think," she told him, her tone stubborn and determined. "I'm not going to give up!"

"Yes, you are," he persisted, just as quietly determined. "You will do what is best."

"I will not go away!" She defiantly threw up her head, hate blazing in her eyes.

He moved to her, firmly clasping her shoulders with both hands. "Good-bye, Jane." It was a statement, a dismissal, the ultimate put-down. He chastely kissed her burning cheek.

The blazing blue eyes closed; she swayed; the color drained, leaving the skin white and chill. Chris opened her slightly puzzled eyes.

"She is gone, Chris," the doctor confidently told her.

"Is she, Dr. Thigpen? I hope so." The tone was also puzzled.

But Jane was not gone. In seeming deliberate defiance of the doctor who had worked so hard to create her and was now striving just as manfully to destroy her, she continued to manifest herself, though weakly, for several days, as if to say,

"If I must go, I will do it when I choose, not when you demand it."

Chris later wrote to Dr. Thigpen telling him that she was entirely well. She never again, no matter how severe her problem became, approached him for help or in any way alluded to her continuing illness. He had pronounced her well; for him, she would be well. The doctor responded, happy for her recovery and instructing her to sit back and live the life of happiness she so richly deserved, never forgetting that the most important thing in her life was to make Don happy and to devote the rest of her life toward that end.

In January, Jim finished the book. The last part had been most difficult, since it had all occurred after her therapy, and there was no case material from the doctors to inform him. For the ending he had had to rely only on Chris's thoughts to guide him. A measure of Chris's impact on the book can be assessed from Dr. Cleckley's advice to Jim when Jim discussed these concerns with the doctors; Dr. Cleckley advised him to project himself into the situation and write events that "could have happened." Even periods in her life of which only she had cognizance were not to be written as she had experienced them, but as the professional writer believed they could have occurred.

The writing was over; the waiting and the hoping began—and all the news was bad. The magazines were just not interested: *McCall's* was unhappy with the publisher's early release date;

Good Housekeeping and *Saturday Evening Post* were too pressed for space; *Look* was interested, then decided against it, saying that the story had already been too widely publicized! Finally, *Life*, after turning down first serial rights, agreed to buy rights to an article and excerpts from the book for four thousand dollars, if they were allowed to publish before the book came out. Willis Wing, having not even the possibility of a better offer in view, accepted. It was arranged that Loudon Wainwright, a writer for *Life*, would interview Chris and Dr. Thigpen for the article.

Why she did it, she, afterward, never really knew. Perhaps she felt that it was her last chance to tell the truth about her illness. Or did she feel vindictive toward those who had "taken away" her story, and deliberately set out to raise questions about their accounts? Whatever the reason, she told Loudon Wainwright that she was not well and that Jane still lived. Corbett Thigpen was concerned. He wrote to Chris that Mr. Wainwright had informed him of the new information she had given him and that it was sure to sabotage her book. He stated that neither he nor Jim Poling had included the material, because a book cannot be written with a "lady or the tiger" conclusion, it had to have a resolved ending; and that knowing that she could handle the Jane affair, he had seen no need to make it public.

He warned her, under no circumstances, to talk with anyone else, not even *Life* magazine, without discussing it with him first, and that if a reporter did find her, she was to absolutely refuse to talk and to feign ignorance. He also suggested that Don attempt to find work in another section of the country and move away from LaPorte, Texas, where she had been interviewed, so that not even *Life* would be able to find her. He emphasized that he was not especially upset with what she had done; he was only concerned with her continued anonymity, which was necessary to her continued good health.

When the *Life* article was published, it devoted half of its coverage to the book and half to the new information that had been omitted. Jim was gentle, calling it simply spilled milk and hoping that the book reviewers would not pick up the discrepancies before they wrote their reviews of the book. Dr. Thigpen urged her to give her agent power of attorney to act for her, thus preventing anyone's having access to her; that way she could just take whatever royalties she could make from the book, use it for whatever happiness she could, and forget about its ever having been published. He admitted that he had always been overcautious about the possibility of exposing her to public view, but that she had absolutely nothing to gain by it except complete misery. Realizing that it might be exciting for her for a short while to have people know who she was, he assured her that the fun would be short-lived and the misery everlasting. Especially, was she not to give out any information to anybody about her sickness, for it wouldn't help anything and would only hold her up to increasing scorn.

Whether Chris's slip sabotaged the book, or whether it simply collapsed under the weight of its many handicaps, *The Final Face of Eve* was a failure as judged by public sales, never reaching ten thousand copies. Foreign sales were even more pitifully small: eighty copies sold in one country, one hundred in another. Chris's one meager triumph came when her book was published in England under her title *Strangers in My Body*. Jim was disappointed, but he characteristically shrugged and admitted that they had been aware of the gamble from the outset. Dr. Thigpen noted that her article had, indeed, scooped her book.

When Chris received her first copy of her book, it was the first time she had seen the edited material. After Dr. Thigpen had made his corrections, he had sent the copy on to Jim, so Chris had been aware of no corrections other than her own. This book was as much of a disappointment to her as had been the first book —it was, in fact, essentially the same book, bearing none of the changes or corrections that had been the impetus behind its inception. The deliberately altered events and the "could have happened" events were so distorted that, if taken out of context, even she would not have recognized them. And the ending was a lie. She put it down after the first reading and did not pick it up again for fifteen years. Neither did she view the movie in all those years. Even though it played in movie houses all around her, and later invaded her home on television, she made no effort to see it until she watched it in 1975. If the story belonged to others, she would have no part of it.

The literary critics did not rave, but for the most part they did not entirely pan, either. The story, while called marvelous and remarkable, was criticized by all as merely a sequel to the doctors' book, and all admitted that the edge had already been taken off. There were some snide remarks about sequels to come, and several reviewers delineated a host of discrepancies between the two accounts of the story. Alden Hoag of the Boston *Herald* pointed out the disparity between Chris's account and the doctors' account of when the fourth personality was born; and ironically he indicated that they differed in their description of when Jane died, a moot argument in the light of the already published fact that the irrespressible Jane was still living. They all seemed to agree that it was a fantastic story and worth reading, but not worth reading twice.

Jim went on to other assignments. He and Chris remained friends and correspondents over the years, and she asked him to be the godfather of her son, a role that he declined, candidly admitting that he was neither equipped nor inclined to fill such a religion-fraught role.

Corbett Thigpen continued his practice of psychiatry in Augusta. Public knowledge of his work now brought him invitations to lecture around the country and to present papers before learned groups. He and Chris continued to exchange letters several times a year, but never again as doctor and patient; and she occasionally visited him for a friendly chat when she happened to be in the city. He became the godfather of her son, and each Christmas he sent the boy greetings and a gift.

And Chris? She took the last advice Dr. Thigpen ever gave her as her doctor: She gave Willis Wing power of attorney and dropped out of sight as far as her true identity was concerned. The big effort to reveal herself had failed; she admitted defeat and tried no more. Oh, she was still interested, keeping every scrap of information about her story: the movie ads, Joanne Woodward's wedding announcement, Dr. Thigpen's lectures and his brief dabble into politics, every sales slip sent her by Willis Wing, every financial report made by the publisher. But what did she go on to? To fifteen more years of insufferable anxiety, intolerable depression, unbearable pain! Ten times she died, and ten times she rose to live again. Unlike the glorious Phoenix, however, which arose each time, shining and new from its ashes, her worn remains prolifically gave birth to multiple new selfs whose disharmony grated discordantly on the ears of those nearby and whose harsh vibrations repeatedly shattered asunder her sensitive soul, trying to find its enduring manifestation.

17

Bells and Turtles and
Cards and Things

"A star cascaded across the sky and collided with the earth, and the heavens were brighter for its having fallen." Chris (Blind Lady): January 1958. Thus did Jane live and die. To have been born so spectacularly, and to have struggled so valiantly to live, Jane's death was notably inconspicuous; she just, without warning, ceased to return. Chris's period of blessed solitude, however, was short-lived.

Chris and Don had traveled around the country long enough now, following construction jobs, that they began to encounter familiar faces when they pulled into new trailer parks; and when they pulled into LaPorte, Texas, they were especially happy to find their old friends Tom and Sarah Byrd. Sarah was the only real friend Chris had made of all the people she had met on her long cross-country treks, and she now desperately needed a friend. Having just undergone her surgery, she was physically weak and frail; and having just lost Jane, she had no one to "turn to" when she encountered obstacles. Sarah, a competent outdoors woman who could as easily change an automobile tire as bake a cake, had exactly the traits that complemented Chris's fearful lack of confidence and her insecurity. With Sarah to support her, she might have had a long period of peace had not the old specter of death brushed her again.

Stricken with Asian flu, she was seriously ill for several days. Sarah, who generously tended her needs and cared for her family, related to her recuperating patient one day that a small boy in the trailer court had just died with flu. Chris's reaction to this news

375

was sudden and violent: She grasped her head as blinding pain struck her temples and waves of nausea turned her weak and breathless; her head rolled back against her chair, and her eyes tiredly closed. Sarah rushed to her.

"Chris, what's the matter?" Putting her hand on the flushed, damp forehead, she urged, "Let's get you back to bed; you've just gotten up too soon."

Chris lay limply against the pillow, appearing to be almost in a faint; but when the eyes opened, they were calm and clear, showing no trace of pain or weakness. They looked curiously around the room as if they had never before gazed upon these familiar objects, a behavior that concerned Sarah far more than had the sudden attack of pain and illness. The lightning physical recovery was remarkable enough, but the mental about-face was even more startling.

"Is everything all right, Chris?" Sarah asked, watching her friend closely. "Can I get something for you?"

"Oh, no, Sarah, thank you," the voice, calm and confident, assured her. "I'll just lie here and rest awhile." The eyes gazed out, controlled, knowing, inquiring; and they, coupled with the disciplined, cool voice, made for a demeanor and an atmosphere that Sarah had never before observed in her usually shy, dependent friend. She was to see several of these eerie changes, and though never in any way alluding to their strangeness, she must have known that Chris had an unusual problem. No other explanation would account for the obvious, basic changes in her personality and behavior.

That was the Bell Lady. And she was an entirely new and different one. She was certainly not Jane. I know Jane had just left, had been gone only a few weeks; but this one was not anything like Jane—just the opposite. This one was very mature and motherly. Jane was vain and selfish; the Bell Lady was generous and civic-minded, and she was ugly. She knew she was ugly and she simply accepted it, never worrying about it. She was just . . . comfortable! She was called the Bell Lady because she collected bells. She thought the sound of bells was the most beautiful sound in the world. She was the first one who collected things, and I know why she came, too. She came because the Blind Lady could not face the thought of death! There's death again—it always seems to cause another one to come. I wonder why Jane didn't come back; she didn't fear death, she was the one always trying to commit suicide and kill the body. But she struggled so hard to live; perhaps those attempts were all empty threats, just cries for help. Jim and Corbett put in the book that Jane did die in the suicide attempt, but she didn't; they know she didn't. She died like all the others: just weakened and died. There were never any suicides. How do I know all this about them? I still can't find myself anywhere when I look back. Yet I must have been there if I can know what they did, even see them doing it. What does that mean? I don't know yet. . . .

Here began a period of peace and calm for Chris and, thus, also for her family. It was a sustained period not only devoid of hurtful conflict but also filled with meaningful activity. But, once unhappiness has paid a visit, its cloying stench is never completely cleared from the nostrils. The suffering of the mind gathers momentum as it quickens, and time does not erase the mind's ability to suffer, ever anew, each exquisite pang. Once anguished, a being becomes pensive, pondering not only the mysteries of ill fate, but those of good fortune as well; knowing full well that they are, irrevocably, opposite sides of the same coin.

As the Bell Lady, Chris reached her peak of maturity, losing her restless striving for what was beyond her grasp and magnifying the long-neglected treasures languishing at her fingertips. She developed her artistic talents through ceramics, poetry, and sketching, winning prizes and ribbons whenever she offered her creations for competition. The fact that she felt sufficiently confident to enter her work for competitive judging indicated a drastic change from the shy, insecure Blind Lady. She developed an interest in politics, national and local, became very civic-minded, and worked diligently as a Girl Scout leader. She spent long hours in musty old shops appreciating antiques that Jane would have considered junk and of which the Blind Lady would have been totally unaware.

During this period she became pregnant. It did not occur until almost a year after her surgery, and just when she was about to lose hope. Having maintained her contact with Dr. Barfield following her surgery, she immediately made plans to return to Augusta for the birth of her baby. This pregnancy was perhaps the calmest, sweetest period of her entire life: Don, who had earlier rejected the idea of having a child, now responded with tenderness and affection; Taffy was delighted at the prospect of having a baby to play with; and there were scarcely any personality changes to upset the even tenor of their lives. Ironically, while it had been the Blind Lady who had so desperately wanted to give Don a son, it was the Bell Lady who conceived, carried, and bore his child. Chris seldom attained her goals in life, and even the rare times when she did reap the fruits of her labor, the sweetness of success was marred because the personality who had striven so laboriously was not allowed to collect the reward. Each attainment became a bittersweet victory, with one part of her suffering defeat at seeing another benefit from her labors, and the other part not fully able to appreciate a prize for which she had not worked and, perhaps, that she did not even want. An intricate and, surely, unique kind of masochism.

One incident, only, marred this tranquil period. While she was waiting to turn left from a busy street, her car was struck from the rear by a careless driver. An immediate thorough examination determined that her unborn child had escaped injury but that her own back and shoulder were damaged, greatly magnifying her chances of aborting the four-month pregnancy. Above all, she could not travel; she had to change all of her plans for returning to Augusta for the birth. This was a difficult adjustment for her and caused one awkward change. She was in the doctor's office and had just been told that under no circumstances could she travel several hundred miles to give birth to her baby. Bitter disappointment engulfed her; she felt suffocated and faint, her head pounded, and the room turned black. When she opened her eyes, her amazement was utter: She was lying naked under a sheet in an examining room. As she gazed around the room trying to orient herself, she felt strange movements in her stomach, and placing a hand on her middle, she was astounded to discover its enormous size. Tentatively, she ran her hand over the tight, protruding belly, finally gathering enough courage to look down at the round bulge under the sheet. As she did so, the strange movement within her was repeated, causing the sheet to mysteriously move, as if by its own volition. Fascinated, she gently touched the tiny bump. The doctor, watching all this, was slightly perplexed.

"Are you all right, Mrs. Sizemore?" he inquired.

"It's a baby, isn't it?" she softly asked.

"It certainly is! It is very much a baby!" the doctor declared. He was perhaps accustomed to the strange behavior of women caught in the wonder of a live child's voluntary movement within their bodies. He smiled indulgently at her, unaware that he had just witnessed a woman awaken to find herself seven months pregnant and willfully pummeled from within by a child she had not conceived.

It's the Blind Lady. I can remember how she felt, how surprised she was. She loved Don so much and wanted so much to bear his child, and now she awakes to find that another woman has conceived his child and is carrying it in her body. Because it was her body, too! Did that make it her baby, also, even though she had not been in the body when it was conceived? And what about giving birth to the baby? Is the one who gives birth the mother? What happens if one conceives the child and the other gives it birth? Which one would be its mother? And what about me? I have the body now. Does that make me the mother also, even though I neither conceived nor gave birth? But a body is a body! A child could be conceived and given birth by a body that was mindless. Does that mean that it is simply the body that is the mother, not the mind? A mind is not simply a mind, as a body is simply a body. The mind is what it experiences. If it does not experience the conception and birth of the child, it is not the mother of the child. But what about the Blind Lady? She neither conceived nor bore, but she carried the moving embryo in her body, she felt it move, she fed it with her own life's blood. Was she not also the mother? . . .

The change lasted for several days. The Blind Lady, unable to even observe the activities of the Bell Lady, could experience only if she were out, and she was so fascinated by the growing child within her that she fought to remain out. She constantly felt and examined her body, laughing in childish delight when the child moved or kicked. Don seemed unaware of this change, thinking

379

only that his calm, disciplined wife was feeling a moment of uncontrolled joy in her motherhood.

A major concern, since she could not return home for her confinement to doctors who knew her history, was that the trauma of birth might cause a recurrence of her problems. She decided to tell her doctor who she was. Don went with her, and seated in the doctor's office, she began,

"Doctor, there is something we feel you should know about me: I am Eve of *The Three Faces of Eve*." She paused. The doctor looked at her with a completely expressionless face.

"Dr. Thigpen of Augusta, Georgia, wrote about me. We thought you ought to know, since sometimes unpleasant experiences precipitate changes in personality." She stopped. The doctor showed no reaction; he only continued to make notes on his paper.

Whatever Chris expected from her doctor, what she received was nothing, absolutely nothing: no comment, no expression of surprise or disbelief; no smile or friendly pat on the hand; nothing. And, fortunately for her, nothing was needed; it was a perfectly natural childbirth. On May 24, 1959, Bobby, her dark-haired, blue-eyed son, was born. There were no complications and no changes. The Bell Lady gave birth to her child as she did everything else, quietly, confidently, and without undue excitement. It was several weeks before the much-weakened Blind Lady returned, and, strangely, it was again in the doctor's office while lying on the examining table. For no apparent reason, the headache struck and the change occurred. As soon as she felt her flat stomach, she became hysterical, crying and moaning,

"My baby, my baby! Where is my baby?"

The doctor, surprised, but judging this to be only some postpartum disturbance, hurriedly brought in Taffy and the baby who had accompanied Chris. Seeing Taffy holding the tiny blue-garbed baby, she asked,

"Why am I here? Who is that baby?"

"You came to see the doctor, Mother," Taffy answered. "This is Bobby, our baby." She held the child for her mother to see.

Chris looked at the small sleeping face and grew calm. She had not lost her baby! She was, however, so embarrassed over the scene she had created that she could not bring herself to return ever again to that doctor. Bobby was cared for by a pediatrician, and she sought a different physician for herself, causing, no doubt, only relief to the doctor at the loss of such an unpredictable patient.

For two years there were no changes, the longest such period of her entire life, and the greatest contributing factor was her home: She finally got a house, her *own* home. When Don had first learned of his approaching fatherhood, he had immediately bought a larger trailer; then, shortly after Bobby's birth, finding that the construction work was good and, seemingly, plentiful for the future in the Washington, D.C., area, he decided to sell the trailer and buy a home. It was a lovely little white house, surrounded by green lawn on a settled street shaded by huge old trees in Vienna, Virginia. Far from her childish remembrances of the Strother place, it still satisfied her. It had spacious rooms, a wide yard for flowers, a fireplace, and above all it was located in a permanent community. It met her needs.

For the first time she cultivated friends and enjoyed a social life. Theirs was a heterogeneous community, peopled by both professional and blue-collar. Chris preferred the more intellectual, idea worker, while Don gravitated to the "workingman." Thus, though six years married, they discovered for the first time that they differed widely not only in their choice of friends, but also in their philosophies about life in general. Chris's new interest in things civic and political caused her to disagree with some of Don's heretofore ignored union activities, a question they were never to solve between them. It was healthy! She was no longer a confused, clinging dependent who selfishly contemplated her own needs. She was able for the first time to place herself into the proper perspective of things and to look with objective interest at the offerings of her world.

While she and Don were beginning to communicate, though not always agree, on surface matters, on the deeper, more fundamental subjects they never even touched. For two years they lived in their house, and Don knew that she was happy, but she never told him that it was the anchor of the house itself that allowed her the freedom to grow. She now had roots that nourished and sustained her, and provided the permanence she so desperately needed. Her lack of confidence demanded present security; while

Don, having no such need, planned for the future. Their house was old, it needed repairs, and taxes in Vienna were rising faster than in surrounding areas; Don felt trapped by debt and rising costs. Making plans without consulting Chris, who had never shown the least interest in business affairs, he located a cheaper house in a large new subdivision and put his own house on the market. Chris was stunned, hurt, betrayed, but strangely unable to explain what the loss of her home meant. The meaning was too deep, too basic; the need sprang from hurt too old, too severe. She grew silent, retreated from the open world back into her closed mind, and allowed Don to proceed, unknowing, along the path that was sure to destroy her.

At about this time she met Dr. Ham, a man who was to become not only her physician but her friend as well, and who would lend her his considerable strength through years of frustrated pain. Tibor Ham, a general practitioner, ironically entered her life through the Yellow Pages of the telephone book as a result, not of her own illness, but of Taffy's. A man of infinite dignity, both professional and personal, his small, impeccably groomed figure soon became for Chris a bulwark of strength and a haven of security. She did not at first tell him who she was, there was no immediate need, and when she did finally have to tell him, he replied to her in his characteristic manner,

"All right, my dear. Tell me about it."

A bond was established. From then on she could tell him anything and know that he accepted it with neither surprise nor disbelief. He protected her and encouraged her, and though from time to time he insisted that she seek psychiatric help, he never refused to extend to her whatever aid was available to him within the bounds of his medical expertise. She trusted him and could always count on him for thorough honesty.

"Dr. Ham, will I ever be absolutely well?" she once asked him.

"My dear," he solemnly replied, "I do not deal with that kind of absolute."

When she needed him, he was there. Her other stanch friend and constant support was her daughter Taffy. Always a sweet, well-behaved child, she had at fourteen become seriously dependable and conscientious. She remembered her childhood as a most pleasant time in which Acie and Zueline played a very strong part, always making her feel extra special. Ralph White never seemed like her father, and the few bad experiences with him that she could recall were rather like nightmares from which she had awakened into loving security. Never really knowing what was wrong with her mother, only that she was "sick," Chris's unusual behavior became routine for Taffy, and she learned to recognize the bizarre symptoms and to compensate for them. She watched Don for signs of his moods and attempted never to cross him. She early became aware that she could best help him by helping Chris, and that her mother's illness, unlike other sickness, did not need physical care, only constant observation. Taffy grew accustomed to having her mother apparently desperately ill today, and perfectly well tomorrow; and it did not seem strange to hear Chris refer to her own actions as if some other woman had performed them. Taffy was soon herself referring to her mother's various personalities by their distinguishing names, usually given as a result of some peculiarity they displayed: The Blind Lady had periods of blindness, the Bell Lady showed an irrational attachment for bells. Later on Taffy even named some of the personalities herself.

The relationship between them was strange, it was reversed; and neither of them seemed to question it. Taffy was obviously the stronger and more stable of the two, yet she never took advantage of her strength and position. Though gentle and respectful to her mother, she never hesitated to be firm if that quality were needed. Chris, in her turn, leaned heavily on her tiny daughter, yet never abrogated her position as mother. They developed an unusual closeness through the years, with neither seeming to recognize either the strange nature of their relationship or the rare quality of their affection.

Taffy, always a happy child, was especially contented and well adjusted in the little house in Vienna. She had many friends, was active in Scouting and sports, and was elected a cheerleader for the athletic teams. She loved Bobby very much and never felt that his coming in any way threatened her position in the family. Often visiting her loved grandparents, she was delighted when Acie and Zueline once came to live with them for an entire winter.

Only Don wanted a change, and he thought he was doing what was best for his family. He could not have realized when he sold the house in Vienna that he was shattering, perhaps forever, this fragile tranquillity into which his family had settled. They moved into a new green-and-white Cape Cod house in Manassas, Virginia, but it was not the same; it was a new subdivision: raw, treeless, transient. There was no air of security, of permanence, and Chris hated it. She hated the small, cramped rooms, the muddy Bull Run behind her house, the identicalness of the houses, the sameness of the streets; and, above all, she hated living on the wrong side of Manassas. And her confidence had been shaken; she had thought that the house in Vienna, with all of its imperfections, was hers—her home. And it had been taken away from her; she had been moved again after only two years. Regardless of the kind of house she had moved to, the shock would have been great; it was the move itself that was traumatic. Moving, to her, symbolized shiftlessness and insecurity.

Her troubles began immediately. The gradual weight gain, begun before the birth of Bobby, had ballooned during her pregnancy, and instead of losing after the birth, she had continued to gain. While she was happy, her obesity had worried her little; after all, she had borne a son, had a home, and was now contentedly growing mature and plump in the bosom of her loving family. She knew that her weight was unbecoming, but she was complacent with indulging herself. This comfortable complacency concerning her self-image was the first of her qualities of contentment to go, as her happiness evaporated into the thin air. Suddenly, she was not motherly and matronly, she was ugly.

In the midst of her growing unhappiness, her father had a cerebral hemorrhage, a stroke, and almost died. For days he lay unconscious and at the point of death, and then he began to rally. It was a long journey back, and Acie never fully completed the trip. Though his mind was clear and his thoughts as agile as ever, his right side was paralyzed and his speech slurred for the remainder of his life. After weeks in the hospital he was allowed to return home, where Zueline devoted herself entirely to his care. This constant physical and mental strain soon ruined her own health, causing her to develop angina pectoris within a few short months.

Since they had so thoroughly enjoyed their visit in Vienna, as soon as Acie was able to travel, Don brought them to Manassas, hoping that the change of scene would benefit their health. But the scene had vastly altered, and circumstances were different now. Settled in her new home, Chris had developed two driving passions: hate for her house and overprotectiveness for her son. She hovered over Bobby, making the care of him her only important task; and her constant unfavorable comparison of her house with the Vienna house made everybody miserable. Don, desperate to find something to divert her attention, had suggested that she take a job, an idea that met with instant rejection.

"The married women in my family don't work," she informed him. "You just want to make a common woman out of me."

"Chris, the women I know about work and help their husbands. If we could get some money ahead, we could buy a larger house and move away from here." He reasoned with her, but to no avail.

Finally, she told him that she would work if she had her own business. Since she knew about materials and could sew garments beautifully, they decided on a fabric shop. Borrowing six thousand dollars, they rented a shop, stocked material, and bought seven machines on which Chris could teach prospective customers to sew. Bobby was dropped off each day with a baby-sitter, and all might have gone well if this had not been such a traumatic experience. Chris had so nurtured the relationship between herself and the child that he protested any separation from her, and each morning he had to be torn screaming from her grasping arms, a heartrending experience for both mother and child.

Soon she was blaming Don for this problem.

"You're taking me away from my son by making me work," she declared. "If you had not sold my house in Vienna, this would never have happened!"

"You're always throwing that up to me!" Don struck back in anger and frustration. "Most wives try to help their husbands get ahead."

The shop, which had gotten off to a good start, began to suffer. Although she had a woman to help with the work, Chris's own irregular appearances to instruct customers caused her sales to start a steady decline. Some days she was too sick to leave the house; some days she could not force herself to leave the screaming Bobby with his sitter, and simply returned home with him. He soon developed an amazing battery of allergies that, of course, were highly manifested when he became so upset. Chris abruptly stopped eating, and her weight began to drop alarmingly. If this were not enough, Taffy's troubles began. For some reason, she did not fit into the school and community life of Manassas, and she desperately missed her friends and activities at Vienna. Chris made no effort to help her as she had always done before, and Taffy, lonely and unhappy, began a rapid weight gain that was to remain a major problem.

Into this confused scene the Virgin was born. What does a man do when he slips into bed beside his wife of almost ten years, and she turns to him a face filled with surprise, slowly changing to fright?

"Who are you?" she yelped, shocked, her blue eyes staring and dilated with terror. "What are you doing here?"

She jumped from the bed and backed against the wall. Keeping as far from his motionless figure as possible, she edged around furniture until she reached the door; and there, turning her back for the first time, she fled from the room. Don remained as her incredible actions had caught him, his head spun, his breathing was slow and shallow. Suddenly he drew a long, shuddering breath and dropped back against his pillow. How much was there going to be? How much could he stand? They were not appropriate questions; he now had two children to care for; there was no question of his enduring anything for their sakes. He had made a mistake about the house, he knew that now; but it was too late, there was no going back. He simply must carefully control the future, making decisions in the light of his reality, not in the light of a man with a normal life. He did not follow his wife. Hearing her fleeing footsteps on the stairs, he knew that she had not left the house, and that she had run to Taffy.

"There's a man in my bed!" she wildly exclaimed as she burst into Taffy's room. Her eyes stricken with fear and her body trembling uncontrollably, she sank down onto the startled girl's bed. Taffy asked no questions; she put her arms around the shaking figure and held her close.

"It's all right," she soothed. Only a lifetime of exposure to such erratic behavior could have prepared her to so unemotionally accept this impossible scene. Almost instinctively Taffy knew who the "man" was, and just as automatically she did not question

386

that her mother, truly, did not know. When the hysterical sobbing ceased, Chris asked,

"Can I sleep with you? I can't go back down there. Please, lock the door."

"Of course," the girl answered. "Now, just go to sleep, and everything will be all right."

Taffy was reassuring her mother with her own philosophy of how to deal with intolerable problems: Just go to bed and sleep, and everything will be fine. She watched as Chris fell into a troubled sleep, twisting and turning and moaning, as if even in sleep she were pursued and terrified by her waking fears. Does sleep block out the tortures of the mind as it does the tortures of the body? Or does it simply toss the demented into a chasm of confusion, where the laws of logic are unknown and chaos reigns unchecked? Taffy, observing her mother's tormented writhing, would have awakened her except for fear of the physical harm she might inflict upon herself. Thus, to protect the body from physical harm, the mind, locked in sleep, was permitted to wreak havoc upon itself.

Taffy stole from the room and went to her father.

"It's all right, Daddy," she told him. "She's asleep now."

"That's good, honey." They sat silently for a while, neither knowing how to express their thoughts. No words were adequate.

"Your mother is sick, Taffy," Don began. "She has been sick for a long time—probably all her life." He was facing facts himself that he had for years denied. "I thought she was well. The doctors said she was well. But she is still very sick."

"I know, Daddy," the child encouraged him. "Nanny told me she was sick."

How could he explain it when he didn't even understand it himself? "You know the movie you saw, *The Three Faces of Eve?* Well, that was written about your mother. And the book she wrote with Mr. Poling, that was about her, too."

"Really, Daddy?" Taffy was impressed. "She's famous."

"But nobody knows who she is. And we can't tell anybody. Nobody would understand, and people would not accept us if they knew. You must not tell anybody, not even your best friends."

Don paused; he had trouble involving this innocent daughter in these confused affairs that even adults did not understand. "I'm going to have to have help, Taffy. I can't handle this alone." It was a humble confession, born of desperate need. "Your mother needs to be watched. She sometimes takes too many pills. If she does that, call me immediately. And Bobby must be looked after and cared for."

He could not ask her to take on this unfair chore, he could only explain the problem. She understood.

"I'll do it, Daddy," she solemnly promised. "I'll help you."

And so, in the still of the night, the man and the child made a pact. They silently agreed to pick up the discarded life of a woman and to protect her from her most vicious enemy: herself.

At fourteen Taffy, with the conscientiousness that only a child can bring to a task, took over her duties as mother to her little brother, monitor to her mother, and lieutenant to her father. She thought deeply about the movie she had seen, and when viewed in the light of her mother's life, it became extremely offensive to her. Her mother had never behaved like Eve Black! Taffy rejected it totally. She read only a small part of her mother's copy of *The Final Face of Eve*, rejecting it also. That was not her mother, either. Becoming very protective of Chris, she made small effort, thereafter, to enter into the activities of her peers, explaining that her mother was sick and needed her at home. When Chris tried to explain her bizarre behavior, Taffy cut short the embarrassed attempt,

"It's all right, Mother," she reassured her. "I understand about it. Daddy explained everything."

So Chris was spared even the unpleasantness of facing the need to explain her condition to her daughter. After the advent of this new member, Taffy had three personalities to deal with: the insecure, dependent Blind Lady; the capable, overprotective Bell Lady; and the prudish, depressed newcomer, whom Taffy promptly named the Virgin, because she denied being Don's wife and refused to sleep with him. They had only one thing in common: All three were desperately unhappy and blamed Don for their miserably depressed state. The changes now came often and easily. Though always accompanied by the accustomed headache, dizziness, and nausea, no longer was anything dramatic necessary to trigger the process. Taffy became so familiar with the traits of all three that upon entering the room she could determine by several seconds of observation which one was in evidence, and she immediately adjusted her own behavior to match.

The Virgin considered herself to be in her late fifties, about twenty-five years older than the other two; and her mid-Victorian ideas caused her to dress very plainly and to wear no makeup. When she went out, she always sprayed her hair white from a can of cosmetic hairspray, which the others would immediately wash out when they emerged. When several changes occurred in one day, most of the time was spent changing clothes and redoing hair. The Virgin was totally lacking in skills, being unable to cook, keep house, or drive a car; and she rejected any family relationships, referring to Don in the third person and to Bobby as "young'un." She scolded everybody, but it was on Don that she especially heaped her anger, taking him to task at every turn.

It was into this confused scene that Acie and Zueline, both invalids, came for an extended visit. Only a year before, they had spent several months with their daughter, and it had been a pleasant time of sight-seeing, card-playing, and talking together. This time the change was immediately apparent. They, with near horror, watched their daughter rapidly switch from youth to old age, and from a shy wife to an overprotective mother to a raging shrew. As a result of all the turmoil, Zueline had an angina seizure, upsetting both herself and the paralyzed Acie to the point of tears. Chris became immediately contrite and even oversolicitous, but the damage was done; the invalided couple could not endure such extremes of emotion, and they left for home after less than two weeks, never again to return to their daughter's home.

Shortly thereafter, Chris was involved in another accident, of exactly the same sort as the one before: Her car was struck in the rear while she was waiting to make a left turn into her shop. Sustaining a severe whiplash and reinjuring her old shoulder damage, she was hospitalized by Dr. Ham for ten days. She had been seeing him periodically for several years for her problems, for which he had prescribed alleviating medication; but it was only at this point that they felt it necessary to inform him of who she was. His calm acceptance of her won her confidence and lasting trust, and though psychiatrists came and went through her life, he remained the constant stable help she came to reply on so heavily.

389

The accident plus the long period of sedated inactivity left her in a highly nervous state. They had made only two lasting friends in Manassas, Bucky and Fran Kemp; and Don, attempting to shake Chris out of her unhappy state, arranged that the four of them go to a stock car race. At a break in the racing, a demolition exhibition was performed; and as the cars began to crash into each other, Chris's composure cracked and deteriorated with every tearing scream of rending metal. Each ripping screech sent a jagged shard through her being, thudding her heart, splitting her head, and dimming her eyes. Overcome, she fell heavily off the bench and onto the feet of spectators. Her eyes immediately opened, revealing fear and rejection so intense that the look faded even as it sharpened. The lids dropped frantically, only to open again on blue orbs clouded by confusion and anxiety. As they gazed up at the faces bending forward, a thunderous crash of cars shook the stands. Abject terror darkened the wide blue eyes and a high-pitched scream of unreasoning fear tore from the constricted throat. The eyes closed, the contorted face smoothed, color flowed back into the marble cheeks. When the lids raised again, they revealed calm, mildly questioning eyes that scarcely flickered at the grating sounds of the multiple crashes.

Don helped her up, explaining to the Kemps that he had better get Chris home. They agreed, believing that she simply had not yet fully recovered from her accident. The rapidity of the changes plus the general noise and confusion of the race had masked most of the incredible happening, and possibly the Kemps were totally unaware of what they had witnessed; but fearing a recurrence of this disturbing behavior, Chris and Don completely ceased their social life.

Two of them were born at the same time. It was so fast; her face was like a kaleidoscope. There were so many it's confusing to separate them. It was the Bell Lady who went to the races and became frightened of the crashes. No! No, it couldn't have been the Bell Lady because the others could not come out through her; it had to be the Blind Lady at the race. There is always one, the pivot, in each group whom the others come out through, and it was the Blind Lady in this group. When the Blind Lady fainted, the Virgin made a brief appearance, but she did not completely come out. When she disappeared, she never came again. She must have died after that brief flash. The next one was perfectly new and she became the new pivot, because right after she screamed and disappeared, another new one came. And that one stayed and went home with Don. Why would two new ones come simultaneously? What kind of need existed to call out two? And that makes four existing at the same time. That had never happened before. It also makes two pivots there at the same time! The Blind Lady didn't last long, though. . . .

Chris was at work several days later when the telephone rang. At the time she was talking with a friend, a barber, whose shop was just up the street, and drinking a cup of coffee that he had brought to her. The call was from her cousin, a truck driver, and he was asking for her help, explaining that he had just been involved in a wreck. At the word "wreck," both the coffee and the telephone dropped from her nerveless hands and she slumped heavily to the floor. As she lay there, her throat worked and corded, and her face flushed painfully. The man bending over her fascinatedly watched the face grow still and white and the blue eyes open, calm and unperturbed.

"Hello," she greeted him, as casually as if he had just walked into the store, as if lying on the floor in that manner were not at all unusual.

Unnerved by this eerie calm under such exciting circumstances, he helped her to a chair and beat a hasty retreat, murmuring something about "waiting customers." And that was the demise of the Blind Lady. As Chris sat in the chair, her three remaining personalities revolved flashingly through her burning brain, the two new ones inexplicably absorbing memories and experiences stored in the common receptacle. One gathered some skills, bents, and tendencies; the other chose different ones. When it was over, two separate and distinct personalities lurked within the being, ready by turn to motivate the dumb, pliable flesh.

Was that the way it was always done, this kaleidoscoping and absorbing of information? Or was this the first time? I can't remember clearly about the others, the earlier ones. Some of

them just seemed to appear full-blown; others had to learn
gradually, like Jane. Perhaps they all grew as differently as the
combinations that made them up. . . .

Within days the new personalities had demonstrated their dominant traits to the point where Taffy could easily recognize them, and it was she who dubbed each with a distinguishing name. The new pivot became fascinated with turtles and began to avidly collect their images in all sizes and compositions. She would squeal with delight on encountering a turtle reproduction and declare that she just had to have it. The other personality fell in love with playing cards and began a career of acquiring decks of all kinds, colors, and dimensions—even round. Taffy named the first the Turtle Lady, and the second, the Card Girl. A collector is striving to organize, to put things in order. Poor Chris; was this thread, which ran so true throughout the fabric of all her personalities, an attempt to organize her own scattered selves?

At this very bleak period in her life, Chris and Elen's paths cross briefly. The cousins had seen each other only for minutes, several times in ten years, and their knowledge of each other had been by way of sketchy information passed on by relatives. Chris wrote, perhaps annually, but, of course, her letters revealed only trivia, nothing of her deep, torturous problems. Elen, a miserable correspondent, wrote scarcely at all.

They met at the open casket of Elen's father. At seventy, Ellis had been retired for ten years. He was in excellent health and had just bought a house in Edgefield so that he and Mamie Lee could more easily spend considerable time near Acie and Zueline. The four of them loved to sit and recall times past, reliving and laughing over their many years together. Driving cross-country in March 1963, Ellis and Mamie Lee were involved in an automobile accident that critically injured them both.

Elen, hurrying down from Chicago to watch over her parents in the tiny Macon County Hospital in Alabama, cared for them for ten days before Ellis died. Then she took them home to Greenwood, her mother in an ambulance to the hospital, and her father in a hearse to Blyth's Funeral Home. Mamie Lee, hospitalized for nine weeks with multiple injuries, underwent surgery the very day of the funeral; Laura, though married and the mother of a small

392

daughter, still seemed much of a child herself, and she moved about in a state of near shock over the death of her father. Elen was alone. Her father, whom she loved more than life itself, was gone; there was no place where she could go to find him, he was irrevocably gone. She did not weep; there were no tears. When grief can weep, it moves off a distance, becomes a companion, is soft and gentle and pliable; but when grief has no tears, it remains hard and cold and numb within the soul—a marble statue, crowding the vitals and suffusing the being with a constant dull ache.

Suddenly there was Chris. She said nothing; she simply pressed Elen's hand, and Elen was no longer alone. The clan gathered, and for the most part it was Ellis's in-law clan—the Hastings family. He had lived among them for more than forty years, and they showed their love and acceptance by bestowing on him their highest honor: an eternal resting place among their own precious dead. He was placed amid military honors in the same plot with Papa and Mama, who had died peacefully only a short three months earlier. Tears coursing down cheeks for Ellis that day were generously intermingled with those for Mama, whose so recent death still left raw, painful grief. Elen knew that Chris's tears were not only for her and her loss, but also for her own loss. He had been her "Unc," and they had loved each other even before Elen was born. And he had loved Chris all her life, lending her his help and support at her times of dire need. Who had a better right to ride in the first car with his daughters as they followed their father to his grave? Elen asked her cousin to ride with her, and the Family clucked in disapproval. As usual, it was Chris who got the blame instead of Elen. It was talked about for days that "Christine should have known better than to ride in the first car!"

The death of Mama started a march of death that was to wipe out seven members of the Family in four years before it halted. Myrtle, gentle, compassionate, and uncomplaining, died shortly after, after ten years of suffering; and within another year, Zueline, wracked and wearied by her painfully constricted heart, died, leaving her Acie paralyzed and helpless. Chris was totally incapable of accepting her mother's death, coming as it did during one of her weakest periods and immediately following a most debilitating experience.

Don, most concerned over Chris's state of health and her increasing inability to deal with routine living, either at home or in her shop, began to worry that she might again become pregnant. Though he loved Bobby dearly, he firmly believed that his mother's worry and concern over him was unhealthy for both Chris and the boy, and he refused to even consider her having another baby. Stubbornly refusing, for the sake of his own sanity, to learn the personalities and to deal with them individually, he was left to attempt to discuss important matters with a wife who seemed to express a different opinion on the same issue each time it came up. On the matter of contraception, she at one time argued for having a child; the next time she declared that she definitely should not become pregnant; and a third time she was totally indifferent, desiring only what Don desired. Finally seeking medical help, she was fitted for a diaphragm. Don was relieved, but he did not trust Chris; time had taught him lasting lessons regarding her capriciousness. Each time he approached her for lovemaking, he questioned her closely.

"Do you have your diaphragm in?" he cautiously asked.

"Yes, of course, Don," she answered.

"Are you sure?" he pressed, watching her closely for strange behavior.

"I'm sure!" she answered crossly.

"Are you sure everything is all right?" His concern would not be allayed.

"Of course I'm sure, Don!" Gathering anger stained her voice. "Don't you trust me?"

He could go no farther. To continue would spoil the lovemaking, the very act that the diaphragm was intended to enhance. Even this small encounter had brought to the experience a tenseness that made it less than completely satisfying. And shortly, Don's suspicions were proved well-grounded. Both of the new personalities were fragile, webby constructs, containing weaknesses fatal to their growth and development. Existing in a make-believe world, the Turtle Lady fantasized people and events, preferring the world of her mind to the world of reality. Taffy often observed her posturing and murmuring endearingly before a wall, while caressing and bestowing impassioned kisses on its smooth, blank surface, no more featureless, however, than her own unformed façade. Extremely interested in sex, and preferring lonely

394

masturbation to the exhilarating exchange with a partner, she often erotically lifted herself to the dizzying heights of orgasm, after which she would disappear, leaving the Card Girl, who could observe her every act, to endure the empty depression often engendered by the guilt of masturbation. Totally fatalistic, her death wish manifested itself daily in her accident-prone behavior and her constant writing of wills, long before she attempted suicide.

The Card Girl was a thief, shoplifting cheap, inconsequential items that struck her fancy. Very hardworking and dutiful, she lived in deep, debilitating depression, believing strongly in fortune-telling and living daily by astrological charts.

And this was Don's wife: a fantasizing suicide alternating with a thief controlled by her superstitions. The tension created by this duo was only occasionally relieved by the appearance of the comfortably normal Bell Lady.

It was the Turtle Lady who put in the diaphragm, and it was the Card Girl who came out and mischievously removed it. The Turtle Lady, unable to observe the actions of the Card Girl, was unaware of the trick that had been played until her interrupted menstrual cycle heralded her pregnancy. Don was understandably furious.

"You lied to me, Chris!" he thundered. "You told me each time that you had the diaphragm in."

"I did, Don!" the innocent Turtle Lady protested. "I had it in every time. Something just must have gotten by."

"That's not true. Dr. Ham told you it would work if you wore it," he countered. "You just deceived me. Why do you do things like that?"

"Why are you accusing me? I did use it." Hurt and confused, she began to weep.

"Well, we don't need another baby. And we can't afford one either." Just as hurt and confused as she, he was unable to comfort her. His wife had deceived him; how she did it was of small consequence now.

"I won't have the baby, then. I'll get rid of it!" she struck back.

Shock cleared Don's head; he could not believe his ears. "No, no, Chris, we can't do that. It's all right, we'll manage somehow." Whether a baby was planned or not, if one were conceived, it was a member of the family already and would be loved and cherished. But Chris was adamant; she had been accused of trickery and she would disprove the charge by personally erasing the result.

When Don and Taffy left the next morning, she searched the house for something lethal with which to kill herself. Finding a bottle of turpentine, she drank it and blacked out, but she did not fall. Her senses cleared, and her eyes opened on the empty bottle. Connecting it with the burning discomfort in her chest, she gradually lowered her lids over quickly glazing eyes. When the eyes opened again, she surveyed the scene, looked carefully at the empty bottle, and grew dark with anger and fright. Hurrying to the kitchen, she made a strong mixture of salt and water and drank it down. In a moment she was retching violently, and the smell of turpentine filled the air. Her head ached violently, and her stomach cramped and knotted in its violent effort to disgorge itself. She closed her eyes and slumped quietly to the floor. In a moment the eyes opened again and she knew immediately what had occurred, that she had been forced to vomit her deadly drink. She was weak and trembling, but that was fine; perhaps the violence done to her body would discharge the fetus as well.

That was the Turtle Lady who drank the turpentine, and the Bell Lady came out only long enough to see what was happening. She couldn't deal with it, she left; and she never returned. She never came back again. She had been growing weak ever since the other two came out. She couldn't deal with their shocking behavior, the stealing and the perversion, and now suicide. Their bad qualities actually killed her off. Then the Card Girl came out long enough to save the body and then left, forcing the Turtle Lady to suffer the physical results of her actions. It's all so confusing, like a madhouse. These two are crazy, really crazy! What did I need them for? I couldn't have been doing this myself. Nobody would deliberately turn herself into such obnoxious, despicable creatures. And these are only the first of the disgusting ones. . . .

In desperation she sought help from Dr. Thigpen, who after hearing her request suggested that she come to Augusta to discuss the whole matter with him. He admitted her overnight to his psychiatric clinic in the new Cleckley Building, and sent Dr. Barfield to see her the following morning.

"I can understand your wish, Chris," the gynecologist informed her, "and Dr. Thigpen approves, but I cannot do it. We worked too hard to make you fertile. I'm afraid the time will come when you will regret this, and I don't want you to blame me. When something like this comes up, you're emotional and not always aware of what you're doing; but I *do* know what you're doing."

"What can I do, then, Dr. Barfield?" she asked, near tears.

"I do know someone who, I think, might help you," he promised her. "Dr. Robert Greenblatt is in practice with me. I have spoken to him. You need to talk with him."

Dr. Greenblatt performed the uneventful surgery, which included a partial hysterectomy, and after several days, Don came to take her home. It was a silent trip; in fact, it was almost six weeks before he talked to her about anything other than absolute necessities. How did they feel about aborting their child? It is psychologically different from simply deciding not to conceive a child, for after its conception, even at the moment of its conception, its traits and characteristics are fully set. The decision not to join the sperm with the ovum is somehow intricately different from deciding to terminate the result once joined. It was these thoughts and the sight of Bobby, the child they had once made together, that interrupted their normal ability to face each other squarely.

Death could not have chosen a less opportune time than when it again visited Chris. She received a call from her sisters that her mother was scheduled to undergo a gall bladder operation. For more than a year, Zueline had periodically been hospitalized for her heart condition, and Chris, though knowing that her mother's condition had gradually deteriorated, was not unduly alarmed. Zueline weathered the surgery, and for a week continued to regain her strength and good spirits. After talking with the doctor, Chris, assured that her mother was out of danger, returned home. Two days later, Zueline died.

Chris returned to a heartbreaking scene. There sat Acie in his shining metal wheelchair, frail and wan; his dark skin, bleached out by the long illness and confinement indoors, showed its blue network of veins. His look of fragility was magnified by the sad blue eyes, looking strange and alien without their usual merry

397

twinkle. Zueline, active, tireless, laughing, was gone, and she was only fifty-eight! Mamie Lee lost control for the first time in her life. She had lost mother, father, husband, sisters, brother; but this was Sister. There had been scarcely more than a year's difference in their ages, and they had shared their entire lives together. Growing up together and dating together, they had married into the same family and reared their children together, twice even living in the same house. She could not bear this loss stoically; she broke down completely and had to be sedated.

Chris found strength where seemingly there was none to be found; and for the sake of her father and her Aunt Meme, she was calm, too calm. Acie himself selected his wife's last garments, and he dressed her all in blue. Zueline, somehow, still looked like the child she had been all her life, with her uncut hair, which had long since gone salt and pepper, wound into a fat knot atop her youthful face, a face that in death appeared no more pale and lifeless than that of her husband of nearly forty years, who sat beside her casket in his wheelchair, unable to even look on her still face without help.

That night, her first night dead, Acie wanted to go home, back to the house he had shared with her. It was past midnight when Chris, followed by Mamie Lee and Laura, brought him back to his empty house. Helpless even to disrobe himself, the three women got him into the big bed, where his thin, emaciated frame scarcely rippled the covers.

Looking down at him, perceiving his thoughts, Mamie Lee's ravaged heart broke.

"Acie, do you want me to lie down beside you, so that your bed won't be so empty?" Her low voice was choked with emotion, for Acie and for herself; her own bed hadn't been empty long. She knew what he was feeling.

"No," Acie answered her. "I'll be alone from now on. I'll have to start getting used to it." Their eyes met; only they knew what had been shared and what had been lost.

Dr. Dunovant, passing the house on his way from a late-night call, saw the lights and stopped.

"I saw your lights," he said, "and stopped to see if I can help. I heard about your trouble."

They asked that he look in on Acie to determine his condition.

The doctor had been caring for both Acie and Zueline during their long illnesses, only turning them over to specialists for serious complications. He cared for his old friend on this night, and he continued to watch over Acie for the remaining ten years of his life, establishing a friendship bond between the two aging men that went far beyond doctor and patient.

The eyes of the gathered clan were perhaps wetter than usual as the wan, bent Acie in his wheelchair followed his Zueline to her final resting place. Mamie Lee remained by his side, holding his hand; and their sharing seemed to render their own grief more bearable. But the family, seeing these two together and remembering how close the two couples had been, grieved doubly for both their lost mates.

Chris watched all this, and her anxiety and tension built to an insupportable load. She did not break, however, until she took her father back to the cemetery the following day. As she stood there looking down at her mother's grave, knowing that she lay there under all that earth, looking exactly as they had seen her yesterday, but also knowing that she would never see her again, Chris felt the cool, green spring day shimmer as if in deep summer heat. The familiar headstones turned crazily, the tall, straight pines dizzily upended, and her head thundered and buzzed. She heard her father say,

"I guess I'll have to go to the nursing home now."

It was too much. Holding onto her father's chair, she felt cold, thick darkness engulf her, but she did not fall. Suddenly the bright yellow sun was back, and the dizzy world had set itself aright again. She felt young and gay and lighthearted. It was spring; nothing could be really wrong in spring!

"Oh, no, Dad," she answered him cheerfully. "You can live with one of us girls. I'll take you home with me."

Acie looked at his daughter, at her happy, smiling visage on which no trace of grief showed, at her matronly figure and face out of which a childishly immature voice rippled, and his own face registered a deeper resignation to the whims of life. Why had they so whimsically claimed his agile, happy wife, so tortuously twisted the mind of his lovely young daughter, and left his own mind clear and unscathed in a twisted, useless body?

"No, Daughter," he quietly responded to her offer. "I must stay here close to Mother."

Shortly Chris appeared to be herself again, but enough of the anxiety had been drained off by this interchange that she was no longer unbearably immersed in black depression. For a short moment she had rolled back time, had regressed to a happier, less complicated age when Mother was to be found simply by seeking her.

That was the Banana Split Girl, and now I know why she had to come. She brought back childhood simply because the others could no longer tolerate the problems of mature people. They could not bear the finality of death, so she went back to childhood, before the death occurred. What must Daddy have thought, seeing her behave that childishly when he needed mature support to lean on? She was no help to him at all; she only saddened him. Or was it me behaving like an irresponsible child? Did Daddy think that it was me? Was it me? Oh, no! Surely I would not have done that to my father, to my mother, to myself! But I know all about it, all about what they all did; and I even know why they did it. Would I know all that if it hadn't been me? . . .

Chris returned home completely incapable of running her business. She sat for hours in deep study, oblivious of her surroundings, unresponsive to her family; and she moved in and out of personalities so quickly that her conversations, often with strangers or tradespeople, took startling turns, switching ideas in midsentence. When Don or Taffy attempted to correct her mixed impressions, she became violently angry. Soon Chris was not able to deal competently with other people, in business or social encounters.

Don sold the business, paying off whatever debts he could, assuming the rest on a term basis. At about that time, the house was condemned for his veterans' mortgage loan because the property did not meet flood control standards; and seeing his opportunity to eliminate another irritant to Chris, he sold their home and rented an apartment in Fairfax. If it were possible, she was even more unhappy in the apartment than she had been in the house; Bobby's allergies had worsened to a frightening point, and he was so miserable in school that he had to be withdrawn and placed in a private school; and Taffy, also unhappy in school, continued to compensate by overeating, masking her tiny five-foot frame in pounds of excess weight.

Their world was falling apart. In quick succession they were involved in two automobile accidents. In the first, Chris, alone, was struck by a speeding taxi, which totally wrecked the car and put her in the hospital for several days. She was so nervous and distraught that Dr. Ham insisted that she be seen by a psychiatrist, who sedated her for days to force rest and quiet on her hyperactivity. Within two months, just before Christmas, a second accident befell the entire family, in which Don suffered a broken back, Chris and Taffy received multiple cuts and bruises, and only Bobby, through Taffy's quick action, escaped harm. Chris and Don were both hospitalized for several weeks, leaving Taffy to care for Bobby, get both herself and the child ready for school each day, and shop for Christmas presents. Her parents came home from the hospital on Christmas Eve to find the tree trimmed, the house stocked with holiday food, and Santa Claus ready to make his visit to six-year-old Bobby.

The next four years settled into an incredible routine, with the four of them living together in the small, cramped apartment, yet each following his own miserable path. Bobby, beset with myriad allergies, was unable to participate in boyish activities or even to play outside except in the best of weather. Don's concern over his son's health was frustrated into anger over Chris's smothering protection of the child, which he felt was a contributing factor to the boy's condition. Teen-age Taffy passed resoundingly into her rebellious stage. Strangely, however, this expected juvenile cantankerousness was aimed at her father, with whom she had a normal relationship, and did not affect in the least the abnormal, reversed role that she played with her mother. It was as if she played out to the finish the child role with her father, but on another plane, entirely, she continued her performance as the mature guardian of her emotionally juvenile mother.

Chris, at Don's urging, applied for a job as manager in a dress shop, the first of many such positions she undertook over the next few years. They desperately needed the extra money to help pay off debts from the dissolved business, and Chris excelled at the work. She worked diligently and proved very successful in her work before personality changes created awkward behavior that forced her to resign. Not really wanting to work, even feeling that a woman's place was in the home caring for her children and her husband, but having no "home" to be in, her frustration was extreme. Success in business simply proved her failure as a woman. Unable to perform at less than her best, her efforts were rewarded with a success that she could not tolerate. Therefore, when praise and promotion proved her business ability, she changed, shook off that odious businesswoman, and became a helpless, frivolous female who "simply had no head for business."

Don often built plans around Chris's ability to excel at her work and to earn substantial salaries. He once decided, when everything seemed to be going well, to buy a new car to replace their ancient, worn vehicle. He discussed it with Chris, and she urged him to proceed, declaring that her job was secure. Don bought the new car; but within two weeks, Chris collapsed at work and refused to return, leaving Don with not only new-car payments and new medical bills for Chris, but also the loss of her salary. How could he be expected to understand such behavior? She did not look sick, she had no broken bones, she was not feverish or weak. Why could she not work as other women did? This was not a kind of sick that he could sympathize with; it more resembled unwillingness than inability. He felt betrayed.

On these occasions, after quitting a job with no warning, she would be ill for weeks, completely out of touch with reality and needing constant medical care. Dr. Ham usually sedated her at home, but he occasionally hospitalized her for a few days. Twice her condition became so severe that he insisted she see a psychiatrist, even threatening to dismiss her as a patient unless she followed his advice. The first of these psychiatric consultations was a miserable failure. She seemed absolutely incapable of again completely entrusting her mind and her emotions to anyone.

In December 1968, Taffy married James Thomas Fecteau, but she did not desert her mother. Always living close by, Taffy spent many of her days with her mother, doing her own work at night. Tommy, a mild, quiet man, was completely understanding, and never once complained when Don called for Taffy to come to stay with her mother. And it was quite often most unpleasant. Chris's temper on occasion became violent. In one heated argument when Taffy and Tommy were visiting, Chris threw a boiled egg at Don, narrowly missing Taffy, who was seven months pregnant. Don, infuriated by this shocking behavior, slapped Chris, who fell stunned to the floor. The ensuing scene took on madcap proportions. Eight-year-old Bobby knelt beside his stricken mother and vowed that he would take her away and sell papers to support her; Don, appalled at his own frustrated behavior, swore silently; and Tommy worriedly comforted the weeping Taffy.

The only calm person on the scene was Chris. Opening her eyes and finding herself lying on the floor amid this bedlam, she was completely disoriented and simply lay still, attempting to determine where she was. No one seemed to notice that all her anger and hysteria were gone and that a sad, passive woman lay on the floor.

It's the Purple Lady. She came so quietly that no one knew she was there, and she remained silent for a long time, just watching the others and absorbing information from them. Not even the other personalities knew she was there. Then how did I know? . . .

Even after her son, Jimmy, was born, Taffy bundled up her baby, left her own home, and spent the day carefully watching her mother to protect her from harm. She never knew what she would find each day when she arrived. The deeply depressed Card Lady slept most of the time, falling into such deep slumber that she neither ate nor drank. The frivolous Turtle Lady kept mostly to herself, fantasizing with her imaginary lovers or writing numerous wills. Taffy had to watch her closely to abort her many intricately planned suicide attempts. If the Banana Split Girl happened to come out, Taffy simply had two children to watch. Irresponsible and self-centered, she was a willful, spoiled child who vied with Jimmy for Taffy's attention. She ate only banana splits, often consuming several at one sitting. She crammed the gooey concoction into her mouth with both hands, smearing it all over her face. As she ate, she crowed with delight, laughing and squealing as might an ill-mannered child of five.

"Ooooh, that's good!" she giggled, awkwardly and messily smearing her face with her napkin. "I want another one!"

If Taffy protested, this naughty child in a middle-aged woman's body grew angry and had a temper tantrum. What could Taffy do? She could spank Jimmy if he so behaved, but she could neither reason with nor spank a grown woman—her own mother! Often this scene was played out in public, where Taffy could only sit in embarrassed silence until this obstreperous Chris satiated herself and retreated, leaving Taffy to deal with another Chris, who suddenly found herself nauseated by the excess of sickening sweetness in her stomach and had to be rushed someplace to vomit.

Once Taffy and Chris drove to Edgefield to visit Tiny and Becky. While stopping at a filling station for gas, Chris suddenly began to laugh gaily and delightedly. Taffy, who had never learned to drive, was shocked to hear her mother say,

"I can't drive."

Taffy looked at her in amazement. Chris giggled, put her hands experimentally on the wheel, wiggled comfortably in the seat, and said,

"You just tell me what to do."

And Taffy, who had never driven a car, instructed Chris, who had been driving ten years, in how to start, steer, and control the vehicle. Even though she knew that the knowledge of how to drive a car was locked in her mother's head, she did not know if this giggling caricature of her mother would be able to use it. When they arrived at Tiny's, the badly frightened Taffy declared that she would not risk her child's life by returning with Chris. Tiny, unaware of her sister's desperate condition, scolded Taffy for her attitude; and a confused quarrel followed, ending with a call to Don and Tommy in Virginia. While on the telephone to Don, Chris, before Tiny's stunned gaze, changed from a docile, loving woman to a raging shrew. Realizing her sister's condition, Tiny tried to persuade her to see Dr. Thigpen, but she adamantly refused.

It was a terrible trip for Taffy. Whenever they stopped someplace Chris stole small, inexpensive articles; once it was an antique perfume bottle, another time it was a paper bookmarker. They stopped by Mamie Lee's house on the way home, and Taffy was miserably afraid that this very proper aunt would notice something wrong with her mother. Since two of Chris's personalities could not drive the car, and the other one was accident-prone and suicidal, Taffy, nervously upset, never again went on such a trip alone with her mother.

Shortly after this trip, Chris secretly hoarded her carefully doled out sleeping pills until she had collected a lethal dose, and only Taffy's constant vigilance prevented her scheme from working. Surreptitiously, she followed her mother into the bathroom and surprised her preparing to swallow the pills, some of which were already in her mouth. Horrified, she knocked the pills from Chris's hand and then slapped her face smartly to force her to spit out the rest. Trying to black out, Chris closed her eyes and leaned against the wall, waiting. Nothing happened. She opened her eyes, terrified; then quickly closed them again, and waited. Nothing. She began to weep hysterically.

"What have I done? What have I done?" Her body shook uncontrollably.

Taffy took her in her arms and held her close. "It's all right, Mother. It's all right," she soothed, just as she soothed Jimmy when he hurt himself.

That was the Turtle Lady who took the pills. When Taffy found her she tried to leave and make the others come out. But there was no one. The others were gone. Where did they go? They never came back again. I don't know when they died, or when was the last time they came out. I just know that the Turtle Lady tried to get them, and they were gone. The Purple Lady is there, but she never comes out, and the Turtle Lady doesn't know about her yet. There were some who did that when I was young—just disappeared. I thought, perhaps, I just didn't remember what happened way back then. But I remember this all clearly. They just suddenly were not there. I remember how lonely the Turtle Lady felt, just as I feel now, so lonely. . . .

Dr. Ham hospitalized Chris for a few days to allow her to recover, but before she was fully on her feet again, two events occurred that proved to be too much for her to handle in her weakened condition: Don underwent serious emergency hernia surgery; and Mrs. Sizemore, Don's mother, died. Chris for the first time was faced with a weak, helpless Don instead of the strong, independent man she had always taken for granted. His lack of strength and need to depend on her in the face of another death frightened away what measure of maturity she had attained, and produced another child, a selfish, irresponsible child who totally rejected Don.

It happened in the church during the funeral. Seated beside the pale, weak Don, she felt herself retreating, slipping away. The minister's voice grew distant, faint; the air was suddenly suffocating and dense; she closed her eyes and settled deeper in her seat. The eyes opened slowly, almost surreptitiously, and the slumped body straightened, vibrant and strong, and the head raised slowly. Her eyes fell first on the flowers; she had never seen flowers before, and she was absolutely fascinated by the red and white and pink carnations. She stared at them, unable to tear her gaze away from their colorful blossoms; and when Don rose and took her arm, she smiled at him gaily, happily. Even at the graveside, she stared at the flowers, smiling mysteriously to herself.

That night, the family ate at a restaurant, and Chris, completely ignorant of a menu, asked Don to order for her. As she was eating her fish, a waiter passed with an order of strawberry pie on his tray. Chris, spying the red strawberries and white cream, pointed and exclaimed,

"That's what I want! I want that to eat! It looks like flowers."

Don, embarrassed, spoke quietly to her, "That's dessert, Chris. We'll have some later."

"Then I'll wait," she joyously announced, and pushed back her mundane fish to await the glamorous pie.

When it arrived, she clasped her hands like a small child and cooed over the luscious concoction, picking it apart with her fork and experimentally tasting each morsel with zest and rejoicing.

On the trip home, Chris exasperated everybody, even Bobby, by constantly searching for places to eat strawberries, whether fresh, in ice cream, or in pie. She ate nothing else.

The Strawberry Girl. Another death, another personality. The pattern becomes increasingly clearer. When the pressure be-

comes strong on her to behave like an adult and to accept adult responsibilities, she becomes a child. She becomes a child. A child does not come. No one really comes, do they? I only thought others came. She just becomes what she needs to be to face life. She cannot adjust herself to each new situation; she must make herself over into an entirely new self, which in turn cannot adjust either. Each one can only tolerate the situation for which she was created. None of them is a whole person. They are only parts; as the arm is only a part of the body, they were only part of her. But were they parts of her or me? Not yet; I won't think of that yet. . . .

Chris's life became a living hell. It was as if all the demons of bedlam had been loosed within her. The two selves battling within her were truly Jekyll and Hyde. As the Purple Lady she was fifty-eight years old, her mother's age at death; and she was obsessed with all things purple, Mamie Lee's favorite color. She not only felt herself to be a misfit among people, but her body also felt strange and misshapen, with elongated extremities dangling awkwardly from a round, bloated body. Painfully modest, she was humiliated and frightened by her counterpart, the twenty-six-year-old Strawberry Girl, who talked to her and taunted her from inside her head. She would attempt to placate her tormentor by buying her anything strawberry that she desired, but to no avail. The maliciously mischievous voice laughed at her purple clothes, her white wig, and her misshapen body. The Purple Lady, never feeling clean, continually bathed her body; and the Strawberry Girl waited until she was in the tub before she began to taunt her,

"I see your pussycat," she teased, laughing vulgarly.

The poor modest Purple Lady tried to cover her naked body with the washcloth.

"It'll take more'n that little ole washcloth to cover that big fat body," she sneered. "Look how your flabby ole tits hang. You look funny with white hair and that black pussycat. Where'd you get that black pussycat?"

The Strawberry Girl did not seem to realize that the same body that housed her victim was also her own body. She rejected the size and weight of their common body, considering herself, even

407

when she inhabited the overweight body, to be as tall and slender as a wood nymph. She wore only loose-flowing clothes to enhance this illusion.

The shocked Purple Lady began to cry. "Please, leave me alone," she begged.

"You're a funny ole bitch," laughed her tormentor.

Nervous and upset, Chris went to see Dr. Ham, but she was unable to tell him the full story, only that she became very upset when she took a bath. He gave her some pills, instructing her to take them shortly before her bath, to relax her. As she was preparing to take the pill before her bath, the voice warned,

"If you take that medicine you'll go blind."

Chris, ignoring the voice, swallowed the pill, and immediately, to her horror, she was totally blind. The voice laughed.

"I told you! I can do anything to you I want to. That ole doctor can't stop me!"

Chris's misery was unrelieved. She was so afraid of the voice and what it could do to her that she never resisted when it wanted to come out of her head and take over her body, even though she was unable to see what was happening and was sure to take the blame for any mischief done in her absence. At this point, Dr. Ham insisted again that she see a psychiatrist, and over her strong protest, he sent her to Dr. Tony Tsitos. Prepared to be uncooperative and resistant, she was won over by his open, friendly air and his first statement.

"I know all about your problem, my dear; Dr. Ham has told me. We are going to talk about it."

And talk about it they did. At first she saw him twice a week, with all three personalities attending the sessions; and strangely, all three liked him and each thought that he was working to make her the surviving one. A glimmer of light entered her dark life when Chris found this doctor; here was help and hope. Almost simultaneously, another ray shot through the blackness engulfing her. Elen contacted her, requesting permission to relate their life experiences together to a public group; and not realizing that Chris had kept her identity secret all those years, she was expecting to use Chris's real name. It was an opportunity to emerge from hiding! Her hand also rested on a third light in the dark tunnel, if only she had courage to turn it on. Her only close friend,

Harriet Henderson, had introduced her to painting and was now trying to persuade her to begin art lessons.

The way was open. Professional medical help was at hand, an opportunity awaited to live openly and normally, and a medium in which to express her soul was ready for her hand. Could a woman who had for almost half a century run from life do a complete turn and face it squarely? Her soul quaked at the very thought, but her last shred of logical reasoning posed the question "What is my alternative?" The answer was unmistakable: insanity!

IV

THE INTEGRATION
(1973–76)

18

The Face of Eve

"*I look up from the bottom of the darkest pit and I don't see a single hand extending over the edge.*" Shortly after Chris wrote these despairing words in her diary, Elen telephoned her with a request that was to change the entire course of Chris's life. Elen, working on her doctorate at Duke University, was calling to ask Chris's permission to discuss their mutual childhood experiences in one of her psychology classes, and to tell her that she had just mailed to her a manuscript of the proposed remarks. Though not revealing her feelings to Elen, Chris was deeply distressed. Obviously, her cousin was not aware that she had been living in hiding for the past twenty years; that Don's family, who lived quite near the Duke area, did not know who she was; and that even fourteen-year-old Bobby, her own son, was not aware of his mother's identity.

When the manuscript arrived, she read it; and her heart swelled to bursting. She recognized herself in what Elen had written: That's what she was really like—alive, human, a person, not a specimen. For the first time Chris felt like somebody to be proud of, not somebody to be ashamed of, somebody to be kept hidden; and she wanted people to know her like this. But the patterns were too deep and too old to be precipitously broken; she took the manuscript and Elen's request to Dr. Tsitos. He was delighted with this turn of events, especially her voiced desire to come out of hiding, and encouraged her to make this small and protected break with her past. Elen was amazed to learn of these events, never having once, over the years, suspected that Chris was hiding her identity. Elen had, in fact, always freely discussed her famous cousin, using her real name and even telling where she lived, never realizing that she was revealing a carefully guarded secret.

Her psychology professor, Dr. W. Scott Gehman, Jr., had been intrigued when she had told him, as a result of Chris's famous case being documented in her textbook, that she and Chris had grown up together. She had even talked generously about her cousin in class. When Dr. Gehman asked her to prepare a tape of her childhood experiences with Chris, she readily agreed. After all, everybody else had talked about Chris. What could she say that was different. When he asked her to obtain Chris's permission, Elen had no idea that it would be this small effort on her part that would set an irreversible chain of events into motion.

And when the secret was finally revealed no bells rang, no thunder roared, no one stared at her with apprehension and disgust. Chris read and reread the manuscript. That was what she really was; down inside that described her. Then why was she never able to be that woman, to feel that person? Deep depression engulfed her, and her behavior became so bizarre and erratic that she could not be left alone. Don leaned once again on his daughter, and Taffy, bringing her small son, left home each morning around six, often not returning to it before midnight. When she did return home, she was so disturbed and exhausted that restful sleep was impossible. Tommy, in his quiet, positive way, calmed her, telling her that she did not have to go back; but she did, and they both knew that Chris could not be left to her own self-destruction. Tommy did not object, feeling that when he married Taffy he also assumed her responsibilities; and Taffy had been carefully taught by Zueline that one cares for family at whatever the needed sacrifice.

The days were nightmarish. From the moment Taffy opened her mother's door, throughout the interminably long day, she was not able to rest or to relax her vigil for even a moment. Chris kept her constantly busy cleaning, rearranging, cooking; and if that were not exhausting enough, she had to be eternally vigilant for her mother's suicide attempts. Taffy hid all the knives, razor blades, household solutions, and medicines, doling out the carefully counted pills when necessary. Chris's death wish alternated disconcertingly with capriciously immature and irresponsible behavior, and though both severely taxed Taffy's coping ability, it was the live-or-die struggle within her mother that broke Taffy's compassionate heart.

"I want to die. Let me die," begged the suicidal Turtle Lady, as Taffy caught her searching for the hidden pills.

"Mother, you can't feel that way," the girl pled. "You must live on."

Chris turned on her furiously. "You're her friend, you're not my friend!"

"You're my mother. I love you whoever you are," Taffy sensibly reasoned.

"How can you help me? You're helping her!" Chris accused.

"When I help her, I *am* helping you," the girl tried to soothe the distraught woman.

Usually, after such an episode, Taffy immediately found herself facing the sad, cringing Purple Lady, resigned but terrified of dying.

"I'm dying, I know I am, but I don't want to die," she moaned.

"No, Mother, you're not dying," assured the girl, mentally shifting positions in this incredible debate.

"But she is going to kill me, she's pushing me out. I feel myself growing weaker, dying," Chris professed in despair.

"You'll live on, Mother," Taffy explained. "Part of you will live on, live out your whole life."

"But I won't be able to get out!" Panic roughened the voice.

"There won't be any need to get out, Mother," Taffy soothed. "When you're well, you won't need to get out."

And all this alternated in resounding jerks with the selfish, malicious, juvenile behavior of the Strawberry Girl. Turtle, Purple, Strawberry! Poor Taffy; with all this madhouse, round robin of coming and going, she had to give them names to separate them in her own mind, to be able to deal with them. She was the only one, besides Chris herself, and Dr. Thigpen with Chris White, Chris Black, and Jane, who ever recognized them as beings and addressed them by name. Dr. Ham always treated her as one person no matter who came to see him and no matter how many changes occurred in his very office, never magnifying or even referring to other personalities. Dr. Tsitos also refused to acknowledge that he had more than one patient, and he always referred to her

415

as Chris or Mrs. Sizemore, no matter how furious a protest he received to the contrary. He advised Taffy not to separate them, and especially not to choose among them, no matter how much she might prefer one set of behavior over another. However, Taffy was never quite able to ignore her mother's well-developed many facets, and perhaps the advice would have been much easier to accept had she not been constantly exposed to their unbelievably distinct machinations. Don simply ignored—outwardly, at least—the entire melodrama; but Taffy, by her own compassionate heart, was trapped into accepting the bizarre as believable, or losing her own hold on reason.

And sometimes her hold grew weak. She walked into Chris's house one morning carrying her three-year-old child to find her mother stretched out on the couch in a sensuous, revealing manner with a sly, knowing look on her face.

"Good morning," her voice held a youthful, cooing lilt. "Do you know who I am?"

"Yes," Taffy answered. "You're Strawberry, aren't you?"

"*She* told you, didn't she?" Chris furiously stormed. "I'll get her for that. What else did she tell you? Did she tell you that I like men?"

"Yes," answered Taffy.

"Oh, yes. I *do* like men, but I don't like Don. He's not my type."

"But you're married to him, Mother," Taffy protested.

"No, I'm not," she declared. She looked slyly at Taffy for a reaction to her remark.

"I'm pretty," Chris pursued, "and I'm young, younger than you are."

"How can you be younger than I am?" Taffy asked, laughing.

"Because I'm twenty-one and you're twenty-six," explained Chris brightly.

"If you're twenty-one and I'm twenty-six, how can you be my mother?" asked the amused Taffy.

"Well, I *can!*" Chris declared. "I didn't have you, but I am your mother."

The voices were now present all the time, and often Chris talked back to them. Sometimes she simply answered a hidden voice, but often she seemed to be carrying on both sides of an argument, complete with a startlingly different tone quality and strength of emotion for each side. Occasionally she would grasp her head and shout as if at two battling children,

"Stop it, stop it!"

"Mother, what's the matter?" Taffy never knew what to expect next.

"They're arguing, there, inside my head. It's filling up my head. I can't stand it." Chris pushed violently on her temples as if trying to crush the interlopers inside her skull.

"Block it out, Mother," Taffy soothed. "Just try to think of something else."

There was one subject on which all the personalities agreed: None of them wanted to see the doctor, either Dr. Ham or Dr. Tsitos. It was like inviting death, and they all resisted until desperation for relief drove one of them for help. And nobody could force Chris to go. Until her own misery reached its extreme, she and her family were compelled to endure her incredibly frustrating behavior. As the furious pace among the personalities became more frantic; their suspicions grew that the doctors were attempting to eradicate them in favor of the others. Each responded to the doctors in her own characteristic way, usually sincerely seeking help and submitting to treatment; but the Strawberry Girl disliked both doctors intensely and made no effort to hide it. She openly and spitefully referred to Dr. Tsitos as "Titso," and she once wrote Dr. Ham a letter telling him that he had "better not help *her*, that other one." The letter, signed "Strawberry Girl," greatly puzzled the doctor, who was at the time treating several young girls. In the midst of his wondering which of his young patients had written him such a letter, a report of Chris's condition from Dr. Tsitos, which mentioned a Strawberry Girl, cleared up the mystery. Dr. Ham was greatly surprised; the tone and terminology of the letter had convinced him that it had been written by a young girl, not a forty-five-year-old woman. He was further intrigued to learn from Dr. Tsitos that Strawberry Girl insisted that she was only twenty-one years old. Dr. Ham never mentioned the letter or any of the many similar such incidents to Chris. He played a supportive role with her, treating her with antidepressants, and never entered into her larger emotional problems unless he felt that she was being overpowered by them; then he referred her to a psychiatrist.

Chris's need for attention was so constant that it became necessary for Bobby to be made aware of the problem. This chore, as had so many others, fell to Taffy. He was shocked, but he did not question, having known for many years that his mother was not like other people, that she was different. His sister gave him two stern warnings: He must never under any conditions tell anyone who she was and what was wrong with her; and he must watch her constantly, especially to prevent her taking an overdose of pills. And so Bobby, in his turn, assumed the care and responsibility of his mother.

At first he was afraid, and his fear sprang from two causes: fear for her, and fear for himself. Now that he was aware of the situation, he was soon able to recognize the different personalities and to refer to them by name; and he soon became aware that the only one he actually feared and dreaded to be alone with was the Turtle Lady. He did not like the silly, childish Strawberry Girl, but he was certainly not afraid of her; and the mature, motherly Purple Lady seemed like a real mother. He had never been allowed to bring his friends home, and now, at fourteen, he understood why and began to dread coming home himself. But he always came, and on those days when Taffy did not come over, he carefully watched, only calling his sister when something unusual happened. The first thing he always did on entering the house was to determine with whom he had to deal by asking secretly probing questions, noticing what clothes she wore, and observing how she acted. As he grew older and more accustomed to the situation, his fear dissolved, but his embarrassed dislike of the Strawberry Girl only increased. She annoyed him by coming into his room to watch his television and behaving like a naughty five-year-old. She cooed and laughed and clapped her hands, and even rode imaginary horses during the cowboy movies.

Don became a silent, morose man, doing little except working, eating, and sleeping. On weekends he took Chris and Bobby, and often Taffy and Tommy as well, on sight seeing trips to nearby historical spots; but most of these outings climaxed unpleasantly, with Chris becoming ill with headache and nausea. Often the day ended with an emotional scene between Chris and Don, in which

418

hurled accusations caused hurt feelings lasting far into the following week. It was at about this time that Chris began to suspect that Don was seeing another woman. She found notes in her diary indicating that one of the other personalities had talked on the telephone with a Mrs. Anderson, who threatened that Don was going to have Chris committed to a mental institution so that he could live with her. Frantic, she took her troubles to Dr. Ham, who, having listened to her marital problems over ten years, assured her that no one could commit her without his authorization.

No matter how irrational her fears or how outrageous her behavior, her family loyally grouped around her, protecting and supporting her even in the face of her rejection of them. Don, tirelessly if dejectedly, worked and earned money for staggering medical and drug bills which, during this period, averaged more than one hundred dollars per week. Bobby became extremely protective, following her around and calling when he was away to assure himself of her safety. He had arrived at an explanation of his unusual mother that satisfied him: They were all his mom, they just had different brains. And Taffy and Tommy, willingly and uncomplainingly, subjugated their own home life and youthful activities to help Chris maintain her own tenuous hold on normal living. Without this critical support and the ever-present help of Dr. Ham, she surely would have destroyed herself, or become eternally lost in the dark maze of a state mental institution.

Added to all this, she had a good friend, Harriet Henderson, the only person over the long years to whom she told her story. They had been friends over four years before Chris, driven to despair, unburdened her aching heart on this, her one trusted friend. Harriet was amazed but accepting, calmly responding,

"I have known that you had abrupt, erratic mood changes, and I thought you had some kind of problem. But they're all you, Chris; it doesn't matter to me which one you are." And that's the way she treated her, often spending long hours day or night talking to the tormented woman, helping her to keep her weak hold on sanity. Harriet, whose own life had included some severe jolts, had discovered that involvement in artistic endeavors helped her weather the rough spots, and she introduced her friend to the world of art, hoping that it would provide the same outlet for her.

419

She introduced Chris to Ardeshir Arjang, an Iranian artist, and persuaded her to take art lessons from him. It was a giant step forward, awakening in her stirrings of the old desires to color and to draw and to make beauty. Ardeshir lent her technical skill and inspiration, and she began to paint. *They* began to paint! With the exception of the Strawberry Girl, whose one painting—a self-portrait—was atrocious, all the existing personalities plied the brush with equal skill; however, they all exhibited different styles, colors, and choices of subject, from still life through portraits.

Not only did her art provide a vital medium of self-expression, it also offered an opportunity for her to move from her cloistered retreat out into the world of people, exciting people. Her excitement was boundless when Ardeshir invited her to show one of her canvases in an art show he gave at the Arjang Art Gallery in Washington, D.C. She not only met Ardeshir Zahedi, the Iranian ambassador, but also discussed some paintings with him and introduced him to her family. Taffy declared that she would never again wash her hand, which had been briefly held by the handsome, smiling diplomat.

Another artist who touched Chris's work and her life was Tom Piper, the exact opposite of the dark, intriguing Iranian. Tom, an aristocratic gentleman of the Old South, sporting an eye-catching white mustache and goatee, lent to Chris his considerable skill with portraits. But she learned more than simply artistic competence from these two widely different masters, and from Harriet; she also learned that she had that ability to add to the beauty of the world.

Painting gave her a tremendous release from her anxiety, but it was not enough; she still could not handle her overpowering pressures without professional help. Her manifested personalities were so clearly defined that they seldom interfered with each other's activities, and they were also able to view the others' activities only in the order in which they first emerged; the first one out in a group of three could not view the activities of those who followed, but those who followed could view the activities of the ones who had come before them. One could never view the activities of any who came after her; and the first one to emerge in any group became the pivot through which all the others must come and go. This intricate design was as stringently adhered to as if it had been a natural physical characteristic rather than a subconscious mental phenomenon; and when these cardinal rules were, on rare occasion, violated, excruciating repercussions followed.

While Chris, as the pivot Purple Lady, was shopping for food one day, the voice in her head insisted on emerging; and she, afraid to resist, relaxed and faded away. Unexpectedly, however, and contrary to the rules of order, her consciousness remained, and when she realized that the Strawberry Girl had filled the grocery cart with nothing but strawberries, she struggled to emerge and take over. Meeting a fierce resistance to this blatant violation of the vital rules of behavior, she strived harder, causing a blinding headache more severe than any in her experience. Suddenly the Purple Lady emerged and fled from the store, sobbing in pain; and with the last of her strength, she drove to Dr. Ham's office and stumbled inside, crying.

"Oh, help me, I've got to see Dr. Ham; I've just got to see him!"

Eunie Gravely, Dr. Ham's receptionist, came to her and led her out of the crowded clinic waiting room. "All right, dear, just come with me," she urged. "We'll get him for you."

Acting as a confidential liaison between the patient and the doctor, Eunie had over the years established a strange relationship with this unusual woman, about whom she had not even told her own husband. Chris had much information about her condition that she could not bring herself to reveal to the serious, dignified doctor; but she told it all to Eunie, knowing that the concerned, professional receptionist would tell no one but Dr. Ham. Chris had, many times, called on her; and Eunie had always responded, listening for hours as the secret pain and shame poured from the tortured woman. Eunie relayed these deeply buried facts to the doctor, who was then better able to deal with this complicated patient.

Dr. Ham was not in the building on this crucial day, but reached by telephone, he ordered his nurse to inject Chris with a sleeping medication.

"Come on, honey," Eunie urged the moaning woman, who stood in the hall, grasping her thundering head.

Suddenly the moans ceased and the trembling body grew still; and right before Eunie's startled eyes, the hysterical woman became a calm, thoughtful person, who looked at the receptionist with mature, knowing eyes. Trembling herself, now, Eunie led her into a consultation room and helped her to lie down on the table. The nurse administered the shot.

"Just relax now, honey, this will put you to sleep," she said. "Dr. Ham will be here when you wake up."

They both watched as the still figure grew drowsy, and when the sad eyes closed, they thought their patient was asleep. But suddenly the eyes opened again, wide, bright, unclouded by the drug. They waited, but the drug had no effect. When Dr. Ham learned of this strange occurrence, he called Taffy and asked her to come to her mother's home; and he then sent Chris home in a taxi.

That was the birth of the Retrace Lady. She came out of the Purple Lady and was given the shot; and when the medication began to take effect, she went away. The Purple Lady came back out, not knowing of the birth of the other one, and not knowing that she had been injected with a sleeping drug. And the drug had no effect on her. None! She wasn't even sleepy. How can that be possible? Can one receive sleeping medicine that has no effect simply because she is unaware of having it? Or is mind over matter so strong that the physical effects of the drug can be erased by the mind? Because it was the body that got the injection. Why wouldn't it go to sleep no matter which mind was working? Is that like the allergy? One has an allergy and the others don't. I'll have to ask Dr. Tsitos about that. And that was the death of the Turtle Lady. She never came out again after that. . . .

Dr. Ham sent her the following day to Dr. Tsitos, and in the course of the consultation she told him of her unhappiness with the way her life had been portrayed in the two books written about her, and of her recently renewed desire to correct that old image. When she informed him that she was considering asking Elen to help her, he strongly encouraged her to carry out her plans immediately. He explained to her that since she and Elen had grown up together, they would be able to review her childhood as would no one else; and that her dredging up of all that

422

old material could be therapeutically very beneficial. That night she called Elen, and they agreed to meet over the Easter holidays in Durham, North Carolina, to discuss details.

Elen was in no way prepared for the series of revelations that burst upon her that weekend. From the moment they checked in at the Durham Hilton, she noticed attitudes about her cousin and phrases in her speech that shook her senses and caused her to doubt her own perceptions. Chris referred often to "they" and "she" and "the others," and it was some time before Elen realized who these other people were: Chris's other selves! At first Elen thought her cousin was referring to her *past* illness, the personalities treated by Dr. Thigpen—the much-touted Eves—and she asked,

"You're talking about the three personalities that you had before you got well, aren't you?"

"Well, yes, those and the others, too," Chris answered, looking at her warily.

Elen felt her pulse quicken. "Which others?" she asked, striving to make her voice matter-of-fact.

"There have been ten or twelve of them since I saw Dr. Thigpen, but most of them died or just went away. There are only three of us now." Her voice was low and infinitely sad, as if she were speaking of dear, departed relatives.

"Three of us," she had said! Elen's ears buzzed slightly, and she realized that she had been holding her breath. Drawing air deeply into her lungs, she cleared her head and tried to analyze what she had heard. What could she say? "Really?" expressed a skepticism that the prickling hair on the back of her neck belied, and she could not bring herself to ask the incredibly melodramatic questions whirling through her brain, such as "Which one are you?" or "Where are the others?" She looked long at the woman sitting in front of her, and her tension relaxed and melted. It was Chris; no matter what, it was Chris.

"Would you like to tell me about it, Chris?" Elen gently asked.

And there began an incredible three days. Elen had thought her cousin was well. She had heard from relatives that Chris had been ill from time to time, but that had always been explained as an accident or a bad case of overwork and nerves. Chris had even come to Chicago to stay a week with her when she was recuperating from meningitis, and never a word had passed between them concerning Chris's former illness or her present state of health. Elen had told people over the years that her famous cousin had adjusted beautifully to life, and she had even thought that Chris had received a handsome sum of money for *The Three Faces of Eve*, from both the book and the movie.

Chris had brought along a group of her paintings to show Elen, and after displaying them, Chris carefully explained which of the personalities had painted each and the distinguishing characteristics of each artist. Elen was unable to appreciate the finer points of difference among the colorful canvases, but the sober logic with which her cousin delineated the not so subtle differences among her many selves registered indelibly on Elen's senses. The weekend climaxed Sunday night when they attended a dinner theater with Elen's fiancé, Dr. Robert Pittillo, Jr., a professor at Duke, where Elen was studying. All afternoon the two women had discussed plans for writing their book, and several rather ticklish subjects had come up. Elen, unaware then of all the details of her cousin's intricate coping mechanism, had asked several questions that slightly upset Chris.

"Am I going to have to interview all of the personalities?" she naïvely asked, "or can you tell me all about them, too?"

Chris looked stricken. "I can't see them," she said, "but they can see me."

"Are they seeing you now?" Elen asked, feeling hysteria begin to rise in her thoat. If they could see Chris, could they also see her? She resisted a wild desire to look behind her.

"I don't know," Chris answered. "They can if they want to. But I don't know if they're looking."

By the time Bob picked them up for the theater, they were both nervous and excitable from their experience. Chris wore a fur stole, and on the way, she commented several times that the fur bothered her. It was so chilly in the huge, cavernous building that both women kept their wraps, and suddenly, before Bob and Elen's startled eyes, Chris began to break out in fiery red splotches on her face and neck, and to itch furiously. Apologizing, she removed her wrap, which alleviated the itching, but the angry red remained on her skin. Back at the hotel, as they were preparing for bed, Chris began to itch again, and the splotches on her face and neck brightened in color.

"I don't think the allergy is going to go away," she said. "I had better take a pill for it."

She passed by Elen, standing before the mirror in the dressing alcove, and went into the bathroom for water. Elen heard her make a slight noise, like a groan, before she came back by; and as she passed the mirror again, Elen noticed that she had her hand clasped to the back of her neck. She went on into the bedroom, which was screened by a partition from the dressing alcove. Elen, only slightly concerned to this point, heard a groan and the sound of a body falling against the bed, and rushing into the room, she saw Chris slowly slipping off the side of the bed into a kneeling position on the floor. Her face hidden against the side of the bed, she was making low mewling noises, and her hands were nervously working on the coverlet. The allergy pill was lying in the middle of the bed, but the glass of water was sitting safely on the dresser.

Elen's heart was pounding; she stifled an urge to run. Actual physical fear assaulted her. Slowly walking to the huddled figure beside the bed, she put her hand on the trembling shoulder and felt a body alive with writhing motion beneath the thin clothes. Was this just the extreme of the allergy? Should a doctor be called? Elen knew it was not. She had never seen this before, but she had seen Dr. Thigpen hypnotize Chris and call out the personalities; and even though this torturous convulsion bore little resemblance to that long-ago process, Elen knew what she was observing. The body ceased its spasmodic moving and grew quiet. As Elen stood there, her hand on the still shoulder, she could feel wary, expectant life tense the entire body, and a dread akin to terror gripped her heart. As much as she had ever dreaded anything in her entire life, she dreaded for that bowed head to rise. What was going to look out at her from the blue eyes? Her usually pragmatic mind had a momentary flash of wolfmen, vampires, and demons. Her breath was suspended as the black head slowly raised, and her relief was infinite as only expectant curiosity and resigned sadness looked from the clear blue eyes. It was still Chris, indefinably different, but still Chris.

Overcome with emotion too strong to permit clear thinking, Elen said the first thing that entered her dull brain: "Here's your allergy pill. You dropped it. I'll get your water," as if by picking up the thread of the last conversation they could wipe out all that had transpired in between.

"It doesn't matter to you, does it, Elen?" Chris asked quietly, ignoring the proffered pill. "It doesn't matter which one of us is here, does it?"

Elen looked at her cousin. "No, Chris, it doesn't matter," she answered. "They're all you. They're all my Chris."

It was the truth. Chris had been different for as long as Elen could remember, and she had long ago grown used to her "being someone different," and pretending, and even telling lies. It was admittedly a shock to find her cousin still involved in strange behavior and obviously still deeply entangled in her mental problem, but it was only Chris, *her* Chris. However, still finding normal conversation difficult, Elen again offered the pill.

"Do you want to take your allergy pill now?" Elen asked, hopefully.

Chris rose from the floor. "I don't have an allergy," she matter-of-factly stated.

Astounded, Elen looked at her, and amazingly, it was true: The skin was white and clear; not one red blemish stained its cool, smooth surface. It had been no more than five minutes since Elen had seen the angry red blotches glowing on that same skin. She would not have thought it possible for the heart to pump adequately enough to move all that congested blood in so short a time. Chris settled herself crosslegged on one bed, and Elen sat upright against the pillows on the other. It was 11 P.M. It was almost 3 A.M. before the conversation ended. This amazing woman told Elen that she was the Retrace Lady and that it was the Purple Lady with whom Elen had been visiting all weekend. She informed her that they need not repeat the information already discussed because she was able to see and to hear everything the Purple Lady did, and that she had been listening the entire time; but she explained that the reverse was not true: The Purple Lady had no knowledge of *her* behavior.

"I came out," she said, "because she has not told you everything, and I think you should know everything if you're going to write this book."

And she proceeded to tell everything, even that she was going

426

to be the one to live on. "That's why I never retrace my steps," she carefully explained. "I'm not going to make any mistakes. They've all made mistakes; they made them over and over. But I'm not going to make those mistakes or any of my own. If I don't retrace my steps, I can't make the same mistakes over and over. And I will be the one to live on." This logic was intriguing.

She told her dumfounded cousin many fascinating stories that had arisen out of all those "ladies" and "girls" being forced to live together in such close quarters. During this discussion, Elen at times felt hysteria stirring her senses at the thought of being a serious participant in this incredible exchange, and she found herself uttering such supportive statements as, "I don't see how they got along as well as they did living so close together. It's difficult for even two women to live in the same house without serious problems." Chris soberly agreed; and soon Elen, lost in the spirit of the moment, was easily prompting and inquiring, with such comments and questions as "Which one . . . ?" "What did she say when . . . ?" and "I can imagine how she felt."

Elen asked the question, "If the Purple Lady and the Strawberry Girl cannot see and hear you, what are they going to think when they hear your comments on the tapes?"

Chris looked startled. "What tapes?"

"The ones I am going to make when all of you tell your stories to me. I'll have to have the tapes to write the story from when I'm not with you. We can't live together for a year," explained Elen.

"I hadn't thought of that," Chris answered, looking puzzled and a little fearful. Was she afraid that if they heard her tell her story, they would gain an advantage that they did not now have?

Suddenly she lost her bright-eyed vitality; her body drooped and her facial muscles sagged. "I think I'll go," she abruptly said, "I'm very tired."

She closed her eyes and dropped her head forward. When she straightened up, she looked at Elen, puzzled and concerned.

"Do you feel all right?" Elen asked, watching her closely.

"Yes," she answered hesitantly. Then she frowned and asked worriedly, "She was here, wasn't she?"

"Yes, she was," Elen answered quietly, trying to keep her voice matter-of-fact.

"Oh, I'm so sorry, Elen," Chris apologized. "I was hoping that you wouldn't have to see that."

"It's all right, Chris," her cousin answered. "They're all you. Whatever happens, they're all you." Elen sounded as if she were trying to convince herself as well as Chris.

"Did you like her, Elen?" Chris asked curiously.

"Of course I like her. I like you, and she's you, too, honey." Elen was trying to walk a tightrope between reality and fantasy, and the going was rough.

"I think I'll see if I can sleep, Elen," Chris said. "I'm not really tired, but I've got a long drive tomorrow."

Elen lay wide awake, sleep out of the question, and her busy brain whirled through this most incredible experience. No longer was hers merely the simple task of retelling Chris's already documented life experiences and catching up the world on a passive, well-adjusted life over the past twenty years. The untold was the amazing story; the told was simply the tip of the iceberg. Chris stirred in her bed, and in spite of herself, Elen felt a moment's fear. Were the others there watching her? Could they see when the eyes were closed and the body was asleep? Even though she knew intellectually that this was only a coping mechanism, it was amazingly convincing, and her excited emotions could not shake the feeling that truly a host of women of all ages, sizes, and characters did inhabit her cousin's familiar body.

They parted with plans to meet again in the fall, after Elen had completed the course work for her degree, to sign a contract of their agreement and to begin work on their book. Chris's job in the meantime was to employ legal aid to determine just what, if any, were her legal entanglements from the past, and to clear away any such obstacles in the path of their project.

An evaluation of the contracts that Chris had signed for the writing of *The Final Face of Eve* with James Poling and with McGraw-Hill proved to have no bearing on the proposed writing, and the Twentieth Century-Fox contract appeared benign, dealing only with movie rights, not literary rights. But the alluded-to agreement between her and Drs. Cleckley and Thigpen was another matter. Since she had no copy of any such agreement, as well as no memory of ever having seen it, and had only the clause in the Twentieth Century-Fox contract to give any clue of its con-

428

tent or existence, she was forced to appeal to the doctors for a copy of theirs or an explanation of its present status. She had kept up her correspondence with Corbett Thigpen over the years, exchanging not only season's greetings with him and thank-you notes for gifts, but also personal information. She had informed him of her taking up painting, her recurring marital problems, her children's growth and development. From time to time she hinted at her distress, and he always assured her that she seemed to be only depressed, a condition not unusual for women her age, and that neither he nor Dr. Cleckley felt that it was related to her former personality adjustment. She visited him occasionally on her infrequent trips home to see her father, and she told him that she was planning to collaborate with Elen on writing her life story.

He had many suggestions and words of advice, including a reminder of how she had "scooped" her own book before; and he assured her that both he and Dr. Cleckley wished her well. He declared that he would like to read the manuscript before it was published and that he might request that she do some rephrasing and deleting, especially of his name. In no way, however, he affirmed, was he going to give her any problems concerning her project.

But this was not good enough. If, indeed, such a contract as the one described in the Twentieth Century-Fox contract had been signed by Chris giving her doctors "all worldwide rights to her life story forever," it must be dealt with before Chris could write her own account. Chris's lawyer wrote to Drs. Thigpen and Cleckley, sending a prepared statement for them to sign that would release her from the alleged agreement of April 24, 1952. Dr. Thigpen's answer stated that the contract was buried somewhere either in the attic of his former home or garage and would require a great deal of work for him to locate, even though he knew it was there. He indicated that Dr. Cleckley and he would appreciate it if the lawyer would be kind enough to send them a copy of the contract. He maintained that he and Dr. Cleckley were desirous of Chris's writing the story of her long-ago suffering and that they had freely granted her permission years ago to write her story, but that they could not sign a release as sweeping in its coverage as the present one. He promised that if the lawyer sent a release saying simply that Chris wished to write an account of her life, that he and Dr. Cleckley would be more than glad to grant their permission.

It was done. The revised release read:

> We understand that Mrs. Christine Sizemore desires to write a further book and/or other articles about her life, but she feels that some contract she might have signed with us in the past might present a stumbling-block.
>
> At the present time we cannot find a copy of any contract we might have entered into with Mrs. Sizemore during the time she was under our professional care and, therefore, are unable to recall any specific details about it.
>
> However, in view of the professional relationship that existed between us and Mrs. Sizemore, and in view of the fact that we have in the past strongly encouraged her to write her own story, we hereby release Christine Sizemore, her agents, designees and personal representatives from any and all claims which we might have by virtue of any contract she may have executed with us.

This release, sent to Dr. Thigpen in September 1975 along with a request for the signatures of both Dr. Thigpen and Dr. Cleckley, was answered by a short note from Dr. Thigpen stating that he was presently away from his office for business reasons and did not expect to resume practice until the middle of November, when he would try to search through the attics of his former home and garage for the contract. On December 1, 1975, Chris's lawyer next received a letter from Dr. Thigpen containing a reworded version of the release, but making no reference whatever to the elusive 1952 contract. The reworded release stated that Drs. Cleckley and Thigpen would grant to Chris the same rights that they had granted to her when she wrote *The Final Face of Eve* with Jim Poling. It further stipulated that in no way did they assign rights to their own book *The Three Faces of Eve* or to the professional movie entitled *A Case Study of Multiple Personality*. He further stated that they would like to have the privilege of reading any manuscripts and the right to have some say-so if their names were to be used. He admitted that they had used their own names as authors of this famous story when they wrote *The Three Faces of Eve* but that they had been careful not to seek unwarranted publicity. He felt sure that Chris would co-operate with them on these requests, since she had always been so gracious in her thanks and praise for the help that they had tried to render her in her miserable problem and sickness.

When Chris saw the reworded release and read the letter, fear clutched her heart. If the doctors were granting her the same rights as they had before, they could edit and control her story as they had before. And what was the professional movie *A Case Study of Multiple Personality* all about? She had to clear these matters up before she could go further. She instructed her lawyer to refuse the reworded release and to find out about the movie.

Several things began to happen in rapid succession. Her personality changes had become so constant and numerous that often they resembled the rapid flipping of television channels. Especially when she lay in bed at night, the confusing and debilitating round robin of changes so completely possessed her that she was even unaware of time or place. During the day, the battle among her three selves waged continually and fiercely, and their competition for dominance filled her entire life. Each one played her role, never behaving out of character, as if they were following a carefully prepared script. The aging Purple Lady, frightened, ugly, conciliatory, strived for normalcy; the young, mischievous Strawberry Girl, happy, irresponsible, and selfish, maliciously tormented her at every turn; and the mature, conscientious Retrace Lady, determined to become dominant and outlive the others, silently watched their every move to avoid repeating their fatal mistakes.

Chris's condition became so severe that it was no longer possible to conceal it from her sisters, and when they realized the seriousness, they rallied around her. Becky sent her seventeen-year-old daughter, Mary Louise, to live briefly with Chris, hoping that her presence would be a protection for her sister. Mary Louise had become disenchanted with home and school, and her mother hoped, also, that the change would be good for her. Probably both ends were accomplished to a small degree: Chris was forced out of her all-absorbing preoccupation with self for short periods, and her niece quieted her teen-age rebellion and successfully came to grips with life. More important, however, Chris renewed her time-dimmed relationship with Becky, and the two sisters became close at a time when both of them were facing emotional crises. This new closeness was very beneficial for Becky, but for Chris, this re-woven tie with her sister was a hand extended over the edge of her black pit.

Tiny and her son Chuck came to Fairfax to visit with Chris for a week, hoping to draw her out of her troubled condition; and they witnessed an episode that both boggles the mind and insults the normal logic of intelligence. One night Chris and Tiny were sitting in the living room talking when Chris jumped from her chair and began to scream hysterically. Before Tiny's astounded eyes, Chris tore off most of her clothes, fell on the floor, and began rolling over and over, screaming.

"My arm is burning! I'm on fire!"

Tiny, who had started toward her, was shocked into immobility. The very words alone were startling enough, but it was the voice itself, high, piping, and sounding like a child of three, that caused Tiny to call for Chuck and Bobby, who were loudly playing musical tapes in the next room. They and Don entered simultaneously to find Chris, her dress torn from her right shoulder and breast, lying on the floor, rolling from side to side and crying hysterically in her small child's voice,

"Mommy, I'm burning! Mommy, I'm burning!"

Bobby ran for his mother's robe, and the two teen-age boys held her still and covered her naked body while Tiny brought a wet towel from the bathroom. She and Don put the towel on Chris's upper right arm, the one containing the puckered scar from that old burn more than forty-six years before. The arm and scar now burned an angry, fiery red. As the wet towel touched the arm, Chris ceased her tossing and screaming and grew quiet, lying on the floor spent and wet with sweat, as one might whose excruciating pain had been touched and soothed by morphine. When Don removed the towel from her arm, he and Tiny stared at each other over the small square of terrycloth. It was steaming and burning hot to the touch, and the arm that it had just covered and that had so shortly been red and burning itself, was now white and cool to the touch. In a daze, they gave Chris a sleeping pill and put her to bed. They then sat long into the night discussing what they had witnessed. Tiny could not remember if she had wet the

432

towel in cold or warm water, she had simply quickly wet it; but she had absolutely not brought in a steaming hot towel. Don was much disturbed by this experience. His practical mind, his store of information learned from years of working with the processes of heat generation, and just simply his confidence in his ability to understand what he saw were all shaken by this incredible phenomenon.

Tiny, greatly disturbed, consulted with Dr. Tsitos, who, though unable to explain the strange occurrence to her satisfaction, assured her that Chris was not lapsing into an uncontrollable condition, and that this kind of abreaction experience was necessary to her coming to terms with the deeply rooted causes of her problem. Tiny took heart, but this week with her troubled sister left her greatly saddened and concerned. She and Becky kept in close contact with Chris both by letter and telephone, and all three agreed to say nothing about this to their ailing father.

In the fall Chris came back to Durham, and she and Elen signed a contract with each other in which Chris became the "party of the first part," who desired to write her life story and would furnish all the material and information relating to her life, to Elen, the "party of the second part," who agreed to write and prepare the material for publication. Chris reserved the right to make editorial changes in the manuscript and to reject any portion of it. Then they got down to work. Elen could not believe the staggering wealth of information; it came in a trunk, full to brimming. Chris had never thrown away a scrap of information: letters, valentines, newspapers, contracts, pictures, diaries, publishers' sales reports, everything was there. While Chris read, sorted, and labeled, Elen devised her plan of action, working out the format of the story, choosing a point of view from which to write, and devising a plan for gathering information. They decided to make a visit to relatives who knew pertinent facts about Chris's life and to tape conversations with them; and they set up a tentative schedule of their own meetings to tape Chris's lengthy recital of her own account of her life, from earliest memories through the present.

One day as Elen was explaining how she planned to handle the many personalities, she said to Chris,

"Since the whole thing is a coping mechanism, we'll have to try to determine when was the first time you used it. Do you remember when was the first time it happened?"

Chris looked at her strangely, frowning. "What do you mean, 'a coping mechanism'?" she asked.

Elen, thinking that Chris simply did not understand the term, rushed in, unaware that she was barging into virgin territory. "It's a defense technique," she explained. "When you faced a reality situation that you could not tolerate, you just avoided it by splitting off a part of yourself; your ego denied that part of yourself and let it—her—do what you could not do."

Chris sat silently, listening to the fractured psychology in Elen's explanation. "Elen, are you saying that I'm doing all this to myself?"

"Of course, Chris," her cousin declared. "It's a means of protecting yourself from hurt. We all have techniques for defending ourselves from life's blows."

"But I'm not doing it, Elen," Chris positively stated. "It just happens. They just come and go, and I don't have anything to do with it."

Elen was stunned. Chris did not even know what her problem was. She truly thought that other women came and inhabited her body. Had nobody ever told her the nature of her trouble? And if not, why? And what had *she* now done by telling her? Elen was well aware of the first rule of psychology in dealing with defense mechanisms, whether they be phobias, dissociations, reaction formations, or any of the myriad other means human beings choose to avoid hurt: Do not take away the existing crutch unless there exists something better with which to replace it. Frightened, Elen changed the subject, but strongly urged Chris to go immediately to see Dr. Tsitos when she returned home and to discuss it with him. When Chris told the doctor, he informed her that Elen was right, she was doing it to herself. She sat, unbelieving, as he explained to her that since she had had so much therapy, he had thought that she had known; and that since the literature was so full of the facts, he had assumed that she had read about her famous case.

She had no choice but to believe, and once she faced this fact, she discovered that it had been evident around her for twenty-five years. She even found in her diaries where she had become hurt and offended when Dr. Thigpen had told her, after she left Augusta, that she was doing it to herself, and she had accused him of no longer understanding. Why had she not heard what was being said to her, and why was she hearing now? The fact penetrated her brain, and intellectually she knew that it was true; but emotionally she could not believe—all of those people, women and children, had been real: her sisters, her friends, her enemies even, but real.

Who can say whether or not this startling revelation caused it, but for whatever the reason, her life now became a true hell of confusion as her three existing personalities battled. She began to see Dr. Tsitos as often as three times a week, and he tried to help her remember any painful experiences from her childhood that might be trying to surface and cause her such stress. During a therapy session she suddenly stopped talking and stared into blank space, as if seeing a frightening picture.

"What do you see, Mrs. Sizemore?" asked the doctor.

"I see a small white box, a little casket," she answered tremulously.

"Whose casket is it?" he pursued.

"I don't know. Oh, I don't know!" she exclaimed, squeezing her eyes shut to blot out the frightful scene.

"It's all right," he assured her. "You'll remember all about it. Just give yourself time. Talk to your father about it when you next see him."

Her stress was so great that her physical health soon became affected. The Strawberry Girl waited until the haunted Purple Lady was seated on the commode for a bowel movement, to taunt.

"That's just going to smell like hell. That's nasty."

The poor fastidious Purple Lady could not allow her body to eliminate its waste with that voice ringing in her head, and soon she was painfully constipated. The Retrace Lady, observing all this, tried to solve the problem by coming out and taking an enema every day. The Purple Lady, caught between these two, could no longer survive. She packed away all of her purple clothes and possessions, wrote a will leaving her paintings to Bobby, wrote a letter to Taffy telling her good-bye and giving her some philosophical advice about loving people instead of accumulating mate-

435

rial goods, dressed herself in her favorite negligee and nightgown, lay down on the bed, and died.

The Retrace Lady had watched the process, and she immediately called Dr. Ham and told him. Not wanting her to be alone with Bobby under these conditions, he told her to drive over and get Taffy to stay with her. On the way back, she suddenly screamed and slammed on the brakes, exclaiming,

"Oh, my God, I hit her; I killed her!"

She jumped from the car and ran along the road searching. Bobby and Taffy got her back into the car and tried to convince her that she had not hit anybody. But she would not be convinced.

"I did, I did hit her. I saw her. I felt the bumper hit her. She was wearing a purple dress, and I've killed her!" She sobbed uncontrollably.

When they arrived home, she wanted to call the police and report what she had done, and Taffy was able to restrain her only by showing her the Purple Lady's self-portrait. When Chris saw it she gave a hysterical scream and dissolved into a shuddering heap, declaring,

"That's her! That's the woman I hit. That's who I killed."

Frightened, Taffy called Dr. Tsitos, who advised them to bring her in to see him immediately. He sedated her and sent her home with medication to keep her tranquilized and drowsy for two weeks. It was during this time that she relived her two surgery experiences. She felt herself lying on the operating table looking up into green-garbed and masked figures bending over her against a background of blinding lights. She heard the clink and rattle of metal instrument against metal tray, she felt the hard clamps on her body like a vice stretching and pulling, and suddenly she felt the red-hot searing of the blade on her skin. Her limbs were dead, immovable; her silent scream of terror was locked in her closed throat,

"No, no, stop! I'm awake; you're operating on me, and I'm awake!"

And she heard voices, but they weren't speaking to her. They had not noticed that she was awake.

"It's about a three-month-old fetus," she heard the doctor say.

She came out of these experiences terror-stricken and drenched with sweat. But all of her moments relived were not unpleasant and horrible; some were reminiscently sweet and exciting. She lay in bed, supposedly asleep, with her mother on Christmas Eve and watched her father, dressed in his long-handled winter underwear, complete with rear trapdoor, hang apples and oranges on a green cedar tree and wrap it carefully with white popped corn and red holly berries strung on thread. She knew she was supposed to be asleep, but she felt the heady excitement of watching this secret trimming. And wonder of wonders, her father had black, curly hair, parted neatly in the middle of his wide forehead. Acie had been bald for thirty-five years!

The experiences were real, just as if they were happening the first time. The surgery was awful. But the Retrace Lady didn't have surgery; how could she remember it and relive it? Were the ones who had lived in the past giving up their memories to her? Or is it true that the memories are just one, and there have not been separate people to experience and store memories, that it was always just me? But that doesn't make sense either. I can understand how I could remember Daddy trimming the Christmas tree, but how could I remember an operation that occurred while I was under anesthesia? But I did remember; I can remember even now what the reliving of it was like. I don't remember the actual surgery, of course. But maybe I do. Maybe the experience of surgery is buried deep in my subconscious, deep in the subconscious of everybody who has ever experienced it, and that it can be remembered under the right circumstances. It would have to be that way; because if other personalities were simply watching while another had surgery, they could experience sight and sound but not pain. And the reliving had pain, awful pain. Who really knows what the mind can remember?

The problems were astoundingly severe, but the carefully wrought master plan was beginning to break down, to disintegrate. For the first time there was no pivot for the other personalities to travel through. The Strawberry Girl and the Retrace Lady now simply went in and out of each other, easily and quickly, causing no headache unless one wanted to force entry while the other wished to remain out. As the long adhered-to rules broke down one by one, Dr. Tsitos was needed more and more often to administer supportive drugs and to calm hysterical fears. Even the Strawberry Girl expressed a desire to see him, and forced herself out one day just before Chris and Taffy were leaving for the doctor's office. On reaching the car they realized that she could not drive, and in disgust and anger she had to retreat to allow Retrace Lady to emerge and drive the car.

When they reached Dr. Tsitos' office, the Strawberry Girl was so afraid that she would miss her opportunity to talk with the doctor that she tried to force her way out, giving the resistant Retrace Lady a terrific headache. The pain caused her to grasp her head and to contort her face. Taffy, trying to protect her from the staring eyes of those seated in the waiting room, led her, along with Jimmy, into a small back hall and to the door of a rest room. There Chris fell heavily onto the floor, completely overcome by her pain. The receptionist, having seen the difficulty, brought Taffy a glass of water; but before anyone could help her, Chris opened her eyes, rose to her hands and knees, and announced brightly,

"I want to see Titso."

Dr. Tsitos, coming at that moment along the hallway, attempted to help her to her feet; but she ignored his proffered hand and crawled on hands and knees the entire length of the hall into his office, and remained on the floor, sitting with her head and arms leaning across a chair. The doctor trailed his plump, middle-aged patient down the hall, entered his office, and closed the door as if there were nothing at all strange in this unusual behavior. Seated in his usual chair, he looked calmly at Chris, peeping coyly up at him from her seat on the floor, and stated,

"I see you're having problems today, Mrs. Sizemore."

To this master understatement, she airily answered, "No, Tsitos, I'm not having any problems."

"Well, I'm glad to hear that," he answered. He motioned for Taffy, who had also trailed her mother into the office, to be seated.

Chris rose from the floor, pulled a chair close to the desk, and leaning on her elbows, spoke confidentially to the doctor, "I've

438

come to you today to discuss a plan to work all this out, and not have all this flipping back and forth going on. You know the Retrace Lady can't handle all this, because she worries about everything all the time. I don't worry about nothing. So all you need to do is fix it so I'm out all the time. Can't you do that?" She looked at him expectantly, almost flirtatiously.

"No, I don't think I can do that," he answered quietly. "We'd best not make plans that we can't follow through on."

Chris jumped furiously to her feet, declaring haughtily, "Well, I don't need you, anyhow, Titso." And she left, just left—died?—never to return again. Chris's body suddenly lost its youthful life and vigor; and when the eyes looked again at the doctor, they were dull and lackluster, showing none of their just-exhibited fire and sparkle. She sat tiredly in a chair and spoke in a voice infinitely sad and weary,

"I'm sorry, Dr. Tsitos, dreadfully sorry."

"Don't be, Mrs. Sizemore; I understand. It's a part of your illness. My feelings are not involved in this. Don't ever worry about anyone hurting my feelings. I'm here to help you; that's all you ever have to be concerned about."

Taffy took her mother home, but Chris could not seem to shake off her confused feeling. Suddenly she said to Taffy,

"I think I'll go down home and discuss all this with Mother. Taffy, can you go with me?"

Dumfounded, not knowing what to do, Taffy looked quizzically at her.

"I don't think we should go now, Mother," she answered.

"Yes," her mother insisted. "I need to go now. I want to talk this whole thing over with Mother."

Taffy, afraid to go further without help, sent her mother from the apartment on a pretext and called Dr. Tsitos. He told her to tell Chris the truth; and when she returned, Taffy led her to the couch, and putting her arms around her mother's drooping shoulders, said,

"Mother, there's something I have to tell you. Honey, your mother passed away ten years ago." Taffy had been spared nothing in her long years of caring for this sick woman.

Chris broke down completely; her grief was even stronger than when she had first heard those terrible words ten long years before. It was almost as if after all those lonely years without her mother, she had regained her, only to lose her again before she could even gaze once on her dear face or touch once her warm, reassuring hand. She was more than gone this time. With a fresh loss, one does not really know what has been lost, only the empty years reveal that; but to lose when one has already tasted the bitter dregs of loneliness and felt the dull ache of empty arms is a despaired wail in the dark, a high scream of unutterable anguish.

Taffy calmed her sobbing as best she could and took her back to Dr. Tsitos, who talked to her at length about Zueline's death. Without warning she developed a severe headache and began to sob aloud.

"I don't feel well," she moaned.

"That's all right," he soothed her, gently holding her hand. "Don't be upset. It's all right."

She continued to moan and sob incoherently.

"What are you thinking?" the doctor probed.

"I have no definite thoughts," she whispered, her voice trailing off.

She looked up, pain gone, tears ceasing to flow. She saw Dr. Tsitos for the first time, but knew who he was; she saw Taffy for the first time, and knew that she was her daughter.

There I am! That's me! For the first time that's really me. I don't know where I was all that time, but that's the first time I was where I could see me. Does that mean that this was when I was born? No, no, that couldn't be, because I could always see all the others and know what they were doing. I've been there all along; I just couldn't be seen.

As she looked at Dr. Tsitos, her face began to twist and contort, and her eyes started to droop. The doctor grabbed her roughly by the shoulder, shaking her vigorously,

"Don't you do that!" he sternly ordered. "Don't you dare do that. You are free now, if you want to be free." Their glances locked and held. Hers melted and dropped. It was over. He gave her an injection and sent her home.

Oh, I remember how I felt, so alone, so terribly alone, totally empty, everything drained out, wrung out. I didn't think I

440

could tolerate it alone. That's why I tried to create another one, because I couldn't bear it alone. But finally it all became unimportant. So I was alone. I wanted to be well; if this was what it took to be well, I could do it. It was frightening, horribly frightening. But Lord, I didn't know, then, anything about fear. The real fear came later. . . .

There began a week of horror. Taffy stayed with her day and night and watched as her mother lay on the bed, eyes wide open and staring, as the experiences of a lifetime kaleidoscoped through her mind: bright, clear pictures—some amusing, some tender, some horrifying, all jumbled and out of sequence. She saw her little sisters standing nude in the washtub, saw them standing singing on the front bumper of an old-model car; she saw Acie cutting large purple cane, saw the cane mill pulled round and round by a patient horse; she saw her automobile accidents; she saw herself and Elen sitting in a green pasture telling sexy jokes; she saw Mama standing in the nude, with her flap of belly skin stretched by eleven pregnancies, hanging onto her legs; and she saw the little white casket. Interwoven into this childhood parade of pictures were flashes from her entire adult life, leaving slighted not one of her many slivered selves.

During this difficult week, Dr. Tsitos called her often to check on her physical as well as her mental condition; and she went to his office several times for short sessions.

"Is anything worrying you?" he continually asked her. "If anything worries you, call me day or night, and we will talk about it. Do not allow worry to build up."

She had two experiences that deeply concerned her. She went to bed one night in the bedroom, and awoke during the night on the couch in the living room, unaware of how she had gotten from one room to another. Shortly afterward, she started to hem a dress but fell asleep before even beginning her task. When she awoke later, she took up her needle and thread only to find that the job had been finished. She feared that another personality had been born without her knowledge, who had performed these acts, unknown to her; but Dr. Tsitos assured her that these sleep-walking performances were only mild forms of dissociation, and that she was not to be concerned. He placed no emphasis at all on these events.

441

In March of 1975, Chris and Elen started out on their fact-finding tour of relatives, and they planned to make their first stop with Acie. True to his prediction beside the fresh grave of his wife, he did have to go to a nursing home. Ellis's death had greatly weakened his courage and his resolve to walk, a feat that he never attempted to try again after the loss of his brother; but Zueline's death dealt him such a cruel blow that his already fragile physical condition began an inexorable deterioration. He needed constant custodial and medical care, and after two years of living in Tiny's home, he had to be placed in a nursing home, where this specialized kind of attention was continuously available.

The old County Home where he had lived so many years had recently been utilized as a nursing home, but it was full to capacity, with a waiting list; and Acie was taken to the next available location, about twenty-five miles away. Shortly after he had been admitted, Chris came by Charlotte, Elen's home, on her way down to see him, and Elen went with her. It was a scene that broke the hearts of both women. They met him in the hall, pulling himself tortuously along in his wheelchair by grasping a wall rail with his good hand. His pitifully thin, shrunken body looked lost in that strange place among other lost-looking souls, cared for by efficient but impersonal strangers. It was a sad trip, but doubly so for Elen. Chris told her that she had developed angina pectoris, and she took pills for the pain several times on their day-long trip. Angina had, of course, been Zueline's terminal illness, and they soberly discussed the fact that both mother and daughter were stricken with the same disease. Elen was greatly surprised and puzzled, on meeting Chris some months later, to be airily told that she no longer had the painful heart ailment. Did one overcome angina as easily as one did a bad cold?

Acie was soon moved to the nursing home in Edgefield, and it was like going home. Not only had he lived in the very building for almost twenty years, but Tiny also lived within sight, and her children ran in to see him several times a day. Since he had known most of the patients when they had all been young and vigorous, it was almost like a reunion of old friends. The nurses and attendants were also long acquaintances, and his doctor was Raymond Dunovant, that trusted friend and aid for more than forty years. Acie spent ten years observing the passing ironies of life from his wheelchair, but only his body was a captive; his mind was active and alert, and his bold, blue eyes never lost their merry twinkle. He read hundreds of books; and he made small crafts, using his paralyzed hand with amazing dexterity. His passive nature and sharp wit gave him the ability to submit to his cruel fate and to enjoy his life, where the more aggressive would have feverishly chafed in the same bonds.

His sharp, pertinent comments on life often left his visitors uncomfortable and unsure of how to react. He casually commented, "I have sat here in this chair and watched the strong and healthy die. I have outlived them all."

Elen and Bob, visiting him once, promised that they would see him soon. He responded with a merry twinkle in his eye, "You'd better hurry, or you might have to dig me up."

However disconcerting for the listener, it was not morbid; it was for him simply a comment on life, an easy resignation. Life had already dealt him her cruelest blows: crippling him and claiming Zueline; compared to those, death held no terror. He merely waited, an interested observer. And several times a week, he played checkers with Dr. Dunovant. In full command of his mental faculties, Acie had given strict orders that if he were severely stricken, only Dr. Dunovant was to be called, and that if he must be hospitalized, he was to be taken to the tiny Edgefield County Hospital. And that is exactly what happened. When his heart attack struck, he was rushed to the little hospital, but he did not know that his old friend did not practice there and that he would be in the hands of strange doctors.

With an irony that Acie himself could fully appreciate, this, his final illness, struck the day before Chris and Elen were to visit him to gather information from his fertile supply. When they reached him, he was desperately ill, watched over by Becky and Tiny. The four women, feeling frightened and concerned because there was no heart specialist on the hospital staff, requested that a cardiologist be called from Greenwood, thirty-five miles away, to examine the rapidly declining old man. They were refused, and surprisingly, here in her hometown where it had never been a secret who she was, Chris received her one and only mean comment concerning her illness. When she revealed her identity, people all over the world expressed, at least openly, only sympathy and kindness; but there in her hometown, when she insisted that a specialist be summoned for her dying father, one of the doctors on the staff accused her in front of others of being crazy and needing to be locked up.

She was not intimidated, as she might have been just a few short months before; she remained firm in her insistence, and the cardiologist came, confirming the hospital's diagnosis. Acie was dying. But now his daughters knew that they had purchased for their father the best of medical care. Acie died, just before his seventieth birthday, as he had lived, quietly and unspectacularly. He was buried, in a blinding thunderstorm, in the old Mount Carmel Cemetery beside his Zueline; and as nearly as his daughters could arrange it, his funeral duplicated hers, even to having the same minister perform the ceremony. His carved headstone, lacking only the death date, had been waiting for him for almost ten years; and as the tornado winds howled and the driving rain thundered onto the funeral tent, Acie took his last resting place among the departed members of this proud family, with whom he had lived for half a century. And by now he had as many loved ones resting with him beneath the sod as were left to mourn him on the earth above. As Mamie Lee looked at his new grave nestled so close beside Sister's green mound, she thought, "His bed is no longer empty," and her eyes strayed to the spot beside Ellis where someday she would take her own place.

He was missed. When Dr. Dunovant made his rounds in the nursing home, he often found himself going down the hall toward Acie's room to have a game of checkers with his old friend. And Chris missed him.

Another death, another funeral. She watched it all; she watched and endured it all—all by herself. She waited, she wondered; perhaps she even hoped for some help to alleviate her pain, but none came. Her fear reached monstrous proportions. Was this truth? Was this sanity? Was this what it was like to be well? Then she wished that she had never known the truth. Her whole world crashed down around her, and she still stood amid the rubble; she desperately wanted to die, but she lived on. Where were the girls, her ladies? She searched for them, wanted them to lean on; but she could no longer find them. She felt that her real self had disappeared and that she no longer knew who she was. Was it possible that her other selves had kept her in balance, and that in losing them she had lost her own identity? Had she loosed a monster? She was consumed by fear and loneliness and insecurity. She was inundated by guilt: guilt for the abortion, guilt for what her illness had done to her children, guilt for spoiling her marriage. She relived her entire life, taking the blame for every wrong turn. She worried constantly about whether to leave Don or to continue her cool, indifferent marriage. She was unable to make decisions, to establish purpose in her apparently aimless life. She tried to paint, but there was no beauty left in her soul. She seriously considered drowning herself in alcohol to dull the pain of being fully alive and aware.

The agony reached its apex and began to dull. Others began to intrude themselves on the periphery of her vision, and the all-consuming concern with self began to shrink and to lessen in intensity. The tomorrows were no longer so dreadful and terrifying, because she had lived through the horrors of yesterday; and today she could even see the sun and smiling faces, and hear laughter and music. And then she reached a day when she actually enjoyed being *one*. Dr. Tsitos was supportive throughout this painful adjustment period; but he now warned her that there would be recurring periods of depression for which she must be prepared, and that work was the best medicine. She began again to paint.

Becky and Tiny, at forty-two, decided to enroll in school, Piedmont Technical College, to prepare themselves for careers working with children. On a visit, Chris attended classes with them; and when a psychology professor learned who she was, he asked her to speak to one of his groups. Expecting to find only a small number, she was amazed, but strangely pleased, to find more than two hundred people, plus press and television coverage, awaiting her. It was a good experience, like the little girl standing on the stage in the church play looking out at all the warm, smiling faces. She talked about herself and answered questions from the audience: gentle, sympathetic questions; and she afterward shook numerous warm, clasping hands and heard people thanking her for being brave enough to stand up and tell what it was like to be mentally ill.

A few days later she received a telephone call from the Augusta *Chronicle* asking for an interview. They had run the original article about her in 1952 when Dr. Thigpen had reported her case to the American Psychiatric Association, and now they wanted to report on her decision to come out of twenty-five years of hiding. The article ran a picture of her and also pictures of Drs. Thigpen and Cleckley, but this time her face dominated the page. Word got around, and she began to receive offers from colleges to speak to groups of students and professionals. She came to Duke University, where the seed for all this had originally been sown, and spoke to a group of psychologists and psychological interns. She told her story so openly and honestly that listeners were hesitant to invade her privacy further and to expose her to more vulnerability by asking probing questions. Her confidence in herself began to grow.

Chris and Elen had begun industriously to work on their book. They met in Durham and for days talked over their childhood, dredging up every moment from the past that they could remember. Some of it was very painful for Chris, as she relived old memories long buried and forgotten, and her tears flowed freely as the recorder duplicated her emotions as well as her thoughts. Often Elen's memories would cue her to remember what years of psychiatric probing had not been able to touch. Sometimes, as they talked, Chris would stop in amazement and stare into space as if seeing moving pictures, and exclaim,

"My God, Elen, I had completely forgotten that!" And Chris would then relate a tale of hurt or horror, and both women would be cast along their separate emotional paths of remembering. Nothing was kept back. Elen often shivered as she saw her cousin's soul laid bare, and she wondered at the courage required to strip oneself naked in such a manner. She often asked,

"Chris, do you want me to write about that?" after a startling bit of information had surfaced.

Chris's tear-drenched eyes gazed at her sadly, but she calmly answered,

"Elen, I want to tell my whole story. Nobody really knows what made me like this, or what makes anybody mentally ill; if I can tell everything about myself, perhaps it will help other sick people. If I leave out even one thing, it might be just what is necessary to complete a whole picture."

They both sat silent. It was a frightening task they were setting for themselves.

Chris was most concerned about correcting the false image that had grown up about her illness. The world had thought for twenty-five years that she was well, when she had certainly not been; perhaps she was not even well now. Possibly "cure" was not a word that was applicable to those fighting their way out of the maze of emotional disturbance. And something else had been bothering her, something about her father's last illness. She felt that it had been harmful to both her father and to his family to have been forced to fight so hard to obtain specialized care for him, or even a second opinion on his condition. She wished to state her opinion concerning this behavior, to set this record straight. She discussed it with Dr. Tsitos and with Elen; both encouraged her to follow her conscience. At first she thought of writing a letter to the newspaper or in some way making her views public; but that was not really what she wanted to do. She wanted to help correct what she viewed, from personal experience, to be a practice detrimental to the welfare of the patient and devastating to the morale of saddened and upset relatives. She decided to write a letter to the South Carolina Medical Association and explain her views to them. Her habit of keeping a daily diary proved helpful; she had faithfully recorded the happenings of each day. She received a prompt reply from them, graciously offering her an opportunity to tell her story before their Mediation Committee. She, Tiny, and Elen, all of whom had been involved in the four-day struggle for a second medical opinion, met with the Mediation Committee, along with the doctors against whom the complaint was being lodged, explained the events concerning Acie's fatal illness, and answered questions posed by the committee.

Chris stressed that she had no complaint about the hospital or medical care rendered by the doctors, that her primary complaint was that she had wanted a consultant, a second opinion, and that she had been forced to threaten litigation to obtain one. The chairman of the committee asked Chris this question:

"What do you want our committee to do?"

"Whatever the committee normally does in circumstances like this," she answered. "I'm highly opposed to malpractice suits and legalities. I think you have an organization, and it must be a system that works or it wouldn't be here; and that's all I ask, that you do what you normally do in a case like this."

The Mediation Committee found that though Acie's medical care adequately met local standards, the doctors had erred when they did not call in a consultant, and it was recommended that in future cases when a family requested a consultant, the request be complied with. Chris was satisfied. She had faced a real problem and had worked it out logically and unrelentingly to a satisfactory conclusion. She was growing.

In the spring of 1975, Elen received her doctorate from Duke University, and Chris came down for her graduation. During the exercises in the huge stadium, after the graduates had been recognized by their various degrees, the speaker asked the families of the graduates to stand for recognition. Elen, whose husband was robed and seated with the faculty, had expected no one to rise in her behalf. When she looked down at the section reserved for visitors and saw Chris proudly standing and waving to her, her heart melted, and emotion choked her throat. She and Chris had been close all of their lives, often alienating other members of their family by their obvious affection for each other, and they had been growing closer over this past year of exchanging such close confidences; but it was not until that moment, when Chris stood as "her family," that she realized the full extent of what she had always before simply taken for granted.

But Chris's problems with her old illness were not quite over. She and Don were having many difficulties communicating, and she felt that he did not properly appreciate the sweeping changes that had taken place in her and was not supporting her in her extreme efforts to be well. She came down to Durham for a work session and found an Elen, not only completely warmed up to her task of writing, but also ready to take on Chris as well. She had ambitiously decided to revamp her cousin in ten easy lessons. She had also decided that Chris lacked self-confidence, and that her self-image needed improving; so she set about to take care of those little items, too. Chris became her *raison d'être*, and she scolded her, corrected her, and instructed her from morning till night. In the midst of all these "good deeds," Chris looked at her one day and wryly commented,

"Elen, our roles have changed since our childhood, haven't

448

they? You are now the teacher and I am the learner." Perhaps she wondered if Elen were trying to get even for all those earlier lessons.

Elen rushed heedlessly on in her Good Samaritan manner, never realizing that Chris did not find this renovation process as fascinating as she, or that it was putting additional pressure on her. She wrote in her diary that Elen was different, had seemed to change toward her. She had mistaken Elen's clumsy attempt to help her to personally grow as a rejection of her, and this appeared to be the ultimate rejection.

Chris entered a period when she took every semblance of disagreement as a personal insult. When Don would not buy a home and remove her and Bobby from the hated apartment, she felt that he did not love her. She wrote in her diary, "He is well! Why isn't he strong enough to make these decisions?" When Taffy asked to read what was being written about her in the book, Chris felt that she did not trust or love her mother enough to know that she would not write anything to hurt her.

On the day of her expected return to Fairfax from Durham, Chris awoke with a headache that grew worse as the day progressed; and finally, instead of returning, she went to bed sick and nauseous. She remained in bed for almost twenty-four hours, and each time Elen went in to check on her, she answered all queries by a shake or nod of the head, never speaking a word. The next day she rose, pale and listless, and drove home, leaving Elen completely unaware of what had happened.

That was the birth of Andréa. Andréa de Cosná, she called herself. She was mute and had to write everything, and she wrote with her left hand. She was only thirty-three years old, and she called her sisters Bitsy and Tidy, her old childhood names for them. It was awful when she came; I was so depressed. I had thought I was finished with all that, that I would never do that again, because I know now that I was doing it myself. I created her to take the pressure off myself, to face a world I could not face. But, interestingly, she could only partly face my world; I had given her such handicaps that she could never completely take over. She was mute, and she could not drive. In every group, there was one who could not drive.

449

> *But I still wanted to be well. I was depressed because of what I had done, and I knew that I had done it, but I wanted to be well. I sought help immediately from Dr. Tsitos. . . .*

Dr. Tsitos treated Andréa as if she were of no importance at all, telling Chris not to worry about it, that it would all work itself out. He simply refused to recognize her, to in any way help her to emerge and become a full-blown manifestation; and by so doing, he refused to aid Chris in her desperate attempt to revive her old technique of escape and denial. So she sought recognition elsewhere.

She took Bobby to get his driver's license, and while waiting for him to finish his test, Andréa emerged. When Bobby returned, his mother was unable to speak. She wrote him a note saying, "I am Andréa." Bobby drove home.

One day Taffy's telephone rang, but when she answered there was no one on the line, yet the line was open. Always alert for cries of help from her mother, Taffy asked,

"Is that you, Andréa?"

There was no answer, no sound at all except the slight buzz of the open line.

"I know that you are there, Andréa," Taffy assured into the silent telephone. "Just stay there and I'll be right over."

Taffy asked her neighbor to drive her the twenty-three miles to Fairfax; and leaving a note for Tommy, she went to her mother. When Taffy arrived, she simply put her arms around Chris and said,

"Anytime you need me, just call. I know you can't speak, but just stay on the line so that I'll know it is you, and I'll come to you."

And once, after a severe argument with Don, she went to sleep while reading from a book, and awoke to find writing on one of the pages, "I am Andréa."

During her last visit to Durham, she and Elen had planned a trip to Nags Head on North Carolina's Outer Banks. Chris was going to work it out so that they would meet Becky and Tiny there, and the four women could spend a week together. But Chris did not call Elen; she took Taffy and Jimmy with her and met Tiny and her family, leaving her cousin to wonder why the

450

plans never materialized. Elen was greatly surprised, on calling to ask about the trip, to hear Bobby say,

"Mother is at Nags Head with Aunt Tiny, and Taffy."

Chris later had no knowledge of having made these plans with Elen. As soon as she arrived at Nags Head, and there was someone else who could drive, Andréa came out; and, as usual, Taffy fell easily into her old role as protector and monitor.

"I'll run your bath, Mother," she told the mute Chris, "and you can go in and bathe and go to bed, and no one else will know."

As Chris sat in the tub, Tiny knocked on the door and called to her; but, of course, she could not answer, could not talk. Tiny, alarmed, came into the room and spoke to her sister,

"Teeny, are you all right? Speak to me."

Chris could only nod her head. Tiny ran to Taffy,

"Taffy, your mother won't talk. Something is wrong with her," she excitedly informed her. And Taffy had to relate the story.

One other time on this strange trip, Andréa came out in a restaurant. She wrote a note on a napkin, saying that she wanted to eat some tacos. On the way out of the restaurant, she stumbled and fell off the steps into a bed of rocks, severely mutilating both knees and shins; and she never uttered a sound, not even as she fell heavily and flatly onto the sharp stones. The air rushing from her lungs did not even produce a grunt. It was as if there were no sound in her. She remained out for an entire day, shopping for small, inexpensive gifts for everyone. This practice was an old one with Chris—she had always spent most of her time away from home searching for gifts to give when she returned. This time she even bought gifts for those who were present with her.

Back at home, Chris's depression and desperation grew, until one evening, alone in the apartment, she got an overpowering urge to kill herself, to get it all over with, to no longer have to worry about whether "they" were coming back. But paradoxically, she did not want to die; she called for help, to Dr. Ham.

"I will put you in the hospital for several days," he told her, "until you get over this depression."

"I don't want to go to the hospital," she stubbornly refused.

"All right," he agreed, "then I will call Taffy and ask her to come and stay with you."

By the time Taffy arrived, Andréa was out, and she had a note already prepared for her daughter.

"I do not wish to live," she had written. "I do not wish to get involved in all these problems, but there are a few things I wish to do before I die. I want to go to a motion picture and I want to eat a ———." At the end of the sentence was a drawing of a hotdog.

Taffy, as voiced people so often do with those who can only communicate by writing, answered her mother by writing another note, "What movie do you want to see?"

"*Earthquake*," Chris wrote.

Taffy and Tommy took her to see the movie and bought her a hotdog, and afterward she went to bed. Andréa went to sleep, never to wake up. It was Chris who awoke the next morning. After that, her life began to assume a new normalcy. She made chronological lists for Elen, she corresponded with relatives for additional information, and she worked with her lawyer on clearing up her past legal entanglements. As a result of an inquiry from her lawyer, Dr. Thigpen had written a lengthy letter explaining that the professional film that had so puzzled Chris was the one made while she was under his treatment, plus an additional part made some two years after she and Don were married. He stated that he believed that Don was present and observed the last part of the movie being filmed. Don was furious; he had only seen Dr. Thigpen once, just before he and Chris were married, and he had certainly never returned. He had known that Chris had gone back from time to time to see the doctor, but he had not known that she had posed for a film. Chris herself had only knowledge of having gone to Atlanta for the first filming, and could remember no second filming after she was married to Don. But when she was to later view the film, there she was, after an obvious lapse of time, smiling and posing and turning.

Dr. Thigpen stated that the film had been stored all these years in a rental library on the Pennsylvania State University campus, and that he and Dr. Cleckley had shown it numerous times to medical groups and to groups interested in psychology. Chris also learned that it had been available, for a rental fee paid to the doctors, to students of psychology and to general medical groups. When Chris spoke to the Greenwood County, South Carolina, Mental Health Association, a member informed her that she had seen the film and that she would recognize her from the pictures. Chris was surprised and embarrassed. She instructed her lawyer to put an immediate stop to any further showing of the film. Although her lawyer did not receive a formal release from Drs. Thigpen and Cleckley, he advised, after investigation and consultation, that she was free to tell her story without fear of legal recourse.

Chris next sought and received her hospital records from the University Hospital in Augusta. Her chores for Elen nearly complete, she settled down to seriously paint. Noticing in the Fairfax *Journal* that George Mason University was offering to hang the canvases of local artists in their library, Chris, supported by Harriet, called and arranged for a showing of her work. She deliberately picked up the telephone, called the *Journal*, and announced who she was and that her paintings were on display. It was a bold, positive move, and her heart thudded with fear and excitement. The paper was interested, sending out a reporter and a photographer, who photographed Chris and her art, and wrote an article about the woman with many faces who had finally become one.

Immediately, her telephone rang. It was her friend Harriet, surprised, pleased, almost unable to believe that this woman whom she had known for so long, hiding such a secret, had finally revealed her identity. Chris listened fearfully as her friend expressed her pleasure and delight, and nowhere could she detect even the faintest hint of disapproval or reserve. Harriet insisted on taking her to lunch, bringing with her one of her own friends, to whom she proudly introduced Chris. This new acquaintance soon became one of Chris's best friends, helping, advising, and encouraging Chris as she struggled with her book.

Bobby, who had carefully followed his instructions to tell nobody of his mother's illness, brought home with him that day after school two of his friends, Mark Donahue and Bob Nolin. Handing them the newspaper article, he waited for them to read and react. And they did.

"Oh, Size, so what?" They nonchalantly shrugged.

And that was the general attitude of the whole of Fairfax High School. Bobby's basketball team, of which he was the proud manager, his coach, and his friends expressed to him their approval and acceptance. Nowhere could he detect the slightest hint of rejection.

Chris received several more telephone calls from friends and acquaintances who expressed surprise at who she was and at the fact that they had not known about her. It was a good feeling; people seemed actually happier to know her now, than they had before they learned her secret.

Then, on September 14, the Washington *Post* picked up the *Journal* story, interviewed her, and published her story on the front page. The Associated Press picked it up, and it became front-page news around the world. Life for Chris then became utterly chaotic: Her telephone rang day and night, letters flooded her mail, and strangers knocked on her door. The offers poured in: offers to appear on television shows, big and small; offers to have her story printed in books, magazines, and newspapers; offers to give radio interviews; offers from agents wishing to represent her; offers by movie producers to make films of her story; offers from publishers to handle her new book. The offers were international as well as national. Overcome, she called Elen, who came to help. Aware that their unfinished book was more important than these temporary offers of publicity, and wishing to avoid making irreparable mistakes, they held off any more interviews until this vital issue were settled. Requesting all others to call back in one week, they made appointments to talk with agents and publishers, hoping to select a professional to handle their suddenly sought-after property.

And there began a week that was. At the beginning they were literally babes in the woods; but their knowledge grew by leaps and bounds, and their span of interviews was so broad that a consensus of facts soon began to emerge. And it was fun for both of them, but especially for Chris. This was what she had missed before: this excitement, this feeling of plotting her own destiny. She was involved in every decision, had the final say at every turn. It was heady! And nobody was rude to her, nobody made fun of her or shamed her; quite the contrary, they all seemed pleased to know her, complimented her on her courage to tell her story, and sincerely wished her well. She wrote in her diary, "I just can't believe that everyone is so interested in me. Did Corbett experience this same elation when he told the story???"

But she was gun-shy, she would not sign a thing; and her suspicion of putting her signature on anything written probably caused her to avoid many helpful people who asked her to sign a simple contract. Even after she and Elen had agreed on a publisher, she studied the contract, had her lawyer review it, and asked innumerable questions before finally signing the document.

Only two or three persons, of the nearly one hundred who had contacted her, had tried to take advantage of her and lead her away from her main purpose of writing her book; but these were from the Washington, D.C., area and they continued to put pressure on her to exploit her story piecemeal to newspaper Sunday supplements and to magazines. She and Elen talked often on the telephone concerning these temptations to bask in temporary limelight at the expense of the more extended value of their book. Suddenly, and for no apparent reason, Elen became "the enemy." Chris wrote in her diary:

Why do I feel Elen may hurt me?? I trust her! But others I have trusted took advantage of me because I was dumb enough to let them. Surely, Elen won't do that to me. I have to trust someone, and she is the only person I know I can trust!!! Lord, help me, I'm weak—but you know that I only want to do good. Granted, I want something for my efforts, but—not at the expense of hurting anyone else—Elen has to love me enough to understand—

They had had their first argument in almost fifty years. And, ironically, it came just as one of their most cherished "let's pretend" fantasies was coming true in real life: that Chris was a famous woman and Elen was a journalist writing about her. Somehow though, it had been more fun when they had played it as children. Her relationship with Elen smoothed out, but it did not go back to its former status; it was much better, more mature. They now related as two women, not two children.

Am I really prepared to stand before the world naked? This question haunted Chris. She had hidden for twenty-five years, half of her life; and she had grown accustomed to being secretive. Also, as she well knew, her secret was not one that she could be proud of, as one is proud of an anonymous feat or creation. Did people really want to know about her, or just simply to see her as they did a freak, an infamous criminal? She remembered Dr. Thigpen's warning that though the excitement might be momentarily exhilarating, the fun would be short-lived, and the misery would be everlasting; and she should threaten with a slander suit anyone who tried to identify her. She had not been aware of any scorn or disapproval in the faces and voices of all the many who had sought her out; they had all seemed genuinely interested in her and her problem, expressing admiration for her that she had been strong enough to emerge and tell the world her story. Had she been in hiding all these years for nothing? Would people have been this understanding twenty-five years ago? Perhaps. Perhaps not. Social toleration of mental illness had greatly grown in a quarter of a century, passing through the early stage of mere curiosity and wonder into the present acceptance with understanding and compassion. Even though, in her own case, it had been harmful and detrimental to hide, the advice to do so had likely been based on the best medical knowledge of the time.

Her fears and suspicion did not all vanish, but did greatly diminish, and her world gradually fell into proper perspective.

Chris was now growing, she was catching up by leaps and bounds; and it was a painful process. She was like a newborn colt on its weak, shaky legs. Now that she had no place to run, nobody onto which to shift her responsibilities, she daily was faced with situations that forced her to make decisions. Perhaps this is the primary task of man as he weaves his intricate journey through life: to act positively and to stand accountable for his actions. It was not easy, and Chris was surrounded by uncounted hosts of others laboring with the same tortuous task. She discovered that this new aloneness, which could be backed into a corner with no hope of escape, brought to the surface long passive emotions that she had difficulty controlling.

Emotions overcame her. She took on the troubles of other people and hurt dreadfully. None of her emotions were in normal moderation. She had never learned to control them; they had always controlled her. She was tossed uncomfortably on the tempestuous sea of her own uncontrolled feelings; and often she was swamped. Dr. Tsitos and Dr. Ham stood always ready to help her,

456

and, gradually, even these leveled and smoothed out, with only an occasional jarring bump to upset her even tenor.

When Elen began to send her copy, Chris knew she was doing the right thing, no matter what the consequences. As she read, she wept: This *was* her story, exactly how she felt, how she remembered it. And her mother and father: This was precisely what they were like, not perfect, but good and loving and generous. They would have been proud of this. This was the truth. Truth? Truth is relative, and often, in the eye of the beholder; but it was truth as she remembered it, and that was what she wanted told, *her* story —the way she had lived it and the way it had appeared to her. They had held back nothing. Oh, yes, one small incident Chris decided to omit. One small incident only, of all the episodes in her life that seemed to be important, and it was fleeting: a bright flash of beauty.

She and Elen had worked so closely together, and their early lives had been so closely entwined, that virtually no rewriting was necessary. Chris read it over and over until whole parts sang, word for word, through her mind; and as she read, a strange phenomenon occurred: She relived the episodes and discussed them with Dr. Tsitos. Their primary purpose in writing the book was being fulfilled: It was proving to be good therapy. Elen was very proud of Chris's approval, and she did not want to send new copy through the mail; she wanted to *read* it to her and to watch the reaction that the fruit of her labors produced on the face of her cousin. Elen literally wanted to *give* the story to Chris, not just to hand her the typed words on a page.

They shared another experience. In September 1975, Taffy had her second child, a little black-haired, blue-eyed girl, named Christie for her grandmother, and presented to Bob and Elen as their godchild. As Chris and Elen stood before the nursery window proudly viewing the tiny porcelain mite, bearing the exact coloring of her grandmother, Chris declared, "Now, there's the *final* face of Eve!"

Finally, the year-long task was almost finished; there lacked only the ending. The week before Elen was to come to Fairfax to do the final pages with her, Chris began to have a recurring dream —a nightmare in which a small child in diapers picked up a small white casket and walked off with it. The dream repeated itself two or three times each night and she waked Don each time, violently shaking her head from side to side, crying and protesting, "I didn't kill him! I didn't kill him!"

The third time he had been so awakened, he asked her, "Who have you not killed?"

She answered him, "Aunt Meme's baby."

Frightened by this kind of talk under these conditions, Don waked her. The dream was repeated each time she fell asleep, even during the day if she were merely napping.

Elen came and they began to give their material a final proof-reading. Seated across the table from each other, she read passages from the manuscript to Chris. She was reading the account of the death of Mamie Lee's baby, and had just read, "Why did he have to die?" when she heard Chris make an unusual sound. Looking across the table, she saw that her cousin was looking in her direction, but her eyes were staring and unseeing. Chris spoke.

"But I didn't kill him, Elen."

Stunned, Elen answered her, "No, honey, you didn't kill him."

Chris began to childishly sob and rub her clenched fists into her eyes, trying to hide her face. Tears poured down her cheeks and dripped from her chin onto the table. When she spoke, her voice was immature and whining:

"I wanted him to stop crying. When he stopped crying I thought I had killed him. I never again wanted to stop a baby from crying. He might die."

Elen, rigid with surprise and shock, started to answer her, but she realized that Chris was no longer aware of her presence. Elen picked up paper and pen, as much to have something to do to avoid just staring at that contorted face out of which that eerie child's voice was pouring, as to record the incredible event.

The voice sobbed on:

"Babies think and feel. They know a lot more than people realize. They cannot communicate, but they know.

"I looked for him all the time. He was out there in that wet hole all by himself.

"I had his little shoes. I was playing with them. Aunt Meme came into the room and began to cry when she saw them. Daddy came in and took the shoes from me and gave them to Aunt Meme.

458

"The milk soured in my stomach, then. It felt funny. I never again drank milk.

"I missed the baby. He had such pretty black hair. Granny bathed him and put little white things on him. His black hair was pretty on the lace pillow.

"I didn't know he was dead until they shut the lid. I knew he was dead then because it was dark in the box and he could not see. Babies don't like the dark. Daddy put the lid down on him, and I resented that, I know now that he did it so that his brother wouldn't have to. I wasn't thinking clearly.

"I thought everybody knew what I had done. I thought everybody knew my thoughts. I didn't know *I* was the only one who knew my thoughts. I thought that was why I was ugly and bad and nobody loved me.

"I looked for him everywhere over the years. I looked for him on every little face.

"I went with Daddy years later to move his grave to Mount Carmel. I went straight to the grave. Daddy was so surprised. He asked me how I knew where the grave was.

"I thought the little casket was a new bed. I wanted it.

"I was in diapers. I felt guilty because I was living and he was dead. I couldn't enjoy the love I received because I felt that I did not deserve it.

"I used to hear people talk about digging a hole to China, and I thought that must be where Junior was and it must be an awful place. I wondered if he was hungry. I could not take my own bottle. If he could not have any more, I did not deserve any either."

The voice trailed off and ceased. Elen looked up and found Chris's eyes clear and watching her with a puzzled look. Elen's own voice was not quite steady as she asked her,

"Do you feel all right now, Chris?"

"Oh, Elen, I'm sorry. I've interrupted our work, haven't I?" Her tone was now normal and recognizable as her own. "I hate to break down like this and not be able to solve my own problems."

"It's all right, Chris. Perhaps this explains your dream."

"What did I say, Elen?" she almost fearfully asked.

Realizing that she was not even aware of what she had said, Elen read to her from her notes. Glancing at her to be sure that this was not causing her further distress, she caught a strange look

459

on Chris's face, almost as if some strange hand had just grabbed her leg under the table.

"Is something wrong, Chris?" she asked, now prepared for anything.

Chris sat up straight in her chair and whispered, "Elen, I have soiled myself."

Horribly embarrassed, she rose and discovered that her entire lower body was soaked and clammy with cold urine. Sometime during the tearful monologue, she had released her bladder. The wetting itself was a humiliating enough shock, but her greatest trauma came from the fact that she had not even been aware of when it occurred.

Was there no end to it? Were her problems, manifested by abnormal behavior—avoidance, denial, regression to childhood—to stretch out before her in a never-ending path of pain, fear, and embarrassment? She had wanted to tell her story, and she had so wanted it to have a happy ending, wanted to be able to say, "I am well; *now* I am well." Dr. Tsitos had told her that she could be the final face if she wanted to, could at least be well of her dissociative problem; but he had put the burden of the cure on her. What was her alternative?

There is a story told of an ancient king who decided the fate of his disfavored subjects by making them open one of two doors in an arena. As everyone knew, behind one door was a hungry man-eating tiger; behind the other was a lovely maiden. A young man fell into disfavor with the king and, as punishment, had to decide his own fate in the arena. He stood before the doors. Which one would he choose: the lady or the tiger? What would the waiting crowd in the arena see: the young man clasp the beautiful prize of life to his heaving heart and walk off with his happiness, or his very being ripped and torn asunder to the accompaniment of his own terrified screams?

And Chris's story? Which door would she choose? Elen did not know; only Chris could answer this all-important question.

"Chris," she asked, "how does the story end? Tell me how you feel, and I'll write."

Chris's mobile face, at rest, showed the ravages of her years of pain and the extremes of her emotions. She sat thoughtfully staring into space; and suddenly she smiled. Gone were the lines, the tension, the droop; the face, framed by its curly black hair, was sunny, happy. Only the eyes retained a trace of mature wariness which life indelibly imprints on the face of sufferers. In a scene enacted so many times over the past year, as Elen recorded, she began to speak. . . .

"Elen," she whispered, "I loosed the tiger."

Epilogue

A year has passed and many hands reached down and lifted me from the dark pit, and I gratefully accepted each one. But I first had to reach up. I first had to want to help myself. When I look at my family, my grandchildren, I know that it was worth the struggle. Don reading his evening paper, Bobby playing race cars with Jimmy, Christie sitting on the floor making baby noises, Taffy and I preparing dinner while Tommy watches television. As I hold my small granddaughter in my arms, I know that she is indeed the final Eve, because I am in control of my life, I am comfortable in my world. I know that there will be adjustments to make, that there will be grief with the joy, pain with the pleasure, ugliness with the beauty. But this is a part of living. Mine is a story of inspiration and love. I did not come through this maze of confusion alone: My family, my friends, my doctors stood stanchly by my side. I am now stable. I have adjusted to my problem. I now lead a full and rewarding life. It is a great big world and I am a small part, a functioning part. I know that life can be beautiful and I have just begun to live.

"Ye shall know the truth and the truth shall make you free." I know the truth. I know who I am. But, as Dr. Tsitos says, we know not what the future holds.

I hope my story will be a slender light to others along the way. I know what it is to call out for help and find a hand in the dark.

For the first time in over forty-eight years, I am free!

Afterword

Since my first patients came to seek medical help thirty-five years ago, I have always felt humbled by their trust. I am honored that they are willing to share with me their physical or psychological problems. This trust of a human being represents the greatest responsibility of a physician.

I feel this deep sense of respect that Chris Sizemore is willing to share her personal suffering and medical problems with the public, more so because they are of a unique nature. I trust this book will be received in the same manner. If the confession of a human soul provides entertainment only or satisfies curiosity, I strongly disapprove; but this confession permits us to gain an insight into the complexity and mysterious dynamism of the human psyche, and it can be rewarding, especially if we are led to self-reflection. Through it we can better understand our own personality and the unique role and vocation every human soul fulfills in our life and our society.

—*Tibor Ham, M.D.*

Vienna, Virginia
June 18, 1976